Gṛhastha

Gṛhastha

The Householder in Ancient Indian Religious Culture

Edited by

PATRICK OLIVELLE

OXFORD
UNIVERSITY PRESS

OXFORD
UNIVERSITY PRESS

Oxford University Press is a department of the University of Oxford. It furthers the University's objective of excellence in research, scholarship, and education by publishing worldwide. Oxford is a registered trade mark of Oxford University Press in the UK and certain other countries.

Published in the United States of America by Oxford University Press
198 Madison Avenue, New York, NY 10016, United States of America.

CIP data is on file at the Library of Congress
ISBN 978–0–19–069615–3

1 3 5 7 9 8 6 4 2

Printed by Sheridan Books, Inc., United States of America

Contents

PART II: *The Sanskrit Śāstras*

PART III: *Epic and Kāvya Literature*

Preface

AS I WILL point out in greater detail in the Introduction, this book owes its origin to the pioneering work of Stephanie Jamison, who also authored its first and seminal chapter. My biggest thanks, therefore, goes to Stephanie. This volume is also the product of a workshop on the *gṛhastha* held in the Department of Asian Studies, The University of Texas at Austin, in February 2016, with the participation of seven of the contributors to this volume. I want to thank the department, its chair Martha Selby, and the convener Donald Davis for facilitating that workshop.

Thanks are due in a special way to the eleven contributors, who took time off from their other work and responsibilities to produce fine pieces of scholarship: Adam Bowles, Joel P. Brereton, David Brick, Csaba Dezső, Oliver Freiberger, Stephanie Jamison, Timothy Lubin, Claire Maes, Mark McClish, and Aaron Sherraden. Finally, Whitney Cox not only served as an external reader for the Oxford University Press but also generously agreed to write a Prologue to this volume and to undertake the goal he set out for the contributors in his reader's report: "one way to frame this collection as a whole would be as an extended demonstration of how collective philological scholarship operates in order to create new knowledge." Finally, I want to thank the Oxford University Press and, in particular, our editor Cynthia Read for her willingness to take on this "philological experiment."

Patrick Olivelle
Austin, Texas

Contributors

Adam Bowles is Senior Lecturer in Asian Religions at the University of Queensland, Australia. His publications include *Dharma, Disorder and the Political in Ancient India: The Āpaddharmaparvan of the Mahābhārata* (2007); *Maha-bharata, Book Eight: Karna* (2 parts 2006, 2008); "Dharma and 'Custom': Semantic Persistence, Semantic Change and the Anxieties of the Principled Few" (2015).

Joel P. Brereton is Professor of Sanskrit at the University of Texas at Austin. His publications include the three-volume translation of the *Rig Veda* (with Stephanie Jamison, 2014); "Tat Tvam Asi in Context" (1986); "Edifying Puzzlement: *Ṛgveda* 10.129 and the Uses of Enigma" (1999); "Gods' Work: The Ṛbhus in the *Ṛgveda*" (2012); and "Word Positioning in Ṛgvedic Poetry" (2016).

David Brick is Assistant Professor of Sanskrit at the University of Michigan. His publications include *Brahmanical Theories of the Gift: A Critical Edition and Annotated Translation of the Dānakāṇḍa of the Kṛtyakalpataru* (2015); "Transforming Tradition into Texts: The Early Development of *Smṛti*: (2006); "The Dharmaśāstric Debate on Widow-Burning" (2010); and "*Bhoḥ* as a Linguistic Marker of Brahmanical Identity" (2016).

Whitney Cox is Associate Professor in the Department of South Asian Languages and Civilizations at the University of Chicago. His publications include *Politics, Kingship, and Poetry in Medieval South India* (2016); *Modes of Philology in Medieval South India* (2017); and coedited volumes, *South Asian Texts in History: Critical Engagements with Sheldon Pollock* (2011) and *Bilingual Discourse and Cross-cultural Fertilisation: Sanskrit and Tamil in Medieval India* (2013).

Csaba Dezső is Senior Lecturer at the Department of Indian Studies, Eötvös Loránd University, Budapest, Hungary. His publications include the critical edition and English translation of Bhaṭṭa Jayanta's *Āgamaḍambara*; (with

Somadeva Vasudeva) a new edition and English translation of the *Caturbhāṇī*, four Gupta-period comic monologue plays; and (with Dominic Goodall) a new critical edition and English verse translation of Dāmodaragupta's *Kuṭṭanīmata*.

Oliver Freiberger is Associate Professor of Asian Studies and Religious Studies at the University of Texas at Austin. His publications include *Considering Comparison: A Method for Religious Studies* (2019); the edited volume, *Methodical Aspects of Comparison* (2018); *Der Askesediskurs in der Religionsgeschichte* (2009); the edited volume, *Asceticism and Its Critics* (2006); and *Der Orden in der Lehre: Zur religiösen Deutung des Saṅgha im frühen Buddhismus* (2000).

Stephanie W. Jamison is Professor of Asian Languages and Culture and of Indo-European Studies at the University of California at Los Angeles. Her publications include the three-volume translation of the *Rig Veda* (with Joel Brereton, 2014); *Sacrificed Wife / Sacrificer's Wife: Women, Ritual, and Hospitality in Ancient India* (1996), and *The Ravenous Hyenas and the Wounded Sun: Myth and Ritual in Ancient India* (1991).

Timothy Lubin is Professor of Religion at Washington and Lee University. He coedited *Hinduism and Law* (2010), and his publications include "Legal Diglossia: Modeling Discursive Practices in Premodern Indic Law" (2013); "Writing and the Recognition of Customary Law in Premodern India and Java" (2015); and "Customary Practice in the Vedic Ritual Codes as an Emergent Legal Principle" (2016).

Claire Maes is a Postdoctoral Fellow at the University of Texas at Austin. A specialist in early Jain and Buddhist monasticism, her publications include: "A Camouflaged Debate Between Early Buddhists and Jains. A Critical Analysis of Buddhist Monastic Rules Laid Down to Protect One-Sensed Facultied Life" (2011); and "Flirtation with the Other: An Examination of the Processes of Othering in the Pāli Vinaya" (2016); and *Dialogues With(in) the Pāli Vinaya: A Research into the Dynamics and Dialectics of the Pāli Vinaya's Ascetic Other, with a Special Focus on the Jain Ascetic Other* (Dissertation, 2015).

Mark McClish is Assistant Professor of Religious Studies at Northwestern University. His publications include *The Arthaśāstra: Selections from the Classic Indian Work on Statecraft* (with Patrick Olivelle, 2012); "Is the *Arthaśāstra* a Mauryan Document?" (2012); "The Dependence of Manu's Seventh Chapter on Kauṭilya's *Arthaśāstra*" (2014); "The Four Feet of Legal Procedure and the Origins of Jurisprudence in Ancient India" (with Patrick Olivelle, 2015); and *The History of the Arthaśāstra: Sovereignty and Sacred Law in Anciet India* (2019).

Patrick Olivelle is Professor Emeritus in the Department of Asian Studies at the University of Texas at Austin. His publications include *Yājñavalkya: A Treatise on Dharma* (2019); *A Dharma Reader: Classical Indian Law* (2017); *A Sanskrit Dictionary of Law and Statecraft* (2015); *King, Governance, and Law in Ancient India: Kauṭilya's Arthaśāstra* (2013); *Manu's Code of Law: The Mānava-Dharmaśāstra* (2005); *The Early Upaniṣads* (1998); and *The Āśrama System* (1993).

Aaron Sherraden is a doctoral student at the University of Texas at Austin. His dissertation focuses on the social and historical evolution of the Sanskrit epic *Rāmāyaṇa*.

Abbreviations

AiG I	Jacob Wackernagel. *Altindische Grammatik*, vol. I
Alex	Lucian. "Alexander the False Prophet"
AM	Ardhamāgadhī
AN	*Aṅguttara Nikāya* (Pali Text Society edition)
ĀpDh	*Āpastamba Dharmasūtra*. Ed. in Olivelle 2000
ĀpGṛ	*Āpastamba Gṛhyasūtra*
AS I	First book of the *Ācārāṅga Sūtra*. Ed. Jacobi 1882; Schubring 2004
AS II	Second book of *Ācārāṅga Sūtra*. Ed. Jacobi 1882
ĀśGṛ	*Āśvalāyana Gṛhyasūtra*
AV	*Atharva Veda*
AVPar	Atharvaveda Pariśiṣṭas. Ed. Bolling 1909–10.
AVŚ	*Atharva Veda* (Śaunaka)
BDh	*Baudhāyana Dharmasūtra*. Ed. in Olivelle 2000
BGPS	*Baudhāyana Gṛhya Paribhāṣāsūtra*
BGṛ	*Baudhāyana Gṛhyasūtra*
Bh	*Sattasai* in Bhuvanapāla's commentary. Ed. Patwardhan 1980, 1988
BHSD	Franklin Edgerton. *Buddhist Hybrid Sanskrit Grammar and Dictionary*
CDIAL	R. L. Turner. *A Comparative Dictionary of the Indo-Aryan Languages*
Cil	*Cilappatikāram*
Dh	*Dhammapada* (Pali Text Society edition)
DN	*Dīgha Nikāya* (Pali Text Society edition)
EWA	Manfred Mayrhofer. *Etymologisches Wörterbuch des Altindoarischen*
GDh	*Gautama Dharmasūtra*. Ed. in Olivelle 2000
GobhGṛ	*Gobhila Gṛhyasūtra*

Hinz-Koch	*Elamisches Wörterbuch*. Ed. Walther Hinz and Heidemarie Koch
HirGṛ	*Hiraṇyakeśi Gṛhyasūtra*
IAD	Shatavadhani Jain Muni and Shri Ratnachandraji Maharaj. *An Illustrated Ardha-Magadhi Dictionary*
It	*Itivuttaka* (Pali Text Society edition)
JaiGṛ	*Jaiminīya Gṛhyasūtra*
Kane	Kane 1962–75
KAŚ	Kauṭilya, *Arthaśāstra*. Ed. in Kangle 1969; tr. in Olivelle 2013
KauthGṛ	*Kauthuma Gṛhyasūtra*. Ed. in Sūryakānta 1956
KEWA	Manfred Mayrhofer. *Kurzgefasstes etymologisches Wörterbuch des Altindischen*
KhadGṛ	*Khadira Gṛhyasūtra*
KNS	Kāmandaki, Nītisāra
KS	Vātsyāyana, Kāmasūtra
MBh	Mahābhārata
MDh	*Mānava Dharmaśāstra*. Ed. in Olivelle 2005
MIA	Middle Indo-Aryan
MN	*Majjhima Nikāya* (Pali Text Society edition)
MRE	Minor Rock Edict of Aśoka
OIA	Old Indo-Aryan
PārGṛ	*Pāraskara Gṛhyasūtra*. Ed. Bākre 1917
PE	Pillar Edict of Aśoka
Pkt	Prākrit
PSM	Pandit Hargovind Das T. Sheth. *Pāia-Sadda-Mahaṇṇavo. A Comprehensive Prakrit-Hindi Dictionary*
PTSD	T. W. Rhys Davids and William Stede. *The Pali Text Society's Pali-English Dictionary*
PW	Otto Böhtlingk and Rudolph Roth. *Sanskrit-Wörterbuch*
pw	Otto Böhtlingk. *Sanskrit-Wörterbuch in kürzerer Fassung*
RE	Rock Edict of Aśoka
RV	*Rig Veda*
ŚāṅGṛ	*Śāṅkhāyana Gṛhyasūtra*
SK I	First book of the Sūtrakṛtāṅga. Ed. Vaidya 1928
SK II	Second book of the Sūtrakṛtāṅga. Ed. Muni Jambūvijayajī 1978
Skt	Sanskrit
SN	*Saṃyutta Nikāya* (Pali Text Society edition)
Sn	*Sutta-Nipāta* (Pali Text Society edition)
TS	*Taittirīya Saṃhitā*
Ud	*Udāna* (Pali Text Society edition)
UD	*Uttarādhyayana Sūtra*. Ed. Charpentier 1922

V	*Videvdāt*
VaDh	*Vasiṣṭha Dharmasūtra*. Ed. in Olivelle 2000
ViDh	*Vaiṣṇava Dharmaśāstra*. Ed. in Olivelle 2009a
Vin	*Vinayapiṭaka* (Pali Text Society edition)
W	*Sattasai*. Ed. Weber 1881
YDh	*Yājñavalkya Dharmaśāstra*. Ed. and tr. in Olivelle 2019

Introduction

Patrick Olivelle

FOR SCHOLARS OF ancient Indian society, culture, or religion, the forest hermit (*vānaprastha*) living in isolated forest dwellings and, even more especially, the wandering mendicant (*pravrajita, parivrājaka, bhikṣu*) who left home and family, lived a celibate life, and was devoted to the search for liberation (*mokṣa, nirvāṇa*) represented an enigma. They are not found in the early Vedic texts, and the Vedic religion, centered on the married householder (*gṛhápati*), had no place for the celibate ascetic. Some scholars take celibate and itinerant asceticism to have its origins in non-Vedic or even non-Āryan religious traditions (Bronkhorst 1993), drawing a sharp contrast between the Vedic householder and the world-renouncing ascetic (Dumont 1960). Others take it to be an orthogenetic development from the Vedic tradition itself (Heesterman 1964). Still others have related it to the development of complex polities and urbanization (Olivelle 1993). More recently, Bronkhorst (2007) has argued that world renunciation is a unique feature of the Greater Magadhan culture. Forest-dwelling and itinerant forms of asceticism were viewed as cultural innovations that required an explanation.

In contrast, the married householder with wife and children was considered unproblematic. Scholars have assumed, explicitly or implicitly, that the householder who occupies the central position in the religio-legal texts called Dharmaśāstra, texts that defined for two millennia or more the essential features of what we call Hinduism, was identical to the Vedic householder. One certainly does not need to question the origin of the institution of the Hindu householder, with its roots in the Vedic religion, as one does that of the ascetic institutions. The former required no historical explanation.

This scholarly consensus was challenged in a seminal paper written for the 2015 annual meeting of the American Oriental Society by Stephanie Jamison. This paper was occasioned by her participation in a volume edited by Donald

Davis and me for the Oxford University Press dealing with the history of the Dharmaśāstra tradition (Olivelle and Davis 2018). In that paper, which provided the basis for the first chapter of this volume, Jamison demonstrated that the term *gṛhastha,* the most common and, indeed, the only term for "householder" in the Dharmaśāstras and even in other kinds of Brahmanical literature contemporary with the Dharmaśāstras—and the dominant term in medieval religious, legal, and philosophical literature—is completely absent in the Vedic texts. When a term is used in the Vedas for householder, it is invariably *gṛhápati* ("house-lord"). As Jamison states: "This terminological demarcation hints at a conceptual discontinuity as well, and the linguistic history of the term *gṛhastha* illuminates the conceptual renewal." The question, then, is why the later tradition abandoned the traditional term *gṛhápati* and adopted a totally new one. What makes Jamison's paper *seminal* is that she actually answers this question, an answer that revolutionizes our understanding of the ancient Indian religious history of the second half of the first millennium BCE and provides the impetus for this volume.

The term *gṛhastha,* Jamison points out, although new to the Sanskrit vocabulary, is found in several Prakritic forms such as *gahattha* and is already used by Emperor Aśoka in the middle of the third century BCE. In his usage, *gṛhastha* is always coupled with and contrasted to *pravrajita,* the ascetic who has gone forth from home into the homeless life. As Jamison points out, *gṛhastha* should be properly viewed as the "stay-at-home" in contrast to the "gone forth," rather than simply as any married householder: "The *gṛhastha* is, in fact, no mere layman, but one who pursues his religious duties no less than the 'gone forth,' although he pursues them at home" (p. 17). The term is thus derived from śramaṇic discourse.

So, the Hindu *gṛhastha* is conceptually different from the Vedic *gṛhapati.* The *gṛhastha* is a member of a religious group who, instead of going forth from home (*pravrajita*) as a wandering mendicant opts to remain at home. But significantly, the *gṛhastha* is also devoted to a religious lifestyle, to the same or similar goal as the "gone-forth." The Dharmaśāstras, thus, are texts devoted to the pursuit of legitimate religious goals in the Brahmanical communities, a pursuit that may take different forms (for example, the wandering mendicant) but, in the view of the Dharmaśāstras, is centered on the "stay-at-home," on the *gṛhastha.*

This volume includes chapters on most genres of literature from ancient India covering the last half of the first millennium BCE and the first half of the first millennium CE. The contributors investigate the position of the householder (both conceptually and in terms of vocabulary) in these texts in relation to the emergence of this figure for the first time in the Aśokan edicts with the term *gṛhastha*. The volume is divided into three parts focusing on (1) the Vedic literature, Aśokan inscriptions, and Buddhist and Jain texts written in Pāli and Prakrit; (2) the Sanskrit scientific literature (*śāstra*); and (3) epics and belle-lettres (*kāvya*).

The first part opens with Stephanie Jamison's groundbreaking chapter on the householder in the Vedic period. It discusses the pivotal Vedic term *gṛhápati*, "house-lord," as applied to the divine lord, Agni, the ritual fire present in a house, and to the human occupants, especially the *gṛhápatnī* (housewife). The absence of *gṛhastha* in the Sanskrit Vedic sources is amplified by its use in a variety of Prakrit sources, including the Aśokan inscriptions, and Buddhist and Jain canonical texts. The chapters by Brereton and Olivelle focus principally on the Aśokan inscriptions. Brereton offers the first scholarly treatment of the term and category *pāṣaṇḍa* and its semantic history. The term came to be used commonly in later literature, both Buddhist and Brahmanical, to refer to "the other," especially other ascetic groups than one's own. Thus, the term is often translated as "heretical sect." Brereton shows that in its earliest usages the term had a neutral meaning, referring to organized religious groups. A precise understanding of this category, moreover, is crucial because in the writings of Aśoka the term *gṛhastha* is always in close proximity to *pāṣaṇḍa*. The precise connection, if any, between the two terms and institutions represented by them is not altogether clear. Brereton sees the connection as minimal, taking *pāṣaṇḍa* and *gṛhastha* as complementary, while Olivelle gives a maximalist interpretation, taking *gṛhastha* and *pravrajita* as two classes of members that constituted *pāṣaṇḍa* groups. What is, however, clear from the three first chapters is that the *gṛhastha* is *always* contrasted to the *pravrajita*; the former "stays at home" while the latter "goes forth" from home into a homeless life of itinerancy. Both are, nevertheless, devoted to a "religious" or "holy" life.

The remaining two chapters of Part I deal with the householder vocabulary in early Pāli Buddhist and Jain texts. In a statistically rich study of the Pāli canon, Freiberger points out that among the several terms referring to lay people living at home the term *gṛhastha* (Pāli *gahaṭṭha*) is the least common. Clearly, it did not serve a significant theological purpose within the Buddhist vocabulary. In the few places it occurs, the context shows that it is used in relation or opposition to the ascetic who has left home, thus conforming to the Aśokan usage. It is, however, suggestive that some passages identify the typically Buddhist layman called *upāsaka* as a *gṛhastha*. Turning to three of the earliest texts of the Jain canon, Maes finds that *gṛhastha* (AM *gihattha, gihittha*) is quite rare, occurring just six times. The basic opposition of the term to the homeless ascetic is maintained, but it is instructive that Maes finds the use of *gṛhastha* within Jain texts may have been due to the influence of its use in Brahmanical texts, especially the early Dharmasūtras.

The second part of the volume focuses on scientific disciplines and treatises generally referred to as *śāstra*. The four chapters focus on domestic ritual (*gṛhya*), law (*dharma*), statecraft (*nīti*), and erotics (*kāma*). Lubin's exploration of the Gṛhyasūtras shows that, even in these late śāstric texts connected to the Veda and its vocabulary, the term *gṛhastha* is absent, making its appearance only within appendices and additions dating to a period after the early Dharmasūtras. The term is also absent in the Śrautasūtras, the aphoristic texts on the Vedic ritual; thus, we do not have a chapter devoted to them. It is in the Dharmaśāstric texts that we encounter *gṛhastha* as a central theological term. As Brick's study of the dharma literature and Olivelle's chapter on the *āśramas* show, in all likelihood, the term entered the vocabulary of the Dharmaśāstric tradition within the context of the *āśrama* system, itself a theological innovation within the Brahmanical tradition. Even in later Dharmaśāśtric texts and, as McClish's chapter indicates, in texts on statecraft and erotics, *gṛhastha* is most frequently used within the context of the *āśrama* system and in juxtaposition to ascetics who have left home and family.[1]

Narrative literature occupies the three chapters of the third part. One surprising finding is the almost total absence of the term *gṛhastha* in the Sanskrit epic *Rāmāyaṇa*. Sherraden offers several plausible reasons, but it is noteworthy that the epic also completely ignores (or is ignorant of) the *āśrama* system. The two seem to go hand in hand. It is in the *Mahābhārata* that *gṛhastha* and *gārhasthya*, as Adam Bowles's statistically rich study shows, appear much more frequently than other terms for a householder. It is also clear that discussions of the *āśrama* system are much more frequent in this epic, once again pointing to the close connection in Brahmanical texts between *gṛhastha* and the *āśrama* system. As Csaba Dezső shows, the picture is complex in the early Kāvya literature he examines. It is present in Aśvaghoṣa's works and in Kālidāsa, often within a context reflecting the ideology of the *āśrama* system, whereas the Prakrit poetic works ignore it and use most frequently the term *gahavaï* (Skt *gṛhapati*).

So, we are faced with a dilemma. Given its absence in the entire Vedic corpus and its presence in Aśoka's vocabulary and other Middle Indo-Aryan

1. Another group of śāstric texts that, due to unavoidable circumstances, we have not been able to study in detail is the medical literature (*āyurveda*). Briefly, though, I have gone through the electronic versions of the *Caraka Saṃhitā* and the *Suśruta Saṃhitā*, and the term *gṛhastha* is conspicuous by its rarity. In the *Caraka*, the term occurs only twice (Cikitsāsthāna 1 and 22), both within the context of the *āśramas*. The term does not occur in the *Suśruta* at all.

sources, Jamison has rightly pointed out that *gṛhastha* "is actually a coinage of and a borrowing from śramaṇic discourse, which discourse, at this period, was conducted in various forms of Middle Indo-Aryan" (p. 18). Jamison further states: "This contrastive pairing [*gṛhastha* and *pravrajita*] implies that the householder of the Hindu dharma texts was not simply a married man and *pater familias* in what we might, anachronistically, consider an essentially secular role, but a man with a religious life equivalent to that of a wandering ascetic, but a religious life pursued and fulfilled within the context of a sedentary family existence. So, not only is this most dharmic of dharmic words an importation from *śramaṇa* circles and most likely from Middle Indic, but it also seems to reflect a division of religious roles that is more at home in those heterodox circles than in the Vedic milieu from which the Brahmanical dharma system supposedly developed" (Ch. 1, p. 19) The dilemma, as Jamison herself points out (Ch. 1, n. 35), is that the term and category of *gṛhastha* does not play a central role in the śramaṇic discourses preserved in the two śramaṇic traditions of Buddhism and Jainism. This is evident from the analysis of Freiberger and Maes in Chs. 4 and 5. While it remained marginal in these śramaṇic discourses in Middle Indo-Aryan languages from which it probably originated, ironically, it is the mainstream of the Brahmanical tradition, represented by the Dharmaśāstras and the *Mahābhārata*, in which the term assumes a central role, theologically and institutionally.

Can this history of the term be explained through the historical vicissitudes of early Buddhism and Jainism? Did this particular term for householder never occupy a central role in the vocabulary of these two śramaṇic traditions? Or, perhaps less likely, did the term gradually lose its cachet and importance as these traditions developed their institutions and theologies? Did its marginal status result from the centrality of Buddhist and Jain monastic institutions within these traditions, a centrality that left little room for a competing institution like the *gṛhastha?* The far more significant development, however, was the emergence of a *gṛhastha*-centered theology within the Brahmanical tradition, along with the construction of the *āśrama* system in which the *gṛhastha* played a central role (see Ch. 7). It is, of course, unknown whether at the time when Aśoka wrote his letters the term *gṛhastha* was more commonly used within the Brahmanical tradition of asceticism than in Buddhist or Jain discourse. At least from the vantage point of the Dharmaśāstras, however, it was the Brahmanical *pāṣaṇḍa,* to use the Aśokan category, in which the *gṛhastha* and the *pravrajita* played central and perhaps equal and competing roles. This tension and the resultant question—who is better, the *pravrajita* or the *gṛhastha?*—will remain part of the Brahmanical tradition until modern times. As Jamison (2018: 126) states: "This terminological demarcation hints at a conceptual discontinuity as well, and the linguistic history of the term *gṛhastha* illuminates the conceptual renewal." This discontinuity is put into sharp focus within the Brahmanical tradition. Jamison's conclusion is apposite: "That *gṛhápati* was replaced by a term adapted from a very different conception of religious life suggests that the lexical replacement was not simply the result of a desire for linguistic novelty, but signals a sharp conceptual break from the Vedic religious landscape" (Ch. 1, p. 19).

The Hindu *gṛhastha* is thus conceptually different from the Vedic *gṛhápati*. The *gṛhastha* is a member of a religious group who, instead of going forth from home (*pravrajita*) as a wandering mendicant, opts to remain at home; the term *gṛhastha*, as we have seen, can properly be translated as the "stay-at-home" in contrast to the "gone-forth." But significantly the *gṛhastha* is also devoted to a religious life, to the same or similar goal as the "gone-forth"; there is a competition as to who is the true *homo religiosus*. This tension is absent in the śramaṇic traditions: there is no parallel between the ascetic and the householder. The former is superior and the only one capable of reaching the ultimate goal of liberation. In the Brahmanical tradition, the *gṛhastha* is thus not simply a married person living at home with his family, that is, a general descriptor of a householder, for whom there are many other Sanskrit terms, but a religiously charged concept that is intended as a full-fledged and superior alternative to the concept of a religious renouncer.

The insightful comments of Whitney Cox in his Prologue lays out a program for the future: "In the light of this metanarrative, a task for future scholarship would be its colligation with other sorts of evidence. . . . If we can indeed write a new history of the *gṛhastha*, it is a history imbricated very deeply into the fabric of social life in early India." This is very much our hope, that this extensive yet limited study of *gṛhápati* and *gṛhastha* will stimulate further explorations, taking into account other kinds of evidence, including archeology and social and economic history.

Prologue

Whitney Cox

THE INDOLOGIST CAN seem like a solitary figure. The scholar of classical India's textual legacy, at least one working in North America,[1] tends to appear alone, in the front of the classroom, on the title page, or on the masthead of her article. The model is a heroic one: the sole scholar, emerging from her office or the library to deliver a lecture or to send off the draft of an article or monograph. The structures of blind peer-review and of tenure and promotion committees across the profession all work to reinforce this.

But it isn't all lonely work. We have our university colleagues, former teachers, and fellow-students and—if we're lucky—pupils of our own with whom we can share ideas. Online fora and email allow for the frictionless dissemination of research, enabling a scholar to share sources, data, interpretations, and new research questions at any time and from anywhere. But the annual conference endures as a premiere form of academic sociability and exchange. Within this admittedly specialist field, there are relatively few options on offer: to continue to be parochially American, there are perhaps four such conferences the professional Indologist can choose from each year. Being based in the Midwest (and a lazy man), I usually attend the annual South Asia Conference at the University of Wisconsin–Madison; early-career job aspirants and institutionally responsible senior scholars gravitate toward the American Academy of Religion or the Association of Asian Studies. But the crucial forum for most of this volume's participants is the annual meeting of the American Oriental Society. It was at the two hundred and twenty-fifth such meeting, in New Orleans in March 2015, that Stephanie Jamison presented

1. Western Europe, with its *unités mixtes du recherche* and its *Exzellenzcluster*, presents a different situation. The continued centrality of the single-author publication, however, demonstrates that the heroic model persists there as well.

the paper "Houses, Housewives, and Householders," the descendant of which opens the present volume.

In the course of this paper, Jamison drew attention to the non-existence in the early Vedic corpus of the term *gṛhastha,* the male "householder" who is the protagonist of much of the classical Sanskrit religious imagination. This occasioned Jamison's philological exploration of the actual or potential terminological equivalents of the "householder" within the corpus, the *dámpati/patír dán,* the *dámūnaḥ,* and especially the *gṛhápati* ("houselord"), all three much more often given as epithets of the fire god Agni than the adult human male in Ṛgvedic. The semantic centrality of the *gṛhápati* continues into the *Atharvaveda* and into the ordinances of the domestic cult. And so Jamison shows that the sudden irruption of the *gṛhastha* in the earliest texts on dharma to the permanent expense of the *gṛhápati* marks a truly radical break, representing in her words a lexical as well as a conceptual discontinuity. Jamison suggests that the vector for the *gṛhastha*'s introduction might be found in the Middle Indic languages and the non-Brahmanical religious cultures that made use of them; she further proposes that *gṛhastha* ("stay-at-home") represented a kind of religious professional, instead of any unmarked married adult male of high caste, and so the counterpart to and not the antitype of the *pravrajita* or wandering ascetic. Patrick Olivelle, who happened to be chairing that particular American Oriental Society panel, evidently took notice.

The essays collected in this volume all take Jamison's now much expanded essay as their point of departure. If, they ask, we change our accepted ideas of the *gṛhastha,* whom Indology has for over a century complacently understood to be the unchanging and central figure in the Brahmanical lifeway, what else must we change? And how do we understand the *gṛhastha* now that this figure is newly endowed with a semantic and (more tentatively) a social history?

Beyond the excellence of the individual contributions, and their interest to specialists in the various genres of Indic literature here surveyed, this volume thus possesses a further value, in that it neatly documents a series of philological experiments in light of a single changed variable. My recourse to the language of experimental science is deliberate: this collection serves as an extended demonstration of how collective philological scholarship operates: of the ways that it creates, tests, and calibrates new knowledge. The figure of the solitary Indic philologist recedes, and in his place we see the field's collective workings in vivo. Within this volume's two covers, the interested reader can trace how a single scholar's (in this case Jamison's) hypothesis can be tested, debated, extended, and refined, and a new scholarly consensus produced.

In suggesting that the current practices of Indology can and should be viewed from the perspective of the history of science, or that of the history of knowledge more generally, I am indebted to the ideas of Lorraine Daston and Glen Most. Writing together, they have detailed not only the ways in which the histories of Western philology and Western science remained entangled until the cusp of modern times, but how even in the contemporary disciplinized university, these practices of knowledge-formation can be profitably understood together.[2] In offering a common definition for these philological and natural-scientific activity as instances of "a rational, disciplined, and institutionalized form of interpersonal research," Daston and Most point to ways in which the history and the sociology of humanistic knowledge—or just its self-aware and self-critical performance—may be aided by the insights gleamed from the modern discipline of the history of science.[3]

Elsewhere, Daston has identified her object of inquiry to be what she calls the "epistemic virtues" of a science of a particular place and time, those "norms that are internalized and enforced by appeal to ethical values, as well as to their pragmatic efficacy in securing knowledge," which are responsible for the parallel creation of the knowable experimental phenomenon and the subjectivity of the experimenting scientist.[4] It is in this light that we can frame a second order question: What might be the epistemic virtues on display in this collection of essays? Most obviously, it documents the latent cooperative structure to the philological and historical research into early and classical Indic texts, something that the norms of publication and assessment typically suppress. But other, equally potent virtues are here to be found. I will detail just a few, and encourage readers to look for their own lessons in the creation of Indological knowledge in the pages that follow.

There is, first of all, the signal mark of scholarship, the willingness to revise received opinion and conventional wisdom, embodied in Jamison's opening move of unseating the *gṛhastha* from his ahistorical place of honor at the

---

2. Daston and Most 2015; especially in tracing the early entanglements of textual and natural science, this duo expands to a triumvirate with the addition of Anthony Grafton: see, e.g., Grafton 1994, 1999.

3. Daston and Most 2015: 386.

4. Daston and Galison 2010: 40; in this study, the epistemic virtues whose history is reconstructed from atlases of scientific images are the overlapping historical series of "truth-to-nature," mechanical objectivity, and the virtuosically trained judgment of the observer; in another publication, Daston has traced a cognate sequence of nineteenth-century humanistic virtues of impartiality and objectivity (Daston 2014). Refer also to Hacking's early appreciation of this method (2002: 8–14), to which he gives the rebarbative (to me, anyway) title "historical meta-epistemology."

center of early Indic religion. This urge to revise seemingly settled conclusions becomes all the more significant when the conclusions in question were earlier advanced by the author him- or herself. Thus the reader should notice that Olivelle, as the volume's editor, most dogged contributor, and tutelary spirit, here publicly revises and even discards some of his own earlier ideas, both from his classic monograph *The Āśrama System* (1993) and more recent work, while leaving his own new provisional conclusions open to yet more debate.

This permits the reader to observe what I find to be the volume's greatest virtue, the congenial practice of principled disagreement. Scholarship is as much about argument as it is consensus, and despite the collegiality that so clearly radiates from these contributions, significant differences of opinion remain, and are acknowledged throughout. At a time when disagreements—be they scholarly, aesthetic, ethical, political, or some cocktail thereof—have a tendency to escalate beyond any semblance of reasoned argument, to see such differences of interpretation recorded, considered, discussed, and left to the judgment of the reader is to find oneself in a Habermasian oasis in the midst of a vast Trumpian desert.

The leading instance of this here is the different reading of the evidence of the Aśokan inscriptions found in Olivelle's and Brereton's chapters. Following Olivelle's characterization, these represent respectively a "maximalist" and a "minimalist" interpretation. Olivelle advances a strong interpretation of a passage from Aśoka's twelfth Rock Edict suggesting that as a matter of policy, the philo-Buddhist emperor folded the two categories called *gṛhastha* and *pravrajita* in Sanskrit into a wider rubric of *pāṣaṇḍa* or 'religious community' (see Ch. 3, pp. 45–46; cf. Ch. 7, pp. 109–110). Brereton, adopting a slightly but significantly different reading of the text of the twelfth edict, and marshaling additional Aśokan evidence, sees juxtaposition rather than subordination (Ch. 2, pp. 33–37): minimally—thus Olivelle—for Aśoka these are all ethically coherent lifeways, to be encouraged by the officers of the Mauryan imperial apparatus, but with the Aśokan *gihittha* (et cetera) forming a totally separate category from the several varieties of ascetic virtuosi.

Other instances of difference are less direct, but equally significant as evidence of how a working scholarly consensus is arrived upon. Maes's and Freiberger's essays take up the conjectural conclusions of Jamison's opening contribution, examining whether in fact the earliest portions of the Buddhist Pāli and Jain Ardhamāgadhī canons might have supplied the raw materials, as it were, for the *gṛhastha* of the Brahmanical dharma theorists. Their studies, however, find consistency with rather than disjunction from late Vedic sources—the Vedic *gṛhápati* finding its counterpart in the statistically prominent Pāli *gahapati* and Ardhamāgadhī *gāhāvaï*—and so do not directly support

Jamison's hypothesis.[5] Such a reminder of the complexity of our temporally remote and fragmentary sources embodies a virtue in its own right, an object lesson in the messily contingent reality of our texts. Freiberger suggests that the Dharmaśāstric *gṛhastha*, with its cognates thinly attested in Pāli (and in the Jain canon), might have seemed like something of a blank slate for the Brahmanical theorists looking to strike out on their own. This, then, suggests a revised hypothesis in the light of the negative evidence he and Maes assemble: rather than the uptake of a well-established term, the recourse to the *gṛhastha* in the texts on Brahmanical dharma may have been an attempt to repurpose a term with no great prior history of use, and so little interpretative or polemical baggage attached to it.

Sherraden's contribution traces a different sort of negative evidence, a "known unknown" about the anomalous absence of the *gṛhastha* or the *āśrama* system *tout court* in Vālmīki's *Rāmāyaṇa*. As this is a major cultural monument of classical India if ever there was one, this is important to any such comprehensive theorization of the *gṛhastha* or of the wider structure that the Brahman dharma theorists articulated around it. This absence had earlier been earlier noted by Olivelle himself, but the expanded evidentiary horizon that Sherraden provides—exhaustiveness being another key Indological virtue—places this anomaly in higher relief. The *Rāmāyaṇa* thus presents a contrast to the narrative and ethical sprawl of the *Mahābhārata*, amply documented in Bowles's chapter: concerned in its details with the vicissitudes of a single prince within a single patriline (and so with the cosmic deeds of Rāma the *avatāra* of Viṣṇu), the domestic concerns of *gārhasthya* simply failed to figure into the moral imagination of the Vālmīki text.

Classical Indic literature is immense, and the volume's constituent chapters readily suggest each of its many domains is possessed of independent dynamics and priorities. But it is important not to lose sight of the bigger picture here, and so the historical reconstruction offered by Olivelle in Chapter 7, while necessarily conjectural, is very welcome. Olivelle, drawing in part on Bronkhorst (2016), suggests that a social and political crisis of the late centuries BCE, following upon the unwinding of the Mauryan imperium, contributed to the formation to two alternative Brahmanical social theories, one that valued renunciation as framed within a system of four *āśramas* and another arguing for *aikāśramya*, the centrality of a single life-way, that of the *gṛhastha*.

5. Though as Jamison points out, the *pravrajita* versus *gṛhastha* dichotomy is later clearly instituted in Pāli, Gandhārī, and Buddhist Hybrid Sanskrit (Jamison, chapter 1, p. 18). Whether, as Freiberger's and especially Maes's data suggest, this is a later phenomenon influenced by Brahmanical usage, will have to await exploration elsewhere.

While the latter was the dominant current in the early Dharmasūtras, notably Gautama and Baudhāyana, the former supplied the raw materials for the conceptual revolution later embodied in the *Manusmṛti* (Ch. 7, pp. 115–117). The ongoing intramural argument between these two theories, moreover, took place in the wider context of debates and competition with the renunciate *śramaṇa* traditions of the Buddhists, Jains, and others; and this complex situation established the ideological lines of force, as it were, which were to endure into early medieval times.

In the light of this metanarrative, a task for future scholarship would be its colligation with other sorts of evidence. This is an idea that Lubin gestures toward in the conclusion to his contribution (Ch. 6, p. 105–106), where he links the centrality of the *gṛhastha* with the practice of the meritorious feeding of Brahmins, and with the establishment of the *brahmadeya* estates that are the subject matter of the vast corpus of copper-plate charters that comprises a major sector of Indic epigraphy. As these documents are often localizable in space and time, the creation of a social geography of the extension of the institution of *gārhasthya* becomes at least a theoretical possibility. Lubin's intelligent focus on the sociality of food, moreover, suggests still other, nontextual sources that could possibly supply further evidence. Here I am thinking of the excellent archaeological and paleobotanical research into food choice and agrarian intensification in early historic India. *Gārhasthya* as a social form traveled alongside the cultivation of rice, which provided—in addition to the nutritional resources that allowed for the demographic possibility of both the noncultivating Brahmin householder and his renunciate cousin—the necessary ingredient for the *piṇḍa*-balls offered in the central domestic offering to the ancestors, the *śrāddha* (see, e.g., Smith 2006; Morrison 2016). This material-cultural evidence presents just as complex a picture as Olivelle's intellectual historical narrative, with some of the same institutional actors, as can be gathered from the history of the extension of riziculture from the north-east—the erstwhile Mauryan heartland!—into the central Indian plains, in which Buddhist, and not Brahmanical, institutions played a decisive role (Shaw, Sutcliffe, et al. 2007; Shaw 2013: 250–53). If we can indeed write a new history of the *gṛhastha*, it is a history imbricated very deeply into the fabric of social life in early India.

I CONCLUDE WITH a small offering in the spirit of the essays that follow. But my subject is not the *gṛhastha* himself, the volume's titular protagonist, but instead the *pāṣaṇḍa*, the institution central to Brereton's and Olivelle's chapters. To highlight the transformations undergone by the term, I draw upon the scant evidence of it found in classical Tamil. These data do not, alas, cast any light on the term's interpretation in its Aśokan epigraphical appearances, but nor do they accord with the position into which later Brahmanism slotted the *pāṣaṇda* or *pāṣaṇḍin*, as "heresy" or "heretic." What I find here, then, is a genuine anomaly.

I limit myself to the *Cilappatikāram* (*Cil*), attributed to Iḷaṅko Aṭikaḷ ("The Reverend Prince"). This long poem is one of the unquestionable masterpieces of early Tamil literature. Its dating is uncertain: I would cautiously, if vaguely, date its composition to some point in the second half of the first millennium.[6] It is, in David Shulman's words, "a highly crafted, exquisitely polished literary composition, enlivened by the whole range of ancient Tamil poetry and story" (2016: 101), one that encompasses every possibility of cultured life of its time and place, ranging over Sanskritic liturgical, mythological, and musical traditions, through the elegant performance of classical Tamil love lyrics, to the rituals of village goddesses and the dances of pastoralist hillfolk. The central arc of its plot is an account of apotheosis: it tells of a quite ordinary, sheltered young woman, Kaṇṇaki of the city of Pukār, and of her eventual transfiguration into an awesome goddess, the resulting fiery destruction of the ancient city of Madurai, and the establishment of worship of the new deity in what is now Kerala. The poem's supposed author, Iḷaṅko, is only mentioned in its opening metaliterary prologue and as a witness to the institution of the cult of the goddess, now called Pattiṉi (=Skt. *patnī*, "the [Good] Wife"), a scene to which we will return.

Though what in Tamil orthography is rendered *pācaṇṭa-* is found only sparsely in the *Cilappatikāram*—there are only four total occurrences in the whole of the long poem—with two very minor exceptions, these appear to be its *only* occurrences in all of early Tamil literature.[7] *Pācaṇṭam* itself, as a common noun, is found late in the text, in the 26th canto's description of the northern conquests of the Kerala king Cĕṅkuṭṭuvaṉ, the putative author's brother, which were preliminary to his establishment of the new Pattiṉi cult. At the start of his campaign, as Cĕṅkuṭṭuvaṉ was encamped beyond the Western Ghats, he is

6. On the portentously named "Gajabāhu synchronism," which supposedly secures the text's date due to the mention of the firmly dated Sri Lankan king of that name (r. 171–93 CE) as a contemporary of the poet Iḷaṅko (*Cil* 30.1160 *kaṭalcūḻ ilaṅkai kayavāku ventaṉum*), see Obeyesekere 1984: 361–80; Tieken 2000: 206; and Shulman 2016: 101, all of whom reject its validity. On the possibility of the poem's expansion through the later addition of its third division (*kāṇṭam*), see below. insert XR to p. 40 of this file.

7. Such is my conclusion, based on electronic searches, the *Madras Tamil Lexicon*, and the *Historical Dictionary of Tamil Literature* (s.v.). I would like to record my gratitude to my colleague E. Annamalai, for discussion of this point, as well as for reading through the *Cilappatikāram* with me over the period 2015–2017.

met by the delegation of an allied king, the large entourage of which included "a hundred comic performers familiar with the ninety-six varieties of the *pācaṇṭam* orders" (26.130–31 *tŏṇṇūṟṟaṟuvakaip pācaṇṭatturai / naṇṇiya nūṟṟuvar nakaiveḷamparum*). "Comic performers" renders *nakaiveḷampar*, "whose sport is laughing." While it might surprise the modern reader to find a troupe of comedians in the midst of a diplomatic embassy, one which includes dancing women, singers, chamberlains, horses, and elephants, this makes sense in the context of early Indian court culture.[8] That the *pācaṇṭam* groups are supposed to number ninety-six parallels their description in the Pāli *Dīpavaṃsa* (6.25b), in a passage cited by Brereton (Ch. 2, p. 24); this appears to be a commonplace throughout early Indian Buddhism.[9] I am uncertain what to make of this connection; it may be that ninety-six is simply a proverbially high number. But this idea is found elsewhere in Tamil: indeed, it seems that the one thing that Tamil authors knew about *pācaṇṭams* was that they numbered ninety-six, for such is testimony of the early *Tivākaram* dictionary, and that of a fragment of a lost poetic work.[10]

This reference to the *pācaṇṭams* as a collection, however, is an outlier in the usage of the *Cilappatikāram*, while the other three occurrences form a bloc. The first of these is found in the opening lines of the poem's ninth canto or *kātai*. The previous canto had ended in suspense, with Kovalaṉ, Kaṇṇaki's husband, ending his affair with the dancer Mātavi. What would happen next? After a briefly sketched erotic scene of women preparing themselves to meet their lovers in the evening, the narrative abruptly dives into a flashback. The audience is suddenly introduced to another woman, named Mālati, as she is feeding milk to the child of her senior co-wife. The little boy chokes and dies, and the grieving and anxious young Brahmin woman wanders from temple

8. Ali 2004: 66, citing among other sources the autobiographical second chapter of Bāṇa's *Harṣacarita*. Parthasarathy translates this as "jesters," which risks confusion with better-known figures from Sanskrit literature, such as the *vidūṣaka*.

9. In Sanskrit, this is found in the Mahāyāna *Gaṇḍavyūhasūtra*: during the ascetic Sarvagāmin's teachings to Sudhana in the he describes "the ninety-six *pāṣaṇdas* found in Jambudvīpa, all of them overly set in their varied philosophical views" whom he attempts to teach (p. 137 *ye 'pīme kulaputra jambudvīpe ṣaṇṇavatiyo pāṣaṇḍā vividhadṛṣṭigatābhiniviṣṭāḥ*). It is also attested, e.g., in the Pāli *Sāratthappakāsinī* (II 401 *chanavutipāsaṇḍino*) and in a Gāndhārī fragment held in the British Museum (fragment 13, ln. 52: *ṣaṇavadi [r]paṣaḍa*); I am grateful to Stefan Baums for these latter two references, the second of which I cite from his edition (Baums 2009: 515–17).

10. The *Tivākaram* is cited by U. Ve. Cāminātaiyar in his notes to Aṭiyārkkunallār's discussion of 9.15 (p. 246), discussed p. 39: *pācaṇṭatturaiyum ivaṟṟuṭ palavām, peciṟ tŏṇṇūṟṟaṟuvakaip paṭume*. In this same passage, Aṭiyārkkunallār cites a verse from the lost *Vaḷaiyāpati* also attesting to this number, and little else.

to temple, the dead child in her arms, across the city. Successively, she visits the temples of the *kalpavṛkṣa*, of Airāvata (? "the white elephant," *vĕḷyāṉai*), of Ādiśeṣa, of the rising Sun, a shrine to Mt. Kailāsa, those dedicated to the weapons of Murukaṉ and Indra, perhaps the temple of Aiyaṉār, a temple of the Jina, and finally one dedicated to the Moon.[11] At each of these, she cries out "Oh gods, cure me of this affliction!" before throwing herself down before *pācaṇṭa cāttaṉ* (9.15). The first word here derives, of course, from *pāṣaṇḍa*; the latter, the commentator Aṭiyārkkunallār attempts to convince his readers (and perhaps himself), refers to the promulgators of these doctrines, which he declares—consistent with what we read later in the poem—to number ninety-six: "the creator of the *śāstras* that are the source of these" is thus named *makācāttiraṉ* (= Skt. *mahāśāstṛ*), from which *cāttaṉ* can be derived.[12] Here the learned commentator appears overmatched by his material, a problem that he discusses explicitly in his remarks on other sections of the *Cilappatikāram*. As the sequel bears out, the figure described here seems less the promulgator of religious dissidence and more of a piece with the world of localized Tamil cults, and indeed *cāttaṉ* is commonly recorded as a synonym for the village deity Aiyaṉār.[13]

A mysterious woman next appears to Mālati and, after telling her that the gods give nothing to those who do not practice *tavam* (=*tapas*), takes the dead child from her hands and leads her to a cremation ground. A corpse-eating *ḍākinī* ghost appears, takes the child's body and devours it, to Mālati's horrified cries. Cāttaṉ himself then speaks to Mālati, soothes her, and assumes the form of the resurrected child (9.16–25). Mālati then returns this illusory child (*māyak kuḻavi*) to her co-wife. The Brahmin boy grows up, studies the Veda, and eventually marries a woman, Tevanti, to whom he reveals his divine,

11. *Cil* 9.9–13. There are some uncertainties here: I follow Aṭiyārkkunallār in understanding *ūrkkoṭṭam* (ln. 11) as "a temple to Kailāsa, which is the natal village of the Lord" (*iṟaivaṉ ūrākiya kailāyam niṟkum koyil*); Parthasarathy prefers "the temple / of the guardian deity of Pukār" (88, ll. 17–18). *Puṟampaṇaiyāṉ vāḻ koṭṭam* (ln. 12) is literally "the temple where dwells he of the fields outside of town"; Aṭiyārkkunallār glosses this as *cātavākaṉaṉ koyil* (on this [=Skt. Śātavāhana] as a name for Aiyaṉār, see Adiceam 1967: 12, who interprets *cāta/sāta/śāta* as "cheval," after Pryzluski 1929, and cf. Ollett 2017: 68).

12. Aṭiyārkkunallār *ad loc* (pp. 246–47): *ivaṟṟiṟku mutalāyuḷḷa cāttiraṅkaḷaip payiṉṟavaṉ ātaliṉ makācattiraṉ ĕṉpatu avaṟku pĕyar āyiṟṟu; cāttaṟku: uruvumayakkam.*

13. On Aṭiyārkkunallār's self-professed limitations, see the discussion in Cox 2017: 87–90. As noticed in n. 11, this identification with Aiyaṉār may have been foreclosed for Aṭiyārkkunallār by his earlier association of *puṟampaṇaiyāṉ* with this deity. Cf. Adiceam's discussion of early lexicographical references identifying these names (1967: 12–13), and her unanswered questions on this particular passage: "Aurions-nous affaire à deux dieux différents? . . . Ne peut-on pas penser plutôt qu'il s'agit de deux aspects différents de même dieu?"

eternally youthful form, tells her "Come to my temple," and disappears (9.26–36). Tevanti, claiming her husband had gone off on pilgrimage, became a *habituée* of Pācaṇṭa Cāttaṉ's temple; it is there that she meets Kaṇṇaki and interprets a prophetic dream of hers.

It is a strange story. For all that it appears to be an unmotivated aside, in its focus on female characters, on domestic tragedy, and on the uncanny irruption of the divine into everyday life, it resonates deeply with the *Cilappatikāram*'s main narrative. This is equally, and even more surprisingly, the case in the other references to *pācaṇṭaṉ*, in the thirtieth and final canto. This, like the reference to the ninety-six *pācaṇṭams*, falls in the *Vañcikkāṇṭam*, the poem's third major division, sometimes regarded as a later addition. Shulman, in his recent survey of the text, rejects this idea, finding its account to be "utterly integral to the work as a whole" (2016: 99). In particular, it is in the third division where the story connects with both royal power, in the form of Cĕṅkuṭṭuvaṉ, the Kerala king, and with the worship of Pattiṉi, which Shulman sees as contiguous with Kerala's *tĕyyam* possession cults of more recent times.[14] I find this idea to be appealing, but believe it possible that the *Vañcikkāṇṭam* is *both* a later addition *and* the imposition of a larger integrative vision onto the narrative.

This is suggested by the reappearance, so late in the story, of Tevanti (or Tevantikai) and her absent husband, the god Cāttaṉ. The Brahmin lady, "who lives with the god Cāttaṉ" abruptly reappears, along with two previously unmentioned characters, Kaṇṇaki's nurse and handmaiden, just after the institution of the new cult.[15] The whole of the *Cilappatikāram*'s twenty-ninth canto forms an extended liturgical text, with sung lyrics allotted these three female figures, the Kerala king, a chorus of the women of Vañci, and to Kaṇṇaki herself, who appears "in divine ornaments,"[16] presumably at the climax of a possession ritual. The *Cilappatikāram*'s final canto, returning to narrative verse, appends a conclusion to this. Here, Tevantikai herself becomes possessed—in a vivid, practically ethnographic, description—and identifies herself as being none other than the god Pācaṇṭaṉ, calling upon the Brahmin Māṭalaṉ (another minor character from early in the poem, present now in Vañci) to attest to this.[17] Some more narrative business follows, involving Māṭalaṉ's recapitulation of Mālatī's story, where the god is once again called Pācaṇṭaṉ, and

14. On *tĕyyam*, refer to Freeman 2003.

15. *Cil* 29, opening prose (*uraippāṭumaṭai*, p. 570): *kaṭavuṭuṭaṉuṟainta tevantiyum*.

16. Proem to 29.10 (p. 573): *kaṇṇakiyār kaṭavuṇallaṇi kāṭṭiyatu*. I hope to discuss this passage elsewhere.

17. *Cil* 30: 69–70: *pācaṇṭaṉ yāṉ pārppaṉi taṉ mel / māṭala maṟaiyoy vanteṉ ĕṉṟalum*.

the recovery of past life memories of some little girls present at the temple's opening. Tevantikai is given ritual perquisites in the new Pattiṉi temple by the Kerala king, who acts as its first devotee. The king, the Brahmin, and the assembled kings of the earth and their armies all enter the temple's sacrificial hall together. Then, something unexpected: "I entered the temple, too" (30.171 *yāṉuñ cĕṉṟeṉ*): after many thousands of lines, the poet speaks for the first time *in propria persona.* He is then addressed by Tevantikai, or rather by Kaṇṇaki, who possesses her and hails his renunciation of kingship and embrace of the path of *mokṣa,* through which he acquired his name ("the reverend prince"). Tevantikai, now established as priestess of the new temple, is transferred it seems from Pācaṇṭa Cāttaṉ to Kaṇṇaki. But it is thus this mysterious deity who made this all possible.

But what to make of this? What especially to make of the presence of *pācaṇṭam* throughout? If we understand, as I think we should, the *Cilappatikāram*'s final cantos to be a secondary addition, both a guide to the cult of Kaṇṇaki and a tying together of the narrative threads of her story made by devout authors who were completely versed in the earlier tale of her apotheosis, the choice of Tevantikai and Cāttaṉ must have been motivated by some element in the earlier part of the text that suggested them as a conduit for the charisma of the new cult. The story of Mālati's domestic tragedy and the revenant child was surely a factor. But so too was the strangely liminal figure of Pācaṇṭa Cāttaṉ, at once a part of a wider cosmopolitan pantheon and an outlier, connected with the impurities of death and the terrifying culture of the cremation grounds. It is here, perhaps, that we make contact between the semantics of *pāṣaṇḍa* as it is more widely distributed in classical India, given the slippage between the "irreligious" *pāṣaṇḍa* and the extreme figure of the Kāpālika.[18] But Cāttaṉ is explicitly not a bearer of antithetical religious values, and so is certainly not a "heretic" in any sense. Within the concluding logic of the final *kātai,* Cāttaṉ is more like a place-holder, a figure of power and charisma who exists to be superseded in the new, more fully feminized dispensation of the cult of Pattiṉi. This liminality that does not cross the line into antimony is perhaps what the *Cilappatikāram* seeks to capture by its use of *pācaṇṭam.* But in any case, we certainly find ourselves a world away from the *pāṣaṇḍa* of the Aśokan edicts.

I was confused by these passages when I first read them, and I remain so now. But in publicly displaying my own confusion, I hope to have internalized

18. Cf. Doniger 1976: 164, 277–85. I adopt Sanderson's phrase "culture of the cremation grounds" (see Sanderson 1985: 200, *inter alia*).

one of the foremost of this collection's virtues: a willingness to ask questions, to present evidence and interpretation, in the hope of provoking others to do the same. I can only hope that some reader, somewhere, might find this mysterious case of Pācaṇṭa Cāttaṉ interesting enough to improve upon my own, tentative understanding.

Gṛhastha

PART I

Vedic and Prakrit Sources

I

The Term Gṛhastha *and the (Pre)history of the Householder*

Stephanie W. Jamison

THE CHAPTER BEFORE you owes its genesis to a particular circumstance and can be blamed on the same Indologist regularly responsible for my flights into unfamiliar scholarly territory—Patrick Olivelle. When Patrick and his colleague Don Davis set about producing an updated and reconceived version of P. V. Kane's *History of Dharmaśāstra* (Olivelle and Davis 2017), I was assigned the chapters on *strīdharma* and on marriage and the householder (*vivāha* and *gṛhastha*). This was all fine up to a point—I've written on various topics involving women and dharma and specifically on marriage. But the point after which it wasn't so fine was the householder—about whom I knew nothing and to whom I had never given any thought. He obviously fell to my lot because an ancient Indian householder had to be married, and I am known to "do" wives. But I was a little resentful.

But I am also dutiful, at least to Patrick, and so I set about digging up what I could and figuring out how to frame what I thought was going to be a fairly predictable and predetermined assignment. Since I'm a philologist above all,

This paper has been presented in various versions to various audiences—the American Oriental Society annual meeting (New Orleans), March 2015; "New Approaches to the Householder in Ancient India," Workshop, University of Texas (Austin), February 2016; "Buddhist Studies in Leiden" conference, Leiden University, May 2017—and has benefited considerably from comments from those audiences, especially the participants in the Texas workshop. I'm especially grateful to Patrick Olivelle for in-depth comments and encouragement.

the first thing I thought to do was to examine the word—*gṛhastha*—where it appears and what it means in texts other than dharma texts. I figured that this was just necessary due diligence, that these facts were generally known, and that nothing much would come of it. But, as it turns out, it seems no one had bothered to look at the word (at least no one I could unearth), and when one does, some unexpected things emerge. The first unexpected thing I came across was, in fact, absence.

As is well known, the (brahmin) householder (*gṛhastha*) is the linchpin of the dharma system, the unmarked subject and agent of most of the multiple provisions in the Dharmasūtras and śāstras and the economic support of the society envisioned there. In order to enter the householder's state, a man must marry, allowing him to establish a household and produce the progeny so necessary for the extension of his family line, both economically and ritually. So far, this figure, the *gṛhastha*, sounds very like the similarly dominant figures in the Vedic Śrautasūtras and Gṛhyasūtras. The latter, which give the rules for the domestic ritual, have as their central focus the married head of household; the Śrautasūtras, which give the rules for the more elaborate śrauta rites, presuppose as their central actor the sacrificer (*yajamāna*), who arranges for and presides over the rites. He too must be married, and his wife must be present and active for such rituals to take place.[1] So the householder of the dharma texts at first seems like a simple continuator of these earlier, Vedic figures, with simply a different aspect of his duties and responsibilities emphasized.

But—as it turns out—there's a total break in lexical realization. The term *gṛhastha* is nowhere encountered in Sanskrit before the dharma texts, and what we think of as the corresponding figure is called by different names. However, once encountered, *gṛhastha* silently replaces previous terms with no signal in the texts themselves as to where the term comes from or why older terms needed replacement. Now, lexical replacement is a common linguistic phenomenon, and it need not signal a conceptual break. But I argue that, in this case, this is not merely a lexical change but a conceptual one, that part of the impetus for the change was a set of conceptual asymmetries, and that the source of this new term is both surprising and, I hope, illuminating.

In order to understand this change, it is helpful to put it in historical context by examining previous terms for something like the same role, since, as was noted above, the generic married head-of-household was not an entirely new invention of post-Vedic India. The terms that identify that role in Vedic

1. See at length Jamison 1996.

text shift over time and participate in different terminological clusters, and this instability may be one of the factors contributing to the apparently abrupt lexical replacement we find in the dharma literature.

I begin at the beginning, and though what I choose to call the beginning would not surprise Indo-Europeanists, it may be unfamiliar to Indologists—namely the Rig Vedic compound *dámpati-* (12×) "master of the house," which has good Indo-Iranian and Indo-European counterparts: Old Avestan *dǝ̄ṇg paiti-*, Greek δεσπότης. It contains an old word for "house" (represented indirectly in our "domestic" vocabulary) as first member. The phrasal equivalent *patír dán* (5×),[2] with the archaic genitive to the root noun (<**déms*), is also found, as is the curiously formed and apparently archaic *dámūnas-* (25×) of approximately the same meaning.[3] Both the extra-Indic cognates and the archaic formation(s) identify this collocation as the old designation for what we will come to call the householder.

But, showing a pattern that we will encounter again, these terms are almost never used of the human householder but applied rather to gods, especially Agni (*dámpati-*, e.g., V.2.4; *patír dán*, e.g., I.149.1; *dámūnas-*, e.g., V.1.8), apparently assimilated to that role. Only once[4] is any one of these terms clearly applied to the human male head of household, *dámūnas-* in X.41.3, a late Aśvin hymn, in which the Aśvins are urged to bypass various other priests and come to our sacrifice:

adhvaryúṃ vā mádhupāṇiṃ suhástyam, agnídhaṃ vā dhṛtádakṣaṃ dámūnasam
víprasya vā yát sávanāni gáchathò 'ta ā́ yātam madhupéyam aśvinā

2. Oddly, given the evident archaism of the phrase, *patír dán* and the root noun *dám-* by itself are confined to Maṇḍalas I and X, save possibly for VI.3.7 . . . *dáṃ supátnī*, which I interpret differently (see Jamison and Brereton 2014 ad loc. and my online commentary at http://rigvedacommentary.alc.ucla.edu/ also ad loc.). The compound *dámpati-* is more widely distributed through the *RV*.

3. On its usage and formation see, most recently, Pinault 2000 (esp. 67–84). Pinault (esp. 72–84) argues strenuously that *dámūnas-* does not mean the same thing as *dámpati-* but rather "bénéficiaire de la maisonnée," and certainly I agree that the semantic range of the former seems wider than the latter. But even Pinault (82–84) admits that it can be used for the houselord. His semantic investigation is in service of his proposed morphological derivation and accounts for his insistent denial of an original "houselord" sense.

4. Pinault (2000: 81) cites also VIII.50.10 (Vālakhilya) with loc. *dīrghánīthe dámunasi*; in this he is following the standard interpretation (see, e.g., Geldner 1951 ad loc.), which takes Dīrganītha as a personal name. Although this is possible, I prefer to take the phrase as referring to Agni "the domestic leader of long counsel." Even if it does refer to a human, the lateness of the passage does not affect my general characterization of the usage of *dámūnas-* in the *RV*.

> Whether you are going to an Adhvaryu-priest of good hands with honey in his palms, or to an Agnidh-priest of steadfast skill, master of the house,
> or to the soma-pressings of an inspired poet, from there drive here to honey-drinking, o Aśvins.

However, there is an exception to this restriction to divine reference: the dual *dámpatī*, which is twice as common as the singular (8× versus 4×), is used exclusively of the human "household pair" (married couple).[5] In other words, when the wife is included under the rubric of *dámpati-*, both members of the pairing are human and form a symmetrical couple, as in the following marital context:

> *añjánti mitrám̐ súdhitaṃ ná góbhir yád dámpatī sámanasā kṛṇóṣi*
>
> They anoint [you (=Agni) as] Mitra with cows, like a well-established [ally], when you make the married couple to be of one mind.[6]

As we will see again later, in this early period it is the house-*wife* who generates and terminologically anchors her house-*husband*, the house-*lord*. After the *Rig Veda* the singular forms of the compound essentially disappear; dual *dámpatī* in the same usage as the Rig Vedic occurrences continues in the *Atharva Veda*[7] and in a few *Yajur Veda* mantras, and it surfaces occasionally in the Gṛhyasūtras (*GobhGṛ* I.4.17; *KhadGṛ* II.1) and even in dharma texts (e.g., *VaDh* 11.11, *MDh* III.116).[8] Its persistence is probably owing to the fact that there is no other established one-word way to refer specifically to the married couple, but it is perhaps surprising that no new term was coined and generally adopted.[9]

---

5. Or once of a pair with semi-divine ancestry who are presented as human or human-like, namely Yama and Yamī in X.10.5.

6. *Rig Veda* V.3.2cd. Unless otherwise noted Rig Vedic translations are taken from Jamison and Brereton 2014, with occasional minor modifications. Translations from other texts are my own, though often filtered through the standard published translations.

7. In addition to repeated passages from the *RV*, there are six new passages: VI.11.3; XII.3.14, 27, 35; XIV.2.9, 64 (wedding hymn).

8. On the use of *dampatī* in the dharma literature, including several occurrences in Yājñavalkya, see Brick, Ch. 8, this volume.

9. A few exceptions: *JaiGṛ* I.22 *jāyāpati-; PārGṛ* II.9.14 *gṛhapatiḥ patnī ca; GobhGṛ* III.3.30 *kulapatī*; in dharma material, specifically *ĀpDh*, the duals *gṛhamedhinoḥ ĀpDh* II.1.1, 15,

Thus, although *dámpati-* is likely to have been the oldest Sanskrit term for what we later call the householder, it is already recessive in the *Rig Veda*, disappears as a designation in the singular for males after that text, and even in the *Rig Veda* it is not used of human householders but only of gods who perform similar roles. It is already being replaced in the *Rig Veda* with *gṛhápati-* (approximately 20×), showing the same formation but a less archaic word (and morphological form) for "house." Nonetheless, this word *gṛhá-* has almost as distinguished a pedigree in Indo-Iranian and Indo-European as *dám-*. Its Iranian cognates include Younger Avestan *gərəδa-*, designating a daevic dwelling (V. 3.7, 10, 22; Skjaervø [unpubl.] translates "den"), and, transmitted in the so-called Nebenüberlieferung (=parallel transmission of Old Persian), several compounds with **grδa-* as first member, possibly including exactly our *gṛhápati*: **grδa-pati-*, found in Elamite *kur-da-bat-ti-iš*, Akkadian *ga-ar-du-pa-tu$_4$*,[10] as well as in Middle Iranian. It also has numerous cognates outside of Indo-Iranian, where the same etymon gives us both English "yard" and "garden" (by different routes).

However, the phonological form of this word for "house" suggests that it may belong to a lower sociolinguistic register and that it is therefore a more colloquial replacement for the more elevated *dám-/dáma-*. For one thing, the medial *-h-* is unexpected: given the cognates just cited, the Indo-Iranian preform should be **ghṛdhá*, which should yield Sanskrit **gṛdhá-* with a dental voiced aspirate. I cannot go into the messy technical details of the development of intervocalic voiced aspirates to *-h-* in Indo-Aryan,[11] but such loss of

II.3.12; *jāyāpatyoḥ ĀpDh* II.14.16; *kuṭumbhinau ĀpDh* II.29.3; *svāminau ĀpDh* II.4.13. For more on the Āpastambha materials, see below.

10. See Hinz 1975: 107; also Hinz and Koch 1987: 520, 534; *EWA* s.v. *gṛhá-*. However, Elizabeth Tucker (personal communication) points out that this kind of compound is so easily formed that it may well have been created independently in the two branches.

11. Intervocalic *-h-* for original **bh* and **dh* is not rare even in Vedic (see AiG I.250–53) and is found not only in individual lexical items but also in the morphology, in desinences like medial first-person plural *-mahi*, *-mahe*, act. second-person singular impv. *-hi* (~ *-dhi*). The data are messy, and whether the *-h-* outcome in any particular case is by phonological rule, dialect mixture, or a combination of both (or neither) is unclear. Since, as noted in the text, loss of occlusion in medial aspirates is common in MIA (see, e.g., Hinüber 2001: §184), the *-h-* outcome is often considered to be the result of dialect mixture or MIA influence (see references in Kobayashi 2004: 85), although this is not a particularly satisfying explanation for the elements deeply embedded in the morphological system. This deocclusion phenomenon has been most recently and fully treated by Kobayashi (2004: 84–91), who tests the phonological conditioning suggested by Wackernagel (AiG I.252: between vowels and specifically after unaccented vowels), which, as Kobayashi points out, leaves too many counterexamples unaccounted for. Kobayashi himself proposes some further refinements to this conditioning, which narrow the list of counterexamples, but he still concludes that

occlusion is very common in Middle Indic. Although I remain agnostic about the cause of the deocclusion in morphological elements like those given in note 11, I do suggest that a dialectal or—perhaps better—register difference may account for it in certain lexical items, and, in particular, as noted above, I suggest that lower-register *gṛhá-* replaced the more elevated *dám-/dáma-*, which by then would have been confined to hieratic archaizing discourse. Middle Indic provides support for this view: forms related to *gṛhá-* are widely distributed in Middle Indic,[12] while *dám(a)-* barely exists there, if it is found at all (see *EWA* s.vv. *dámūnas-*, *dámpati-*), a distribution that suggests a more demotic quality to *gṛhá-* than the *dám(a)-* words. This likely vernacular source will be worth keeping in mind when we investigate the source of *its* replacement, the *gṛhastha* that is our focus here.

The semantic overlap of the terms and the process of replacement of one by the other are suggested by the fact that *gṛhápatir dáme* "houselord in the house" is found in several passages in the *Rig Veda* (II.1.2 [=X.91.10], IV.9.4) and that *dámūnas-* and *gṛhápati-* occur several times adjacent to each other and with the same referent (IV.11.5, V.8.5, and note especially the triple representation of "house" in I.60.4: *dámūnā gṛhápatir dáma ā́* "house-master, houselord in the house").

And what is that referent? Here the usage of *gṛhápati-*, which is only singular in the *Rig Veda*, almost entirely tracks that of *dámpati-* in the same number and in fact is even more restricted. That is, *gṛhápati-* in the *Rig Veda* is almost never used of the human householder, but always of the god Agni, in his role as the fire lodged in the household. Although *pátir dán/dámūnas-* occasionally have other divine referents besides Agni (e.g., X.105.2 *patír dán* = Indra; VI.71.4 *dámūnas-* = Savitar), *gṛhápati-* is never used with any other referent than Agni, save for one passage in a Pūṣan hymn (VI.53.2) that seems to refer to the human houselord. In a typical passage with Agni as referent, the god's various ritual roles are laid out:

tvám agne gṛhápatis tváṃ hotā́ no adhvaré
tvám pótā viśvavāra prácetā yákṣi véṣi vā́ryam

"no single phonological formulation or dialectal generalization can satisfactorily explain all case of deocclusion" (89) and specifically includes *gṛhá-* among examples of "sporadic" deocclusion between vowels (90).

12. For an overview, see *EWA* s.v. *gṛhá-* and *CDIAL* 4240, 4242–45, as well as the discussion of various such forms p. 15–16.

Agni, you are the houselord; you the Hotar in the rite;
you the attentive Potar, o you who grant all wishes—sacrifice and seek out a desirable reward [for us]. (*RV* VII.16.5)

Although we might presume that Agni is called *gṛhápati* because he is the divine counterpart of the human head of household, it is still striking that that human has been essentially elided, at least in the Rig Vedic usage of the term. Although we often hear in the *Rig Veda* about the human who arranges and performs the rituals, about the soma-presser and the singer and the man who labors over the sacrifice, that sacrificer is never identified as a *gṛhápati*, except possibly in the Pūṣan passage just mentioned. This is of course also true of the usage of *dámpati-*/*dámūnas-*, save for X.41.3 quoted above. And I, in fact, sometimes wonder whether that presumption is wrong and whether we are misled by the prominent later role of the human householder to assume that in the earlier material the god as houselord is secondary to the human one. Certainly the Rig Vedic usage of the terms *dámpati-* and *gṛhápati-* gives no reason to take the human referent as primary.

Where then does the human houselord come from? Here we must focus on the housewife. Remember that though *dámpati-* in the masculine singular is not used of humans, the dual *dámpatī* is used of the human married couple and indeed in at least one context where it's clear they are performing ritual together:

yā́ dámpatī sámanasā sunutá ā́ ca dhā́vataḥ

The household couple who with one mind press and rinse (the soma) . . . [13]

Unlike *dámpati-*, *gṛhápati-* is never found in the dual. There seems to be no way to refer to the married householder couple with a term that includes *gṛhá-*. There is, on the other hand, a feminine: *gṛhápatnī*, which occurs once in the *Rig Veda*, in X.85.26cd, and clearly refers to the human "mistress of the house" in the wedding hymn:

gṛhā́n gacha gṛhápatnī yáthāso vaśínī tvám̐ vidátham ā́ vadāsi

Go to the house, so that you will be mistress of the house. Exerting your will you will announce the ceremonial distribution.

13. *Rig Veda* VIII.31.5ab. It should be noted, however, that *RV* VIII.31 is almost unique in the *RV* in depicting the later śrauta model with the *pátnī* a necessary participant in ritual. I have argued elsewhere that the introduction of the *pátnī* in that role came only in the late Rig Vedic period and encountered considerable conservative opposition. See Jamison 2011, 2016, and 2018b.

Here the new bride, on her wedding journey, is exhorted to take her *place* in the house so that she can take up her *role* in the house. The term *gṛhápatnī* seems almost a definitional one, and it is therefore especially striking that there is no corresponding term for her husband—for, as we saw, *gṛhápati-* names not her husband, the lord of the house, but rather the ritual fire established in the house, the fire that will later be called the *gā́rhapatya-*, a transparent vṛddhi derivative. But, interestingly, this last term, which occurs four times in the *Rig Veda*, does not refer to the fire as it does later, but is used rather as a noun for "the ruling/arranging of the household." It is found twice in the same wedding hymn, once in the verse immediately following the one just quoted and also addressed to the new wife:

asmín gṛhé gā́rhapatyāya jāgṛhi

Here in this house be vigilant for the ruling of your household. (*RV* X.85.27b)

It is found once in a verse addressed to the wife by the husband:

máhyaṃ tvādur gā́rhapatyāya devā́ḥ

The gods gave you to me for the ruling of the household. (*RV* X.85.36d)

The other two occurrences are in Agni verses: in VI.15.19 Agni is addressed as *gṛhapate janānām*, "houselord of the peoples," and it is hoped that our *gā́rhapatyāni* will be to his satisfaction; in I.15.12 Agni is called the leader of the sacrifice (*yajñanī́-*) by virtue of his *gā́rhapatyena*.

Putting this all together, it seems that, at least for the Vedic bards, the counterpart to the *gṛhápatnī*, "mistress of the house" is not her husband, but rather the household fire, which is named by the corresponding term *gṛhápati*; both wife and fire are characterized by their *gā́rhapatya-*. The pairing is radically asymmetrical, for the husband, the expected houselord, is not part of the pairing. What I'm saying here is that at least terminologically the human householder, the houselord, is secondarily generated from his wife, whose original opposite number is the fire, not the man. The wife creates her husband. In a sense, this seems on the surface to be no different from the conceptualization of the householder's state in the dharma literature—what defines a man as a *gṛhastha* is the fact that he is married and has therefore set up a household—but, on the one hand, the Rig Vedic evidence makes the dependence of the householder on the housewife much clearer, and, on the other, as I argue below, this superficial impression may conceal a deeper disjunction between the two householders.

Here, briefly, let us place the emphasis not on the second members of the compound but the first, *gṛhá-*, for if the housewife generates the householder, the house itself generates the housewife. Note the verse in which the only Rig Vedic occurrence of *gṛhápatnī* occurs, right after the command *gṛhā́n gacha*. The locative *gṛhé* is also found in verse 27, right before *gā́rhapatya-*. The happy couple is also depicted as "rejoicing in your own house" (*módamanau své gṛhé*) in verse 42 and in additional verses in the *Atharva Veda* version of the wedding hymn (*AVŚ* XIV.1–2) houses figure prominently (e.g., *AVŚ* XIV.2.12, 17, 26, 27, 43). It is the housewife's exclusive association with the house that provides her with her title and role. Indeed, in a repeated passage in the Gṛhyasūtras she is identified as the house itself: in *Khadira Gṛhyasūtra* I.5.17 as in *Gobhila Gṛhyasūtra* I.3.15, *gṛhāḥ*[14] *patnī*, "the wife is the house."

The *Atharva Veda* shows us the next step in the production of a human houselord. The word *gṛhápati-* is found only four times in that text, and, in sharp contrast to the Rig Vedic usage, in only one of them (in identical adjacent passages) is the referent Agni:

> *sāyám̐-sāyam̐ gṛhápatir no agníḥ prātáḥ-prātaḥ saumanasásya dātā́*
>
> Evening after evening is Agni our houselord, morning after morning the giver of benevolence. (*AV* XIX.55.3 = 4)

In the other three passages the word refers to the human houselord. In one, in a wedding hymn, he becomes *gṛhápati-* by oppositional association with his new wife:

> *pátnī tvám asi dhármaṇāhám̐ gṛhápatis táva*
>
> You are (my) wife by dharma; I am your houselord.[15]

Note the migration of *gṛha-* from the wife, who is now just *pátnī*, not *gṛhápatnī* as in the *Rig Veda*, to the husband, who was not a *gṛhápati-* in the *Rig Veda*

14. The plural of *gṛha-* is often used of a single homestead, presumably because it was made up of a number of separate structures.

15. See *AV* XIV.1.51. This verse immediately follows a repetition from the *RV* wedding hymn, X.95.36 = *AV* XIV.1.50, partially quoted above because it attributes *gā́rhapatya-* ("household management") to the wife. The same verse also contains *páti-* referring to the husband, but, significantly, not *gṛhápati-*: *RV* X.95.36b, *máyā pátyā jarádaṣṭir yáthā́saḥ*, "so that with me as your husband you will reach old age."

(see the passage cited in n. 15). In another *Atharva Veda* passage he becomes *gṛhápati-* by knowledge of the Gārhapatya fire, now so named:[16]

> *sódakrāmat sā́ gā́rhapatye nyàkrāmat / gṛhamedhī́ gṛhápatir bhavati yá evám̐ véda*
>
> She [=Virāj] ascended; she descended into the householder's (fire); he who knows thus becomes a house-sacrificing houselord.[17]

Thus a man becomes a *gṛhápati-* by virtue of his association with the asymmetrical pair found already in the *Rig Veda*, the housewife and the house fire.

In the *Atharva Veda*, quite distinctly from the *Rig Veda*, the term *gā́rhapatya-* (approx. 20×) now only designates a fire,[18] the householder's fire, and in a number of passages it is paired with the other two classical śrauta fires (VIII.10.2–4; IX.6.30; XV.6.5; XVIII.4.8–9). There is still some evidence for the association between housewife and house fire, however; in the wedding hymn XIV.2, the new wife serves this fire (in a verse not found in the *RV* wedding hymn):

> *yadā́ gā́rhapatyam ásaparyait pū́rvam agním̐ vadhū́r iyám*
>
> When this bride has served the householder's (fire), the former (?)[19] fire . . . (*AV* XIV.2.20)

Thus the *Atharva Veda* shows a more natural symmetrical pairing of the (house)wife (*pátnī*) with her human houselord/house-husband (*gṛhápati-*), while her divine consort of Rig Vedic times, Agni, mostly shorn of his *gṛhápati-* title, is designated rather by the vṛddhi adjective *gā́rhapatya-* "belonging to/

16. It is clear that *gā́rhapatye* here refers to the fire, because it is the first in a series of parallel verses referring to the three śrauta fires (verse 3 is on the Āhavanīya; verse 4, the Southern fire).

17. *Atharva Veda* VIII.10.2 [prose]. The third passage containing the human houselord is XIX.31.13, where an amulet of udumbara wood is identified as a *gṛhamedhín-* and credited with the ability to make the man in question a *gṛhápati-*: *gṛhamedhī́ gṛhápatim̐ mā kṛṇu*, "being house-sacrificer, make me a houselord."

18. Except for two Rig Vedic repetitions in the wedding hymn, XIV.1.21, 50.

19. I am not certain of the sense of *pū́rvam* here. Does it refer to a transformation upon marriage of a previous fire into the householder's fire? Is the Gārhapatya fire "previous" because the Āhavanīya has been taken out of it and installed to the east? Or does it simply mean something like "foremost"?

stemming from the houselord." However, the conditions for a new asymmetry have been established.

Let us now fast-forward to the Gṛhyasūtras, the manuals for the domestic ritual. For us, the trouble with these texts is that the central figure, whom we may think of as the householder, often has no designation, since he is the default and therefore unnamed subject of all verbs of ritual action. However, when he *is* named, he is generally called the *gṛhapati* (cf. *ŚāṅGṛ* I.1.2; *PārGṛ* II.9.14–15; *KhadGṛ* I.5.36; III.3.16, 24; *GobhGṛ* I.4.24).[20] Thus the term seems finally to have settled down as the name for the human head-of-house exactly in the texts devoted to the rituals of the house, the Gṛhyasūtras. But curiously the wife has lost her domestic prefix, a development we saw already beginning in *Atharva Veda* XIV.1.15. Though, as discussed above, the housewife, *gṛhapatnī*, seems to precede and indeed generate the human houselord in the *Rig Veda*, in later texts she is no longer referred to as *gṛhapatnī*, but simply as *patnī* (*ĀśGṛ* I.9.1, 3; *PārGṛ* II.9.14; *KhadGṛ* I.5.17, III.4.8; *GobhGṛ* I.3.15, 6.9), and sometimes *jāyā* (*ŚāṅGṛ* III.4.9; *PārGṛ* III.2.6) or *bhāryā* (*ĀpGṛ* III.8.7; *KhadGṛ* III.3.22 [pl.]); *strī* is also found, though not always designating the wife per se but simply a woman as opposed to a man (*GobhGṛ* I.4.19; *ĀpGṛ* III.8.3; *PārGṛ* II.17.18 [pl.]). The married couple may be referred to as *gṛhapatiḥ patnī ca* (*PārGṛ* II.9.14), though the old dual *dampatī* is also found (*KhadGṛ* II.1.4; *GobhGṛ* I.4.17). Thus, it is no longer the wife who is identified with the house, but the husband.[21]

As I mentioned above, another asymmetry has been created by this terminological shift. The houselord is now properly so called, but the domestic cult over which he presides is centered on a single fire, and that fire is *not* named by the vṛddhi derivative of his title, Gārhapatya—because that term was long ago (beginning in the *Atharva Veda*, as we saw) co-opted by the śrauta ritual system, as one of the three fires on the ritual ground and the fire from which the other two śrauta fires, particularly the Āhavanīya, are taken. In the śrauta system the man who sponsors the sacrifice is called the *yajamāna*, not the *gṛhapati*. So the *gṛhapati* is terminologically severed from what we might expect to be his fire, *gārhapatya*. The fire for the domestic cult is generally just called *agni* or *gṛhya agni* (*ŚāṅGṛ* I.25.11; III.7.3; *ĀśGṛ* I.9.1; *KhadGṛ* I.5.1; *GobhGṛ* I.3.15; *MDh* III.84), as well as *āvasthya* (*PārGṛ* I.2.1) and *aupāsana* (*PārGṛ* I.9.1; *HirGṛ* I.7.26.1; II.1.3.4, 4.7). It is often derived from

20. Also *svāmin-* in *PārGṛ* 6; *gṛhamedhin-* in *GobhGṛ* I.4.18.

21. Though see *KhadGṛ* I.5.17 = *GobhGṛ* I.3.15, quoted above, where she is equated with the house itself.

the nuptial fire, *vaivāhya* (*ŚāṅGṛ* I.1.3, 17.8) or *vivāhāgni* (*ĀśGṛ* I.8.5, 9),[22] and in Manu III.67 the householder is enjoined to perform the domestic rites (*gṛhyaṃ karma*) in his nuptial fire (*vaivāhike 'gnau*). My working assumption is that the disjunction between the *gṛhapati* and the *gārhapatya*, which inhabit two different ritual systems, caused some discomfort—that is, a feeling that the standard householder performing domestic rituals perhaps shouldn't be called *gṛhapati* because that is associated with śrauta rites—and that, given the higher prestige of the śrauta system, the term *gṛhapati* for the central figure of the gṛhya system passed out of use or, rather, was not carried over into the dharma texts.

Whatever the reasons, pass out of use—or at least of this usage[23]—it certainly did. Although we might expect that the houselord of the Gṛhyasūtras would be the obvious prototype of and model for the householder of the dharma system, the *gṛhapati* of the Gṛhyasūtras is completely absent from the dharma texts. And in place of this venerable word we find what is for us the familiar term *gṛhastha-*. But though it is familiar to us, it is a complete innovation in the tradition. The word is not ever found in Sanskrit before the Dharmasūtras, but it suddenly appears in all four Dharmasūtras and the legal tradition seems never to have looked back: *gṛhastha* is *the* word for householder, and that's that. Although some synonyms do get used (*kuṭumbin-*, e.g., *ĀpDh* II.6.5, 7.1; *gṛhin-*, e.g., *MDh* III.67), the term of art is clearly *gṛhastha-*.

Before inquiring into the source of the term, I first call attention to a telling discrepancy in the early dharma literature, well described and analyzed by Brick (Ch. 8, this volume). The blanket statement I just made, "it [*gṛhastha*] suddenly appears in all four Dharmasūtras," needs to be qualified, for the usage in Āpastamba, probably the earliest of the four Dharmasūtras, is different from the texts that come later. In fact, the term *gṛhastha* is found only once in Āpastamba, in a quoted verse (II.9.13), so not as part of the text's own discourse. Otherwise there is only the vṛddhi derivative *gārhasthyam*, in a passage (II.21.1) in which it is identified as the first of the four *āśramas*. Āpastamba prefers other terms, and, significantly, all those other terms are used in the dual, referring to the household pair (see n. 9): *gṛhamedhinoḥ*

22. See also Gonda 1980: 163–64.

23. However, *gṛhapati* does not disappear from the scene in non-dharma texts, but has a prominent career in later Sanskrit and, especially, Middle Indic texts in a somewhat different meaning: the houselord as a rich or substantial man, a merchant or the like, especially of the Vaiśya *varṇa*. See Jamison forthcoming.

(*ĀpDh* II.1.1, 15, II.3.12); *jāyāpatyoḥ* (*ĀpDh* II.14.16); *kuṭumbhinau* (*ĀpDh* II.29.3);[24] and *svāminau* (*ĀpDh* II.4.13). It appears from this preponderance of duals that Āpastamba continues to adhere to the older Vedic model that focuses on the household pair, the married couple, and indeed, judging from *gṛhamedhin-* ("possessing/performing the house sacrifice"),[25] on an older *ritual* model. (For further discussion of this model in Āpastamba, see Jamison 2006: 192–95.)

But let us return to *gṛhastha* and ask—where does it come from? Compounds in *-stha-* are reasonably common already in the *Rig Veda*, and at least one goes back, in one form or another, to Indo-Iranian: *ratheṣṭhá-* ("standing on the chariot, charioteer"), the thematized version of root-noun-final *ratheṣṭhā́-* with its Younger Avestan cognate *raϑaēštā-*. All the other clear Rig Vedic examples, however, refer not to people but to places, such as *go-ṣṭhá-* ("place for cattle, stall"), *bhayá-stha-* ("fearful place").[26] But these parallel formations are of limited value in explaining the coinage.

Much more important is the evidence of Middle Indic, for forms of this very word are attested throughout Middle Indic beginning with Aśoka—that is, dating from approximately the same time as the early Dharmasūtras. Before examining the usage of the term there, we must take a slight detour into several of the words for "house" in Middle Indic. The ordinary Middle Indo-Aryan reflex of our Sanskrit *gṛha-* is *gaha-* (Pāli, Pkt.), but *giha-* also occurs (in *agiha-*, "homeless").[27] In Northwestern dialects the typical *saṃprasāraṇa*-like *-ra-*/*-ri-* outcome of syllabic *ṛ* is found in Shāhbazgarhī *graha-* and Gāndhārī Prakrit *griha-*. All of these forms unequivocally go back to **gṛha-*. However, there are

24. The word *kutumbhin-* also occurs in the singular in *ĀpDh* II.6.5, 7.1. For discussion, see Brick (Ch. 8, this volume).

25. The terms *gṛhamedhá-* (*RV* VII.59.10, where it has an initial accent because it's a vocative) and *gṛhamedhī́ya-* (*RV* VII.56.14) go all the way back to the *Rig Veda* and refer to an offering to the Maruts. Despite the *gṛha-* prefix, this offering is later found in śrauta, not gṛhya rites, as part of the Sākamedha, the last of the Caturmāsyāni rituals, another instance of the disconnect between earlier "house"-related ritual and the gṛhya ritual system. I do not understand why the Maruts, the least domestic of gods, receive an offering so named, but it is not material to our purposes, since the association with the Maruts is not evident in the use of the term here or even in the attestations in the *Atharva Veda* quoted above (*AV* VIII.10.2; XIX.31.13, text and n. 17). Note the *-medha-* ("sacrifice"), the second component also of *aśvamedha-*, etc.

26. Though compounds with the root-noun *-sthā́-*, rather than the thematized *-stha-*, show agentive value; e.g., *giriṣṭhā́-*, "standing on the mountain."

27. Berger (1955: 40) considers *gaha-* the standard reflex in Pāli and derives *-giha-* from *gihi(n)-*, "possessor of a house, householder" by vowel assimilation.

two other "house" words that are phonologically similar but quite possibly etymologically separate, *ghara-* and *geha-* (the latter also Sanskrit, found already in the Rig Vedic derivative *gehyà-*). The tangled and much-disputed history of these words is unimportant for our purposes;[28] what *is* important is that the three words in their various Middle Indic guises become hopelessly confused, and all three show up as the first member of the compound that I'll represent with the cover term **gṛhastha-*.

Let us now consider the usage of this compound in the Aśokan inscriptions,[29] where it appears three times, starting with the beginning of the 12th Rock Edict. I give first the reading of the first sentence in Girnār (the most [pseudo-]Sanskritic of the versions), with Bloch's (1950) translation:

> Girnār (Rock Edict XIIA.): *devānaṃpiye piyad[a]si rājā savapāsaṃḍāni ca [pa]vajitāni ca **gharastāni ca** pūjayati*
>
> Bloch: Le roi ami des dieux au regard amical honor toutes les sectes, **les samanes et les laïques.**[30]

The other readings,[31] showing variant forms of the first member, are

> Kālsī: *pav[a]jitā[n]i gahathāni vā*
> Shāhbāzgaṛī: *pravrajita[ni] grahathani ca*
> Mānsehrā: *[p]ravra[ji]tani gehathani ca*

The important thing to note here is the pairing in which our compound finds itself, what in Sanskrit would be *pravrajita-/gṛhastha-*, "the 'gone forth' and the *gṛhastha-*," rendered by Bloch as "the śramaṇas and the laymen." There is another occurrence, in the 7th Pillar Edict, where Aśoka claims that his agents of dharma occupy themselves in numerous types of benevolent action with

28. For this see *EWA* s.vv. *gṛhá-* and *gehá-*, with further literature, including Berger.

29. Rock edicts cited after Schneider 1978; the pillar edict after Hultzsch 1925. For detailed discussion of the Aśokan evidence, see Olivelle (Ch. 3, this volume), and for *pāṣaṇḍa* in particular, Brereton (Ch. 2, this volume).

30. On the ambiguous syntax of the object noun phrase, particularly whether the *pravrajitas* and *gṛhasthas* are included among the *pāṣaṇḍas* or not, see Brereton (Ch. 2, this volume), and, differently, Olivelle (Ch. 3). The issue is not of importance for my point, which is the conjunction of *pravrajitas* and *gṛhasthas*.

31. The relevant word is missing in Eṛṛaguḍi.

regard to various groups of people. Again we meet the pairing *pravrajita-/gṛhastha-*, along with *pāṣaṃḍa-*, as in Rock Edict XII:

> *dhaṃmamahāmātā pi me te bahuvidhesu aṭhesu ānugahikesu viyāpaṭāse pavajītānaṃ ceva gihithānaṃ sava[pāsaṃḍ]esu pi ca viyāpaṭāṣe.* (PE Dehli-Topra 7.25)

Adopting Brereton's translation (Ch. 2, this volume) of this syntactically ambiguous passage (for which see his careful and convincing discussion), we get "The officers of the *dharma* also are engaged in benevolent affairs of many kinds: [those] for both renunciates and householders. They are engaged also among all religious communities." In the third occurrence in Aśoka, in the Rock Edict XIIIG, the word appears with *śramaṇa*, in a larger set of personnel:[32]

> Shāhbāzgaṛhī : *bramaṇa va* ***śrama[ṇa]*** *va a[ṃ]ñe va praṣaṃḍa* ***gra[ha]tha*** *va*
> Kālsī: *b[ā]bhanā va ṣama va ane vā pāśaṃḍā gih[i]thā vā*
>
> Hultzsch: the Brāhmaṇas or Śramaṇas, or other sects or householders. . . .

For further discussion of the structure of this passage, again consult Brereton (Ch. 2, this volume). He convincingly argues, on the basis of the distribution of relative pronouns in the larger passage, that the "Brahmaṇas, śramaṇas, or other religious communities" form one constituent, opposed to the other, which consists entirely of householders.

In other words, in the Aśokan occurrences the *gṛhastha* is either found in a two-way contrastive pairing with ascetics who have "gone forth" or contrasted with a collection of ascetic types. This, I think, is the solution to the question of where this word came from. The term *gṛhastha* in these contexts does not refer to the householder per se, but rather to the "stay-at-home" as against the "gone-forth" ascetic; he is one pole of the two extreme possibilities. He may seem to represent the layman, but the literal meaning of the term refers to his staying put, as opposed to the wandering of the renouncing ascetic. The formation of the word makes perfect sense in this contrastive polarity, and it makes clear the participation of the householder in the larger system of religious roles and activities. The

32. A further list of sects is also found in PE 7, though not in the same syntactic unit.

gṛhastha is, in fact, no mere layman, but one who pursues his religious duties no less than the "gone forth," although he pursues them at home.

In any case, the evidence is not confined to Aśoka. Most[33] of the early Middle Indo-Aryan corpora contain the same contrastive pairing. For example, in Gāndhārī Prakrit the Niya Document 489, concerning the rules for the saṅgha and disobedient monks, contains two occurrences of *grihastha*. In the first a monk (*bhic̄ḱu*) who appears at a certain ceremony "in householder's dress" (*grihasta coḍ'ina*) must pay a fine. Even more telling is the final phrase (before the tablet breaks off): *yo* ***grihasta śramaṃnas̱a*** *pra*, "whichever householder to/of [etc.] a śramana . . ." Whatever one was going to do to, for, or with the other, they are paired.

The pairing is also found frequently in Pāli; see Margaret Cone's (2010) definition under *gahaṭṭha*: "one who lives in a house; a householder; a layperson (very often contrasted with *pabbajita*)."[34] Compare, for example, Khaggavisāṇasuttam (Rhinoceros Sūtra) 9, *dussaṅgahā* ***pabbajitā*** *pi eke, atho* ***gahaṭṭhā*** *gharam āvasantā* and *Vinaya* III.89.35, *pūjita apacito* ***gahaṭṭhānaṃ c'eva pabbajitānaṃ ca***. The word *gahaṭṭha* is also contrasted with other words for the gone-forth ascetic; compare *Suttanipāta* 134 [= Vasalasuttaṃ. 19], *yo buddhaṃ paribhāsati, atha vā tassa sāvakaṃ /* ***paribbājaṃ gahaṭṭhaṃ*** *vā, taṃ jaññā vasalo iti* and *Dhammapada* 40 *asaṃsaṭṭhaṃ* ***gahaṭṭhehi anāgarēhi*** ["homeless"] *cūbhayaṃ* (with the identical pairing, mutatis mutandis, in the parallel versions of the *Dhammapada*: Gāndhārī Dharmapada 32; Patna 44; Udānavarga 33.20).

Buddhist Hybrid Sanskrit also attests this contrast. Edgerton (BHSD, s.v. *gahastha*) cites *Saddharmapuṇḍarīka* 291.11 (verse) with *gahastha* contrasting with *pravrajita*. Note the Middle Indo-Aryan non-Sanskritized form of the word.

The implications of this word history are quite striking, at least to me. It indicates that the *gṛhastha-*, so thoroughly embedded verbally in the orthodox Brahmanical dharma texts and so explicitly the foundation of the social system depicted therein, is actually a coinage of and a borrowing from śramaṇic discourse, which discourse, at this period, was conducted in various forms of Middle Indo-Aryan. The *gṛha-stha*, literally the "stay-at-home," is thus defined against a contrastive role, that of an ascetic of no fixed abode and no domestic

---

33. Or, rather, those I have investigated, with the partial exception of Jaina Ardhamāgadhī, whose terminology and usage will be treated briefly below (n. 35) and in more detail by Claire Maes (Ch. 5, this volume).

34. See the similar definition in *PTSD* of "a householder, one who leads the life of a layman [opp. *anagāra, pabbajita, paribbājaka*]." For other passages containing the contrastive pairing, see further citations in Cone 2010 and *PTSD*.

entanglements, a role well recognized in heterodox circles, but not available in Brahmanical orthodoxy save as a later, post-retirement life stage. This contrastive pairing implies that the householder of the Hindu dharma texts was not simply a married man and *pater familias* in what we might, anachronistically, consider an essentially secular role, but a man with a religious life equivalent to that of a wandering ascetic—but a religious life pursued and fulfilled within the context of a sedentary family existence. So, not only is this most dharmic of dharmic words an importation from *śramaṇa* circles and most likely from Middle Indic, but it also seems to reflect a division of religious roles that is more at home in those heterodox circles than in the Vedic milieu from which the Brahmanical dharma system supposedly developed.[35] The older term *gṛhapati*, which we might have expected to name the foundational "householder" of the dharmic social structure, was replaced or set aside, perhaps in part because of the asymmetrical usage with attendant drawbacks, as outlined above, but also because the role of the householder in the social structure seems to have radically changed. That *gṛhapati* was replaced by a term adapted from a very different conception of religious life suggests that the lexical replacement was not simply the result of a desire for linguistic novelty, but signals a sharp conceptual break from the Vedic religious landscape. And once again, as in the replacement of *dámpati* by *gṛhápati* discussed above, the new term comes from a more vernacular, less formal level of language.

---

35. As it happens, of course, most of the reflections of śramaṇic discourse that we have preserved are Buddhist oriented, but I would predict (or would have predicted) that this terminology for the gone-forth and the stay-at-home was general in heterodox circles. But this assumption is challenged by the material in Jaina Ardhamāgadhī, and I confess I don't know quite what to make of it. Ardhamāgadhī does attest *gihattha*, the *lautgesetzlich* equivalent of *gṛhapati*, glossed as "householder" in the IAD with a respectable number of citations, as well as *gahavai*, glossed "householder, merchant," with at least the latter gloss matching those of other MIA representatives of **gṛhapati* (see n. 23). But the older and extremely well-attested term for "householder" as contrasted to "wandering ascetic" is *gāhāvai*, whose Sanskrit equivalent is also supposed to be *gṛhapati*: the IAD gives *gṛhapati* as its Sanskrit correspondent, though it also suggests a **gāthāpati*, and Pischel also takes it as the phonological development of *gṛhapati*. But I am somewhat dubious about this derivation. Pischel (§78) explains the first long *ā* in *gāhāvai-* as due to (sporadic) "Vokalsteigerung," with the second long *ā* resulting from occasional lengthening of final vowels in first compound members (§70). Neither of these developments is impossible, but the coincidence of the two, especially given the attestation in AM of clearer correspondents to *gṛhastha* and *gṛhapati*, is surprising. On the other hand, *gihattha* and *gahavai* could have been later, secondarily Prakritized borrowings of the Sanskrit/Buddhist Middle Indic terms, to bring the terminology more into line with Buddhist lexical choices, while *gāhāvai* represents the older stratum. Whatever the source of *gāhā* in *gāhāvai*, we seem to have the "houselord" term in the "stay-at-home" slot. In other words, instead of the formulaic pair of "stay-at-home" and "gone-forth" that we find in the Buddhist texts, we seem to have the older term for "householder" preserved. Does this signal non-parallel conceptual structures as well? For a detailed discussion, see Maes (Ch. 5, this volume).

2

Pāṣaṇḍa

RELIGIOUS COMMUNITIES IN THE AŚOKAN INSCRIPTIONS AND EARLY LITERATURE

Joel P. Brereton

FOLLOWING[1] AN OBLIQUE course from the discussions of *gṛhastha* in this volume, I have been looking at Aśoka's understanding of the role of *pāṣaṇḍas*,[2] which in his inscriptions refer to religious communities of one kind or another (cf. Freiberger 2013: 33–39).[3] My purpose here is to clarify the nature of

---

1. I wish to thank Claire Maes for sharing with me the parts of her dissertation bearing on the interpretation of *pāṣaṇḍa*. I am also very grateful to Stephanie Jamison and Oliver Freiberger, who offered observations about and corrections to a draft of this chapter and, of course, to Patrick Olivelle, for enlightening me with his ideas about this topic and so much else.

2. *Pāṣaṇḍa* is the Sanskrit form of this word, which I will be using throughout this chapter, except in specific passages that use a Middle Indic form.

3. Unfortunately, etymology is of doubtful help in trying to refine the meaning or history of *pāṣaṇḍa*. Hesitantly, Mayrhofer in *KEWA* II: 265–66 and *EWA* II: 101–2 suggested that *pāṣaṇḍa* is related to *parṣad*, "assembly," a view supported by Bollée (1977: 219) in his comments on AM *pāsattha*. But even were this etymology correct, the attestations of *parṣad*, *pārṣad*, and *pārṣada* in late Vedic and Epic literature are not of much use in explaining *pāṣaṇḍa*. A *parṣad* or *pārṣad* is any sort of assembly; it does not have the more specific reference to a religious group that *pāṣaṇḍa* has. For example, Draupadī says in *Mbh* 4.17.2, *yan māṃ dāsīpravādena prātikāmī tad ānayat / sabhāyāṃ pārṣado madhye tan māṃ dahati bhārata*, "This burns me, Bhārata [=Yudhiṣṭhira], that a servant then brought me to the hall, in the middle of the assembly, calling me a slave!" Here the *pārṣad* is the assembly of Kauravas and Pāṇḍavas at the court of Dhṛtarāṣṭra into which Draupadī has been dragged. Or again, *Śāṅkhāyana Āraṇyaka* 8.9: *sa ya evam etāṃ daivīṃ vīṇāṃ veda śrutavadanatamo bhavati bhūmiprāsya kīrtir bhavati suśrūṣante hāsya parṣatsu bhāṣyamāṇasyedam astu yad ayam īhate yatrāryā vāg vadati vidur enaṃ tatra*, "If he thus knows this divine *vīṇā* [=the human body], he becomes the best of those whose speech is heard; his fame comes to fill the earth. They are

pāṣaṇḍas and to understand their role within Aśoka's larger political and religious purposes. However, the *pāṣaṇḍas* of Aśoka present an odd situation. In the inscriptions, *pāṣaṇḍa* carries a positive connotation—Aśoka encourages, honors, and supports *pāṣaṇḍas* (e.g., RE 7[A], 12[A])—while standard lexica attribute to Sanskrit *pāṣaṇḍa* and its equivalents in Middle Indic a largely negative one. For example, the *Petersburg Wörterbuch* defines Sanskrit *pāṣaṇḍa* as "Irrlehre, Ketzerei" ("false teaching, heresy") and as an adjective, "ketzerisch" ("heretical"), and most translations of *pāṣaṇḍa* reflect this general interpretation. Similar definitions of *pāṣaṇḍa* are common in later Sanskrit lexical and commentarial literature from the late first millennium, which characterizes the *pāṣaṇḍas* as those who teach doctrines opposed to the Vedas or who perform non-Vedic rites. That is, the *pāṣaṇḍas* are "unorthodox" Hindu sects, such the Śaiva Kāpālikas, Kaulas, and Pāśupatas, as well as non-Hindu traditions, specifically Buddhist and Jain (Doniger O'Flaherty 1971: 272–73).

Such a critical view of *pāṣaṇḍas* is shared by non-Brahminical traditions as well. Pāli texts call groups that are *not* Buddhists *pāsaṇḍa*, and in Ardhamāgadhī *pāsaṃḍa* or *pāsattha* refers to communities that are *not* Jain, so for Buddhists and Jains too, the *pāṣaṇḍas* are groups opposed to one's own. However, even when they are hostile to *pāṣaṇḍas*, Middle Indic texts also provide information about them that is relevant to the Aśokan inscriptions. The *Sūyagaḍa*, which belongs to the oldest stratum of Jain literature (Dundas 2002: 23), discusses doctrines of opponents of the Jains. *Sūyagaḍa* 1.1.2.1 begins a discussion of the teachings of Niyativādins, "Fatalists," who believe that people's happiness or misery is their destiny, not the result of their action (Bollée 1977: 80). The text calls such adepts *pāsatthas: evam ege u pāsatthā te bhujjo vippagabbhiyā / evaṃ p' uvaṭṭhiyā santā na te dukkhavimokkhayā*, "Surely some adepts (*pāsatthā*) (speak) in this way; they are very rash. Those being admitted (to their community) are not those who attain release from suffering" (*Sūy* 1.1.2.5).[4] As the

---

eager to hear from him when he speaks in the assemblies, (thinking), 'Let that be what this man desires!' Where Āryan speech is spoken, there they know of him." In a personal communication to Patrick Olivelle, Oskar von Hinüber suggested that *pāṣaṇḍa* might be "one of the eastern words like *muṇḍa* or *paṇḍita*, which seems to belong to a non-aryan language of ascetics in the broadest sense of the word." I find this an appealing suggestion, but in any case, an attempt to establish the meaning of *pāṣaṇḍa* through its origin or derivation appears to provide little headway.

4. This translation generally follows that of Bollée (1977: 86): "In dieser Weise (reden) einige Häretiker. Sie sind sehr verwegen (in ihren Ansichten). Wenn (Leute) in dieser Weise ordiniert worden sind, führt sie das nicht zur Befreiung von Leiden."

technical term *uvaṭṭhiyā* "admitted" or "ordained" implies,[5] membership in this *pāsattha* community was by a formal, ritual act. Here, the *pāsatthas* likely formed an organized mendicant or ascetic order, and admission to that group involved adoption of a mendicant or ascetic life. Also note that this *pāsattha* community is defined not only by its way of life but also by its doctrines.

A passage from the Pāli canon also illustrates the character of *pāṣaṇḍas* as mendicant or ascetic communities characterized by a way of thought and a way of life. In a passage from the *Saṃyutta Nikāya* (I, 133–34), Pāli *pāsaṇḍa* refers to a religious community that is contrasted to the community of the Buddha:

2. *atha kho māro pāpimā yena sīsupacālā bhikkhunī ten-upasaṅkami* ||
upasaṅkamitvā sīsupacālam bhikkhunim etad avoca || ||
kassa nu tvaṃ bhikkhuni pāsaṇḍaṃ rocesīti || ||
3. *na khvāham āvuso kassaci pāsaṇḍaṃ rocemī ti* || ||
4. *kiṃ nu uddissa muṇḍāsi* || *samaṇī viya dissasi* ||
na ca rocesi pāsaṇḍaṃ || *kim-iva carasi momuhā ti* || ||
5. *ito bahiddhā pāsaṇḍā* || *diṭṭhīsu pasīdanti ye* ||
na tesaṃ dhammam rocemi || *na te dhammassa kovidā* || ||
atthi sakyakule jāto || *buddho appaṭipuggalo* ||
sabbābhibhū māranudo || *sabbattham aparājito* ||
sabbatthamutto asito || *sabbam passati cakkhumā* || ||
sabbakammakkhayaṃ patto || *vimutto upadhisaṅkhaye* ||
so mayhaṃ bhagavā satthā || *tassa rocemi sāsanan ti* || ||

Now then, the evil Māra approached the *bhikkhunī* Sīsupacālā and said this: "Whose religious community (*pāsaṇḍa*) do you choose, *bhikkhunī*?"
"I do not choose anyone's religious community, sir."

(Māra:)
"Signifying what, then, are you shaven-headed?
You appear like a *samaṇī* [=a female ascetic or mendicant]
but you do not choose a religious community (*pāsaṇḍa*)!
Why do you wander as a fool?"

5. The term *uvaṭṭhiyā* (Skt. *upasthita*) belongs to the verbal system of the stem *uvaṭhāv*, which according to the *IAD*, means "establish (a fresh disciple) in right conduct, administer the great vows (to a disciple)," and it is related to the nominal form *uvaṭhavaṇa* (Skt. *upasthāpana*) "fresh admission after expulsion from the order of monks."

(Sīsupacālā:)
"Outside (the Buddhist community) here, religious communities (*pāsaṇḍa*)
find satisfaction in false views (*diṭṭhi*).
I do not choose their dharma.
They are not skilled in the dharma.

"This is the truth: one born in the Sakya clan,
the Enlightened One, unrivalled,
overcoming all, expelling Māra,
unconquered everywhere,
everywhere free and unbound—
(that) clear-sighted one sees all.

"Having attained the destruction of karma,
free by the destruction of attachments,
that Blessed One is my teacher.
His teaching (*sāsana*) do I choose."

By her shaved head, Māra identified Sīsupacālā as a *bhikkhunī* and a *samaṇī*, and therefore he asks her what doctrine she follows that she has adopted this way of life. She denies that she follows the doctrines of any religious community, and in doing so, she excludes the Buddhist community from the category of *pāṣaṇḍa*. Like Buddhists, *pāṣaṇḍas* have dharmas, but for Sīsupacālā, the *pāṣaṇḍas'* dharmas are not the real dharma; the real dharma belongs exclusively to the Buddha and his community. Its sole possession of the true dharma sets the Buddhist community apart from other communities and its teaching from other teaching. Sīsupacālā is asserting something similar to the contention of Christian theologians when they say that Christianity is not "a religion." For such thinkers, to categorize Christianity as *a* religion appears to make Christianity just one choice among many and does not acknowledge Christianity's claim to a unique truth.[6] Sīsupacālā removes Buddhism from *pāṣaṇḍas* because for her it is not just one community among others or one teaching among many but the right community and the true teaching. This example illustrates how

6. Compare, most famously, Karl Barth, who said in his *Church Dogmatics*: "The revelation of God denies that any religion is true. No religion can stand before the grace of God as true religion." Or more recently, Robert Capon colloquially expresses a similar sentiment in *Between Noon and Three: A Parable of Romance, Law, the Outrage of Grace*: "Religion, therefore, is a loser, a strictly fallen activity. It has a failed past and a bankrupt future. There was no religion in Eden and there won't be any in heaven; and in the meantime Jesus has died and risen to persuade us to knock it all off right now." Both these passages and others to similar effect are quoted in Fowler 1998.

pāṣaṇḍa developed from a positive or neutral term to a pejorative one as communities distanced themselves from the category of *pāṣaṇḍa* in order to assert their uniqueness, leaving only rejected communities and teachings in that class.

A passage from the Buddhist *Dīpavaṃsa* (ca. third–fourth century?) illustrates another, perhaps even more negative view of *pāṣaṇḍas*. The following is Oldenberg's text with his translation and queries and my additions in brackets:

Dīpavaṃsa 6.24–27

24. *paripuṇṇavīsavassamhi piyadass' ābhisiñcayuṃ*
pāsaṇḍaṃ pariganhanto tīṇi vassaṃ atikkami.
25. *dvasaṭṭhidiṭṭhigatikā pāsaṇḍā channavutikā,*
sassataucchedamūlā sabbe dvīhi patiṭṭhitā,
26. *nigaṇṭhācelakā c' eva itarā paribbājakā*
itarā brāhmaṇā 'ti ca aññe ca puthuladdhikā.
27. *niyantisassatucchede sammūḷhe hīnadiṭṭhike*
ito bahiddhā pāsaṇḍe titthiye nānādiṭṭhike
sārāsāraṃ gavesanto puthuladdhī nimantayi.

24. They crowned Piyadassi [=Aśoka] after full twenty years (?); he passed three years doing honour to Pāsaṇḍa infidels. 25. (There were) adherents of the sixty-two false doctrines, ninety-six kinds of Pāsaṇḍas, who proceeded from the Sassata and Uccheda [Eternalist and Nihilist] doctrines, all of them established on these two principles;—26. Nigaṇṭhas [Jains] and Acelakas [naked ascetics] and other ascetics [*paribbājakā*] and other Brahmans and sectarians [*puthuladdhikā*]. 27. Searching where truth and where falsehood [*sārāsāraṃ*] was, he invited the infatuated [*sammūḷhe*], infidel [*hīnadiṭṭhike*] Nigaṇṭhas (?)[7] and sectarians of the Sassata and Uccheda doctrines, and Pāsaṇḍa and Titthiya infidels of different creeds [*nānādiṭṭhike*] outside the Faith, sectarian people [*puthuladdhī*].

The passage mentions Aśoka and religious communities that Aśoka also names in his inscriptions, but it stands in contrast to the inscriptions. While Aśoka says that he honors Brahmins, Jains, and those of other *pāṣaṇḍas*, this

7. In his notes, Oldenberg suggests emending the opening of 27a to *niyatisassatucchede* or *nigaṇṭhasassatucchede*. His translation reflects the latter.

passage is eager to denigrate these communities. The text also links *pāṣaṇḍas* with *titthiyas*. In a lengthy note on *tīrthika*, Edgerton says *tīrthika* was probably Sanskritized from Middle Indic *titthiya*, and he glosses *tīrthika/titthiya* as "heretic" (*BHSD*, s.v. *tīrthika*). As Maes (2015: 173–207) demonstrates in detail, however, *titthiya* draws on the frequent religious metaphor of "crossing" or "fording" danger and difficulty to arrive at a place of safety. For that reason, we would have expected Pāli *titthiya* to have a positive connotation. Maes argues that it can and once did, and that it came to have a negative sense, as in the passage above, only as the term became restricted to other religious groups in competition with Buddhists. As the *Dīpavaṃsa* illustrates, it is difficult to say what differentiates *titthiyas* and *pāsaṇḍas*, and their histories are also similar. Both *tīrthika/titthiya* and *pāṣaṇḍa/pāsaṇḍa* followed a path from an originally positive or neutral sense to the negative one dominant in Hindu and Buddhist texts because they were terms for rival religious communities.

Confirming this history, some Sanskrit literature attests instances in which *pāṣaṇḍa* is not used negatively but neutrally to characterize a religious group or individual. In accord with the pejorative sense of *pāṣaṇḍa* observed thus far, the *Atharvaveda Pariśiṣṭas*[8] provide a robustly negative view of *pāṣaṇḍas* in the discussion of omens and portents. Destruction of the country is near, the text says, when there are: *śīlācāravihīnaś ca, madyamāṃsānṛtapriyāḥ / nagnapāṣaṇḍabhūyiṣṭhāḥ* "those who have abandoned moral living, being fond of liquor, meat, and untruth, chiefly consisting of naked religious communities (*-pāṣaṇḍa-*)" (*AVPar* 70b.16.4). There is an implied opposition between these communities and Brahmins in particular, since the passage emphasizes contrasts to Brahminical commitments to truth (*satya*) and to ritual purity through dietary restriction.[9] But in a second passage, in the same section dealing with omens and portents, there is another *pāṣaṇḍa*, whose *absence* is a sign of disaster: *tyajanti vāpi yaṃ deśaṃ, pāṣaṇḍā dvijadevatāḥ / vidveṣaṃ*

---

8. The date of the *Atharvaveda Pariśiṣṭas* is uncertain. They are quoted by Sāyaṇa's commentary on the *Atharvaveda* (fourteenth century) and by Hemādri (thirteenth century), so they are no later than these texts (Modak 1993: 198). Modak remarks that the *Atharvaveda Pariśiṣṭas* are a "collection of tracts belonging to different chronological periods" (195), but according to him (472–73), the assembled collection dates between Manu (dated by Olivelle [2005: 25] to the second/third century CE), which it quotes, and *Bṛhatsaṃhitā* (dated by Modak to the fifth or early sixth century), which quotes it.

9. Compare *MDh* 4.175, speaking of a Brahmin teacher: *satyadharmāryavṛtteṣu, śauce caivāramet sadā, śiṣyāṃś ca śiṣyād dharmeṇa, vāgbāhūdarasaṃyataḥ* "He should always take delight in speaking the truth, in following the Law, in conforming to the Ārya ways, and in purifying himself. With his speech, hands, and stomach controlled, he should discipline his disciples according to the Law" (tr. Olivelle 2005).

vāpi gacchanti, so 'pi deśo vinaśyati, "What land religious communities having 'Brahmin-deities' [=learned or pious Brahmins?][10] abandon or (in which land) they find hostility, that land goes to destruction" (*AVPar* 64.4.9). Unlike *Atharvaveda Pariśiṣṭa* 70b.16.4, the *pāṣaṇḍas* in this passage include Brahmins or are constituted by Brahmins, and they are good things for a kingdom to have. For this text, what differentiates a bad *pāṣaṇḍa* from a good *pāṣaṇḍa* is whether it is a non-Brahmin *pāṣaṇḍa* or a Brahmin *pāṣaṇḍa*.

Nor is this passage an isolated instance of a positive reference to *pāṣaṇḍas* in early Sanskrit literature. In *Mahābhārata* 12.292, Vasiṣṭha speaks of all the activities that the self or the soul thinks it has done in the thousands of bodies it has inhabited throughout the course of time. In doing so, he mentions various forms of religious life that the self imagines it has adopted: *cāturāśramyapanthānam, āśrayaty āśramān api / upāsīnaś ca pāṣaṇḍān, guhāḥ śailāṃs tathaiva ca* "(The self) resorts to a path relating to the four holy ways of life, also to places of retreat, both having abided in religious communities (*pāṣaṇḍas*) and likewise in caves and mountains" (*Mbh* 12.292.20). Here life in *pāṣaṇḍas* is contrasted to life in caves and mountains since *pāṣaṇḍa* likely refers to religious groups who normally live together and in proximity to other populations rather than alone in distant areas. But whatever the precise nature of these communities might have been, this passage honors life in them, just as it does life in *āśramas*.

Again in *Mahābhārata* 12.211, Yudhiṣṭhira asks how King Janaka succeeded in attaining release, in verse 1d, *bhogān utsṛjya mānuṣān*, "after he cast off all human enjoyments." Bhīṣma begins his story of Janaka by telling Yudhiṣṭhira, in verse 4, *tasya sma śatam ācāryā vasanti satataṃ gṛhe / darśayantaḥ pṛthag dharmān nānāpāṣaṇḍavādinaḥ*, "A hundred teachers always used to live in his palace, exhibiting to him their individual dharmas, advocating for various religious communities (*nānāpāṣaṇḍa*)."[11] Ultimately Janaka became dissatisfied with the answers these teachers presented him, but he finally finds a master in Pañcaśikha, the son of Kapila, who was accomplished, according to verse 7ab, *sarvasaṃnyāsadharmāṇāṃ tattvajñānaviniścaye*, "in his firm grasp of the knowledge of the truth belonging to all the dharmas of renunciation."[12] As

---

10. According to the *pw*, *dvijadeva* means a "Brahman" or a "Ṛshi," with reference to *Bhāgavata Purāṇa* 3.1.22 and 5.5.22. Monier-Williams expands Böhtlingk's explanation of *dvijadeva* to " 'god among the twice-born,' a Brāhman, a sage." In the *Atharvaveda Pariśiṣṭas*, I would expect *dvijadevatā* to mean something similar.

11. Wynne (2009) translates *nānāpāṣaṇḍa* as "various heresies."

12. Pañcaśikha gives Janaka a long discourse that centers on the fate of the soul after death. By this talk Janaka becomes assured that death is not the loss of anything ultimately important

in the passage from the *Saṃyutta Nikāya* quoted above, *pāṣaṇḍas* are associated with the dharmas of the groups teaching them. The *Mahābhārata* text acknowledges that the advocates for the various religious communities were wrong, but it takes for granted that there would be different religious groups teaching different dharmas and doctrines, and it does not fault Janaka for bringing them to his palace. Here *pāṣaṇḍa* does not have a positive connotation, since Janaka wisely rejects their doctrines, but there is no basis for the strongly negative one that a translation "heresy" would imply. The *pāṣaṇḍas* are just other communities whose doctrines are eventually cast aside.

In the *Anuśāsanaparvan*, there is passage that, like *Atharvaveda Pariśiṣṭa* 64.4.9, says that Brahmins can be members of *pāṣaṇḍas: avyutkrāntāś ca dharmeṣu pāṣaṇḍasamayeṣu ca / kṛśaprāṇāḥ kṛśadhanās teṣu dattaṃ mahāphalam* "Those [Brahmins] who have not overstepped with regard to the laws (dharmas) and to the obligations of religious communities, those poor in strength, poor in possessions—what is given to them brings great fruit" (*Mbh* 13.24.56).[13] The obligations of the *pāṣaṇḍas*, their *samayas*, may be voluntary, but here they are placed alongside the dharma of Brahmins and impose a comparable responsibility.

Outside of the *Mahābhārata*, Manu appears to speak of *pāṣaṇḍas* neutrally: *deśadharmāñ jātidharmān kuladharmāṃś ca śāśvatān | pāṣaṇḍagaṇadharmāṃś ca śāstre 'sminn uktavān manuḥ* (*MDh* 1.118). With the substitution of *pāṣaṇḍa* within it, Olivelle's translation (2005) is: "The timeless Laws of regions, of hereditary groups, and of families. Laws of *pāṣaṇḍas* and guilds. All that Manu has set forth in this treatise." Since elsewhere Manu speaks very critically of them, Olivelle translates *pāṣaṇḍas* here as "heretical ascetic groups," but he also notes that this verse might not be consistent with other parts of Manu. I think he is right about that inconsistency, for here *pāṣaṇḍa* does not appear to be disparaging. Rather, Manu acknowledges that membership in a *pāṣaṇḍa* imposes obligations, which one rightly fulfills. Note that these obligations are called dharmas, again attesting to a close connection between *pāṣaṇḍas* and the dharma that defines the *pāṣaṇḍa*.

---

to him. This teaching allows him to live "in the highest happiness" (12.212.51 *paramasukhī*) and brings him release (v. 52).

13. In his translation, Ganguli turns himself inside out in an attempt to give a negative meaning to *pāṣaṇḍa*, but I don't see how to do that without torturing the passage. Here, though, is his interpretation of the passage: "By making gifts unto such Brāhmaṇas as live at

Since the *Arthaśāstra* is not deeply troubled concerning matters of religion, it is not surprising that it too shows a neutral use of *pāṣaṇḍa: Arthaśāstra* 3.16.32–33 declares, *jñātayaḥ śrotriyāḥ pāṣaṇḍā vā . . . paravāstuṣu na bhogena hareyuḥ . . . .* (33) *āśramiṇaḥ pāṣaṇḍā vā mahaty avakāśe parasparam abādhamānā vaseyuḥ*, "Relatives, Vedic scholars, or members of religious orders (*pāṣaṇḍas*) residing in immovable property belonging to others do not obtain ownership over them through enjoyment. (33) Hermits (*āśramin*) or members of religious orders (*pāṣaṇḍas*) should live in a large compound (*avakāśa*) without disturbing each other" (tr. Olivelle 2013). Kauṭilya understands *pāṣaṇḍas*, "members of religious orders," not to have permanent residences, even though they may live in a space or place for such an extended time that they might have claimed ownership. As in *Mahābhārata* 12.292, *pāṣaṇḍas* are closely conjoined with those living in *āśramas*. As Olivelle (1993: 21, 24) has observed, *āśramas* typically were not distant from villages, and *pāṣaṇḍas* also typically were located in or near populated areas.

Such a neutral use of *pāṣaṇḍa* may also occur in Pāli literature. The term *sabbapāsaṇḍika* appears only once in the *Vinaya*, at IV, 74. There an Ājīvika asks the king to provide "a meal for all *pāsaṇḍikas*" (*sabbapāsaṇḍikabhatta*). The king consents, but only if the Ājīvika invites and gives first place to the Buddha and the Saṅgha. The Buddha accepts the invitation and institutes a rule that allows the Saṅgha to participate in such an "occasion for a meal for *śramaṇas*" (*samaṇabhattasamaya*). In commenting on this passage, Maes (2015: 151) questions Horner's translation of *sabbapāsaṇḍika* as "all heretics." Comparing it to the Aśokan edicts, she says that "*pāsaṇḍa/pāsaṇḍika* might have been a neutral and commonly used and understood umbrella denomination to refer to . . . all ascetic/religious folds within early Indian society." Note especially that the Buddha uses *samaṇa* in *samaṇabhatta-* ("meal for *śramaṇas*") as a synonym for *pāsaṇḍika* in *-pāsaṇḍikabhatta*. Since *samaṇa* can be applied to Buddhists, the text would be unlikely to equate them were *pāsaṇḍika* a deprecatory term. Given what we have seen in Sanskrit literature, therefore, Maes is surely correct that *pāṣaṇḍika* is here a neutral term.

On the basis of this brief survey, therefore, I suggest the following: First, especially in literature from around the beginning of the common era, *pāṣaṇḍa* is not always used pejoratively, but it can have a neutral sense or even the positive one that it has in the Aśokan inscriptions. This is true in both Brahminical and non-Brahminical literature. Second, *pāṣaṇḍas* are communities of religious adepts, who practiced some sort of religious discipline. Third, members of these religious communities lived not only in close proximity with one another but also near populated areas, on which they likely depended for their support. And fourth, *pāṣaṇḍas* are associated with rules and doctrines that govern what they do—the dharma of the *pāṣaṇḍa*.

Let me begin with this last point as we turn to the Aśokan inscriptions themselves, for in them too is evidence that Aśoka associated *pāṣaṇḍa* and dharma and that this connection was important to him and to his message. However, some of the evidence pertinent to this topic is slightly roundabout, because it involves not only a Middle Indic text of the inscriptions but also the extant sections of a Greek translation that Aśoka had ordered.

These extant portions belong to Rock Edicts 12 and 13. In them the Greek translator rendered *pāṣaṇḍa* by διατριβή (*diatribḗ*), a word typically glossed as "philosophic school."[14] Although my examples come from the Roman period and therefore are much later than the Aśokan inscriptions, we need to think about διατριβή more broadly than "philosophic school" might suggest. In the second century, Galen mentions "the school (διατριβή) of Moses and Christ," in which (he says) "one might hear talk of undemonstated laws" (νόμων ἀναποδείκτων ἀκούνῃ), rather than the careful analysis characteristic of truly philosophic schools (Walzer 1949: 14). Also in the second century, Lucian has an account of a man named Alexander, whom he considered to be an utter religious fraud. According to Lucian, Alexander acquired a following by means of the oracular advice he gave and the divine descent he claimed. Lucian says that at least Alexander came by his dishonesty honestly, for his teacher and admirer was a follower of another phony named Apollonius. "You may see for yourself," Lucian concludes (*Alex.* 5), "from what sort of school (διατριβή) is the man I describe" (ὁρᾷς ἐξ οἵας σοι διατριβῆς ἄνθρωπον λέγω). So while a διατριβή could be a philosophic school, it could also be applied to Jews or Christians, or even to religious crackpots,[15] that is, to religious communities of almost any sort.[16]

Benveniste (1964: 153) observes that in Rock Edict 13, the Greek translator made an effort to clarify διατριβή by a paraphrase using the cognate verb διατρίβειν (*diatríbein*), here in the sense of "to dedicate oneself to" or "to spend time in speaking about." The Greek translator renders *pāsaṃḍā*

a great distance from the practices that are observed by the sinful and the wicked, as are destitute of strength for want of adequate support, and as are very poor in earthly possessions, one earns great merit." Ganguli 1993, IV, *Anusasana Parva* Part I: 125.

14. Compare Schlumberger 1969: 415. But see the comments of Roth (2007: 156), who notes the wide semantic range of the word.

15. Of course, one person's religious imposter may be another's sagacious thinker. As Oliver Freiberger pointed out to me, even if Lucian considered Apollonius a fraud, others did not, including his biographer Philostratus and those who were devoted to him both during his life and after his death.

16. See Roth 2007: 153, who interprets διατριβή as a "religious group."

in Rock Edict 12[G] as οἱ περὶ τὴν εὐσέβειαν διατρίβοντες "those dedicating themselves to dutifulness." "Dutifulness"—εὐσέβεια (*eusébeia*)—is the Greek inscription's translation of dharma.[17] The translator, therefore, understood that *pāṣaṇḍas* are defined by dharmas, which accords with the connection between *pāṣaṇḍa* and dharma that we saw in the *Mahābhārata* and *The Laws of Manu.*

There is another way in which the inscriptions, especially through their Greek translation, confirm the linkage of *pāṣaṇḍa* and dharma, but this way leads through the interpretation of the disputed compound, *sālavaḍhi*. Aśoka says in Rock Edict 12[B-C], *no cu tathā dānaṃ vā pūjā vā devānaṃpiye maṃnati (-te) athā kiti sālavaḍhi (-ī) siyā savapāsaṃḍānaṃ* [C] *sālavaḍhi (-ī) cu bahuvidhā*,[18] "But the Beloved of the Gods does not regard gifts or honors as much as that there would be a *sālavaḍhi* of all religious communities. But the ways of *sālavaḍhi* are various." The second part of the compound is unproblematic: *vaḍhi* corresponds to *vṛddhi*, "strengthening," so the compound must mean a "strengthening of the *sāla*." But what then is a *sāla*? Bloch, Hultzsch, Sircar, and Thapar all take *sāla* to correspond to Sanskrit *sāra*, "essence, essential part," and therefore translate the compound as "promotion of the essential" (Hultzsch), "advancement of the essential doctrine" (Thapar), or the like.[19] But Norman (1972: 112) notes that the redactors at Shāhbāzgaṛhī and Mānsehrā write *sāla* rather than *sāra*, the expected form

---

17. Benveniste (1964: 139) translates εὐσέβεια as "piété" and Schlumberger and Benveniste (1967: 194–95) as "piety," although Benveniste argues that εὐσέβεια in the inscriptions has more the sense of "reverence" toward people—parents, teachers, members of other religious groups—than "piety" directed to the gods. Roth (2007: 152) questions this translation of εὐσέβεια and argues that especially in the Greek translation of Aśoka's edicts, it is better understood as "Pflichtbewußtsein." In citing passages of the inscriptions, he translates it by "Wohlverhalten ("good conduct"). I have followed his general interpretation of εὐσέβεια and therefore translate it, perhaps not altogether felicitously, as "dutifulness."

18. The texts of the Rock Edicts quoted in this essay are the reconstructions of Schneider (1978), who produced a synoptic text P—P for Pāṭaliputra. Schneider understands this reconstructed text P, or a recension of this text, to be the dictated or written words of Aśoka himself. However, he also believes that there existed two recensions of P; he calls these p^1, which follows closely the Rock Edicts at Girnār, Dhauli, and Jaugaḍa, and p^2, which follows the Rock Edicts of Eṛraguḍi (in the south) but also those of Kālsī, Mānsehrā, and Shāhbāzgaṛhī. Schneider held that of the two recensions, p^2 is the superior and even possibly the source of p^1. For that reason, I have quoted his p^2 reconstruction followed in parentheses by p^1 where it differs from p^2. Underlined *akṣaras* are those Schneider considered doubtful for his reconstruction, but his doubts often concerned whether a vowel should be long or short in Aśoka's dialect.

19. Summarized by Norman 1972: 112. Also following this interpretation, Schneider (1978: 115) has "Wachstum im Wesentlichen."

in their dialect. He argues that these redactors would have changed the Eastern /l/ of *sāla* to a Western /r/ had they understood *sāla* to be *sāra* "essence." Likewise, he notes that the redactor at Kālsī wrote *śālā* or *ṣālā* in the three occurrences of the word. He did so, Norman says, because he mistook *sāla* (masculine) for *sālā* (feminine) and then wrongly interpreted the compound to mean "increase of houses, i.e., of sectarian halls" (*śālās*). So then, according to Norman, the Kālsī redactor's error shows again that he did not recognize *sāla* to be *sāra,* "essence." He concludes that an etymological connection between Aśokan *sāla* and Sanskrit *sāra* is unlikely and therefore that the meaning of *sālavaḍhi* has largely to be conjectured by context. He thinks "that something like 'intercommunion' or 'mutual knowledge' " would be a possible interpretation of *sāla.* Learned though they certainly are, Norman's arguments are not fully persuasive, in part because his alternatives are not compelling. The context of the passages does not strongly suggest that *sāla* means "intercommunion" or the like in preference to various other possible interpretations, including "essence" or "the essential."[20]

But whether Norman is correct or not in rejecting an etymological connection between *sāla* and Sanskrit *sāra,* his attempt to circumvent the uncertainties of etymology is a welcome strategy. However, I think a better approach to understanding what *sāla* denotes runs through the Greek translation of the edicts. Here is the Prakrit for Rock Edict 12[L], which almost replicates the text of Rock Edict 12[B–C]: *devānaṃpiye no tathā dānaṃ vā̱ pūjā vā̱ maṃnati* (*-e*) *athā kiti* (*kiṃti*) *sālavaḍhi* (*-ī*) *siyā savapāsaṃḍānaṃ ti* (∅), "The Beloved of the Gods does not regard gifts and honors as much as that there be a *sālavaḍhi* of all religious communities." For this passage, the Greek translator offers: ἵνα δειαμείνωσιν διὰ παντὸς εὐσεβοῦντες, "so that they have been ever concerned to be living dutifully."[21] As Benveniste (1964: 149) remarks, the Greek translation omits the first part of the Prakrit phrase and leaves a paraphrase of *sālavaḍhi:* δειαμείνωσιν . . . εὐσεβοῦντες "they have been concerned to be living dutifully." In that paraphrase *sāla* is represented by the participle εὐσεβοῦντες (*euseboûntes*), "living dutifully," a verbal form related to εὐσέβεια (*eusébeia*), "dutifulness," the normal translation of dharma. The Greek translator does something similar in the opening of the inscription. The first words are missing, and the extant portion begins [.εὐ]σέβεια καὶ ἐγκράτεια

20. Norman (1972: 112–13) additionally suggests a connection of *sāla* with later Jaina Sanskrit *sārā,* which can mean "information, knowledge," but the evidence of Jaina Sanskrit is much later than the Aśokan inscriptions.

21. For the translation of this phrase, see Roth 2007: 154: "damit sie immer darum bekümmert sind, sich im Wohlverhalten zu üben" and his note on δειαμείνωσιν.

κατὰ πάσας τὰς διατριβάς, "... dutifulness and self-control throughout all religious communities." The translator truncated a great deal, but it appears that [.εὐ]σέβεια ... κατὰ πάσας τὰς διατριβάς, "dutifulness throughout all religious communities," renders *sālavaḍhi* (-ī) . . . *savapāsaṃḍānaṃ*, "a *sālavaḍhi* of all religious communities" in Rock Edict 12[B] and that ἐγκράτεια (*egkráteia*) "self-control" reflects Aśoka's discussion of the virtue of *vacaguti* "control of speech" in Rock Edict 12[D]: *tasa cu iyaṃ mūle a̱ vacaguti* (*vacigutī*), "But this is the root of that (*sālavaḍhi*): the control of speech." If so, then *sālavaḍhi* has again been approximated by [.εὐ]σέβεια "dutifulness." Therefore, at the beginning and end of the Greek version of Rock Edict 12, the translator understands *sāla* to mean or to gloss "dutifulness," which is to say, dharma. The Greek translator may not always be right in his interpretation of Aśoka, but in this case, I think that he correctly understood that *sāla* points to dharma.[22]

One other passage in the inscriptions also supports such an association of *sāla* and dharma. In it, Aśoka speaks of his *dharmamahāmātras*, his officials in charge of the *pāṣaṇḍas*. He describes their work in Rock Edict 5[J] *te savapāsaṃḍesu viyāpaṭā dhaṃmādhithānāye ca dhaṃmavaḍhiyā hitasukhāye ca dhaṃmayutasa* "These (*dharmamahāmātras*) are occupied among all religious communities (*pāṣaṇḍas*) for the establishment of dharma and by the strengthening of dharma for the well-being and happiness of him who is attached to the dharma." The compound *dhaṃmavaḍhi*, "strengthening of the dharma," and its association with the "happiness and well-being of the world" occurs elsewhere in the inscriptions (e.g., PE 6[B, C]),[23] but particularly in Rock Edict 5[J], which connects *dhaṃmavaḍhi* with "all religious communities" through the work of the *dharmamahāmātras*, echoes Rock Edict 12[B, L], where *sālavaḍhi* belongs to "all religious communities."

So, then a *pāṣaṇḍa* was a religious community characterized by a dharma. In the Hindu, Jain, and Buddhist texts surveyed above, we saw that the teaching of a *pāṣaṇḍa* is associated with a community of religious adepts. But are *pāṣaṇḍas* restricted to such groups, or did they have broader membership? A hint that others might be included occurs in the *Mahābhārata*, in which poor Brahmins belong to "religious communities."

---

22. This interpretation does not exclude an etymological connection between *sāla* and *sāra* ("essence"), because the "essence" or "core" of the teaching of the *pāṣaṇḍas* could be their dharma, but it does not depend on or require this analysis.

23. Compare also PE 7[JJ] *munissānaṃ cu yā iyaṃ dhaṃmavaḍḍhi vaḍḍhitā duvehi yeva ākālehi dhaṃmaniyamena ca nijjhatiyā ca* "And the strengthening of dharma among men has been strengthened by just two methods: by dharmic discipline and by reflection."

But that might not expand the scope of *pāṣaṇḍa* much further, since these poor Brahmins might have been Brahmins living in *āśramas* or Brahmin ascetics of some sort.

It is possible that Aśoka may include householders, *gṛhasthas*, along with ascetics as members of a *pāṣaṇḍa*, but the evidence is ambiguous. One of the passages that suggest householders might have been included among *pāṣaṇḍas* is Rock Edict 12[A] *devānaṃpiye piyadasi lājā savapāsaṃḍāni* (Girnār adds: *ca*) *pavajitāni* (Girnār adds: *ca*) *gihathāni vā̱*[24] *pūjayati dānena* (Girnār adds: *ca*) *vividhāya ca pūjāya* (Girnār adds: *pūjayati ne*). Following the text of p^2, the passage could mean, "King Piyadassi, Beloved of the Gods, honors all religious communities—renunciates or householders—with gifts and various honors." That is, the idea would be that renunciates and householders form types of *pāṣaṇḍas*. But there is evidence that this is not what Aśoka intended. The situation is either clarified or complicated by the Girnār inscription, which inserts a connective *ca* after "all *pāṣaṇḍas*" and after "renunciates" (*pavajitāni*). By doing so, the Girnār redactor names two separate groups: "all *pāṣaṇḍas*" on the one hand and "renunciates or householders" on the other. The Girnār redactor's interpretation may be correct for the other versions of the inscription as well. That is, the passage in the Girnār inscription and also in the other inscriptions could be translated, "King Piyadassi, Beloved of the Gods, honors all religious communities and also renunciates or householders with gifts and various honors." This is not the only instance in which the Girnār redactor has added the words *ca* or *vā* where the other redactors have asyndetons, for instance, Rock Edict 11[B], 12[M], 13[O, AA], and in these examples, the Girnār redactor's interpretation of the text is surely right.[25] If the redactor is correct here, Aśoka's point would be that he honors all communities (*pāṣaṇḍas*) and also all religiously dedicated people, whether they stay home as *gihathāni* or leave home as *pavajitāni*.

Whether or not the possibility that householders could belong to *pāṣaṇḍas* is supported by Pillar Edict 7[Y-AA] is also uncertain. Schneider (1978: 138) thinks that it is. He follows Thapar's (1997: 255) translation of Pillar Edict 7[Y] *dhaṃmamahāmāttā pi m' ete bahuvidhesu aṭṭhesu ānuggahikesu viyāpaṭā se pavvajītānaṃ ceva gihitthānaṃ ca savvapāsaṃḍesu pi ca viyāpaṭā se*, in which she takes the genitives *pavvajītānaṃ* and *gihitthānaṃ* with *savvapāsaṃḍesu*: "among

24. The inscription at Girnār reads *ca* also here, as do those at Mānsehrā and Shāhbāzgaṛhī. Schneider reconstructs *vā* on the basis of the Eṛṛaguḍi and Kālsī inscriptions.

25. See also the hesitation of Bloch (1950: 121 n. 2): "Girnar seul a ce *ca*: d'où l'on est tenté de conclure que la suite commente *pāsaṃḍāni*: les sectes, errantes ou sédentaires. Mais le mots qui suivent sont des substantifs et surtout Kalsi XIII l. 37 [= RE 13(G)] sépare bien brahmanes, samanes, autres sectes et maîtres de maisons."

all religious groups of renunciates and householders." But it is more likely that *pavvajītānaṃ ceva gihitthānaṃ ca* follows the verb as a further explanation of *aṭṭhesu ānuggahikesu* "benevolent affairs." A post-verbal expression, often marked with *eva* as it is here, is not uncommon in the Upaniṣads, for example in *Bṛhadāraṇyaka Upaniṣad (Kāṇva)* 1.5.23, *tasmāt ekam eva vratam caret, prānyāc ca evāpānyāc ca, nen mā pāpmā mṛtyur āpnavad iti*, "Therefore he should carry out just a single vow—he should breath in and he should breath out—with the idea that 'evil death will not get me.'" Or again, in *Muṇḍaka Upaniṣad* 1.1.4, *tasmai sa hovāca dve vidye veditavye iti ha sma yad brahmavido vadanti parā ca eva aparā ca*, "He said to him what the knowers of the *bráhman* say, that 'two forms of knowledge must be known,' the higher and the lower." If this is the case, the translation of the passage in Pillar Edict 7 would be:

> (Y) *dhaṃmamahāmāttā pi m' ete bahuvidhesu aṭṭhesu ānuggahikesu viyāpaṭā se pavvajītānaṃ ceva gihitthānaṃ ca savvapāsaṃḍesu pi ca viyāpaṭā se* (Z) *saṃghaṭṭassi pi me kaṭe ime viyāpaṭā hohaṃti ti hemeva bābhanesu ājīvikesu pi me kaṭe ime viyāpaṭā hohaṃti ti nigaṃṭhesu pi me kaṭe ime viyāpaṭā hohaṃti nānā pāsaṃḍesu pi me kaṭe ime viyāpaṭā hohaṃti ti.*
>
> These officers of the dharma of mine also are engaged in benevolent affairs of many kinds: (those) for both renunciates and householders. They are engaged also among all religious communities: I have determined that some are to be engaged in the affairs of the Saṅgha also, that likewise I have determined that these are to be engaged among Brahmins and Ājīvikas. I have determined that these are to be engaged among the Nigaṇṭhas. I have determined that these are to be engaged among various religious communities.[26]

The statement that the officers of the dharma are active among all religious communities sets up the list of specific groups that then follows, beginning with the Buddhist Saṅgha and including also Brahmins, Ājīvikas, and Jains. At the end of this list, in his summing up, Aśoka again says in Pillar

26. This translation is similar to that of Alsdorf (1960: 259): "And as to my dharma-mahāmātras, they are occupied with beneficial affairs, viz., of ascetics and householders; they are also occupied with all sects, to wit, I have ordered 'these shall occupy themselves with the affairs of the (Buddhist) saṃgha,' likewise I have also ordered 'these shall occupy themselves with brāhmaṇas and ājīvikas,' (and) I have also ordered 'these shall occupy themselves with the nirgranthas,' and I have also ordered 'these shall occupy themselves with various sects.'" I believe he is correct in his interpretation of the passage, whether or not he rightly understands *viyāpaṭāse* as *viyāpaṭā se*, that is, as two words rather than one, and *se* in the sense of Pāli *seyyathā* or AM *se jahā*, "that is." His view of *viyāpaṭā se* is supported by von Hinüber 2001: 230. On this passage, also see the comments in Olivelle, Ch. 3, this volume, pp. 51–52.

Edict 7[AA], *dhaṃmamahāmāttā cu me etesu ceva viyāpaṭā savvesu ca aṃnesu pāsaṃḍesu,* ". . . but my officers of the dharma have been active among these and among all other religious communities." That is to say, there might be other religious communities in addition to the Buddhists, Brahmins, Ājīvikas, and Jains among whom his officers of the dharma are active.

Rock Edict 13 contains another reference to *pāṣaṇḍas* alongside *gṛhasthas,* but here too, they likely comprise two different religious categories. In this inscription, Aśoka regrets the harm he has done in his conquest of the Kaliṅgas, during which, he says, 150,000 people were deported, 100,000 were killed, and many others died from other causes (RE 13[B]). Aśoka then goes on to say, in Rock Edict 13[F], *iyaṃ pi cu tato gulumatatale devānaṃpiyasa* (G) *e tata vasati bābhanā vā̠ samanā vā̠ aṃne vā̠ pāsaṃḍā gihathā vā̠ yesu vihitā esa agabhutisusū̠sā* . . . . "This weighs even more on the Beloved of the Gods: that those who were staying there—Brahmins or *śramaṇas* or other religious communities—or householders, among whom there is prescribed obedience to the foremost (one/ones) . . . ."[27] It is unlikely that the "householders" (*gihathā*) are here included with the *pāṣaṇḍas,* since the phrase *aṃne vā̠ pāsaṃḍā,* "or other religious communities," marks an end to the first relative clause. Aśoka often ends a sequence with a reference to "other" (*aṃne, aṃnāni*) similar items, as, for example, in Rock Edict 4[B]: *se aja devānaṃpiyasa piyadasine lājine dhaṃmacalanena bhelighose aho dhaṃmaghose vimānadasanā hathīni agikaṃdhāni aṃnāni ca diviyāni lūpāni dasayitu janasa,* "But today, by the dharmic action of King Piyadassi, Beloved of the Gods, the sound of drums is the sound of 'Hurrah, the dharma!' when he [=the king] has exhibited to the people exhibitions of flying palaces, and elephants, and heaps of fire, and other heavenly forms."[28] After the first relative clause, Aśoka then adds a second that concerns the *gihathā* ("householders"). In this clause, Aśoka lists the various virtues of the householders: obedience to mother and father and to teachers and courtesy to friends, acquaintances, companions, and relatives, and to slaves and servants. Both the phrases beginning *e tata vasati* and *gihathā vā yesu* are resumed by *tesaṃ* "for those" in the conclusion: (G) *tesaṃ tatā hoti upaghāte vā vadhe vā abhilatānaṃ vā vinikhamane,* ". . .—for those (people) there was violence then, or death, or separation from loved ones." As I understand this passage, therefore, we are again dealing with two groups—Brahmins, *śramaṇas,* and other religious communities, on the one hand, and on the other, householders, who adhere to the kind of dharmic

27. On the translation of this passage, see Schneider 1978: 124–27.

28. Or likewise, RE 8[B]: *migaviyā aṃnāni ca hedisāni (edisāni) abhilāmāni,* "hunting and other such pleasures" and RE 2[A], 5[J (quoted below), M], and 12[M].

behavior that Aśoka promotes.[29] In this interpretation of the passage, *vasati* in the first relative clause may have the sense of "stays."[30] That is, if members of Brahmin, *śramaṇa*, and other religious communities were semi-mobile, they might have happened to be in Kaliṅga when Aśoka's invasion occurred, but they were not necessarily permanent inhabitants of Kaliṅga. In that case, they would contrast to the *gihathā*, who were residents of Kaliṅga.

In this case, the Greek translation complicates the interpretation of the 13[F-G]. That translation begins: καὶ τοῦτο ἔτι δυσχερέστερον ὑπείληφε ὁ βασιλεὺς καὶ ὅσοι ἐκεῖ ὤικουν βραμεναι ἢ σραμεναι ἢ καὶ ἄλλοι τινὲς οἱ περὶ τὴν εὐσέβειαν διατρίβοντες, τοὺς ἐκεῖ οἰκοῦντας ἔδει τὰ τοῦ βασιλέυς συμφέροντα νοεῖν, "And this the king has accepted with yet more difficulty: even as many as lived there—Brahmins or *śramaṇas* or also all others dedicating themselves to dutifulness—. . . ." Following the Prakrit versions, the translator starts by naming those who "lived" (ὤικουν [*ōíkoun*]) there: Brahmins, *śramaṇas*, and others "dedicating themselves to dutifulness." As before, those "dedicating themselves to dutifulness" (οἱ περὶ τήν εὐσέβειαν διατρίβοντες [*hoi perì tḗn eusébeian diatríbontes*]) translates *pāṣaṇḍa*. But the translator then veers into a parenthetical construction rather than, like the Prakrit *gihathā vā yesu vihitā* . . . , a nominative with a relative clause. That parenthesis begins τοὺς ἐκεῖ οἰκοῦντας ἔδει τὰ τοῦ βασιλέυς συμφέροντα νοεῖν, "it was an obligation that those living there mind the interests of the king . . . ." and then the translation lists other forms of good behavior of those who lived in Kaliṅga. In this parenthetical construction, he appears to translate *gihathā* with the phrase "those living there" (τοὺς ἐκεῖ οἰκοῦντας [*toûs ekeî oikoûntas*]). This translation may well have been inspired by the translator's association of *giha-* ("house") in *gihatha* with οἶκος ([*oikos*], "house"), a nominal form related to the participle οἰκοῦντας (*oikoûntas*), "living" or "dwelling." This participle belongs to the verbal system of ὤικουν (*ōíkoun*, "they lived," translating *vasati*), which he used before of the "Brahmins, *śramaṇas*, and those dedicating themselves to dutifulness." That is to say, he seems to understand *gihathā* to mean the inhabitants of Kaliṅga, consisting of or including Brahmins, *śramaṇas*, and

29. The catalogue of the householders' virtues is not to differentiate these householders from householders whose deaths he might not regret, but rather to emphasize Aśoka's grief that he has caused pain to people who act in the way that Aśoka encourages.

30. As, for example, in *Rāmāyaṇa* 2.1.6, Bharata and Śatrughna "were staying" (*nyavasat*) with their uncle while all the court intrigue at Ayodhyā took place that resulted in Rāma's exile. Or in 2.41.15, Rāma "stayed the night" (*avasat . . . tāṃ rātrim*) near the bank of the Tāmasa.

those dedicating themselves to dutifulness.[31] After the parenthesis, the translator has the king conclude by saying that he was deeply distressed by the deaths or deportations of those who lived there and behaved in this way.

If this is what he intends, the translator conceives of Brahmins, *śramaṇas*, and other religious communities differently from the way Aśoka did, since, as I understand him, Aśoka did not think of them as necessarily native to Kaliṅga or permanently settled there. The translator also does not appear to be familiar with *gihatha* as a distinctive social or religious category but thought of it as just a word for "resident." He did recognize Brahmins and *śramaṇas* as specific and complementary religious groups because he simply transcribes them as βραμεναι (*bramenai*) and σραμεναι (*sramenai*), a rhythmic and rhyming antithetical pair. In contrast, as he did before, he translates *pāṣaṇḍa*, rather than transcribing the term, because he knew the word as a general description of religious communities. In doing that last, he does reflect Aśoka's understanding.

On the basis of these observations, therefore, I take *pāṣaṇḍa* to refer to religious communities of Brahmins, *śramaṇas*, and the like. We might have a clearer picture of the common features of all these communities, and especially what is meant by "Brahmins" in this context, by a detailed examination of the collocation *bābhane ca samane ca*, "Brahmins and *śramaṇas*." I cannot provide that study here, but instead I can offer a few comments based on the work of others.

In addition to the collocation *bābhane ca samane ca* in Rock Edict 13, Aśoka repeats the compound *samanabaṃbhana/-bābhana* or *baṃbhanasamana* in Rock Edicts 3[D], 4[A, C], 8[E], 9[G], and 11[C]. Brahmins and *śramaṇas* were clearly comparable communities and are mentioned together in a variety of other literatures. A generation before Aśoka, Megasthenes (according to Strabo, *Geography* XV.1.59) described two types of "philosophers" in India: *brakhmanas* and *garmanas* (*śramaṇas*), both of whom live separately and simply. About a century after Aśoka, Patañjali says that the "*śramaṇas* and Brahmins" form a singular compound *śramaṇabrāhmaṇam*, presumably because they form an oppositional pair. Similarly, a masculine compound *samaṇabrāhmaṇā* is

31. This interpretation, which follows Benveniste (1964: 153), contrasts to the opinion of Norman (1972: 115–16), who holds that *gihathā* is omitted in the Greek translation and that by τοῦς ἐκεῖ οἰκοῦντας, "those living there," the Greek translator was restating ὅσοι ἐκεῖ ᾤκουν "as many as lived there," his translation of *e tata vasati*. Certainly, the Greek translator does truncate and rearrange the Prakrit text, but he also paraphrases as we saw in the case of *sālavaḍhi*, which he translated by δειαμείνωσιν . . . εὐσεβοῦντες, "they have been concerned to be living dutifully." While I find it likely that a comparable paraphrase occurs here, Norman's view has this advantage, that it does not imply that the Greek translator misunderstood *gihathā*.

frequent in Pāli (Bronkhorst 2016: 413–14). A passage in the *Dīgha Nikāya* (*DN* II, pp. 150–51; citation and translation in Bronkhorst 2016: 415) attributes a common form to these communities:

> *ye 'me bho gotama samaṇabrāhmaṇā saṃghino gaṇino gaṇācariyā ñātā yasassino titthakarā sādhusammatā ca bahujanassa, seyyathīdaṃ pūraṇo kassapo, makkhali gosālo, ajita-kesakambalī, pakudho kaccāyano, sañjayo belaṭṭhaputto, nigaṇṭho nāthaputto, sabbe te sakāya paṭiññāya abbhaññaṃsu, sabbe 'va na abbhaññaṃsu, ekacce abbhaññaṃsu ekacce na abbhaññaṃsūti?*
>
> Venerable Gotama, all those *śramaṇas* and Brahmins (*samaṇabrāhmaṇā*) who have orders [*saṃghino*] and followings, who are teachers, well-known and famous as founders of schools, and popularly regarded as saints, like Pūraṇa Kassapa, Makkhali Gosāla, Ajita Kesakambalī, Pakudha Kaccāyana, Sañjaya Belaṭṭhaputta and the Nigaṇṭha Nāthaputta—have they all realised the truth as they all make out, or have none of them realised it, or have some realised it and some not?

The teachers mentioned here belong to what we would consider to be *śramaṇa* communities, but even if none is classed as a Brahmin, the passage implies that Brahmins also form similar communities of teachers and students and live lives of holy restraint. As such, they should be comparable to non-Brahmin *śramaṇa* communities. Aśoka usually refers to Brahmins in conjunction with *śramaṇas*,[32] and such lumping *brāhmaṇas* together with *śramaṇas* might overstate the similarity of the two groups. But some distortion of its constituents does not affect the conception of a *pāṣaṇḍa* as a religious community, even it diminishes the differences among communities classified as *pāṣaṇḍas*.

Understanding Aśoka's *pāṣaṇḍas* to consist of communities of religious adepts would bring the inscriptions into concert with the attestations of *pāṣaṇḍa* in Sanskrit and Middle Indic discussed above, since whether they are viewed negatively, neutrally, or positively, *pāṣaṇḍas* consist of such groups. Even limited to this kind of community, Aśoka understands *pāṣaṇḍas* to be a universal phenomenon. All societies have similar religious communities, as he says in Rock Edict 13[J]: *nathi ca se janapade ata nathi ime nikāyā aṃnatā yonesu bābhane ca samane ca nathi ca kuvāpi janapadasi ata nathi munisānaṃ*

32. But there are instances in which he refers to Brahmins but not *śramaṇas* in MRE 2, RE 5, and PE 7, quoted above, although in the last in conjunction with the Buddhist Saṅgha, Ājīvikas, and Nigaṇṭhas.

ekatalasi pi pāsaṃḍasi no nāma pasāde, "There is no land where there these classes (*nikāyā*)—Brahmins and *śramaṇas*—do not exist except among the Greeks; in any land in which (Brahmins and *śramaṇas*) do not exist, there does not exist among men no inclination [=men have an inclination] toward one religious community or another."[33] Aśoka recognizes that the specific categories of Brahmins and *śramaṇas*—the latter including Buddhists, Ājīvikas, and Jains—are not everywhere, but groups belonging to the more open category of *pāṣaṇḍa* are everywhere.

Aśoka wants to foster these religious communities, but he recognizes that there are differences among the *pāṣaṇḍas* and that their competition, especially their competition for patronage, could lead to conflict. Since such conflict would be dangerous to the empire, Aśoka is concerned to minimize disagreement among the *pāṣaṇḍas* and to tamp down *pāṣaṇḍas'* self-promotion and criticism of others. Attempts at such self-promotion and criticism, he says, do more harm than good even to one's own religious community: Rock Edict 12[H] declares, *e hi kechi* (*keci*) *atapāsaṃḍaṃ pūjayati palapāsaṃḍaṃ vā galahati save atapāsaṃḍabhatiyā vā̱* (∅) *kiti* (*kiṃti*) *atapāsaṃḍaṃ dīpayema ti se ca mana tathā kalaṃtaṃ* (add: *atapāsaṃḍaṃ*) *bāḍhatale̱ upahaṃti̱ atapāsaṃḍaṃ* (∅), "For whoever honors one's own religious community or denigrates the religious community of others—all only through their devotion to their own religious community, thinking that they would glorify their own religious community—if he is acts thus, he even injures his own religious community more greatly (than the religious community of others)." Aśoka's hope is that all religious communities will respect all other religious communities, according to Rock Edict 12[E-F]: *pūjetaviya̱ va cu palapāsaṃḍā tena tena ākālena | hevaṃkalaṃtaṃ atapāsaṃḍaṃ* (*ca*) *bāḍhaṃ vaḍhayati palapāsaṃḍasa pi* (∅) *ca upakaleti*, "But the religious communities of others ought to be honored in one way or another (that is appropriate).[34] By acting thus, one greatly strengthens one's own religious community and serves the religious community of others also." That is to say, religious communities are all better off if they do not engage in attacks on one another.

If religious communities have the potential for conflict, why is the king so favorably inclined to them? The reason is that for Aśoka *pāṣaṇḍas* are not simply a problem. As we have seen, the *pāṣaṇḍas* teach dharmas, likely different dharmas to be sure, but Aśoka believed that there was a common

---

33. On the translation of this sentence, see Schneider 1978: 141.

34. Compare Schneider (1978: 139): "Ich glaube, der Gedanke dabei ist: man soll in derjenigen Form Lob spenden . . . welche den jeweiligen Umständen usw. angemessen ist."

dharma, which is or which includes the dharma that he seeks to promote. Like Rock Edict 13[J], Rock Edict 5 also connects the universality of *pāṣaṇḍas* with the universality of the dharma: *te savapāsaṃḍesu viyāpaṭā dhaṃmādhithānāye ca dhaṃmavaḍhiyā hitasukhāye ca dhaṃmayutasa yonakaṃboc̲agaṃdhālānaṃ laṭhikapet̲inikānaṃ e vā pi aṃne apalaṃtā* (*āpa–*), "They [=the officers of the dharma] have been active among all religious communities for the establishment of the dharma by strengthening the dharma and for the well-being and happiness of those dedicated to the dharma among the Greeks, Kāmbojas, Gāndhāras, Laṭhikas, Pitenikas, and others on the western borders" (RE 5[J]). For Aśoka, the existence of *pāṣaṇḍas* means the existence of dharmas, since *pāṣaṇḍas* are communities that teach dharma. The universality of such religious communities and therefore the universality of their dharmas make practical his idea that his dharma can be universal. Similarly, in Rock Edict 12 Aśoka connects the *pāṣaṇḍas* with dharma and their dharma with his dharma in a passage quoted before, Rock Edict 12[L]: *devānaṃpiye no tathā dānaṃ vā̲ pūjā vā̲ maṃnati* (*-e*) *athā kiti* (*kiṃti*) *sālavaḍhi* (*-e*) *siyā savapāsaṃḍānaṃ ti* (∅), "The Beloved of the Gods does not respect gifts or honors so (much) as that there should be a strengthening of the *sāla* [≈ the dharma] of all religious communities." As a result of his efforts to promote this *sāla* of *pāṣaṇḍas* by what he himself does and by the work of his officials, the outcome will be, according to Rock Edict 12[N], *yaṃ atapāsaṃḍavaḍhi* (*-ī*) *ca hoti dhaṃmasa ca dīpanā*, "that there comes to be a strengthening of one's own religious community and a glorification of the dharma." In the middle of the twentieth century, there were public service announcements promoting "religion in American life,"[35] because there were thought to be common religious values within the small number of traditions then understood to constitute American religion. For the sponsors of these announcements, these values were good for the country. Aśoka appears to have believed something similar about the *pāṣaṇḍas*. Their dharmas were, at their basis, also his dharma, and therefore they were good for the empire, good for its citizens, and just plain good.

Here, then, is what we can say about *pāṣaṇḍa* in the Aśokan inscriptions. Aśoka's use of the term reflects its original sense as a "religious community" or more specifically a community of mendicants, ascetics, or other religious adepts. The examples of such religious communities that Aśoka mentions are Ājīvikas, the Buddhist Saṅgha, Jains, and Brahmins, but he understands that there are other religious communities, which he does not name. And as we have seen, Aśoka imagined such communities to exist even outside the Indian

35. Compare https://www.youtube.com/watch?v=kırVqFT8H4M, accessed June 3, 2017.

cultural world. Not every social segment that we would call "religious" might have been classified as a *pāṣaṇḍa*. The *pāṣaṇḍas* were communities, among which Aśoka may not have included individual and independent renunciates, who neither live as part of a group nor identify themselves with any recognized sect and, even more importantly for him, might not have taught dharma. The evidence for this claim is admittedly an absence: Aśoka does not include *parivrajitas* "religious wanderers" or all *pravrajitas* "religious renunciates" among the groups he *explicitly* designates as *pāṣaṇḍas*. Whether or not Aśoka would have included householders as members of *pāṣaṇḍas* remains uncertain. As I understand the inscriptions, nowhere does he explicitly include *gṛhasthas* within *pāṣaṇḍas*. However, both for Aśoka and elsewhere (e.g., AVPar 64.4.9 and Mbh 13.24.56 above), Brahmins could constitute *pāṣaṇḍas*, and it is likely that many of these Brahmin *pāṣaṇḍas* were householder communities or communities that included householders. If that is the case, then the collective of Brahmins would provide an example of a householder *pāṣaṇḍa*. As Lubin (2013: 34–35) discusses in more detail, in Minor Rock Edict 2[J-K], Aśoka mentions Brahmins alongside "elephant drivers" (Eṛṛaguḍi, *hathiyārohāni*), "accounts officers" (?) (Niṭṭur, *kāranakāni*), and "horse-training masters" (Eṛṛaguḍi, *yūgyacariyāni*), who teach resident students (*aṃtevāsīni*).[36] These students, in turn, ought to respect and obey their teachers (MRE 2[O] Niṭṭur, *[ā]cāli[y]e apacāyitaviye ca susūsitaviye ca*). Although they are here mentioned among professionals, such Brahmin teachers who studied and taught dharma would remain analogous to *śramaṇas*. And since they form a community teaching the dharma, then Brahmins are classifiable as *pāṣaṇḍas*. As Lubin (2013: 31) astutely observed: ". . . if Asoka understood by the label *brāhmaṇa* a class of religious professionals constituted by a system of training,

---

36. On Brahmins in Magadha during the Maurya period, see Lubin 2013: 30–35 and on this passage, pp. 34–35. The gloss of *hathiyārohāni* follows and the gloss of *yūgyacariyāni* approximates his translations. With regard the latter, Olivelle (2013: 167) translates the similar Sanskrit word *yogyācārya* as "training master" in *KAŚ* 2.30.42, a passage cited by Silk in Lubin 2013: 34 n. 18. Lubin translates *kāranakāni* as "record-keepers" with a query. Bloch (1950: 151 n. 18) compares *kāranaka* to Sanskrit *kāraṇika*, attested in the *MBh* 2.5.23, where van Buitenen (1975: 41) translates the word as "judicious teacher" and in *KAŚ* 2.7.22 and 34, where Olivelle (2013: 113) translates it as "accounts officer." I have followed the latter, although keeping a query. In n. 18, Lubin also mentions that Norman (1966: 116–17) interprets *hathiyārohāni, kāranakāni,* and *yūgyacariyāni* to refer not to professionals but to religious groups: "elephant worshippers" (=Ājīvikas), "causationists" (=Buddhists or Jains), and "yoga teachers" respectively. Such an interpretation would bring the passage in line with the communities who usually accompany Brahmins in the inscriptions, but leaves puzzling the reason Aśoka would employ such terms and, as Lubin points out, sets aside likely equivalent expressions in Sanskrit and Pāli.

a disciplinary regime, and a distinctive set of teachings, an analogy with ascetic orders would make sense. . . ."[37]

These *pāṣaṇḍa* communities, including Brahmins, depended for support on the king and on others outside of their communities. For this reason, members of *pāṣaṇḍas* lived live near to or even within populated areas. Their proximity allowed them not only to teach within their communities but also to instruct those who were not members of their communities as part of their interaction with them. That instruction was of particular importance to Aśoka. In Aśoka's view, the *pāṣaṇḍas* were characterized by dharmas, and while their dharmas might differ, Aśoka understood that there was a common core of their teaching that applied to all, and this common core was or included the dharma that Aśoka taught. This dharma encompassed ideals such as respect for parents and teachers and consideration for all people, whether socially higher or lower. It was both this connection of the *pāṣaṇḍas* to dharma, as well as his own close relationship to one *pāṣaṇḍa*, the Buddhist Saṅgha, that recommended them to the king.

37. Were there were other householder communities in addition to these Brahmins? Obvious possibilities are Buddhist *upāsakas* and *upāsikās*, male and female lay followers who had formally taken refuge in the "three jewels" (Bloch 1950: 145 n. 4). Aśoka was certainly familiar with Buddhist *upāsakas*, since he was one himself (MRE 1[C] in Andersen 1990: 112) and since he refers to both *upāsakas* and *upāsikās* in the Bairāṭ edict and to *upāsakas* in the Schism edict. In chapter 3 of this volume, Olivelle argues that Aśoka would have included these *upāsakas* and *upāsikās* as *pāṣaṇḍas*, and he might be right. However, it is difficult to demonstrate this from the inscriptions themselves. In Aśoka's lists of *pāṣaṇḍas*, he refers to the Buddhist religious community as the *saṃgha* and for the early period, the *saṃgha* likely refers only to monks and nuns.

3

Gṛhastha *in Aśoka's Classification of Religious People*

Patrick Olivelle

AS STEPHANIE JAMISON'S seminal study in Chapter 1 has shown, the category of *gṛhastha*[1] was a neologism in Sanskrit; it appears for the first time in the Dharmasūtras perhaps around the third century BCE. As she also points out, the Prakrit forms of the term, however, are found frequently both in the Aśokan inscriptions and in Pāli and Prakrit texts. It is in the former that we have the sole datable occurrences of the term—first around the year 256 BCE in the 12th and 13th Rock Edicts (RE), and then in 241 BCE in the 7th Pillar Edict (PE). Thus we have a total of three occurrences of the term in Aśokan inscriptions. Several Prakritic forms of the term are used at different sites: *gharasta* (Girnār), *gahattha* (Kālsī), *grahatha* (Shāhbazgaṛhī), *gehatha* (Mānsehrā) and *gihittha* (Kālsī, Delhi-Toprā), which were dialectical or regional variants. Jamison has also pointed out that *gṛhastha* is always presented in opposition to or at least in close proximity to *pravrajita*, the ascetic who has "gone forth." In the Aśokan inscriptions, moreover, there is another category with which *gṛhastha* is closely associated, and that is *pāṣaṇḍa*, a term that Joel Brereton has discussed in Chapter 2. Finally, all three of these terms are in some way juxtaposed to the compound *śramaṇa-brāhmaṇa* (or *brāhmaṇa-śramaṇa*), which occurs frequently in the inscriptions in a variety of Prakrit forms.

1. Unless citing Prakrit texts, I use the Sanskrit forms: *gṛhastha*, *pāṣaṇḍa*, *pravrajita*, and so on.

Within the context of that related vocabulary, this chapter will attempt to tease out the meanings and significance attached to *gṛhastha* in the Aśokan vocabulary, in the hope that this focused study will throw light on the broader adoption of this term in Brahmanical texts composed during the three or four centuries before and after the Common Era, as well as on the sociology of religious groups of the time encapsulated in the terms *pāṣaṇḍa, pavrajita, śramaṇa*, and *brāhmaṇa*. I will refer to Brereton's essay in Chapter 2, noting any differences from his views and attempting to extend his conclusions by taking into account the broader context and evidence from the Dharmasūtras.

Before proceeding further, however, a word may be appropriate regarding the Aśokan inscriptions.[2] They consist of three classes of major texts: Minor Rock Edicts (MRE, with several versions), Major Rock Edicts (RE; a total of fourteen inscribed in several locations), and Pillar Edicts (PE; six inscribed on six pillars, and a seventh on the Delhi-Toprā pillar), as well as several other inscriptions, including two Separate Edicts, the Schism Edict, and edicts translated into Greek and Aramaic. Even though they have been traditionally referred to as "edicts," they are better seen as letters from the emperor to his officials, subjects, the Buddhist monastic order, and other religious groups. Their significance lies also in the fact that they are the earliest written and datable texts from ancient India, and, since they were inscribed on stone, we have the added benefit of having them exactly as they were originally inscribed. The consecration of Aśoka as king probably took place in 268 BCE. His first dated inscriptions (RE 3 and 4) were inscribed twelve years after his consecration (i.e., 256 BCE), although his inscriptional activity probably began earlier with the Minor Rock Edicts that are thought to predate the Major Rock Edits. Norman (2012: 51) dates them to the eleventh year (257 BCE), that is, one year before the beginning of the Rock Edict series. The last inscription, the 7th Pillar Edict, was done twenty-seven years after his consecration, that is in 241 BCE. If we accept that Aśoka died in 233–232 BCE (Thapar 1997: 196), then there is an absence of writing, or at least extant writing, during the last decade or so of his life. We should also keep in mind that the Rock Edict and Pillar Edict series are anthologies of Aśoka's writings[3] compiled either by him and/

2. In a previous study (Olivelle 2012a), I have pointed out that "edict" does not adequately indicate the nature of Aśoka's writings, which are best described as letters. There I also commented on the fact that the inscriptions as we have them, especially in the major Rock Edicts, are anthologies, probably collected initially and inscribed in batches (Falk 2006: 111–12). For the uniqueness of Aśoka's inscriptions within the context of royal inscriptions in India and worldwide, see Salomon 2009.

3. I use "writings" to refer to the texts that were authored by Aśoka and written and inscribed on stones and pillars subsequently. It is, of course, unknown how Aśoka himself composed

or by his officials. It is more than likely that the writings that have survived are only a portion, possibly a small portion, of Aśoka's writings.

We have thus a period of about seventeen years during which Aśoka wrote his extant messages. Although it is difficult to assign specific dates to each edict—only a few contain a date—I think it is important to our understanding of Aśoka and his literary, political, and religious activities that we recognize that his ideas and policies may have changed and developed over that period of time. We know, for example—because he says so—that his creation of a new senior level of bureaucracy, the *dharmamahāmātras*, was an unprecedented innovation introduced by him during the thirteenth year after his consecration (255 BCE), that is, five years after the end of the Kaliṅga war, probably four years after his conversion to Buddhism, and three years after he started his program of dharma instruction through inscriptions.

It is in Rock Edict 12, a message completely devoted to the conduct of the various *pāṣaṇḍas* or religious groups and written sometime after 255 BCE,[4] that we get the first mention of the term *gṛhastha* and the clearest statement both of its meaning and about its relationship to the two other categories: *pāṣaṇḍa* and *pravrajita*. The beginning of this inscription reads in Schneider's (1978) reconstruction:[5]

> [A] *devānampiye piyadasi lājā savapāsaṃḍāni pavajitāni gihathāni vā pūjayati dānena vividhāya ca pūjāya.*
> The king Devānāṃpriya Priyadarśin venerates all *pāṣaṇḍas, pravrajitas,* or *gṛhasthas,* with gifts and diverse kinds of veneration.[6]

---

these texts, or even whether he was himself literate. It could well have been that he composed his messages orally, which were written down by scribes and dispatched to the various locations where they were inscribed.

4. Given that this inscription mentions *dharmamahāmātras*, it must be after 255 BCE when Aśoka tells us that he created this institution. Falk (2006: 111–12) thinks that RE 12 constituted the third batch (the first batch, RE 1–8, were sent in or shortly after 256 BCE), while RE 13 and 14 were the fourth batch of edicts to be sent to the inscription sites. Rock Edict 12 may have been written a few years after 256 BCE, and RE 13 sometime after that.

5. Unless otherwise stated, I follow Schneider's reconstructions when citing RE texts, as does Brereton in Ch. 2. This gives some coherence to the cited texts, because otherwise, given the fragmented state of texts in some sites, the citations would have to be taken from different sites. Schneider's reconstruction also gives the most plausible original version of the texts.

6. Besides the spellings of different words, the major differences in the readings at the various locations where RE 12 is inscribed are the following. Girnār adds *ca* after *savvapāsaṃḍāni* and *pavajitāni*. Girnār, Mānsehrā, Shāhbazgaṛhī read *ca* in place of *vā* after *gahatthāni*.

The maximalist way to read this is to take *pavajitāni* and *gihathāni* as subcategories under *ṣavapāṣaṃḍāni*. This, I think, is supported also by the placement of *vā* ("or") after *gihathāni*,[7] perhaps indicating that the categories of *pravrajita* and *gṛhastha* are linked to the *pāṣaṇḍas* mentioned just before them. Even if we follow Brereton's interpretation in Chapter 2, the minimalist way would be to take *gṛhastha* as being in some manner related complementary to *pāṣaṇḍa*. Otherwise it is difficult to explain why the term always occurs in close proximity to *pāṣaṇḍa* and never in some other context. It is clear even from Brereton's perspective that *gṛhasthas* were not simply any kind of married householder; they were, as Jamison has pointed out, presented in a manner that contrasts them, the "stay-at-home" individuals, to the *pravrajitas*, those who have "gone forth." The fact that Aśoka speaks of *gṛhasthas* in the same breath as *pāṣaṇḍas* shows that in his mind the two were in some sense related.

If the former interpretation is correct, then the various religious groups classified as *pāṣaṇḍa*, in Aśoka's eyes, had within them two kinds of members: the *pravrajitas*, who "went forth," and the *gṛhasthas*, that is, those who belonged to a *pāṣaṇḍa* group but chose to remain at home or in a house. If we follow Brereton, then at a minimum the *gṛhasthas* constituted a special group of people who were in some way affiliated with or connected to various *pāṣaṇḍas*. In either case, I want to argue that what follows in this inscription is also related to *gṛhasthas* in their association with *pāṣaṇḍas*. Otherwise the mention of *gṛhasthas* and *pravrajitas* in the opening sentence would make little sense.

Taking a cue from his own gifts and acts of veneration to these groups, the rest of Aśoka's message to the *pāṣaṇḍas* in Rock Edict 12 tells them that he considers it far better than any gift or act of veneration he may bestow on them that all *pāṣaṇḍas* attend to their *śālāvaḍḍhi* (G. *sāravaḍḍhī*), a term that is a hapax unique to this passage and quite obscure, but which I think refers to the "essential core or pith" of what a *pāṣaṇḍa* is all about.[8] Let me cite this long text again in Schneider's (1978) reconstruction:

> **[B]** *no cu tathā dānaṃ vā pūjā vā devānaṃpiye maṃnati athā kiti sālavaḍhi siyā savapāsaṃḍānaṃ* / **[C]** *sālavaḍhi cu bahuvidhā* / **[D]** *tasa*

---

7. Brereton (Ch. 2, p. 33) bases his interpretation on the insertion of *ca* ("and") after both *savapāsaṃḍāni* and *pavajitāni* in the Girnār version.

8. For a different analysis and interpretation of this term by Brereton, see Ch. 2. He argues that *sāla* approximates "dharma," although with a different semantic shading.

cu iyaṃ mūle a vacaguti kiti atapāsaṃḍapūjā vā palapāsaṃḍagalahā vā no siyā apakalanasi lahukā vā siyā tasi tasi pakalanasi / [E] *pūjetaviya va cu palapāsaṃḍā tena tena ākālena* / [F] *hevaṃkalaṃtaṃ atapāsaṃḍaṃ bāḍhaṃ vaḍhayati palapāsaṃḍasa pi ca upakaleti* / [G] *tadaṃnathā kalaṃtaṃ atpapāsaṃḍaṃ ca chaṇati palapāsaṃḍasa pi ca pi apakaleti* / [H] *e hi kechi atapāsaṃḍaṃ pūjayati palapāsaṃḍaṃ vā galahati save atapāsaṃḍabhatiyā va kiti atapāsaṃḍaṃ dīpayema ti se ca mana tathā kalaṃtaṃ bāḍhatale upahaṃti atapāsaṃḍaṃ* / [I] *se samavāye va sādhu kiti aṃnamanasa dhaṃmaṃ suneyu ca susūseyu ca* / [J] *hevaṃ hi devānaṃpiyasa ichā kiṃti savapāsaṃḍā bahusutā ca kayānāgamā ca huveyu ti* / [K] *e ca tata tata pasaṃnā tehi vataviye* / [L] *devānaṃpiye no tathā dānaṃ vā pūjā vā maṃnati athā kiti sālavaḍhi siyā savapāsaḍānaṃ ti* / [M] *bahukā ca etāye aṭhāye viyāpaṭā dhaṃmamahāmātā ithidhiyakhamahāmātā vacabhūmikā aṃne ca nikāyā* / [N] *iyaṃ ca etasa phale yaṃ atapāsaṃḍavaḍhi ca hoti dhaṃmasa ca dīpanā* //

[B] Devānāṃpriya, however, does not prize gifts or veneration as highly as this: namely, that the essential core[9] may grow among all *pāṣaṇḍas*. [C] The growth of the essential core, however, takes many forms, [D] but this is its root: guarding speech—that is to say, honoring one's own *pāṣaṇḍa* or disparaging the *pāṣaṇḍa* of others when it is inappropriate,[10] and, even when it is appropriate, doing so in moderation. [E] The *pāṣaṇḍas* of others, on the other hand, should be honored whenever it is appropriate. [F] Acting in this manner, one certainly enhances one's own *pāṣaṇḍa* and also benefits the *pāṣaṇḍa* of others. [G] When someone acts contrary to that, one hurts one's own *pāṣaṇḍa* and also harms the *pāṣaṇḍa* of others. [H] For, should someone honor his own *pāṣaṇḍa* and disparage the *pāṣaṇḍa* of others wholly out of devotion to his own *pāṣaṇḍa*, thinking, that is, "I shall make my *pāṣaṇḍa* illustrious"—by so doing he harms his own *pāṣaṇḍa* even more grievously.

[I] Consorting together is indeed a good thing. That is—one should learn and strive to learn each other's dharma. [J] For this is Devānāṃpriya's

9. See Norman 1972: 112–13 for its possible meaning of "knowledge, information."

10. The terms *apakalana* and *pakalana* used here are ambiguous. Norman (1972: 113), comparing them with their Greek translations, takes *pakalana* to mean "topic" and its opposite as "off topic," and translates the terms as "without reason" and "with reason" Others translate them as "appropriate/inappropriate occasions."

wish, namely, that all *pāṣaṇḍas* become highly learned and have excellent teachings. [K] And whichever of these they may fancy, they should be advised: [L] "Devānāṃpriya does not prize gifts or veneration as highly as this: namely, that the essential core may grow among all *pāṣaṇḍas*."

[M] And large numbers have been dispatched for this purpose: high officials in charge of dharma, high officials in charge of women, officials in charge of cattle and farms, and other classes of officials. And this is its fruit: one's own *pāṣaṇḍa* is made to flourish and dharma is made illustrious.

The central point Aśoka wants to make is that he values what he calls *sālavaḍḍhi* more than gifts or veneration that he speaks of in the opening statement. Leaving aside the exact meaning of that term, it is curious that Aśoka appears to compare what he is giving to *pāṣaṇḍas* with the inner development of the *pāṣaṇḍas* themselves, and he finds the latter better than the former. When a similar comparison is made, for example, in Rock Edict 9, he compares the useless ceremonies (*maṅgala*) to the highest ceremony that is the *dharmamaṅgala*; but both are performed by the same people. It seems that Aśoka is here telling the *pāṣaṇḍa* his wish—as he explicitly does in the last part of the inscription. He is saying in effect that, "even though I give you gifts and pay you homage, my true wish is that you develop your inner quality." But this is also Aśoka's gift, the *dharmadāna* he speaks of so highly in other inscriptions. He is here preaching to the *pāṣaṇḍas*, giving them the gift of dharma, by teaching them what is most important to the life of a member of a *pāṣaṇḍa*.

Aśoka points out that the root of *sālavaḍḍhi* is the control or guarding of speech (*vacaguti*). And this consists especially of not disparaging the *pāṣaṇḍas* of others (*parapāṣaṇḍa*) and not praising one's own *pāṣaṇḍa* (*ātmapāṣaṇḍa*). The thrust of Aśoka's plea is that members of the various *pāṣaṇḍas* should live in harmony and mutual respect. But Aśoka wants them to take a further step and recommends *samavāya*. This term has been translated as "concord" (Thapar 1997; Nikam and McKeon 1959), "réunion" (Bloch 1950), and "restraint" (Sircar 1975, taking the reading to be *sayamo*). I agree with Norman (1972: 114) that "the meaning required here is the usual one in Skt., 'coming, meeting together, contact,' since Aśoka's aim of increase in communication between the sects would be helped if they all met together so that they could hear each other's doctrines." In this way, Aśoka says, they will become truly learned (*bahuśruta*) and both honor their own *pāṣaṇḍas* and assist the *pāṣaṇḍas* of others. Even though *bahuśruta* (literally, "much heard") is a common term in early Sanskrit literature to refer to a learned man, I think Aśoka appears to play on the term *śruta*, which is related to listening. Earlier he had said that members of *pāṣaṇḍas* should consort with each other and "should learn (*sruṇāru*) and strive to learn (*susuṃsera*) each other's dharma." The terms here for learning actually refer to hearing or listening (from the verb √*śru*), and etymologically are connected to *śruta*. So in a sense one can become *bahuśruta* only by listening to each other.

Broadly, then, Aśoka outlines a program for different *pāṣaṇḍas* to live in harmony with each other, to respect and interact with each other, and to come to know each other's doctrines (dharma). It is clear, I think, that Aśoka's advice is given to both *pravrajitas* and *gṛhasthas* associated with *pāṣaṇḍas*, given that he addresses both groups in his opening statement. Aśoka's view parallels the indictment of groups who disparage each other given in the *Aṭṭakavagga* of the Buddhist text *Sutta-Nipāta*, one of the most ancient texts of the Buddhist canon (tr. Norman, modified):

> *sakaṃ sakaṃ diṭṭhi paribbasānā viggayha nānā kusalā vadanti | yo evaṃ jānāti sa vedi dhammam idam paṭikkosam akevalī so || evam pi viggayha vivādiyanti bālo paro akusalo ti cāhu | sacco nu vādo katamo imesaṃ sabbe va h' ime kusalā vadānā ||* (*Cūḷaviyūhasutta* of the *Sn*, 878–79)
>
> Each abiding by his own view, contending, experts say various things: "Whoever knows thus, knows the *dhamma*. Whoever rejects this is imperfect." Thus contending they dispute, and they say: "My opponent is a fool, no expert." Which of these is the true statement? For indeed all of these say they are experts.

> *yam āhu dhammaṃ paraman ti eke tam eva hīnan ti panāhu aññe | sacco nu vādo katamo imesaṃ sabbe va hīme kusalā vadānā || sakaṃ hi dhammaṃ paripuṇṇam āhu aññassa dhammaṃ pana hīnam āhu | evam pi viggayha vivādiyanti sakaṃ sakaṃ sammutim āhu saccaṃ || parassa ce vambhayitena hīno na koci dhammesu visesi assa | puthū hi aññassa vadanti dhammaṃ nihīnato samhi daḷhaṃ vadānā ||* (*Mahāviyūhasutta* of the *Sn*, 903–5)
>
> The *dhamma* that some people call the highest, others call the lowest. Which of these is the true statement? For all these people indeed call themselves experts. They say that their own *dhamma* indeed is superior, but they say another's *dhamma* is inferior. Thus contending they dispute. They each say his own opinion is true. If a doctrine is inferior because of the reviling of an opponent, then among *dhammas* none would be outstanding. For many people, speaking firmly about their own *dhamma*, declare another's *dhamma* to be inferior.

It is clear that inter-religious rivalry and doctrinal disputes were, on the one hand, prevalent among religious groups and, on the other, considered deleterious to spiritual advancement even within these religious groups, such as the Buddhists. For Aśoka there was an added layer of concern: he wanted to maintain harmony in his empire, and it is evident that he also believed in the importance of religious pluralism (Freiberger 2013 and Ch. 4, this volume) where no single religion would occupy a privileged position. Further, his advancement of dharma included its success within the groups devoted exclusively to religious pursuits, that is, the *pāṣaṇḍas*. He believed that none of them had a complete insight into the true dharma; they had to be humble enough to listen to and learn from each other. Perhaps a fool's errand, but then Aśoka was not your run-of-the-mill king.

The connection between the three categories—*pāṣaṇḍa, pravrajita,* and *gṛhastha*—is even less clear in Rock Edict 13, in which Aśoka speaks about his remorse at the devastation caused by his war against Kaliṅga, in particular his remorse at the violence and death visited on various *pāṣaṇḍas*:

> **[F]** *iyaṃ pi cu tato gulumatatale devānaṃpiyasa* **[G]** *e tata vasati bābhanā vā samanā vā aṃne vā pāsaṃḍā gihathā vā yesu vihitā esa agabhutisusūsā mātāpitusu susūsā gulususūsā mitasaṃthutasahāyanātikesu dāsabhaṭakasi samyāpaṭipati diḍhabhatitā tesaṃ tata hoti upaghāte vā vadhe vā abhilatānaṃ vā vinikhamane.*
>
> This, however, weighs even more heavily on Devānāṃpriya. Those living there—*brāhmaṇas*, or *śramaṇas*, or other *pāṣaṇḍas* or *gṛhasthas*[11] in whom these are established: obedience to superiors, obedience to mother and father, obedience to elders, treating properly friends, acquaintances, companions, and relatives, as well as slaves and servants, and firm devotion—they are visited with injury, killing, and separation from their loved ones.

Here for the first—and last—time we have a connection between *pāṣaṇḍa* and *gṛhastha*, on the one hand, and the two common categories *brāhmaṇa* and *śramaṇa*, so often used in the compounds *śramaṇa-brāhmaṇa* or *brāhmaṇa-śramaṇa*, on the other. The expression *aṃne vā pāsaṃḍā* probably implies both that *śramaṇas* and *brāhmaṇas* fall under the category of *pāṣaṇḍa*, and that there

11. In the Greek translation of this passage, *gṛhastha* is, in the opinion of Norman (1972: 115–16), missing. But for the opposite view, see Brereton in Ch. 2 (p. 36–37).

are other *pāṣaṇḍas* not falling under *śramaṇa* or *brāhmaṇa*. But who could they be? In the list of specific *pāṣaṇḍas* given in Pillar Edict 7 that we will examine below, all the known ascetic groups such as Ājīvakas, Nirgranthas (Jains), and the Buddhist Saṅgha would, I assume, fall within the category of *śramaṇa*. Now, it is possible that "other *pāṣaṇḍas*" is a throw-away line, used also in Pillar Edict 7, to make sure that *all pāṣaṇḍas* are comprehended, or the expression may refer to *pāṣaṇḍa* groups we are ignorant of. In any case, the category *gṛhastha* here also is used in close proximity to the three others given before, especially to *pāṣaṇḍa*.

There is a problem with the exact syntax of this passage that affects our understanding of *gṛhastha*, and Brereton has analyzed this in Chapter 2 (pp. 35–37). Most translators take the relative clause beginning with "in whom these are established" (*yesu vihita eṣa*) as going with all the preceding (so, apparently, Hultzsch 1925) or just with *gṛhastha* (so Thapar 1997; Sircar 1975; accepted by Brereton). If the latter is accepted, the virtues Aśoka enumerates (which are given elsewhere as prominent features of his dharma) are practiced by *gṛhasthas*. It is significant that two major features of Aśoka's dharma, namely, not killing and giving to *śramaṇas* and *brāhmaṇas*, are omitted in the list of virtues. Perhaps these were either superfluous or inappropriate in the case of *gṛhasthas*. Given that Aśoka had already spoken about the hundreds of thousands of people who had been killed, deported, or taken prisoner, many, perhaps a majority, of whom would have been householders, the mention here specifically of *gṛhasthas* shows that the latter fell into a different category. In Aśoka's mind they were part of a cluster of religious people that included also *pāṣaṇḍa*, *śramaṇa*, and *brāhmaṇa*.

The individual missing in this enumeration is the *pravrajita*, who is generally paired with the *gṛhastha*. I think the omission may be due to the mention of *śramaṇa*, a category that probably overlaps with *pravrajita*.

The third and final use of *gṛhastha* in the Aśokan corpus occurs in Pillar Edict 7 in a rather long and somewhat clumsy construction. This inscription probably consists of nine or ten separate messages strung together, each beginning with: *devānaṃpiye piyadassi* (*lājā*) *hevaṃ āhā*—"The king Devānāṃpriya Priyadarśin says thus" (Tieken 2012). The sixth in this list begins:

> *devānaṃpiye piyadassi hevaṃ āhā. dhaṃmamahāmāttā pi m'ete bahuvidhesu aṭṭhesu ānuggahikesu viyāpaṭāse pavvajītānaṃ ceva gihitthānaṃ ca savvapāsaṃḍesu pi ca viyāpaṭāse.*

This has been translated in two ways. Sircar and Thapar are representative:

> **Sircar**: "Those Dharma-Mahāmātras of mine are occupied with various kinds of activities which are beneficial both to ascetics and to householders. And they are occupied with all the religious sects." **Thapar**: "My officers of *Dhamma* are busy in many matters of public benefit, they are busy among members of all sects both ascetics and householders."

Sircar connects the two genitive plurals (*pavvajītānaṃ* and *gihitthānaṃ*) following the finite verb *viyāpaṭāse* with *bahuvidhesu aṭṭhesu ānuggahikesu* that precede the verb. Thapar takes the two words in the genitive with *savvapāsaṃḍesu* and thus with the second *viyāpaṭāse*. The issue with this interpretation, however, is how these two words in the genitive plural can be related to the word in the locative plural. Further, everywhere that it is used, *viyāpaṭāse* takes the locative. Brereton's translation in Chapter 2 (p. 34) agrees broadly with that of Sircar, and I think this is correct.

It is clear, however, that here *pravrajitas* and *gṛhasthas* are closely connected to *pāṣaṇḍa*. We saw a very similar phrase in Rock Edict 12: *ṣavapāṣaṃḍāni pavajitāni gihathāni vā*, where the relationship of the three terms is clearer. The meaning here is that Aśoka's officials are occupied with various matters beneficial to *pravrajitas* and *gṛhasthas*. And as in other places, Aśoka recapitulates this theme by saying that they are occupied with all the *pāṣaṇḍas*.

The conclusion thus from our survey of Aśoka's use of *gṛhastha* and *pāṣaṇḍa* is that *gṛhastha* was one of the two subcategories of *pāṣaṇḍa*, the other being *pravrajita*. This is maximalist position, which I share. Thus, a person could belong to a *pāṣaṇḍa* either as a *pravrajita* or as a *gṛhastha*, which is the how the two categories of persons are viewed within the *āśrama* system, without, however, using the term *pāṣaṇḍa*. There it is the Brahmanical religious community within which the two are incorporated. But even if we take the minimalist position suggested by Brereton in Chapter 2, still in Aśoka's eyes the *gṛhastha*, *pravrajita*, and *pāṣaṇḍa* were closely related categories, all referring to people and organizations devoted primarily to religious pursuits.

A linguistic issue that emerges pertains to the meaning of *pāṣaṇḍa*: does the term refer to individuals (called *pāṣaṇḍin* in later literature) or to a demographically identifiable group, such as Buddhists or Ājīvikas. I think Aśoka's usage indicates that the term could be used with regard to both. In Rock Edict 12, for example, when Aśoka refers to *ātmapāṣaṇḍa* and *parapāṣaṇḍa*, or in Rock Edict 5 and Pillar Edict 7, when he says he has appointed *dharmamahāmātras* to various *pāṣaṇḍas*, he is clearly referring to groups and group identities. In Rock Edict 13, however, when *pāṣaṇḍa* is associated with *brāhmaṇa* and *śramaṇa*, it appears that the term refers to individual members of a *pāṣaṇḍa* group.

A more significant question relates to whether the dual category of *pravrajita* and *gṛhastha* applied to all or most *pāṣaṇḍa* groups, or whether some *pāṣaṇḍa* groups consisted of only *gṛhasthas* or of only *pravrajitas*, while others may have contained both kinds of members. This is important, because if we go with the former, then the term *pāṣaṇḍa* would approximate what we take to be a "religion," as noted by Oliver Freiberger (2013; Ch. 4, this volume). The Aśokan texts themselves do not provide a clear path to resolving this issue. Yet, the *āśrama* system developed within what could be called the Brahmanical *pāṣaṇḍa* (see Ch. 5, this volume) points to the presence of both *gṛhasthas* and *pravrajitas* within it.

After the introductory statement given above, Pillar Edict 7 continues with concrete examples of *pāṣaṇḍa* groups:

> *saṃghaṭṭhassi pi me kaṭe. ime viyāpaṭā hohaṃti ti.*
>
> I have directed: "These should be occupied also with the Saṅgha."
>
> *hemeva bābhanesu ājīvikesu pi me kaṭe. ime viyāpaṭā hohaṃti ti.*
>
> Likewise, I have directed: "These should be occupied also with *brāhmaṇas* and Ājīvikas."
>
> *nigaṃṭhesu pi me kaṭe. ime viyāpaṭā hohaṃti.*
>
> Likewise, I have directed: "These should be occupied also with the Nirgranthas."
>
> *nānāpāsaṃḍesu pi me kaṭe. ime viyāpaṭā hohaṃti ti.*
>
> I have directed: "These should be occupied also with various *pāṣaṇḍas*."
>
> *paṭivisiṭṭhaṃ paṭīvisiṭṭhaṃ tesu tesu te te mahāmāttā.*
>
> To each specific group have been assigned specific Mahāmātras.[12]
>
> *dhaṃmamahāmāttā cu me etesu ceva viyāpaṭā savvesu ca aṃnesu pāsaṃḍesu.*
>
> And my *dharmamahāmātras* are occupied with these, as also with all other *pāṣaṇḍas*.

Here we are faced with a conundrum. The very first entry, *saṃgha*, clearly refers to the Buddhist monastic order in the other places where Aśoka uses the term. It is very unlikely that here he would use it to refer in general to the Buddhist *pāṣaṇḍa* or religious group, which would include both monastics

---

12. The meaning of *paṭivisiṭṭhaṃ*, repeated here to emphasize its distributive aspect, is not altogether clear. It appears to mean that to each separate *pāṣaṇḍa* groups (*tesu tesu*) he has dispatched specific *mahāmātras*. Professor Oskar von Hinüber, in a personal communication, says that the term is used with a very similar meaning in Pāli, for example in the *Majjhima Nikāya* I: 372, 22.

and lay people, *upāsakas* in the Buddhist vocabulary. They would, indeed, be *gṛhasthas*, because, after converting to the Buddha's message, they remained at home rather than "going forth" (called *pabbajjā* in Buddhism), which signals the initial entry of a novice into the Buddhist order. If, then, in the case of Buddhism, Aśoka here refers to just the monastic order, it is reasonable to assume that Ājīvika and Nirgrantha, likewise, refer to their respective ascetic orders. That leaves *brāhmaṇa*, which, as we have seen, is an open category that can include both *pravrajitas* and *gṛhasthas*. Yet I think the conclusion we can draw is that when Aśoka says that he is sending his *mahāmātras* or his *dharmamahāmātras* to various *pāṣaṇḍas*, he is most likely referring to ascetic or monastic communities of these *pāṣaṇḍa* groups rather than to the *gṛhasthas*, although here as elsewhere the *brāhmaṇa*, constituting its own category, may be an exception.

Yet the passage of Pillar Edict 7 also demonstrates what we have seen in the other two instances in which Aśoka uses the term *gṛhastha*, namely, that *gṛhasthas*, along with *pravrajitas*, are either members of religious groups identified as *pāṣaṇḍa* or closely associated with them.

In this context, we need to consider whether the uniquely Buddhist term *upāsaka* refers to what may be called Buddhist *gṛhasthas*. Aśoka refers to himself as an *upāsaka* in his Minor Rock Edicts and refers to both male and female *upāsakas* in the Bhabra edict. In the so-called Schism Edict, moreover, he instructs his officers to deposit a copy of his letter with *upāsakas* and instructs the *upāsakas* to endorse his royal order every *uposatha* day. Although scholars are in disagreement about the actual role of the *upāsakas* in the affairs of the Saṅgha, it is clear that there was some interaction between the *upāsakas* and the monks and nuns with a view to making sure that the monastic members abided by their rules and did not create dissension (*saṃghabheda*) within the *saṃgha*. Although one cannot be totally sure, it appears very likely that the *upāsakas* were the Buddhist variant of the generic *gṛhastha* of all or most of the *pāṣaṇḍas*. At least in some contexts, as Freiberger has shown (Ch. 4, pp. 62–63), Pāli texts refer to the Buddhist *upāsaka* as *gṛhastha*.

One other important issue relating to membership in a *pāṣaṇḍa* concerns gender. Were there female members within the *pāṣaṇḍas*, and if so, were they *pravrajitas* and/or *gṛhasthas*? The Aśokan texts themselves do not permit us to answer these questions conclusively, even though some light is thrown on the issue in his Bhabra inscription directed at the Buddhist Saṅgha. There, after giving a list of Buddhist texts, he instructs both monks (*bhikkhupāye*) and nuns (*bhikkhuniye*) to listen to them, as also male and female lay followers (*upāsakā* and *upāsikā*; see the Bhabra Edict). That there was a parallel order of nuns within Buddhism is clear from Buddhist canonical texts as well. Although

Aśoka is silent on this point, Jain texts also point to the existence of Jain nuns. So, in the list of *pāṣaṇḍas* given in PE 7, at least the Buddhist Saṅgha consisted of both male and female religious professionals. It is thus possible and even likely that at least some of the other groups mentioned there may have had a similar distribution of members.

There is still the issue of female *gṛhasthas*. Was there room for female *gṛhasthas*? One obstacle to a female *gṛhastha* has to do with grammar: we do not find in the literature, whether in Prakrit or in Sanskrit, a feminine form, such as *gṛhasthā*, whereas the Vedic *gṛhápati* has the feminine *gṛhápatnī*, a form, according to Jamison (Ch. 1, this volume), that is even more prevalent than its masculine counterpart. The other common term for a householder, *gṛhin* (possessor of a house: see Ch. 8, this volume) also has its feminine *gṛhiṇī*. In spite of the lack of a feminine form of the term *gṛhastha*, it is clear from the Buddhist evidence that there may have been female *gṛhasthas* who were part of their respective *pāṣaṇḍas*, if we accept that the *upāsaka/upāsikā* were Buddhist versions of *gṛhastha*. The lack of a feminine form may go back to the origin of the term in its opposition to the *pravrajita*. Originally the term did not indicate a householder per se but a person who has decided to stay at home rather than go forth as a *pravrajita*. When, for example, in the Dharmaśāstras, we have discussions of the family life of *gṛhasthas*, their authors had to find terms to refer to the wives of these *gṛhasthas*. As Brick (Ch. 8, this volume) has shown, they chose from a range of options, such as *gṛhamedhinī*. But the most common term was *patnī*, derived from the old Vedic term *gṛhápatnī* as the female counterpart to *gṛhápati*.

A further question flowing from the issue of gender is whether Aśoka's *gṛhasthas*—male or female—were married and raised families. There is no evidence in the Aśokan inscriptions themselves that permits us to draw a clear conclusion. It is, however, more likely than not that the *gṛhasthas* were married family men and women. We see this in Buddhist sources with regard to *upāsakas* and in Brahmanical sources with regard to the *gṛhastha* of the Dharmaśāstras. It is also clear, however, that the Aśokan *gṛhastha* was not simply any married person with a family. Aśoka addresses and tells his officials to instruct his subjects, who, we must suppose, were people with families and heads of households. Yet he never identifies these subjects by a special term. But the *gṛhastha* within the Aśokan discourse, as we have already noted, was a special person, a counterpart of and parallel to the ascetic *pravrajita*. By definition he is a person dedicated to religious pursuits. In an interesting, and perhaps ironical, twist, it is within the Brahmanical tradition as represented by the Dharmaśāstras that the term *gṛhastha* continues as a central term within the religious discourse of ancient India. There, as we will see in Chapters 5 and 7, *gṛhastha* and a religious ideology focused on him occupy a central position.

Besides *pāṣaṇda* and the related terms *pravrajita* and *gṛhastha*, Aśoka, as we have seen, uses frequently the compound *śramaṇa-brāhmaṇa*, sometimes inverted to *brāhmaṇa-śramaṇa*, as a broad classification of religious people. Here I want to investigate how the two classificatory systems are related within the context of the pair *pravrajita* and *gṛhastha*.

Some version of the compound *śramaṇa-brāhmaṇa* occurs seven times (RE 3, 4 [twice], 5, 8, 9; PE 7), while the two terms uncompounded are juxtaposed twice, both times in Rock Edict 13. The order of the two terms—*brāhmaṇa-śramaṇa* or *śramaṇa-brāhmaṇa* —is probably not overly significant. In most instances, we find *brāhmaṇa-śramaṇa* used in some locations (most frequently in Girnār) and *śramaṇa-brāhmaṇa* in others; the sequence seems to be determined to some degree by local preferences.

The semantic compass of *śramaṇa-brāhmaṇa* does not coincide with that of *pravrajita-gṛhastha*. Further, even though the category *pāṣaṇḍa* includes the former pair, its extension is broader and it refers to institutional groups. The category of *gṛhastha* is excluded from that pair, even though *brāhmaṇa* may theoretically include it also. And the category of *śramaṇa*, at least in Aśokan discourse, appears to exclude *brāhmaṇa*, while *pravrajita* can include the latter. At the level of idiom, furthermore, the terms in these pairs were probably not interchangeable. It would have been jarring to the ear to use the pair *brāhmaṇa-pravrajita* or *śramaṇa-gṛhastha*. Many such linguistic pairings are fixed: note, for example, "men and women" and "male and female"—while "men and females" would be viewed as unidiomatic.

Beyond the linguistic register, however, the two classifications in Aśoka operate at two different, though interrelated, levels. The *śramaṇa-brāhmaṇa* classification relates specifically to Aśoka's definition of dharma and the virtues he wants his people to develop. The compound is used four times in his definition of dharma (RE 3, 9, 11; PE 7), once in the context of his journeys to see and donate to these two classes of people (RE 8), and twice in the context of virtues that were lacking under previous kings but are practiced now due to Aśoka's instructions (RE 4); the two are used together but uncompounded in Rock Edict 13. It appears that *śramaṇa-brāhmaṇa* identified the dual class of religious/ascetic people to whom honor and donations are due both from the king and from ordinary people wishing to lead lives according to dharma.

The classificatory term *pāṣaṇḍa*, on the other hand, is the one used most frequently by Aśoka, and he uses it especially when speaking of his official or regulatory activities as emperor. It thus appears to refer to religious/demographic groups with which government agencies interacted and which they probably wanted to influence and regulate. The term is used a total of twenty-five times.[13] As we have seen, it is in the context of *pāṣandas* that Aśoka introduces the category *gṛhastha*. Given that Aśoka in Pillar Edict 7 includes *brāhmaṇa* within the category of *pāṣaṇḍa*, and given that *pravrajita* and *śramaṇa* refer broadly to the same or similar class of religious people, the category of religious people left out of the *śramaṇa-brāhmaṇa* classification is the *gṛhastha*. It must, however, be acknowledged that in actual usage the term *pāṣaṇḍa* may have referred specifically to ascetics, that is, to *pravrajitas*, as Maes's study (Ch. 5, p. 85) has shown within its usage in Jain texts.

Thus, *pāṣaṇḍa* refers to a wider slice of religious people than the compound *śramaṇa-brāhmaṇa*. The former is used when Aśoka speaks about or to such religious organizations. If, as seems likely, the specifically Buddhist term *upāsaka* refers to Buddhist *gṛhasthas*, then the Schism Edict indicates that such "lay" people may have been used by the state to enforce proper order within the *pravrajita* segment of a *pāṣaṇḍa*.

The conclusion that *pāṣaṇḍa* groups generally had as members or at least in an affiliated capacity both *pravrajitas*, that is professional religious people who left home, and *gṛhasthas* who stayed at home, is confirmed by the novel institution of the four *āśramas* invented by some segments of the *brāhmaṇas* responsible for the creation of the new genre of literature known as Dharmaśāstra, to which I will turn in Chapter 5.

13. See RE 5, 7, 12 (seventeen times), 13 (twice); PE 6, 7 (thrice).

4

Gṛhastha *in the Śramaṇic Discourse*

A LEXICAL SURVEY OF HOUSE RESIDENTS IN EARLY PĀLI TEXTS

Oliver Freiberger

AS RECENT STUDIES of ancient Indian literature have demonstrated, the early Brahmanical vision of society centers on the householder (Olivelle 1993; Olivelle 2006c). From the early dharma literature onward the technical term for the Brahmanical householder has been *gṛhastha*, literally "house resident." In her study of the concept's history Stephanie Jamison (Ch. 1, this volume) shows that *gṛhastha*, a term so common and familiar in Brahmanical literature, is actually relatively late. It does not seem to appear before the Dharmasūtras and then replaces earlier designations for householders. While the Brahmanical authors' motives for introducing and establishing this very term remain obscure, Jamison makes an interesting suggestion. Since both Aśoka, in his inscriptions, and Buddhist texts in various Middle Indic dialects regularly juxtapose the "gone-forth" ascetic and the house resident, she assumes that "the *gṛhastha*-, so thoroughly embedded verbally in the orthodox Brahmanical dharma texts and so explicitly the foundation of the social system depicted therein, is actually a coinage of and a borrowing from śramaṇic discourse" (p. 18). The present chapter pursues one aspect of this argument a little further. It takes a closer look at early Buddhist texts in Pāli and surveys the vocabulary for householders therein. If these texts represent one expression of the "śramaṇic discourse" that may have been the source for the

Brahmanical *gṛhastha*, their usage of this—and other—terms might yield useful insights.

While Jamison's suggestion is appealing, the dating of the sources makes it notoriously difficult to provide hard evidence for an act of "borrowing." Thankfully we can date Aśoka's inscriptions fairly accurately to the third century BCE. The Dharmasūtras, in which, according to Jamison, the term *gṛhastha* appears for the first time in Brahmanical literature, are less precisely datable, but Patrick Olivelle makes a convincing argument for dating them around the same time (Olivelle 1999: xxxiv; Olivelle 2010: 37–38). So "borrowing" between these texts seems possible in theory. But when Aśoka's inscriptions serve as evidence, we must keep in mind that although he was likely influenced more by the śramaṇic than by the Brahmanical discourse, his voice is that of the emperor. When he juxtaposes renouncers and householders in his inscriptions, this should probably be viewed, at most, as a *reflection* of the śramaṇic discourse. Furthermore, it seems rather unlikely that the authors of the Dharmasūtras would turn directly to the inscriptions of Aśoka—of all people—to find inspiration in their pursuit to establish the arguably most important category of their ideology. While Aśoka's inscriptions are a very appealing source because they can be dated so well, I believe that they can serve merely as an indirect source for the śramaṇic discourse. Aśoka is not a primary voice in that discourse, and—who knows?—he may have gotten it wrong.

The earliest source for a primary voice in the śramaṇic discourse are Buddhist texts. Dating the early Buddhist texts, however, is difficult because there is little to no external reference to them, or vice versa. Thus, for our present question we seem to have two options: Either we dismiss the Buddhist texts entirely because they cannot serve as a reliable source for showing that the term *gṛhastha* was commonly used among *śramaṇas before* the Dharmasūtras were composed. Or we enter the realm of uncertainty and assume that the earliest extant Buddhist texts have preserved features of the pre-Dharmasūtra śramaṇic discourse. The fact that Jamison refers to various Middle Indic Buddhist texts as evidence for the juxtaposition of ascetic and house resident shows that she decided to take the latter route.

This approach has great potential. Aside from the fact that insisting on dateable sources would not get us very far, the Buddhist texts provide a multitude of aspects that may enrich the discussion, as I will try to show. My limited focus here is exclusively on early Buddhist texts that were composed in Pāli. While an absolute dating of the so-called Pāli canon is difficult, scholars have been able to establish some relative chronology within the canon. Some texts are clearly much younger than others, and a case can be made for a certain corpus that broadly contains the earliest layer of Pāli texts.[1] This corpus, which is the basis for the discussion in this paper, includes the four major *nikāyas* (*Dīgha, Majjhima, Saṃyutta*, and *Aṅguttara Nikāya*) as well as four old collections from the fifth, the *Khuddaka Nikāya*, namely the *Dhammapada, Udāna, Itivuttaka*, and *Sutta-Nipāta*. Within this corpus some short individual collections, such as the *Aṭṭhakavagga* and the *Pārāyaṇavagga* of the *Sutta-Nipāta*, are regarded as being very old (Gómez 1976: 139; Vetter 1988: 101–106; Hinüber 1996: 49).[2] But for most texts in this corpus it is difficult to establish a firm chronological position, also because of processes of borrowing and exchange between *nikāyas*. The benefit of the corpus, which consists of twenty volumes in the edition of the Pāli Text Society, is that it constitutes a rich source for our discussion.[3]

In order to supplement Jamison's study with regard to this single point and possibly to find more evidence to support her suggestion, I did a word search of *gahaṭṭha* (Pāli for *gṛhastha*) in those early Pāli texts. I will discuss the results in greater detail below, but what immediately struck me was that the term is, in fact, rather rare. It does not show up once in the entire *Dīgha Nikāya* (three volumes in the edition of the Pali Text Society), much of which is often regarded as belonging to the older layers within the corpus. Since the *Dīgha Nikāya* also includes many of the Buddha's extended conversations with Brahmins, a robust presence of the term *gṛhastha* would have allowed for exciting speculations. Among all the mentioned collections, it is in the *Aṅguttara Nikāya* (five volumes), which is normally seen as slightly younger, that the word appears most often, but even there it is attested only twelve times. In total, I found a mere twenty-seven instances of the term *gahaṭṭha* in the corpus of earliest Pāli texts.

---

1. See the respective sections in Hinüber 1996.

2. The word *gahaṭṭha* (Skt. *gṛhastha*) does not appear in them.

3. Other texts that probably belong to this early layer too are the *Pātimokkha Sutta*, the list of individual monastic rules for monks and nuns, and the *kammavācās*, formulas of formal acts of the monastic community. In the *Bhikkhupātimokkha Sutta*, of all the potential terms, *gahapati/gahapatānī* appears eleven times (all in the *Nissaggiya Pācittiya* section) and *gihin* once (*Pācittiya* 29). In the *Bhikkhunīpātimokkha Sutta, gahapati/gahapatānī* appears, in addition, in two rules (*Saṅghādisesa* 1 and *Pācittiya* 36), *gihin* in one (*Pācittiya* 44), and *agārika* in two (*Pācittiya* 28 and 46). In the *kammavācās, gahapati* has three occurrences (in *Vin* II 18; 19–20; 160) and *gihin* one (*Vin* II 288). The usage corresponds to the findings below. The term *gahaṭṭha* does not appear at all in any of these texts.

I was puzzled because I knew from my earlier work that those texts talk about house residents quite often, but I had never looked closely at the distinctions between the respective Pāli terms. In her chapter, Jamison mentioned other Middle Indic terms for "house" as well, which led me to conduct word searches for multiple possible combinations of "house" and "resident," as well as other terms used for such persons. I will discuss the results below. While most compounds that I checked are not attested at all or extremely rare, three stood out—in terms of quantity—in a startling way. While *gahaṭṭha* appeared 27 times, *gihin* (Skt. *gṛhin*) yielded 65 hits, and *gahapati* (Skt. *gṛhapati*) yielded 224.[4]

This shows, first of all, that *gahaṭṭha* is not the only term, and by far not the most common one, that the authors of the early Pāli texts had at their disposal when they wanted to refer to house residents. The point of Jamison's argument was, of course, that *gṛhastha* might have been particularly attractive for Brahmanical authors because it often appears in the contrastive pair of house residents and ascetics. As she notes, Margaret Cone's new *Dictionary of Pāli* says that *gahaṭṭha* is "very often contrasted with *pabbajita*." In the light of the search results above, however, it is important to note that Cone's entry for *gihin* says almost the same: "often contrasted with *pabbajita*" (Cone 2010: s.v. *gihin*). As we will see, its frequency and its usage make *gihin* a serious contender indeed. And what do we do about the overwhelming presence of *gahapati*, a term that, as Jamison argues, the Brahmanical authors of the Dharmasūtras had good reason to dismiss for their purposes? In order to draw further conclusions, it seems useful to examine the usage of these terms in greater detail.

---

4. For my search I used the electronic versions of the Pali Text Society editions available on the website GRETIL (http://gretil.sub.uni-goettingen.de/). Since the search function does not seem to recognize a word that carries over a line break, some occurrences may have not been found. A term is counted only once for each narrative setting; only the first occurrence is noted here. Sometimes the term appears very often in one *sutta*, for example when the Buddha repeatedly addresses his conversation partner as *gahapati* in the vocative, but here it will be counted only once. I did not consider the—omnipresent—formula, "he goes forth from home into homelessness" (*agārasmā anagāriyam pabbajati*). Aside from the three terms discussed here, the fourth most frequent term is *gharāvāsa* (15 occurrences), which appears almost exclusively in the stock phrase *sambādho gharāvāso rajopatho, abbhokāso pabbajjā* (*DN* I 63,3; *DN* I 250,11; *MN* I 179,12; *MN* I 240,20; *MN* I 267,24; *MN* I 344,30; *MN* II 211,29; *SN* II 219,25; *SN* V 350,23; *AN* II 208,23; *AN* V 204,17; *Ud* 59,31; *Sn* 72,4; also in *MN* II 198,21 and *AN* III 295,22). Other terms are *agārikabhūta/agāriyabhūta* (*DN* III 235,11; *MN* I 504,18; *SN* II 219,24; *SN* V 89,16; *AN* II 124,3; *AN* III 375,9; *AN* IV 370,22; *AN* IV 372,9; *Ud* 18,29; *Ud* 57,22); *gharamesin* (*SN* I 215,3; *Sn* 33,11; *It* 112,6); *agārin* (*Sn* 66,15), and *gharaṭṭha* (v.l. *It* 112,6). See the table in the appendix for a quantitative distribution of the terms.

The Term Gahaṭṭha *in Early Pāli Texts*

In the examined corpus of early Pāli texts, the contrastive pair of *gahaṭṭha* and ascetic (*pabbajita, anāgara*, et al.) appears in two different ways, which may be referred to as an inclusive and an exclusive usage, respectively. For the inclusive usage the speaker makes a statement that applies to both groups equally. Instances of this are the idea that the "true" Brahmin (=the ideal ascetic) does not mingle with either *gahaṭṭhas* or *anāgaras*[5] or the note that the Buddha does not praise bonding (*saṃsagga*) with *gahaṭṭhas* and *pabbajitas*.[6] Living together too closely with *gahaṭṭhas* and *pabbajitas*[7] leads to a *bhikkhu's* decline.[8] A famous poem in the *Sutta-Nipāta* includes a verse that says that some *gahaṭṭhas* and some *pabbajitas* were not kindly disposed and that one should wander solitary as a rhinoceros horn.[9] The pair appears in an inclusive usage also when the text states that if a *paribbājaka* or a *gahaṭṭha* reviles the Buddha or a disciple of his, he should be known to be a low person or outcaste (*vasala*, Skt. *vṛṣala*).[10]

While all these are connoted negatively, there are just as many instances of a positive inclusive usage. When asked by non-Buddhist ascetics about what makes the *bhikkhus* so confident, they are supposed to say, as one of four points, that both *gahaṭṭhas* and *pabbajitas*, as their "*dhamma*-fellows" (*sahādhammikā*), were dear and pleasing to them.[11] The fact that *gahaṭṭha* can refer to a Buddhist lay follower is confirmed by another passage in which the god Sakka (=Indra) pays homage to *pabbajitas* and to "merit-making house residents" (*gahaṭṭhā*

---

5. *Asaṃsaṭṭhaṃ gahaṭṭhehi anāgārehi c' ūbhayaṃ / anokasāriṃ appicchaṃ tam ahaṃ brūmi brāhmaṇaṃ* (*Dh* 113,18–19; *Sn* 120,16–17).

6. *Sagahaṭṭhapabbajitehi kho ahaṃ Moggallāna saṃsaggaṃ na vaṇṇayāmi* (*AN* IV 88,2–3).

7. And socializing in a way typical of *gihins*; see below.

8. *Sekho bhikkhu saṃsaṭṭho viharati sagahaṭṭhapabbajitehi ananulomikena gihisaṃsaggena* is one of the five things that cause the decline of a *bhikkhu* (*bhikkhuno parihānāya saṃvattanti; AN* III 116,16–17 and 27–29) and one of the five disadvantages of dwelling too long at one place (*ādīnavā atinivāsa; AN* III 258,2 and 5–6).

9. *Dussaṅgahā pabbajitā pi eke / atho gahatthā gharam āvasantā, / appossukko paraputtesu hutvā / eko care [khaggavisāṇakappo]* (Sn 7,19–22). Or "solitary like a rhinoceros." *Khaggavisāna* (lit. "sword-horn"), in conjunction with *kappa* ("like") can refer both to a rhinoceros and to the horn of a rhinoceros, and scholars have different opinions about how to translate this phrase. I follow K. R. Norman here, but this translation is not relevant for the argument of the present essay.

10. *Yo buddhaṃ paribhāsati atha vā tassa sāvakaṃ / paribbājaṃ gahaṭṭhaṃ vā, taṃ jaññā ['vasalo' iti]* (Sn 23,10–11).

11. *Sahadhammikā kho pana no piyā manāpā gahaṭṭhā c' eva pabbajitā ca* (*MN* I 64,13–14).

puññakarā) that are "virtuous laypeople" (*sīlavanto upāsakā*) (*SN* I 234,28). Here *upāsaka*, the Buddhist technical term for a committed lay follower, and *gahaṭṭha* refer to the same persons. This positive inclusive usage is apparent also when a non-Buddhist ascetic who is about to join the Buddhist Saṅgha remarks that the Buddha's assembly included both *gahaṭṭhas* and *pabbajitas* (*parisā sagahaṭṭhapabbajitā, MN* I 493,26), or when the Buddha says about the ideal elder monk (*thera*) that he had a large retinue of *gahaṭṭhas* and *pabbajitas* (*sagahaṭṭhapabbajitānam bahujanaparivāra, AN* III 114,20). In the *Aṅguttara Nikāya* the Buddha states that five things should often be contemplated by women, men, *gahaṭṭhas*, and *pabbajitas*,[12] namely old age, illness, death, impermanence, and *kamma*.[13]

All these instances have in common that the respective statement applies to both the *gahaṭṭha* and the ascetic equally. In contrast, the exclusive usage juxtaposes the two, either as mutually complementary groups or to indicate tensions. The idea of complementarity is reflected in statements that present the *gahaṭṭha* as the ideal lay follower. An *Itivuttaka* passage states that house residents and houseless ascetics are beneficial (*bahūpakāra*) to each other because the former donate material goods while the latter teach the *dhamma*. The passage uses three different terms for "house resident" (*sāgāra, gahaṭṭha, gharamesin*) synonymously and *anāgāra* for the ascetic.[14] In the *Dhammika Sutta* of the *Sutta-Nipāta*, one who "goes from the house to the houseless state" (*agāra anagāram eti*) is juxtaposed to the "*upāsaka* with a house" (*agārin upāsaka*). The latter is the ideal *gahaṭṭha*, whose way of life is in accordance with the ethical norms (*pañcasīla*, etc.) (Sn 69,3–70,22).[15] In the *Cunda Sutta*

---

12. *Pañc' imāni bhikkhave ṭhānāni abhiṇhaṃ paccavekkhitabbāni itthiyā vā purisena vā gahaṭṭhena vā pabbajitena vā* (*AN* III 71,23–25).

13. In a terminologically complicated passage, Subha, a Brahmin youth, asks the Buddha to comment on the statement of Brahmins that *gahaṭṭhas* were accomplished in the right conduct (*ñāya*), the *dhamma*, and the good (*kusala*), while *pabbajitas* were not (*Brāhmaṇā, bho Gotama, evam āhaṃsu: Gahaṭṭho ārādhako hoti ñāyaṃ dhammaṃ kusalaṃ; na pabbajito ārādhako hoti ñāyaṃ dhammaṃ kusalan ti. Idha bhavaṃ Gotamo kim āhāti? MN* II 197,6–9). The Buddha responds that both house residents (*gihins*) and *pabbajitas* can accomplish—or not accomplish—the right way. House residents and ascetics are juxtaposed here, but with varying terms. Note that only Subha uses *gahaṭṭha*—prior to this passage a householder was called a *gahapati*. And the Buddha does not adopt the same terminology in his response (as he usually does) but speaks of *gihins* (*MN* II 197,10–18).

14. *Sāgāresu ca cīvaraṃ paccayaṃ sayanāsanaṃ / anāgārā paṭicchanti parissayavinodanaṃ // Sugataṃ pana nissāya gahaṭṭhā gharamesino / saddahānā arahataṃ ariyapaññāya jhāyino //* (*It* 112,1–8).

15. In the final verse the good householder (here: *gihin*) is born in heaven (*etaṃ gihī vattayaṃ appamatto Sayampabhe nāma upeti deve ti*; Sn 70,21).

the *gahaṭṭha* is a learned, wise lay disciple (*sutavā ariyasāvako sapañño*) who can distinguish between four kinds of *samaṇas* (the knower, teacher, and practitioner vs. the defiler of the way [*magga*]) and understands that not all *samaṇas* are corrupt.[16]

Aside from this exclusive usage, which stresses the complementarity of house residents and ascetics, there are a few passages that make a qualitative distinction between the two. When the Buddha, while talking with the Brahmin Subha, asks him whether he observes five things for doing good, as proclaimed by the Brahmins, more among *gahaṭṭhas* or among *pabbajitas*, Subha declares that he observes them abundantly among *pabbajitas*. He explains that *gahaṭṭhas* were permanently busy with their worldly affairs, while *pabbajitas* could focus on asceticism, celibacy, study, and renunciation. The Buddha agrees implicitly by reiterating the accomplishments of ascetics (*MN* II 205–206). In a short *sutta* of the *Saṃyutta Nikāya*, a *deva* appears before the *bhikkhu* Nāgadatta and urges him not to spend too much time among house residents, because the entanglement with society was harmful to his spiritual development.[17]

Finally, in several passages *gahaṭṭha* appears independently, outside of the contrastive pair and unconnected to *pabbajita* or other terms for houseless ascetics. Here a *gahaṭṭha* is a wealthy and generous donor (*yācayoga dānapati*) who intends to make merit (*puññatthika*) (Sn 87,22).[18] Along the same lines, a number of passages describe qualities of a *gahaṭṭha* by which his generosity and merit increase.[19] Elsewhere the Brahmin Vassakāra, chief minister of Magadha, lays out four qualities of a great man before the Buddha, one of them being skillfulness and diligence in attending to the various duties of a householder (*tāni gahaṭṭhakāni kiṃkaraṇiyāni*). The Buddha neither rejects nor approves these four but lists his own four qualities that do not include a specific relationship with house residents. Then everyone agrees that the Buddha possesses these (*AN* II 35,25). And Nakulamātā, who is often listed as one of the most prominent female lay followers, assures her sick husband

---

16. *Ete ca paṭivijjhi yo gahaṭṭho sutavā ariyasāvako sapañño sabbe n' etādisā ti ñatvā, iti disvā na hāpeti tassa saddhā, kathaṃ hi duṭṭhena asampaduṭṭhaṃ suddhaṃ asuddhena samaṃ kareyyā ti* (Sn 17,25–18,4). This is the response to a question raised by the smith Cunda.

17. *Kāle pavissa Nāgadatta divā ca āgantvā ativela- / cārī saṃsaṭṭho gahaṭṭhehi / samānasukhadukkho // bhāyāmi Nāgadattaṃ suppagabbhaṃ / kulesu vinibandhaṃ / mā heva maccuraññо balavato / antakassa vasam eyyā ti //* (*SN* I 201,3–10).

18. Note that the question about the right "sacrifice," or gift (*huta; yajamāna*) is asked by a wealthy young Brahmin.

19. See *AN* III 354,16; *AN* IV 285,14; *AN* IV 289,17; *AN* IV 322,20; *AN* IV 325,12.

that if he died she will not remarry, noting that they had lived a "a house resident's celibate life" (*gahaṭṭhakaṃ brahmacariyaṃ*) for sixteen years (*AN* III 296,8).[20]

The Term Gihin *in Early Pāli Texts*

Another term for house resident, *gihin*, appears in the corpus more than twice as often as *gahaṭṭha* (sixty-five versus twenty-seven occurrences). Like *gahaṭṭha*, it is used for contrasting the house resident and the ascetic, but it almost always appears in the exclusive usage.[21] The two are often presented as two alternative ways of life,[22] sometimes also in a diachronic order, when the text refers to an ascetic's pre-ascetic life.[23] Often *gihins* appear in groups (*gihiparisā*), which an ascetic addresses and instructs in religious matters.[24] This is presented as an attractive situation for ascetics. In one passage a group of ascetics sends one of them off to become a Buddhist *bhikkhu*, learn the *dhamma*, and then tell them about it, so that they can teach it to the house residents (*gihīnam*) and become equally revered (*SN* II 120,5). Some groups of *gihins* are white-clad (*gihī odātavasanā*)[25] and, as such, are sometimes identified as followers (*sāvakā*) of

20. For more on Nakulamātā see below, under *gahapati*. Note also that in this passage she addresses her husband as *gahapati*. This seems to be the only occurrence of the phrase *gahaṭṭhakaṃ brahmacariyaṃ* in the corpus. In his translation Bhikkhu Bodhi notes (n. 1278) that "[i]t is not unusual in traditional Buddhist cultures for devout couples who have begotten several children to mutually agree to observe celibacy."

21. Only three passages have the inclusive usage, two of which are literal parallels: When the Buddha declares that he does not praise the wrong path, whether for *gihin* or for *pabbajita* (*SN* V 18,28; *AN* I 69,18), and when a prideful fool puts himself above both *gihins* and *pabbajitas* (*Dh* 20,13–15 [74]).

22. See *DN* III 147,15; 151,3; 152,11; 162,4; 163,21; 165,23; 167,5; 169,1 (here: *gihin* and *samaṇa*); 171,21; 174,18; 176,11; 179,7; *AN* I 49,15.

23. This is indicated by the compound *purāṇagihīsahāya* ("friend from house-resident times"): One *bhikkhu* was another *bhikkhu's* friend when he was still a house resident (*MN* III 124,28); and an ascetic who is a *purāṇagihīsahāya* visits the *gahapati* Citta (*SN* IV 300,9).

24. See *SN* I 111,11 (the Buddha in a Brahmin village); *MN* I 373,30 (Nigaṇṭha Nāṭaputta); *AN* III 184,6 (a *bhikkhu*). In *AN* IV 281,10, a man introduces himself and his company to the Buddha as house residents who enjoy sense-pleasures (*gihī kāmabhogī*) and asks the Buddha for a teaching about welfare in this and the future life; similarly in *AN* IV 438,19.

25. The *gahapati-putta* Kevaddha asks the Buddha to tell a monk to perform a miracle for the white-clad house residents (*DN* I 211,15); and Pessa, the elephant trainer, self-identifies as one of the "white-clad house residents" (*MN* I 340,13).

an ascetic teacher, such as the Buddha,[26] Nigaṇṭha Nāthaputta,[27] and perhaps also Purāṇa Kassapa.[28]

The authors of our texts explain the proper conduct and the duties of *gihins* (*gihīsāmīcipaṭipadaṃ; gihisāmīcikāni sikkhāpadāni; gihidhamma*), which include caring for family, friends, servants, ascetics, et alia and providing the Saṅgha with robes, food, shelter and medicine.[29] In return, one of the purposes of the Buddhist Saṅgha's rules is compassion for *gihins*. The *bhikkhus* express this compassion by instructing them in religious matters and informing them about merit-making opportunities.[30] One passage says that when the *bhikkhus* behave well in a village, *gihins* will do their duty, and the novices will emulate the elder monks (*SN* II 269,24). But this relationship between *bhikkhus* and house residents is not without problems. *Upāsakas* can express their lack of confidence (*appasāda*) in a *bhikkhu* when he possesses eight qualities many of which cause harm to *gihins* (*AN* IV 345,21);[31] and Ānanda, who is busy talking to house residents (*gihisaññattibahulo*), is exhorted by a *deva* to stop excessive chatting.[32]

When juxtaposed directly, the life of *gihins* is regularly marked as inferior to that of *pabbajitas*. The *Sutta-Nipāta* says that having removed the marks of a house resident (*gihivyañjanāni*) and cut the house resident's bonds (*gihibandhanāni*), one should walk solitary as a rhinoceros horn (*Sn* 7,23 and 8,1; *Sn* 10,25). Similarly, other passages speak of the fetters and enjoyments

---

26. See *MN* II 23,27. In one passage, non-Buddhist *paribbājakas* see the Buddhist lay follower Anāthapiṇḍika approaching and remark that he was one of *samaṇassa Gotamassa sāvakā gihī odātavasanā* (*AN* V 185,21); the same with Vajjiyamāhita (*AN* V 190,1). In an assembly that values worldly things *bhikkhus* praise each other in the presence of white-clad *gihins* (*AN* I 73,29). And before his awakening the Buddha dreamed that many white-clad *gihins* would take refuge in him (*AN* III 242,11); see also *DN* III 124,6. When a *bhikkhu* tells the lay follower (here only: *kulaputta*) Hatthaka about the praise the Buddha had for Hatthaka, the latter shows modesty (*appiccha*) by saying that he hoped that no white-clad house resident (*gihin*) was present to hear it (*AN* IV 217,26).

27. See *DN* III 117,17 (=*DN* III 210,13); *MN* II 244,5.

28. According to Purāṇa Kassapa the *gihī odātavasanā acelakasāvakā* are one class of people; they may perhaps be regarded as lay followers of the Ājīvikas (*AN* III 384,2).

29. See *DN* III 192,6; *AN* II 65,7; *AN* III 41,3; see also *DN* II 196,6; *DN* III 188,16. The *gahapati* Anāthapiṇḍika follows the *gihisāmīcikāni sikkhāpadāni* taught by the Buddha (*SN* V 387,10).

30. *AN* I 98,20; *AN* III 263,17; *AN* III 263,27.

31. The Saṅgha can punish him too when he does that (*AN* IV 346,15). See also *AN* III 124,7, where the disciples of an unpurified teacher hesitate to report him to the *gihins*.

32. See *SN* I 199,27; see also *AN* III 116,28; *AN* III 258,6.

of house residents (*gihisaṃyojana; gihibhoga*), which come with being bound in society (*saṃsaṭṭha*).[33] Unlike the *muni* (or *bhikkhu*), the *gihin* is not totally restrained in respect of the killing of living creatures (*Sn* 38,3–10). Thus, of the two kinds of happiness, the *gihī-sukha* and the *pabbajjā-sukha*, the latter is superior (*AN* I 80,13). *Gihins* also do not have the capacity to discern whether a person has attained liberation and is an *arahant* or even on the path to arahantship.[34]

Nevertheless, there are four kinds of happiness that a *gihin* who enjoys sensual pleasures (*kāmabhogin*) can achieve, namely happiness of ownership, enjoyment, freedom from debt, and blamelessness.[35] And one passage says that a white-clad *gihin* who follows five rules can become a stream-enterer, which is the first of four Buddhist stages of spiritual achievement (*AN* III 211,22). But normally the term *gihin* is not used when the texts speak about spiritual accomplishments of house residents—the regular term in such contexts is *gahapati*, as discussed in the next section. In one passage Ānanda and Sāriputta give the *gahapati* Anāthapiṇḍika a *dhamma* talk that, as they point out, white-clad *gihins* normally do not receive (*MN* III 261,22). Another extraordinary *gahapati* is Citta who, in one passage, explains the four *jhānas* to an ascetic who is stunned as to how a white-clad *gihin* can have such superhuman wisdom (*uttarimanussadhammā*) and seeks to be ordained (*SN* IV 301,27). Note how in these two passages a house resident is called a *gahapati* when, from a religious perspective, he is identified as extraordinary. The ordinary people, among which he stands out, are called *gihins*. Finally, when the Buddha boasts that hundreds of white-clad *gihins* have attained *nibbāna*, he also calls them *upāsaka* and *sāvaka* (*MN* I 490,31). These three passages seem to be the only ones in the corpus that ascribe a high spiritual status to a *gihin*, and even here the term is always accompanied by a synonym that is normally used for this purpose (*gahapati* or *upāsaka*).[36]

---

33. See *MN* I 483,6; *It* 90,7; *SN* IV 180,18. See also Ud 21,21 + n. 5, where a sentence in which a *bhikkhu* decided to return to the "lower life" (*hīna*) has a variant reading which adds *gihibhāva* ("the lower condition of a house resident").

34. The Buddha addresses King Pasenadi and explains that, as a *gihin*, the king does not have that capacity (*Ud* 65,24; *SN* I 78,20). See also *AN* III 391,13.

35. See *AN* II 69,9; the Buddha is talking to the *gahapati* Anāthapiṇḍika.

36. In *AN* III 296,24, the extraordinary female lay follower Nakulamātā portrays herself as a white-clad *sāvikā gihī*, but in this passage no special accomplishments are associated with her.

The Term Gahapati *in Early Pāli Texts*

By far the most common term for a house resident in the here-examined corpus is *gahapati* (or *gahapatika*).[37] Its number of occurrences (224) is more than three times the number of *gihin* and more than eight times the number of *gahaṭṭha* occurrences. One reason for this frequency lies in the fact that the term often occurs in stock phrases. Here the most frequent compound is the plural *brāhmaṇa-gahapaṭikā*, an ambiguous term that could be translated either as "Brahmins and householders" or as "Brahmin householders." The compound, which appears almost exclusively in the plural, often refers to inhabitants of certain villages who hear that the Buddha is arriving and then listen to his *dhamma* instructions. Sometimes Māra incites or possesses some *brāhmaṇa-gahapaṭikā*, which makes them hostile; sometimes they take refuge at the end of the story. Curiously, I. B. Horner, in her *Majjhima Nikāya* translation, speaks of "brahman householders" whenever the text identifies the respective village as a Brahmin village (*brāhmaṇagāma*), but of "brahmans and householders" when there is no such identifier.[38] That the latter may be the more likely reading is suggested by a *Dīgha Nikāya* passage that says that Mahāgovinda has been "a Brahmā for the Brahmins and a *devatā* for the *gahapatikas*."[39] Other passages too suggest that the compound refers, in a generic way, to a group of house residents that is viewed as separate from, but somehow complementary to, Brahmins.[40] A number of times, when the king's care for all his subjects is discussed, the *brāhmaṇa-gahapatikā* appear alongside "town and country folk" (*negama-jānapadā*).[41] The compound *brāhmaṇa-gahapatikā* is used descriptively to denote a certain part of society; it is generally not used for normative statements about the distinction between house residents and ascetics.

37. For a discussion of some meanings of *gahapati* see also Chakravarti 1996: 65–93 and Yamazaki 2005: 131–34.

38. *Brāhmaṇa-gahapaṭikā* of a Brahmin village are mentioned in *DN* 127,15; *MN* I 285,5; *MN* I 400,30; *MN* II 164,10; *MN* III 290,29; *SN* I 114,6; *SN* V 352,17 and 353,21; *AN* I 180,18; *AN* III 30,10; *AN* III 341,17; *AN* IV 340,26; *Ud* 78,7. Without the identifier in *DN* I 111,9; *DN* II 317,2; *MN* I 290,15; *MN* I 334,6; *MN* II 54,27; *MN* II 140,32; *MN* II 185,17; *SN* I 184,6.

39. *Brahmā ca brāhmaṇānaṃ devatā ca gahapatikānaṃ* (*DN* II 248,25). Note, however, that the compound does not appear in the passage.

40. See *DN* II 178,2; *MN* III 176,23; *SN* I 59,15; *It* 111,9.

41. See *DN* II 202,10; *DN* III 61,7. A similar wording is found in *DN* III 148,13; 153,6; 167,19; 169,16; 170,23; 172,11; 177,16; *MN* II 78,29; *MN* III 116,3–4; *AN* I 110,1; *AN* II 74,31; *AN* III 149,30. See also *DN* I 136,25.

In another stock occurrence the *gahapatikā* are listed as a group or assembly (*parisā*) among others, most often as the third after *khattiyas* and *brāhmaṇas*,[42] and with *samaṇas* as the fourth.[43] These *parisās* are described as important assemblies in society that a virtuous person approaches confidently. Some passages refer to smart members (*paṇḍitā*) of each of these four assemblies, who question the Buddha, cannot refute him, have faith in him, or take care of his relics after he dies.[44] In some lists the first three of these assemblies are wealthy (*mahāsāla*),[45] and while wise and virtuous people are born into them,[46] some of their members speak lies out of worldly desire or engage in misconduct and will therefore be born in hell after death.[47] Yet another list adds four divine assemblies (*Cātummahārājika-parisā, Tāvatiṃsa-parisā, Māra-parisā*, and *Brahma-parisā*), making it a total of eight assemblies in which the Buddha preaches.[48]

As Stephanie Jamison notes (Ch. 1, this volume), it is tempting to assume that in the list of three (*khattiya, brāhmaṇa, gahapatika*) *gahapatika* represents the Vaiśya class of the Brahmanical *varṇa* system. While it may certainly resonate in the respective passages, the authors do not specify features of the individual assemblies, or even differentiate them. The list always appears in an inclusive usage—what applies to one, applies to all. The fact that most lists also include divine beings or *samaṇas*—which, from the Buddhist perspective, would not exactly constitute a proper replacement of the fourth Brahmanical category, the Śūdras—further complicates the matter. In any case, since the link to the *varṇa* system is not explicitly made in the examined corpus, we should probably consider it as nothing more than a distant echo.

Another stock list in which *gahapati* regularly appears is the list of seven jewels (*ratana*) that belong to a person with thirty-two extraordinary marks when this person becomes a Cakkavattin, not a Buddha. The *gahapati-ratana*

42. See *DN* I 8,23; *DN* I 67,3; *MN* I 86,19; *MN* I 88,7. Queen Mallikā has command over the girls (*kaññā*) of these three assemblies at her court (*AN* II 205,11), and all such girls have soft hands and feet (*AN* IV 128,17).

43. See *DN* II 85,23; *DN* II 145,18; *DN* III 44,2–4 (here *titthiyā* instead of *samaṇā*); *DN* III 236,8; *AN* II 133,10; *AN* III 39,17; *AN* III 253,3; *AN* III 328,9; *AN* IV 80,33; *AN* IV 114,32.

44. See *DN* II 141,24; *MN* I 176,34; *MN* I 395,25; *MN* I 502,18; *MN* II 123,9; *SN* III 8,3.

45. *DN* II 146,17; *DN* II 169,13; *DN* III 16,20; *SN* I 71,11; *AN* IV 129,19.

46. *MN* I 289,8; *MN* III 100,8; *MN* III 177,28; *AN* IV 104,17; *AN* IV 239,9; *AN* V 290,23. See also *DN* III 258,21.

47. *SN* I 74,17; *AN* II 86,3; *AN* III 386,11.

48. *DN* II 109,7; *DN* III 260,4; *MN* I 72,19; *AN* IV 307,15.

(besides the elephant-jewel, the horse-jewel, the woman-jewel, and so on) is always part of the list.[49]

Aside from the appearance in stock lists, *gahapati* is the most common designator for house residents in the daily life of the Saṅgha. Some *nikāyas* have entire chapters devoted to them (*Gahapativaggas*).[50] Many individual and well-known Buddhist lay followers (*upāsakas*) are referred to as *gahapatis*: Anāthapiṇḍika,[51] Nakulapitā,[52] Hāliddikāni,[53] Ugga,[54] Citta,[55] both Citta and Hatthaka,[56] Uggata,[57] Tapussa,[58] Dasama,[59] Upāli (*SN* IV 110,6), Ghosita (*SN* IV 113,29), Dārukammika (*AN* III 391,3), Vajjiyamāhita (*AN* V 189,11), and the *gahapatānī* Nakulamātā.[60] Some, like Soṇa[61] and Sigāla/Siṅgāla (*DN* III 180,5), are called "son of a *gahapati*" (*gahapati-putta*). The *gahapati* Sandhāna is identified by the ascetic Nigrodha as a house resident (*gihin*) and white-clad follower of the Buddha (*Samaṇassa Gotamassa sāvakā gihī odātavasanā*) (*DN* III 37,15–16). One *gahapati* named Upāli starts out as a Jain follower sent by Nigaṇṭha Nātaputta to the Buddha to refute him, but in the end

49. See *DN* I 89,3; *DN* II 16,18; *DN* II 176,7; 188,1; 191,32; 193,28; 195,14; 197,9; *DN* III 59,6; *DN* III 75,25; *DN* III 142,14; *DN* III 177,9; *MN* II 134,22; *MN* III 175, 14–15; *SN* V 99,5; *AN* IV 89,17; Sn 106,14. Only five gems are listed in *AN* III 167,29.

50. See, for example, *SN* II 68–80; *SN* IV 109–124; *AN* IV 208–235.

51. See *MN* III 258,4; *SN* I 56,8; *SN* I 210,30; *SN* II 68,7; *AN* I 62,33; *AN* I 261,16; *AN* I 262,21; *AN* II 63,26; *AN* II 65,2; *AN* II 65,26; *AN* II 69,5; *AN* III 45,4; *AN* III 47,15; *AN* III 204,28; *AN* III 206,24; *AN* III 211,18; *AN* IV 91,7; *AN* IV 392,13; *AN* IV 405,16; *AN* V 176,18; *AN* V 182,17; *AN* V 185,4; as the best of alms-givers: *AN* I 26,3.

52. See *SN* III 1,10; *SN* IV 116,15; as the best of those who converse intimately: *AN* I 26,15; *AN* II 61,20; *AN* III 295,15 (see also under *gahaṭṭha*).

53. See *SN* III 9,14; *SN* III 13,1; *SN* IV 115,4.

54. See *SN* IV 109,5; *SN* IV 109,23; *AN* III 49,9; *AN* IV 208,23; *AN* IV 212,22; as the best of those who give pleasant gifts: *AN* I 26,11. In the list of ten outstanding *upāsakas* and *upāsikās* in *AN* I 26, only some are referred to as *gahapati*. Only these are considered here.

55. See *SN* IV 281,25; *SN* IV 283,23; *SN* IV 285,20; *SN* IV 289,1; *SN* IV 291,15; *SN* IV 293,4; *SN* IV 296,1; *SN* IV 298,3; *SN* IV 300,10; *SN* IV 302,21; as the best of *dhamma*-teachers: *AN* I 26,5.

56. See *AN* I 88,23; as model *gahapatis*: *SN* II 235,21; as model *upāsakas*: *AN* II 164,14.

57. He is the best of those who wait for the Saṅgha: *AN* I 26,12.

58. See *AN* III 450,23; *AN* IV 438,15.

59. See *MN* I 349,10; *AN* V 342,17.

60. See *AN* II 61,20; *AN* III 295,15 (see also under *gahaṭṭha*); *AN* IV 268,4; *AN* IV 348,4; as the best of those who converse intimately: *AN* I 16,25.

61. See *SN* III 48,8; *SN* IV 113,16.

he becomes a Buddhist lay follower.[62] The texts report that some *gahapatis* have reached certain stages on the Buddhist spiritual path, such as that of a "stream-enterer" (*sotāpanna*)[63] and a "non-returner" (*anāgāmin*).[64] One passage has a list of named *gahapatis* who have realized the "deathless" (*amata*).[65]

It is also important to note that *gahapati* frequently appears as a vocative used by the Buddha to address the conversation partner in the course of a dialog (which is counted here only once for every narrative context). While this normally remains without further comment, in one curious passage a certain Potaliya complains that the Buddha calls him *gahapati*. He says that he had given up all obligations and occupations (*sabbe kammantā paṭikkhittā sabbe vohārā samucchinnā*) by handing his wealth over to his sons. But the Buddha replies that in the discipline of the Noble One (*ariyasse vinaye*), giving up occupations means eight items of moral behavior and more—up to arahantship. In the end, Potaliya takes refuge and becomes an *upāsaka* (not a *bhikkhu*!) (*MN* I 359,12). Persons that are otherwise identified as *upāsakas* are regularly addressed as *gahapatis*, also in groups.[66] Some addressees have particular occupations like a carpenter (*thapati*),[67] a farmer (*kassaka*),[68] or a village headman (*gāmaṇī*) (*SN* IV 315,11).[69] The term is also used within families, when a woman addresses her husband as *gahapati* (*MN* II 62,18; see also *AN* III 296,8), and their son, now a *bhikkhu*, his father (*MN* II 62,27).

The *gahapati* and the ascetic are implicitly juxtaposed in phrases that describe a *gahapati's* going-forth. In a common phrase a *gahapati* or his son or

---

62. See *MN* I 374,15. See also the *gahapati* who is a follower of the Ājīvakas (*ājīvakasāvaka*), then talks to the Buddha and becomes an *upāsaka* (*AN* I 217,24).

63. Anāthapiṇḍika: *SN* V 380,19; *SN* V 385,14; *SN* V 387,17.

64. Sirivaḍḍha: *SN* V 176,14; Mānadinna; *SN* V 178,3. The *upāsaka* Dīghāvu, who is later identified by the Buddha as a non-returner, is sick and sends his father, the *gahapati* Jotika, to ask for the Buddha's visit: *SN* V 34.

65. Bhallika, Sudatta, Anāthapiṇḍika, Citta Macchikāsaṇḍika, Hatthaka Āḷavaka, Mahānāma Sakka, Ugga Vesālika, Uggata, Sūra Ambaṭṭha, Jīvaka Komārabhacca, Nakulapitā, Tavakaṇṇika, Pūraṇa, Isidatta, Sandhāna, Vijaya, Vajjiyamāhita, Meṇḍaka (*AN* III 451,9). See also *MN* II 173,32, where a *gahapati* or his son examines a monk concerning the monk's states of greed, hatred, and delusion; only then he trusts him and learns the *dhamma* from him and awakens to truth (*saccānubodha*).

66. See *DN* II 85,13; *AN* V 58,21; *Ud* 86,25.

67. See *MN* I 396,30; *MN* III 145,30.

68. See *AN* I 229,32; *AN* I 239,28; *AN* I 241,31.

69. The name of the *gahapati-putta* Kevaddha has the variant Kevaṭṭa (fisherman) (*DN* I 211,4).

someone from the family (*gahapati vā gahapati-putto vā aññatarasmiṃ vā kule*) hears the *dhamma* and decides to leave home for homelessness.[70] It is particularly noted when a very wealthy (*mahaddhana mahābhoga*) *gahapati* or *gahapatiputta* gives up all his wealth and goes forth (*MN* I 451,36). Another implicit juxtaposition is present in descriptions of the relationship between house residents and the *saṅgha*. As householders, *gahapatis* provide the Buddhist monks—other ascetics are not mentioned in this usage—with food, robes, lodging, and medicine;[71] often they are called devoted (*saddhā gahapatikā*).[72] As seen above, we regularly encounter affluent *gahapatis* in the texts[73]—gaining wealth is regarded as their aim (*AN* III 363,9). It is taken for granted that they enjoy sensual pleasures,[74] and only a very few passages make a negative value judgement about their way of life.[75] In fact, in talking about *gahapatis* the texts' tone is generally benevolent and caring, and the *gahapatis'* concerns are taken seriously.[76]

---

70. *DN* I 62,33; *DN* I 250,8; *MN* I 179,9; *MN* I 267,21; *MN* I 344,27; *AN* II 208,19; *AN* V 204,14. It is a fruit of *sāmañña* when a *gahapati* becomes a monk and is respected as such (*DN* I 61,22).

71. See *MN* I 369,17; *MN* II 7,16; *SN* II 202,14; *AN* I 274,7. Sometimes the Buddha simply instructs *gahapatis* and *gahapatāniya* who travel the same road (*AN* II 57,17). See also the way the Buddha describes the "three fires" of *āhuneyyaggi* (for father and mother), *gahapataggi* (for family, workers, and servants), *dakkhiṇeyyaggi* (for *samaṇa-brāhmaṇā*) (*AN* IV 45,1; see also *DN* III 217,20).

72. See *MN* I 222,3; *MN* I 448,10; *MN* I 461,12; *AN* II 125,1; *AN* V 350,5.

73. See *SN* III 112,28; *AN* I 117,1; *AN* V 40,6; a wealthy merchant (*seṭṭhi*) *gahapati* in *SN* I 89,32 and *SN* I 91,28. One passage says that to a *bhikkhu*, the rag robe is what a chest full of garments is to a *gahapati* or *gahapatiputta* (*AN* IV 230,24).

74. See *MN* I 461,27; *MN* I 505,3; *AN* IV 55,17.

75. The Buddha puts it mildly when he remarks that *gahapatis* and *gahapatiputtas*, despite their luxurious houses, sleep badly because of disturbances caused by greed, hatred, and delusion, while he himself sleeps well because he has overcome those (*AN* I 137,17). Another passage says that unlike an otherwise-gentle female householder (*gahapatānī*) who is provoked by her slave and gets mad at her, monks should be gentle in a deeper way (*MN* I 125,4; see also *MN* II 106,4). In a polemical passage directed at the non-Buddhist ascetic Kassapa, the Buddha claims that the latter's ascetic practices could easily be performed by a *gahapati*, his son, or even a slave girl carrying a water-jar—in contrast to living a life as a Buddhist *bhikkhu* (*DN* I 168,24). Probably the most explicit contrast made between ascetic and *gahapati* is found in a passage about a *bhikkhu* who sees a *gahapati* or a *gahapatiputta* enjoying sense pleasures and then returns to the "low life" (*hīnāyāvattati*) (*AN* II 125,16).

76. The Buddha says that a "son of good family" (*kulaputta*) should associate with virtuous and wise *gahapatis* or *gahapatiputtas* (*AN* IV 282,9; *AN* IV 286,18; *AN* IV 323,13). In making a point about lying, he brings up the case that a person ruined a *gahapati* or *gahapatiputta* with false speech (*AN* III 210,18; *SN* IV 247,23). And he declares that the danger in singing rather than reciting the *dhamma* is that *gahāpatikā* may complain that the monks sing just

Conclusion

The starting point of this chapter's discussion was Stephanie Jamison's assumption (Ch. 1, this volume) that the term *gṛhastha* may have been borrowed by the Brahmins from the śramaṇic discourse of the time with its pronounced distinction between householders and ascetics. Has surveying the usage of the most frequent terms for house residents in early Pāli texts yielded any insights that would help to test this hypothesis? I wish to couch my conclusion in a somewhat playful way. Let us imagine, most presumptuously and only for a moment, that we were Brahmanical legal scholars of the third century BCE looking for inspiration in our pursuit to coin what would become the most central category of our ideology. Let us also imagine, most inadequately, that the presented usage of terms in the early Pāli texts somewhat represented the śramaṇic discourse of that time. Considering the findings of this chapter, which one of the three terms would we Brahmins find most appealing?

Clearly, *gahapati/gṛhapati* would not be high on our list. Not only might it create internal discomfort within the Brahmanical discourse, as Jamison argues, but the Buddhist use is rather unattractive too. The term is associated with householders who, as a group in society, most often appear separate from Brahmins; it regularly refers to Buddhist lay followers who are in a close relationship with the Saṅgha; and it is never used as an idea or a concept that sets the *gahapati* fundamentally apart from the ascetic. The term *gihin/gṛhin* works much better in this respect because it is more abstract. It is used as a generic, highly normative category that emphasizes the (non-*pabbajita*) status of house residents. However, in this concept a *gihin* is generally presented as being inferior to the *pabbajita* and as a person who is supposed to carry out a variety of duties for the ascetics. When they appear in groups, *gihins* are a faceless and nameless mass. All this—and the fact that *gihin* never seems to refer to a Brahmin—does not make the term very attractive either. That leaves us with *gahaṭṭha/gṛhastha*. Unlike *gahapati*, it is used conceptually in the contrastive pair of house resident and ascetic, but it is less ideologically charged than *gihin*. It is generally not as specifically defined as the other two and has both positive and negative connotations, neither one of which is very strong. In fact, its sparsity in the texts may be regarded as an advantage since it is the least specific and the most flexible of the three terms.

---

like them (*AN* III 251,5). Elsewhere I argued that depicting *gahapatis* as spiritually accomplished and generally in a positive way—especially in contrast to *gihins*—might have been an attempt to attract affluent members of society who self-identified as *gahapatis* in the sense of an influential group in society (Freiberger 2018).

Clearly, none of this provides hard evidence to verify the hypothesis that third-century BCE Brahmins borrowed the term *gahaṭṭha/gṛhastha* from the śramaṇīc discourse of the time. But if—and that is a big "if"—the earliest extant Pāli texts represent one expression of the third-century śramaṇic discourse, and if the Brahmins did want to reinterpret the śramaṇic contrastive pair of ascetic and householder in favor of the latter, *gahaṭṭha/gṛhastha* would have suggested itself more strongly than any other term.

Appendix

Quantitative Distribution of Attested Terms

	DN	*MN*	*SN*	*AN*	*Dh*	*Ud*	*It*	*Sn*	Total
gahapati	38	47	47	88	—	2	1	1	224
gihin	10	9	12	26	1	2	1	4	65
gahaṭṭha	—	4	2	12	1	—	2	6	27
gharāvāsa	2	6	2	3	—	1	—	1	15
agārik/y/ abhūta	—	—	2	4	—	2	—	—	8
gharamesin	—	—			—	—	1	1	2
gharaṭṭha	—	—			—	—	1	—	1
agārin	—	—			—	1	—	—	1

Unattested in this corpus are: **agāraṭṭh*°, **agārapat*°, **agārames*°, **agāravās*°, **agārāvās*°, *kuṭimbik*°, *kuṭimbiy*°, *kuṭumbik*°, *kuṭumbiy*°, **gahames*°, **gahavās*°, **gahāvās*°, **gihaṭṭh*°, **gihapat*°, **gihames*°, **gihavās*°, **gihāvās*°, **gehaṭṭh*°, **gehapat*°, **gehames*°, **gehavās*°, **gehāvās*°, **gharapat*°, **gharavās*°.

5

Gāhāvaï *and* Gihattha

THE HOUSEHOLDER IN THE EARLY JAIN SOURCES

Claire Maes

THIS CHAPTER BRINGS the Jain materials into conversation with the central argument of this volume: that the Sanskrit term *gṛhastha* is a neologism in the Dharmaśāstra texts.[1] Being the principal and technical term for the twice-born householder in the dharma literature, *gṛhastha* represents the central institution of the ideal society imagined by early Brahmins. As Jamison states, it is the *gṛhastha* who is "the linchpin of the dharma system, the unmarked subject and agent of most of the multiple provisions in the Dharmasūtras and śāstras and the economic support of the society envisioned there" (Ch. 1, p. 4). Given this fact, it is surprising that the term did not evolve from an orthodox Brahmanical context. A logical antecedent for *gṛhastha* would have been the Vedas. Jamison, however, shows that the term is absent in Vedic texts, where *gṛhápati-* is used instead. Observing how in Middle Indic sources, Prākrit equivalents of *gṛhastha* often occur in a contrastive pair with ascetics or those who go forth from home into homelessness (*pravrajita*), Jamison suggests that the Brahmanical term *gṛhastha* must have been adopted from the śramaṇic

1. I would like to thank Patrick Olivelle for inviting me to contribute to this volume, and Stephanie Jamison for her many stimulating questions regarding the Jain materials. I hope this chapter succeeds in answering some of her questions, while generating other, new interesting questions. The research presented in this paper has been made possible thanks to a generous postdoctoral fellowship of The Robert H. N. Ho Family Foundation. I presented an earlier version of this chapter at the Annual Meeting of the American Oriental Society at Pittsburgh (PA) in March 2018.

discourse. This is an important argument for our understanding of ancient Indian religious history, since it throws new light on both the history of the development of the Brahmanical institution of the householder, and the interaction and circulation of ideas between the *brāhmaṇas* and *śramaṇas* of early India.

I seek to contribute to this fascinating discussion by offering a critical examination of the vocabulary used for householders in three Jain canonical texts—the *Ācārāṅga Sūtra* (AM *Āyāraṅga*), the *Uttarādhyayana Sūtra* (AM *Uttarajjhayaṇa*), and the *Sūtrakṛtāṅga* (AM *Sūyagaḍaṅga*).[2] If the *gṛhastha* of the Dharmaśāstra texts was indeed inspired by a *śramaṇa* discourse, then the Jain materials need to be brought into the discussion. Predating the historical start of the Buddhist tradition in North India, Jainism is the oldest *śramaṇa* community with a body of canonical and paracanonical texts which, unlike the Ājīvikas, did not get completely lost.[3]

The dating of ancient Indian texts is known to be notoriously difficult, resting on shaky grounds or, as Lariviere once put it, on "a chronological house of cards."[4] This is no less true for the dating of ancient Jain texts. According to a Jain tradition itself, the collecting and writing down of the Jain "canonical" texts did not occur before the middle of the fifth century CE, implying a long and complex textual development of the Jain "canon."[5] Although the date of *composition* is late, parts of the *content* of the Jain "canon," however, may have a greater

2. Despite the fact that these three texts are composed in Ardhamāgadhī Prākrit, they are best known under their Sanskrit titles. I therefore use their Sanskrit titles throughout this chapter. Note that though AM *Sūyagaḍaṅga* is rendered in Sanskrit with *Sūtrakṛtāṅga*, AM *sūya* does not correspond to the Sanskrit *sūtra*. The AM word for *sūtra* is *sutta*. The "*sūya*" component of the title *Sūyagaḍaṅga* most probably corresponds to *sūcī*, with the meaning of *dṛṣṭi* ("view"). For more information on the meaning of the title *Sūyagaḍaṅga*, see Schubring 2000: § 45.2.

3. While Digambaras reject the Śvetāmbara classification of sacred texts, both Jain sects agree that their oldest scriptures (the Pūrvas) have been lost. For a discussion of the Jain canon and the Jainism presented therein, see Deo 1956; Dundas 2002; Schubring 2000; and Winternitz 1999.

4. Lariviere 2003: 11.

5. The Jain tradition I am alluding to is the Śvetāmbara tradition regarding the "second council of Valabhī." This council was supposedly held during the middle of the fifth or the beginning of the sixth century CE and presided over by Devarddhi Kṣamāśramaṇa. According to tradition, it was during this council that the Jain canon was collected and written down, in an attempt to prevent the complete loss of the Jain *Sūtras*. See Deo 1956: 21; Winternitz 1999: 416.

antiquity.[6] Indeed, based on an investigation of meter and language, Jacobi suggests that the most ancient parts of the Jain canon must approximately date from the end of the fourth or the beginning of the third century BCE.[7] Jacobi considers the first two *aṅgas* (the *Ācārāṅga Sūtra* and the *Sūtrakṛtāṅga*) and the first *mūlasūtra* (the *Uttarādhyayana Sūtra*) to constitute the oldest strata of the Jain canon. Both the *Ācārāṅga Sūtra* and the *Sūtrakṛtāṅga* are divided into two books; of these the first of each is considered more ancient (Jacobi 2002: xli–xliii and Jacobi 2004: xxxviii–xl). Because of their relative antiquity, I have chosen to concentrate on these three texts in my investigation of the Ardhamāgadhī terminology for householders. If we follow Jacobi's dating, then some parts of these Jain texts might predate the early Dharmasūtras, while other sections might be contemporaneous or younger.[8] In fact, the mapping out of the development and use of the different terms for householders might prove to be a helpful tool for the relative dating of ancient Indian texts.

Terms for Householder in the Early Jain Sources

The Ardhamāgadhī equivalents of the two Sanskrit terms central to Jamison's argument are *gāhāvaï* and *gihattha*. While *gihattha* presents itself as a straightforward development from the Sanskrit *gṛhastha*,[9] the connection between *gāhāvaï* and *gṛhapati* is, admittedly, less clear. The term *gāhāvaï* does not follow the common laws governing the phonological development of Sanskrit words into Ardhamāgadhī. Let us take a closer look. The compound may be broken up into *gāhā* and *vaï*.[10] To begin with the second part *vaï*: with the weakening of the labial -*p*- to -*v*- and the dropping of the intervocalic -*t*-, *vaï*

---

6. My choice to put the words "canon" and "canonical" between quotation marks is to avoid creating the idea that our given concept of canon as a closed and authoritative body of texts would agree with the manner how early and pre-colonial Jains approached their "texts." On this subject (but for Buddhist texts) see Collins 1990.

7. On meter as a tool to the relative dates of various parts of the *Ācārāṅga Sūtra* and other Jain texts, see Schubring 2004a: 1–32. See also Winternitz 1999: 414.

8. For the absolute and relative dating of the four Dharmasūtras see Olivelle 2010.

9. With the Old Indo Aryan vowel -*ṛ*- developing into -*i*-, and the dominant assimilation of the consonant cluster -*sth*- into -*tth*-, *gihattha* is an anticipated form for Sanskrit *gṛhastha*. For a concise grammar discussing the phonological and morphological features of Prākrit see Van Den Bossche 1999.

10. In the Roman transliteration of Prākrit words, it is common practice to mark the vowel -*i*- with an umlaut (ï) when following immediately the vowel -*a*-. This is meant as a visual aid to read the two vowels as separate and to not confuse it with the Old Indo-Aryan diphthong *ai*.

is an anticipated development of the Sanskrit *pati*, meaning "husband," or, when compounded, "lord," "owner." More difficult, however, is the connection between Ardhamāgadhī *gāhā* and Sanskrit *gṛha*. The Old Indo-Aryan (OIA) vowel *-ṛ-* disappears in the Prākrit languages. When in medial position, Old Indo-Aryan *-ṛ-* commonly evolved into *-i-*, sometimes into *-a-*, or, when followed by labials, Old Indo-Aryan *-ṛ-* could also change into *-u-*, but never into a long *-ā-*. So how can we explain the first *ā* of *gāhā*, not to mention the second one? One dictionary of the Prākrit languages, recognizing the difficulty of linking *gāhā* with Sanskrit *gṛha*, suggests that *gāhā* must be a *deśi* word for "house."[11] But as Jamison notes, "the trouble with a deśi explanation is that it's a black box explanation."[12] In other words, it is no explanation at all. A solution to this phonological crux may be found in Pischel's *Grammatik der Prakrit-Sprachen (1900)*. Pischel explains the first long *-ā-* of *gāhāvaï* as being the result of a sporadic "vocalic elevation," while the second long *-ā-* as being due to the "occasional lengthening of final vowels in the first compound members."[13] Though both rules are perhaps indeed "ad hoc" explanations, we must, for now, settle for this explanation.

In Table 5.1, I give an overview of the distribution of *gāhāvaï* and *gihattha* in the first and second book of both the *Ācārāṅga Sūtra* (*AS* I and *AS* II) and the *Sūtrakṛtāṅga* (*SK* I and *SK* II), and the *Uttarādhyayana Sūtra* (*UD*). In addition, the table lists other words the authors of the sūtras employ to refer to householders. We have the terms *gihi, gihittha, gihivāsa, giha,* and *gehavāsa,* next to several words developed from *(a)gāra*. The term *(a)gāra* stresses the fact that the individual referred to is a house owner or, at least, one who lives in a house as opposed to the ascetic, who is *anāgāra* or houseless. Meaning literally "stay-at-home," the terms *gārattha* and *agārattha* should both be viewed as semantic equivalents of *gihattha/gṛhastha*. In his *Jaina Sūtras*, Hermann Jacobi sometimes translated the terms *asaṃgaa* and *para* with "householder."[14] I have chosen not to include these two words in our discussion, since both are generic in meaning and do not necessarily refer to a householder. The

11. See *PSM*: s.v. *gāhā*.

12. Personal communication: email December 8, 2017.

13. Jamison, Ch. 1, n. 35, of this volume. See Pischel 1900: §70 and §78.

14. Jacobi translated into English the *AS*, the *SK*, and the *UD* for the *Sacred Books of the East* series, a fifty-volume set of Asian religious writings in English translation edited by Max Müller. For *AS*, see Jacobi 2002. For *SK* and *UD*, see Jacobi 2004. The first book of the *AS* has also been translated into German (and this, in turn, into English) by Schubring. See Schubring 2004b.

Table 5.1 Terms for Householders in the Early Jain Sources and Their Distribution

	AS I	*AS* II	*SK* I	*SK* II	*UD*	Total
gāhāvaī	9	57	—	19	—	85
gihattha	—	—	—	1	4	5
gihittha	—	—	—	—	1	1
sāgāri(y)a	—	9	1	—	—	10
gārattha	—	4	—	5	1	10
agāra	—	1	—	4	3	8
agāri	—	—	2	2	1	5
agārattha	1	—	—	—	—	1
agāravāsa	—	—	—	—	1	1
gāri	—	—	1	—	—	1
giha	—	—	—	—	1	1
gihi	—	—	2	1	4	7
gihivāsa	—	—	—	—	1	1
gehavāsa	—	—	—	1	—	1
	AS I	*AS* II	SK I	SK II	*UD*	Total
	(10)	(71)	(6)	(33)	(17)	137

term *asaṃgaa* (also spelled *asaṃjaa* or *assaṃjata*) corresponds to the Sanskrit *asaṃyata*. Etymologically, an *asaṃyata* refers to an unrestrained individual. He is one who is not (*a*) connected (*sam*) to restrains (*yata* < *yam*). In the *Ācārāṅga Sūtra*, the *asaṃgaa* is often a well-meaning individual, desirous of donating alms or other items to Jain mendicants, but unaware of the rules he should be mindful of to ensure that his gift is acceptable.[15] The term *para*, on the other hand, is a highly unspecific term, meaning "other [than oneself]."

When noting the different Ardhamāgadhī terms for householders and their distribution in the three Jain sūtras, we can make the following observations. First, with just five occurrences, *gihattha* is neither the predominant nor a common term for householder in the ancient Jain texts. Four out

15. I counted fifteen occurrences of the term *asaṃgaa* in the *AS* and one in the *UD*. The typical setting is the *asaṃgaa* who cooks, prepares, or buys something "for the mendicant's sake," making it thus an impure and unacceptable gift. Jain ascetics should ideally refrain from accepting anything that has been purposefully prepared for their sake. The main concern here is to avoid a situation where others perform acts of *hiṃsā* on their behalf. For an example of a typical *asaṃgaa* reference, see *AS* II.6.1.1.

of five references occur in the *Uttarādhyayana*, a text generally considered younger than both the *Ācārāṅga* and the *Sūtrakṛtāṅga* (Jacobi 2004: xxxviii– xl). Second, the dominant term for householder is *gāhāvaï*, which accounts for more than half of the references I have counted in the three texts. While most of the *gāhāvaï* references occur in the *Ācārāṅga* and the second book of the *Sūtrakṛtāṅga*, the term is notably absent in the first book of the *Sūtrakṛtāṅga* and the *Uttarādhyayana*. What does this mean? And how does this fit into the larger argument of this volume, namely, that the term *gṛhastha* of the dharma literature might have been adopted from the *śramaṇa* milieu? Considering these questions, the following sections examine more closely the conceptual use of the terms *gāhāvaï* and *gihattha* in the early Jain sources.

Gāhāvaï *in the* Ācārāṅga Sūtra

The *Ācārāṅga* is the oldest extant Jain text devoted to ascetic conduct (*ācāra*). Through hundreds of precepts and guidelines, the *Sūtra* regulates every aspect of the daily life of Jain monks and nuns, from how a Jain *bhikkhu* and *bhikkhunī* should walk, talk, sleep, and go to the bathroom, to how they should wade through a river or enter a boat. Significant sections of the text deal with two other daily activities of the Jain mendicant's life: the collection of alms and the searching for appropriate lodgings. During these two activities, the Jain mendicant is in direct contact with householders, which in part accounts for the higher frequency of householder references in this text than in the *Sūtrakṛtāṅga*, which deals with incorrect views, the tortures of hells, and the hardships mendicants face, and in the *Uttarādhyayana Sūtra*, which contains thirty-six lectures on a wide variety of subjects, from the principal duties of the monk to the nature of the soul (*jīva*), karma, and inanimate substances.

The nine *gāhāvaï* references in the first book of the *Ācārāṅga Sūtra* occur in lecture 7.[16] Among other things, the lecture instructs the Jain ascetic about inappropriate gifts and how to refuse these. He is told not to accept from a *gāhāvaï* any item the latter procured violently or specifically for his sake. Within the context of the *Ācārāṅga*, violence is defined broadly as any act causing harm (*samārabbha*), whether to oneself or to other living beings, however minute. The *Sūtra* sketches an ideal—or one should say, implausible— scenario in which a *gāhāvaï* goes up to a Jain mendicant and truthfully

---

16. Note that Schubring in his edition of the first book of the *AS* considers lecture 7 as missing. He consequently refers to this lecture as lecture 8. See Schubring 2004b: 121–22 (tr.) and 212 (ed.).

declares: "O long-lived śramaṇa! I shall give you what I have bought or stolen or taken, though it was not to be taken, nor given, but was taken by force . . . by committing violence on lower animals, plants, higher creatures [and], other living beings" (*AS* I.7.2.1, tr. partly following Jacobi 2002: 64).[17] If a *gāhāvaï* is not as transparent, an ascetic can still find out whether his gift is appropriate or not, the text tells us, through his own keen powers of observation, the instructions of the Jinas, or, more mundanely, because others told him so. While the lecture encourages ascetics not to succumb to inappropriate gifts, we incidentally learn how the *gāhāvaï* in the first book of the *Ācārāṅga Sūtra* is one who provides Jain ascetics with the requisites necessary for leading a mendicant life. The *gāhāvaï* is thus presented as approaching Jain ascetics to offer lodgings (*āvasaha*), in addition to "food, drink, dainties and spices, robes, an alms-bowl, blanket, or a broom."[18]

In the second book of the *Ācārāṅga Sūtra*, *gāhāvaï* references occur predominantly in sections regulating (1) how an ascetic should enter the abode of a householder (*gāhāvaïkula*), and (2) how he should inspect and, if found appropriate, also accept food, lodgings, and other requisites from the householder and his family. To quote a short but typical example, *Ācārāṅga Sūtra* II.6.2.1 (p. 104) reads:

> *se bhikkhū vā* 2[19] *gāhāvatikulaṃ piṃḍavāyapaḍiyāe pavisamāṇe puvvam eva pehāe paḍiggahagaṃ avahaṭṭu pāṇe pamajjiya rayaṃ tato saṃjayam eva gāhāvatikulaṃ piṃḍavāyapaḍiyāe pavisejja vā nikkhamejja vā.*

> A monk or a nun, entering the abode of a householder [*gāhāvatikula*] for the sake of alms, should after examining their alms bowl, taking out any living beings, and wiping of the dust, circumspectly enter or leave the householder's abode. (tr. Jacobi 2002: 169)

Similar passages with the terms *gāhāvaï* or *gāhāvaïkula* instruct Jain ascetics to put their complete outfit on "when entering or leaving the abode of a

---

17. See Schubring 2004b: 121–22.

18. See *AS* I.7.1 (ed. Jacobi): "*asaṇaṃ vā* 4 [= *pāṇaṃ vā khāimaṃ vā sāimaṃ vā*] *vatthaṃ vā paḍiggahaṃ vā kaṃbalaṃ vā pāyapuṃchaṇaṃ.*" In the edition of the *AS* one frequently encounters the numbers "2" and "4". Manuscripts from the 1500s onward use numbers to indicate that words or groups of words mentioned previously should be repeated. The numeral reflects the number of words that needs to be supplied. I thank Wu Juan for enlightening me on this subject.

19. The number "2" means that *bhikkhuṇī* mentioned earlier should be supplied here. On the use of numbers, see the previous note.

householder to collect alms," except, we are told, when it rains. On their alms round, they should not enter a householder's place if they notice a cow is being milked or food is being cooked. We further read how Jain ascetics should be respectful when collecting alms at a householder's abode by not leaning against a wall or object, peeking through wall fissures, or pointing their finger at the householder or his wife. [20]

Numerous other passages could be cited, but these suffice to show, on a most basic level, that ascetics and *gāhāvaïs* were often in contact for alms and lodging. While these references confirm that a *gāhāvaï* was an important supporter of Jain mendicants, they unfortunately fail to provide much insight into the *gāhāvaï's* life, role, and status in the society. The multiple injunctions of the *Ācārāṅga Sūtra* never shift from the ascetic's perspective. When reading the *Sūtra* we, together with the ascetic, take up our begging bowl, walk circumspectly, stop at the abode of a *gāhāvaï*, and stretch out our bowl. But while entering, we never seem to go really inside the *gāhāvaï's* house to have a look around and see how and what the *gāhāvaï* is doing.

The word *gāhāvaï* often occurs at the start of a stock formulation that enumerates the various people the Jain ascetic could meet when entering a householder's residence. Next to the *gāhāvaï* himself, the monk could meet the *gāhāvaï's* wife (*gāhāvatiṇī*) and their son (*gāhāvatiputta*) and daughter (the *gāhāvatidhūyā*), in addition to *suṇhās, dhātīs, dāsas, dāsīs, kammakaras,* and *kammakarīs*, these being various types of domestic aides, workers, and slaves.[21] In sum, within the second book of the *Ācārāṅga*, the word *gāhāvaï* seems to denote the head of a household who gives alms and lodgings to the Jain ascetic.

While a *gāhāvaï* was affluent enough to provide for the material needs of Jain ascetics, there is no—or insufficient—indication that the *gāhāvaïs* of the *Ācārāṅga Sūtra* formed an exclusively wealthy group within society. In this context, it is worth noting that the term *gāhāvaï* also occurs in the vocative case in both *Ācārāṅga Sūtra* I and II as a respectful appellation. Apart from the obvious suspect (the "*gāhāvaï*" himself), also other members of society could have been addressed with *gāhāvaï*. *Ācārāṅga Sūtra* II.3.1.21 and II.3.2.3 are two instructive passages in this matter. They both incidentally show how

---

20. See *AS* II.1.3.6; *AS* II.3.9; *AS* II 1.4.3; II.1.6.2; and *AS* II.1.6.2.3 respectively.

21. For the complete enumeration, see *AS* II.1.4.4. I counted 17 occurrences of this stock enumeration, though most of these are abbreviated in the manuscript with "*jāva*." See, e.g., *AS* II.1.6.4.

a boatman (*nāvāgata*) could be addressed with "*āusaṃto gāhāvai*" ("long-lived householder") by Jain ascetics.[22]

Gāhāvaï *in the* Sūtrakṛtāṅga

The story of the term *gāhāvaï* seems to be different in the *Sūtrakṛtāṅga*. As we see in Table 5.1, the term *gāhāvaï* disappears in the first book of the *Sūtrakṛtāṅga* and reappears in the second book. Unlike the *Ācārāṅga Sūtra*, the *Sūtrakṛtāṅga* provides more information about the *gāhāvaï*. In *Sūtrakṛtāṅga* II, the *gāhāvaï* is clearly a well-respected member of society, very wealthy, a landowner, and a cattleman. We know this because of the incidental references to the possessions of the *gāhāvaï* and the *gāhāvaïputta* in two lectures of the *Sūtrakṛtāṅga*.

Lecture 2.44–53 of *Sūtrakṛtāṅga* II deals with the type of violence men turn to when possessed by anger. Anger, we read, can move a person to set fire to the cornfields and stables of a *gāhāvaï* and a *gāhāvaïputta*; it can lead one to stab the limbs of the camels, cows, horses, or donkeys belonging to a *gāhāvaï* and a *gāhāvaïputta*; or to steal the earrings, jewels, or pearls of a *gāhāvaï* and a *gāhāvaïputta*.[23] While these sūtras warn us about the dangers of anger, we thus incidentally learn how the *gāhāvaï* and the *gāhāvaïputta* are associated with a wide range of possessions, from fancy jewellery to fields and cattle.

The seventh lecture of the *Sūtrakṛtāṅga* consists of a conversation between Gotama, the *ganadhara* or chief disciple of the twenty-fourth Tīrthaṅkara, Mahāvīra, and Udaga, a follower of the twenty-third Tīrthaṅkara, Pārśva. They debate the question of whether householders are as capable as ascetics in avoiding harming living beings, alternatively classified as movable and immovable, or beings with one to five sense faculties. The lecture begins by describing the debate's setting. The debate takes place in a park called Hastiyāma in Nālandā, a wealthy suburb of the thriving town Rājāgṛha. Providing precise directions, the text locates the park northeast from a public bathing-hall belonging to the householder Leva (*gāhāvaï leva*). As part of the opening setting, the text describes in

---

22. See *AS* II.3.1.21, which instructs how the Jain mendicant should act when noticing a leak in the boat he or she is traveling in, while *AS* II.3.2.3 informs the mendicant what he should say in case the boatman and his crew are planning to throw him overboard, for whatever reasons. Concerning (in)appropriate forms of address, see also *AS* II.4.1.8 and 9.

23. See *SK* II.2.44–47; ed. *SK* II: pp. 214–15. Similarly, for one who is devoid of consideration, see *SK* II.49–53. These sūtras are considered to be a later addition to the lecture, whose principal topic is the discussion of merit and demerit. See Jacobi 2004: 365, fn. 3.

details the opulent wealth of this householder Leva. We read how the *gāhāvaï* Leva was "prosperous, famous; rich in high and large houses, beds, seats, vehicles, and chariots; abounding in riches, gold, and silver; possessed of food and drink; owning many male and female slaves, cows, buffaloes, and sheep; and inferior to nobody" (*SK* II 7.2, tr. Jacobi 2004: 420).[24] In other words, the *gāhāvaï* of the *Sūtrakṛtāṅga* coincides with the idea of a wealthy and influential citizen.

Gihattha *in the Early Jain Sources*

This section examines how the *gihattha* of the Jain sources relates to the *gṛhastha* of the Dharmasūtras. It begins with a brief overview of the use of the term. *Gihattha* occurs five times in the early Jain texts: four times in the *Uttarādhyayana Sūtra* and once in the second book of the *Sūtrākṛtāṅga.*

A first reference to *gihattha* is found in *Uttarādhyayana Sūtra* II. Expounding the hardships (*parīsahā*) of Jain mendicancy and in particular the difficulty of leading a constant itinerant lifestyle, *Uttarādhyayana Sūtra* II.19 reminds the monk how:

> *asamāṇe care bhikkhū | neva kujjā pariggahaṃ / asaṃsatte gihatthehiṃ | aṇieo parivvae ||*
>
> Different from others, a *bhikkhu* should wander about. He should not acquire possessions (*pariggaha*). Not attached to *gihatthas,* he should roam without a fixed residence.

The choice of the term *gihattha* is quite appropriate, since its literal meaning effectively underlines the contrast between the wandering lifestyle of the houseless monk and the stay-at-home lifestyle of the householder, which the Jain monk should not yearn for. Lecture 25 of the *Uttarādhyayana* similarly uses the expression "*asaṃsattaṃ gihatthesu*" when redefining the real *brāhmaṇa,* that is, the Jain ascetic, as "one who is not attached to *gihatthas*" (*UD* 25.28).

Another *gihattha* reference occurs in lecture 18. The lecture recounts the well-known debate between the Jain ascetics Gotama and Kesi on the

---

24. *Tatthā ṇaṃ nālaṃdāe bāhiriyāe leve nāmaṃ gāhāvaï hotthā, aḍḍhe ditte vicchiṇṇavipu labhavaṇasayaṇāsaṇajāṇavāhaṇāïṇṇe bahudhaṇabahujāyarūvarajate āogapaogasaṃpautte vicchaḍḍiyapaurabhattapāṇe. bahudāsīdāsagomahisagavelagappabhūe bahujaṇassa aparibhūe yāvi hotthā.* Ed. *SK* II: pp. 271–72.

differences between the Law of Mahāvīra and the Law of Pārśva.[25] As it befits the religious communities of ancient India, the debate takes place in a park (*ārāma*) and in the public eye. For the event, there "assembled many *pāsaṇḍās* out of curiosity, as well as thousands of *gihatthas*" (*UD* 23.19).[26]

The fourth and final occurrence of *gihattha* in the *Uttarādhyayana* appears in a section that discusses two types of death: "death against one will" and "death according to one's will." For a good death morality is the key. Those who are moral can die assured. A good rebirth is determined not by one's status in society, but by one's actions. The discussion is interesting as it uses next to *gihattha* various other terms for householder, such as *agāra, agārattha, gārattha, gihivāsa,* and *gihittha.*[27] While meter might determine which of these terms is preferred, all the terms are used interchangeably insofar as they serve to stress the fact that the person referred to lives at home, as opposed to the wandering mendicant. To quote the verse with *gihattha*:

> *piṇḍola evva dussīle naragāu na muccaī,*
> *bhikkhāe vā gihatthe vā suvvae kammaī divaṃ.* (*UD* 5.22)
>
> One who is immoral, even a mendicant (*piṇḍola*), will not escape hell.
> The pious one, be he a *bhikkhu* or a *gihattha*, will ascend to a heavenly realm (*diva*).

The sole occurrence of the term *gihattha* in the *Sūtrakṛtāṅga* appears in book II in a section that treats the subject of demerit. It is an overtly negative reference. The lecture starts by describing how there are men on this planet, *gihatthas*, who live a life devoid of morality. They are *adhammiya* in every sense of the word: they live unrighteously, think unrighteously and they, among other things, are characterized by an unrighteous character and conduct. These are the five *gihattha* references in the early Jain sources.

With this overview, we can now turn to consider how these *gihattha* references fit into the larger argument postulated in this book, namely that the Brahmanical term *gṛhastha*, being a neologism in the Dharmasūtras, might have been adopted from the śramaṇic milieu. First, I would like to reiterate

---

25. Pārśva would have stipulated a Fourfold Restraint (*caujjāma*) for his ascetic followers whereas Mahāvīra would have stipulated five restraints, i.e., his five Great Vows (*mahavvaya*). For more details, see Dundas 2002: 30–31.

26. For a discussion of the term *pāsaṇḍa* (Skt. *pāṣaṇḍa*) see Brereton (Ch. 2) and Olivelle (Ch. 3) of this volume.

27. See *UD* 5.19–28.

the fact that, with just five occurrences, *gihattha* is not at all a common term in the early Jain literature. This limited use of the term, combined with the fact that the context, as we have just seen, usually does not provide much—if any—additional information on the *gihatthas*, make it difficult to discern any pattern in the use of the term in the early Jain *Sūtras*. Second, being absent in both the *Acārāṅga Sūtra* and the first book of the *Sūtrakṛtāṅga*, the term only occurs in the younger parts of the *Sūtras* we have examined. Third, we have seen how in a few sūtras the term *gihattha* underlines well the conceptual distinction between the "stay-at-home" householder and the ascetic. It should be noted, however, that this binary construct, lying at the heart of the *śramaṇa* discourse, is in the early Jain texts more frequently expressed with the terms *agāra* and *anāgāra*. A paradigmatic example is the standard expression for "one who goes forth from home into homelessness" (*agārāo aṇagāriyāṃ pavvaïttae*). Fourth, while the evidence presented in the early Jain sources might not allow us to determine the degree of influence Jains exerted on the development of the Brahmanical term *gṛhastha*, we can be certain, however, that once the term *gṛhastha* did start to represent the central figure of the twice-born householder in the dharma literature, the term, or better, the Brahmanical worldview embedded in the term, circled back to the *śramaṇa* milieu, where its validity became contested. To illustrate this point, let us examine more closely the *gihattha* reference in the twenty-fifth lecture of the *Uttarādhyayana Sūtra*.

The Twice-Born Householder in the Early Jain Sources

Lecture 25 of the *Uttarādhyayana Sūtra*, as we have seen above, redefines who the real *brāhmaṇa* is. According to this lecture, the one who can rightly be called a *brāhmaṇa* is not the knower of the Vedas, nor the conductor of sacrifices, but the Jain ascetic "who," we read, "is not greedy, who lives unknown, who is without a house, who has nothing, and who is not attached to *gihatthas*" (*UD* 25.28). Considering the larger narrative setting of the reference, I think the term *gihattha* carries here the Dharmaśāstric connotation of the twice-born householder.

The larger narrative setting is a conversation between two *brāhmaṇas*, named Jayaghosi and Vijayaghosi. Jayaghosi is a famous and well-respected *brāhmaṇa*. Though born in a good Brahmin family, he dedicates his life to the Jain dharma. He observes the fivefold restraints of Jain ascetics, fasts regularly, and as befits a true mendicant he wanders from place to place. Vijayaghosi, on the other hand, is a more traditional *brāhmaṇa*. Being a priest, he conducts the sacred sacrifices.

One day, during his wanderings, Jayaghosi arrives in the town of Varanasi. Searching for a suitable lodging, he goes to a park just outside the town. Jayaghosi was about to complete a month-long fast when he heard that the *brāhmaṇa* Vijayaghosi was conducting a sacrifice in Varanasi. He decides to go to Vijayaghosi's sacrifice for alms.[28] This, however, did not please Vijayaghosi. When he saw Jayaghosi approaching his sacrificial ground, Vijayaghosi tried to shoo him away, saying how he is unworthy of offerings because of his mendicant status. "Those who are worthy of offerings," Vijayaghosi continues, "are priests well-versed in the Vedas, chaste, and grounded in the science of sacrifice." Being thus refused alms, Jayaghosi is neither angry nor pleased, but he feels compelled to instruct Vijayaghosi on the real essence of the Veda and sacrifice. Jayaghosi proceeds smartly. He does not begin with the well-known strategy of redefining the Vedic sacrifice in Jain ascetic terms, but he starts by showing his Vedic knowledge to the priest Vijayaghosi. This is not without effect. Soon he is praised by Vijayaghosi himself, who declares him to be "the most learned of those who know the Vedas" (*UD* 25.38).

Showing his mastery of the Brahmanical tradition, Jayaghosi establishes his authority to speak on this subject. Only then does he proceed to redefine some cornerstones of the Brahmanical tradition in Jain terms. He begins with a classical reinterpretation of the "real" *brāhmaṇa*. In his view, the true *brāhmaṇa* is the ideal Jain ascetic, who is free from love, hatred, and fear, and who shines forth like purified gold. A true *brāhmaṇa* is the one who knows the movable and immovable living beings and refrains from harming them in thought, word, or deed. He is the Jain mendicant who does not take what is not given, who has no sexual relationships, and who remains undefiled by pleasures. It is in this context that he refers to *gihatthas*. Further extolling the virtues of the true *brāhmaṇa*, Jayaghosi declares, as we have seen at the beginning, how a real *brāhmaṇa* should have no house, no possessions, and be unattached to *gihatthas*. This is followed by a few more verses that are counterintuitive to the traditional Brahmanical worldview. We learn how, according to Jayaghosi, a *brāhmaṇa* should cut all ties with his relatives and relations.[29] And how:

---

28. For a similar trope of a Jain ascetic approaching the sacrificial grounds of a *purohita* to break a month-long fast, see also lecture 12 of the *Uttarādhayana Sūtra*. For a discussion of this lecture, see Charpentier 1908.

29. See *UD* 25.29, tr. 139.

> *pasubandhā savvaveyā ya jaṭṭhaṃ ca pāvakammuṇā,*
> *na taṃ tāyanti dussīlaṃ kammāṇi balavanti hi.* (*UD* 25.30)
>
> The binding of animals (to the sacrificial pole), all the Vedas, and sacrifices, being causes of sin, cannot save the sinner; for his works (or Karman) are very powerful. (tr. Jacobi 2004: 140)

To this, Jayaghosi adds: "One does not become a *śramaṇa* by the tonsure, nor a Brāhmaṇa by the sacred syllable *oṃ*, nor a Muni by living in the woods, nor a Tāpasa by wearing (clothes of) kuṣa-grass and bark. [But] one becomes a *śramaṇa* by equanimity, a Brāhmaṇa by chastity, a *muni* by knowledge, and a *tāpasa* by penance. By one's actions one becomes a Brāhmaṇa, or a Kshattriya, or a Vaiśya, or a Śūdra. The Enlighted One [i.e., the Tīrthāṅkara] has declared these (good qualities) through which one becomes a (true) Snātaka; him who is exempt from all Karman, we call a Brāhmaṇa. The most excellent twice-born men who possess these good qualities, are able to save themselves and others" (*UD* 25.31–35, tr. Jacobi 2004: 140).

When considering this larger narrative, it is safe to suggest that *gihattha* does not refer to just any house resident. We have seen how the whole passage is permeated with Brahmanical concepts and terminology. When Jayaghosi uses and redefines words and concepts such as *brāhmaṇa*, *snātaka*, and sacrifice, he is speaking to the *brāhmaṇa* Vijayaghosi in a thoroughly Brahmanical language. Given these facts, it is sound to assume that the term *gihattha* also should be understood within such a Brahmanical vocabulary. If our assumption is correct, then we have here an example of a lecture that should be read as a Jain response to the Brahmanical idea of "*gṛhastha*." This is an important conclusion, as it not only shows how Jains actively engaged with Brahmanical ideas, but also because it throws light on the relative chronology of (the different layers) of our texts. If *gihattha* is indeed referring to the twice-born householder, then this lecture of the *Uttarādhyayana* must be either contemporaneous with or younger than the Dharmasūtra texts.

A final point I would like to make regarding this lecture concerns the question of audience. Who was its intended audience? Though this lecture could be addressed to multiple audiences for multiple reasons, I would like to suggest that Brahmins both inside and outside of the Jain ascetic community must have been an important intended audience. The reason, I think, is that the lecture establishes the worthiness of the Jain ascetic path to Brahmins via the authority of a Brahmin. Let us not forget that Jayaghosi, the pious Jain ascetic, was a Brahmin himself. Furthermore, when he spoke of the superiority of the Jain path, he did so in a thoroughly Brahmanical language. In the end, he wins over the *brāhmaṇa* Vijayaghosi, who enters the Jain order. The superiority of the Jain path is thus confirmed to a *brāhmaṇa* priest through the authoritative voice of another *brāhmaṇa*. Lecture 14 of the *Uttarādhyayana Sūtra* employs a similar strategy. It is worth taking a closer look at this lecture since, just as lecture 25, it critically engages with the Brahmanical values of domesticity, while also rejecting the compromising view formulated in the classical *āśrāma* system that converts asceticism to, as Olivelle put it, "an institution of old age."[30] This, in turn, both suggests the relatively late date of the lecture and further corroborates the possibility that some sections in the *Uttarādhyayana Sūtra* must be contemporaneous with, or later than, the Dharmasūtras.

Lecture 14 tells the story of a Brahmin family. It is the story of a husband, who is a Brahmin *purohita*,[31] his wife Jasā, their two sons, and their collective decision to renounce domestic life and become ascetics.[32] As Olivelle noted (1995: 540), this story must have been part of the ascetic folklore, since it also occurs in a Buddhist Jātaka tale, a Pūraṇa, as well as in the *Mahābhārata*, suggesting both its enduring popularity and thematic relevance.

The story recounts how one day, the two sons of the Brahmin priest become overwhelmed by a fear of birth, old age, and death. Urged by a strong desire to escape the cycle of birth and death they approach their father, saying:

> *asāsayaṃ datthu imaṃ vihāraṃ bahuantarāyaṃ na ya dīhamāuṃ,*
> *tamhā gihaṃsi na raiṃ lahāmo āmantayāmo carissāmu moṇaṃ.* (*UD* 24.7)
>
> Seeing that the lot of man is transitory and precarious, and that his life lasts not long, we take no delight in domestic life; we bid you farewell: we shall turn monks (tr. Jacobi 2004: 62).

Their father is not pleased at all by their announcement. Trying to dissuade his sons, he reminds them how "those versed in the Vedas say that there will be no better world for men without sons." He further pleads: "My sons, after you have studied the Vedas, and fed the priests, after you have placed your own sons at the head of your house, and after you have enjoyed life together with your wives, then you may depart to the woods as praiseworthy sages" (*UD*

---

30. Olivelle 1995: 540.

31. Ardhamāgadhī, *māhaṇa purohiya*; Skt. *brāhmaṇa purohita*.

32. For a discussion of family relations in early Indian asceticism, see Clarke 2014 and Granoff 2006.

24.9, tr. Jacobi 2004: 63). The sons remain unaffected by their father's plea. Standing firm in their decision to go forth, they reply:

> *veyā ahīyā na bhavanti tāṇaṃ bhuttā diyā ninti tamaṃ tameṇaṃ,*
> *jāyā ya puttā na havanti tāṇaṃ ko ṇāma te aṇumannejja eyaṃ.* (*UD* 24.12)
>
> The study of the Vedas will not save you; the feeding of Brāhmaṇas will lead you from darkness to darkness, and the birth of sons will not save you. Who will assent to what you said? (tr. Jacobi 2004: 63)

The sons did not settle for the compromise. Focused on the goal of *mokṣa* and realizing the urgency of it, they adopt the Jain law and become ascetics. Upon this, their father too decides, against all odds, to become a Jain ascetic. Without sons, he ceases to find meaning in domestic life. His wife, left all alone, follows in their footsteps. The story shows well how Jains debated the two dominant but conflicting value systems of that time: the Brahmanical ideal of the married householder devoted to the Vedas, sacrifice, and the begetting of male offspring, versus the ascetic ideal of the celibate mendicant devoted to *mokṣa*. While the sons extol the virtues of asceticism, their father holds on to the centrality of domestic life. When the father begs his sons to first have their own sons before turning to asceticism, he echoes the compromise articulated in the classical *āśrama* system.

Conclusion

In light of Jamison's argument that the Sanskrit word *gṛhastha* is a neologism in the Dharmaśāstra texts that might have been adopted from the *śramaṇa* milieu, this chapter examined the terms for householders in the early Jain sources. We focused in particular on two terms: *gāhāvaī* and *gihattha*.

Being the Ardhamāgadhī equivalent of *gṛhapati*, the term *gāhāvaī*, as we have seen, is the most common term in the early Jain sources to refer to a householder. In the oldest extant Jain text named the *Ācārāṅga Sūtra*, the *gāhāvaī* appears to designate the head of a family, who most probably was a house owner. In the *Ācārāṅga Sūtra*, the term *gāhāvaī* does not so much occur in a binary construction of the householder versus the ascetic, or the stay-at-home versus the gone-forth, but, together with his family, the *gāhāvaī* constitutes a social realm with which the ascetics interact and to which they go for alms and lodgings. Though the *gāhāvaī* has sufficient means to provide for ascetics, there is no indication that he was a particularly wealthy citizen. On the other hand, the *gāhāvaī* encountered in the second book of the

Sūtrakṛtāṅga is associated with great riches. As we noted, the term is absent in the first book of the *Sūtrakṛtāṅga*. While *gāhāvaī* appears again in the second book (*SK* II) in sections that are considered to be relatively late, the term does not appear to be an exact clone of the *gāhāvaī* encountered in the *Ācārāṅga Sūtra*. In the *Sūtrakṛtāṅga*, *gāhāvaī* resonates more strongly with the "substantial citizen" or the wealthy merchant class we are familiar with from the Buddhist sources.

Regarding *gihattha*, corresponding to Sanskrit *gṛhastha*, the term appears only in the younger layers of the texts examined, that is, in the second book of the *Sūtrakṛtāṅga* and in the *Uttarādhayana Sūtra*. We observed how, with just five occurrences, the term is not common in the early Jain sources. Buddhists too use the term sparingly in comparison to other words for householders, such as the Pāli terms *gahapati* and *gihin*. Freiberger (Ch. 4 of this volume) suggests that the limited use of the term might have been one of the reasons why Brahmins selected it to denote the central institution of the householder. Because of its rarity in both Jain and Buddhist texts, *gihattha/gahaṭṭha* cannot have been an important carrier of *śramaṇa* ideology, something Brahmins would have disliked. Further, as we have seen in a few verses of the *Uttarādhyayana Sūtra*, the literal meaning of the term *gihattha* establishes well the contrast between the stay-at-home lifestyle of the householder and the wandering lifestyle of the ascetic. This might have added to the term's attractiveness.

To conclude, as I hinted in the introduction, the careful examination of the various terms for householder can help in the relative dating of the different layers of our texts. I argued that one *gihattha* reference occurring in the twenty-fifth lecture of the *Uttarādhyayana Sūtra* must either be contemporaneous with or younger than the Dharmasūtras, as the term seems to carry the Brahmanical connotation of the twice-born householder. Further, as we have seen in our discussion of lecture 14 of the *Uttarādhyayana*, once the institution of *gṛhastha* became a well-established feature of the Dharma literature, Jain authors did not hesitate to try to dispute its validity.

PART II

The Sanskrit Śāstras

6

The Late Appearance of the Gṛhastha *in the Vedic Domestic Ritual Codes as a Married Religious Professional*

Timothy Lubin

Introduction

Considering the centrality of the householder ideal in the classical Indian picture of the world, as exhibited in religious, didactic, and literary sources—an ideal long viewed as a timeless feature of the culture—it might be a matter of astonishment that its chief exponent, the *gṛhastha*, is virtually absent from the works that codify the ceremonies and roles of Brahmanical household life, namely, the Gṛhyasūtras. Stephanie Jamison[1] and Patrick Olivelle observe in their contributions to this volume that the term *gṛhastha* does not seem to appear in Sanskrit texts until the Dharmasūtras, the first works devoted to expounding Brahmanical dharma ideal as the basis for religious life. On the other hand, Jamison further observes that the word *does* appear earlier in Prakrit beginning with three mentions in the edicts of Aśoka (RE 12 and 13, and PE 7), followed by two occurrences in a Niya document (489) in Gandhari. In these contexts, it usually occurs in juxtaposition to words like *pravrajita* ("going forth"), *pāṣaṇḍa* ("religious order"), *śramaṇa*, or *bhikṣu*, all referring to members of a religious order; in these contexts the word is apparently intended to designate an opposite status: "remaining at home." The central

1. Jamison first raised the issue in a paper at the 2015 annual meeting of the American Oriental Society, now chapter 1 of this volume.

question is: Is this alternate status that of an ordinary layperson, or is this another type of religious professional or sectarian?

The Gṛhyasūtras, the rulebooks of household ritual that were the precursor genre to (and largely provided a model for) the Dharmasūtras, might be thought of as a likely place in which to hear about a person labeled *gṛhastha*, since in later Brahmanical Hinduism, this word becomes the standard term for a married householder responsible for performing such rites. But in fact, as Jamison observes, the head of household is rarely named in the Gṛhyasūtras because his is, on principle, the default agent of ritual actions, and in the few cases in which he is identified by a general title, it is *gṛhapati* (*ŚāṅGṛ* 1.1.2; *PārGṛ* 2.9.14–15; *KhadGṛ* 1.5.36, 3.3.16, 24; *GobhGṛ* 1.4.24), or more rarely *gṛhamedhin* (*GobhGṛ* 1.4.18; *BGṛ* 4.11.1) or *svāmin* (*PārGṛ* 6). Still, a search of the Gṛhyasūtra canon as it has come down to us does yield a very few hits for the word *gṛhastha*. The contexts in which the word occurs, though, are restricted, and this restriction itself may inform us about the circumstances of the word's adoption.

Baudhāyana Gṛhyasūtra *2.9.17*, *interpolated:* Gṛhastha *as Honored Guest Fed after a* Bali *Offering*

At first glance, it might seem that the oldest Gṛhyasūtra to use the word is the *Baudhāyana* at 2.8–9, the chapters dealing with the form of the *baliharaṇa* rite, an offering of food to spirits of the earth and air. Following the mantras to accompany the offerings themselves (in 2.8), the next section prescribes that the *vaiśvadeva* ritual (of which *baliharaṇa* forms a part) should be followed by a ceremonial guest-reception. The author here inserts a set of stanzas in praise of the Five Great Sacrifices (to gods, to ancestors, to spirits, to men, and to Brahman), emphasizing the sacrifice to men, on which it quotes a piece of Brāhmaṇa-type exegesis: "This one, namely, the guest, is the fifth sacrifice" (*vijñāyate—yajño vā eṣa pañcamo yad atithiḥ*). Immediately following the stanzas, the sūtra shifts back to prose to define who counts as a potential guest. The text runs, in the standard Mysore edition:

> *athāsmā atithir bhavati guroḥ samānavṛttir vaikhānaso vā gṛhastho vānaprasthaḥ parivrājako gataśrīḥ snātako rājā vā dharmayuktaḥ* | (*BGṛ* 2.9.17 [Mysore edition])

> Now, a guest for him is: one with the same behavior as a *guru*, or a *vaikhānasa*, a *gṛhastha*, a *vānaprastha*, a *parivrājaka*, a *gataśrī*, a *snātaka*, or a king who adheres to dharma (*rājā vā dharmayuktaḥ*).[2]

To find the *gṛhastha* wedged between ascetics of one sort or another seemed quite significant. However my suspicions about the passage were raised by the awkward appearance of *vā* ("or") in the middle of the list of guests, so I consulted the 1905 Grantha-type edition (p. 46), which instead reads: *athāsyātithir bhavati | guros samānavṛttir vaikhānaso gataśrīs snātako rājā vā dharmayuktas teṣām abhyutthāyā 'sanaṃ pādyam arhaṇam arghyaṃ vā prayuñjīta*. The words *vā gṛhastho vānaprasthaḥ parivrājako* are missing there. A quick check of some copies of manuscripts in my possession seems to confirm that those four words, including the latter three *āśramas* in Manu's system, were interpolated in one (northern?) line of transmission of the work, perhaps as a quasi-commentarial expansion.[3]

So most likely no *gṛhastha* was included in the original form of the text; it was inserted by someone who was familiar with the *āśrama* system, perhaps the version that we know from the Dharmasūtras, which (apart from Gautama) also prefer the word *parivrāja(ka)* for the fourth *āśrama*. Still, it is worth considering what the anonymous interpolator understood by the word. If *gṛhastha* here just meant any married head of household, he would not seem worthy of the role of *atithi*. Rather, the *gṛhastha* belongs in the list only in light of his qualifications as a home-based religious professional—a more marked usage than the later, more pedestrian way in which it came to be applied to householders in general.

Baudhāyana Gṛhyasūtra *4 (Penance for a* gṛhastha vidyārthin*)*

Apart from the apparent interpolation at *Baudhāyana Gṛhyasūtra* 2.9.17, the term *gṛhastha* appears only in a chapter on penances (and guest reception) in *Baudhāyana Gṛhyasūtra* 4, as well as similar passages in the *Āgniveśya Gṛhyasūtra* and *Kauthuma Gṛhyasūtra* (both works probably dating to the first

---

2. *Baudhāyana Gṛhyasūtra* 2.9.21 also adds an alternate rule: "One should welcome all who come calling, including dogs and Cāṇḍālas" (*sarvebhyo 'bhyāgatebhya ā śvacāṇḍālebhyaḥ svāgataṃ kāryam*).

3. For example, Institut français de Pondichéry ms. 31577, 32v6–33r. National Archive Kathmandu ms. 5.657 and Baroda Oriental Institute ms. 554 read *asyāthitir*; Baroda omits the first *vā*.

few centuries CE), and other supplements of the *pariśiṣṭa* (appendix) variety, of similarly late vintage. Of all of these, *Baudhāyana Gṛhyasūtra* 4 may be the oldest.

Baudhāyana Gṛhyasūtra 4.11–12 prescribes penances for a wide array of missteps, both ritual and social. Most of these unhappy occurrences, listed in 4.11, pertain to "one who sacrifices in the home" (*gṛhamedhin*) and/or "one who pursues *brahman*" (*brahmacārin*, i.e., a celibate student).[4] On the other hand, 4.12 deals with another sort of person, the "wisdom-seeker who-stays-at-home":

> *athagṛhasthasyavidyārthinaḥ striyābhyanujñātasya ṛtusaṃveśanaviccheda-prāyaścittaṃ vyākhyāsyāmaḥ* | (*BGṛ* 4.12.1)
>
> Now we shall explain the penance for a wisdom-seeker-who-stays-at-home[5] who, [though] allowed to do so by his wife, leaves off cohabiting with her during her fertile period.

He performs a *homa* offering with cooked food, after which both husband and wife should eat the remainder of the ghee and water (*apareṇāgniṃ ājyaśeṣam udakaśeṣaṃ cobhau jāyāpatī prāśnīyātām*). Is this an actual instance of a Vedic text using the word *gṛhastha* as an attributive adjective qualifying a term for a religious aspirant—in other words, using it rather as Aśoka did? Since *vidyārthin* is also an adjectival form, it is difficult to be sure which word modifies which, though the modifier may (weakly) be expected to precede by default. In any case, the fact that this particular circumstance is dealt with separately from the long list of occasions for *gṛhamedhins* and *brahmacārins* to perform penances (4.11) suggests that we may be dealing with a status distinct from either of those.

Whichever way we interpret the collocation of these terms, it is clear that we are dealing with a married man who, out of a desire to gain higher wisdom, adopts a special rule of discipline that includes sexual chastity, the hallmark of both the Veda student and the professional ascetic. This idea is mentioned

4. These occasions include: for both classes of person, ritual defects such as the fire going out, missing the time for performing *homa* or new- and full-moon rites, dribbling of ghee in the first feeding of solid food, performing a mantra too few or an act too many, and neglecting to perform the parting of the hair, and in general any ritual error; but also the birth of twins and social violations such as conversation with a *patita*, sex during daytime or with a Śūdrā, spilling one's seed, and defecating or urinating in water. Also listed are mishaps specific to the *brahmacārin*.

5. Or if one takes *gṛhastha* as already nominalized: "a householder who seeks wisdom."

also in *Āpastamba Dharmasūtra* 1.13.18–20 and 2.3.13–14, and in *Gautama Dharmasūtra* 18.17, where it is treated as a controversial practice.[6]

In the Gṛhya Pariśiṣṭas

The old domestic ritual codes were subject to expansion and modification, and in a few instances in such appendices, the *gṛhastha* makes a cameo appearance. Although the dates of such works are difficult even to estimate with confidence, there is (as I will show) some reason to think that the *gṛhastha*-related passages were inserted at a time after the appearance of the Brahmanical *āśrama-dharma* in *Āpastamba Dharmasūtra* but prior to the *Mānava Dharmaśāstra* (i.e., between the late third century BCE and second century CE).

Pāraskara Gṛhya Pariśiṣṭa

One supplement (*pariśiṣṭa*) to the *Pāraskara Gṛhyasūtra*, dealing with the ancestor offering (*śrāddha*), mentions *gṛhasthas*:[7]

> *śrāddhasūtram | aparapakṣe śrāddhaṃ kurvītorddhvaṃ vā caturthyā(ḥ) | yad ahaḥ saṃpadyeta tad ahar brāhmaṇān āmantrya pūrvedyur vā | snātakān eke yatīn gṛhasthān sādhūn vā śrotriyān vṛddhān anavadyānt svakarmasthān, abhāve 'pi śiṣyānt svācārān | dvir nagnaśuk laviklidhaśyāvadantaviddhaprajananavyādhitavyaṅgiśvitrikuṣṭhikunakh ivarjam anindyenāmantrito nāpakrāmed | āmantrito vānyad annaṃ na pratigṛhṇīyāt | snātāñ cchucīn ācāntān prāṅmukhān upaveśya daive yugmān ayugmān yathāśakti pitrye ekaikasyodaṅmukhān dvau vā daive trīn pitrya ekaikam ubhayatra vā mātāmahānāñcaivaṃ tantram vā vaiśvadevikam | śraddhānvitaḥ śrāddhaṃkurvīta śākenāpi nāparapakṣamatikrāmenmāsi māsi vośanamiti śruter atad ahaḥ śucir akrodhano 'tvarito 'pramattaḥ satyavādī syād adhvamaithunaśramasvādhyāyān varjayed āvāhanādi vāgyata opasparśanād āmantritāś caivam |* 1
>
> The Śrāddhasūtra: in the latter fortnight, he should perform the Śrāddha, or after the fourth. On the day when he would complete it, he should invite Brahmins, or the day before. Some [say one may

6. I discuss this controversy in Lubin 2018b: 119–20.

7. This supplement may not necessarily be much younger than the Gṛhyasūtra proper. Rules related to funerary cult were commonly transmitted separately from contemporary works dealing with other aspects of ritual.

invite] *snātakas, yatis,* or good *gṛhasthas* who are learned, elder, blameless, and continuing to perform their proper rites, and if none of those are to be had: pupils following one's own practice. [Ceremonial details follow.]

This contains (in the underlined portion) a list of types of person worthy to be invited to dine at a *śrāddha* ritual: *snātakas, yatis,* or *gṛhasthas* of a particular sort. This last passage might be thought to imply that *gṛhasthas,* or at least *proper, model gṛhasthas* are being classed along with other ritually delimited religious professional statuses.

Another *Pāraskara Gṛhyasūtra pariśiṣṭa* discussion of *śauca* also refers to *gṛhasthas,* but it is of little interest since it is a formulaic (but pre-Manu) allusion to four *āśramas*:

> *karayoḥ pādayoḥ sakṛt sakṛd eva mṛttikā deyeti śaucaṃ gṛhasthānāṃ dviguṇam brahmacāriṇāṃ triguṇaṃ vanasthānāṃ caturguṇam yatīnām iti* / (*PārGṛ pariśiṣṭa* 1)
>
> Earth is to be applied just once each on the hands and feet—that is the purifications of *gṛhasthas,* twice for *brahmacārins,* thrice for *vanasthas,* and four times for *yatis.*

The four *āśramas* are indeed the operative classification here, though they are not sequential as in the *Mānava Dharmaśāstra,* but rather they seem to be ordered on a scale of worldly to unworldly or from less to more rigorously disciplined, with the *gṛhastha* placed first, as in *Āpastamba Dharmasūtra* 2.21. Nevertheless, these four categories implicitly span the whole range of possible agents; the *gṛhastha* can no longer be set apart from other family men—except by his adherence to Brahmanical Gṛhya norms.

Kauthuma Gṛhyasūtra

A *gṛhastha* shows up in another Gṛhyasūtra discussion of penances (*prāyaścitta*) as well. The *Kauthuma Gṛhyasūtra,* in the incomplete and probably recast form in which we have it,[8] opens with a discussion of the differences between penances for *gṛhastha* and those for a *brahmacārin,* though it is hard to know

8. Gonda 1977a: 608. Its editor Sūryakānta thinks it contemporary with the *Baudhāyana Gṛhya Śeṣasūtra* (early centuries CE), though it may be closer in time to the *Baudhāyana Gṛhya Paribhāṣāsūtra,* i.e., contemporary with the Dharmasūtras.

what is going on, since the edition is based on a single apparently very corrupt manuscript:

> *athātaḥ prāyaścittāni / athātaḥ kramāṇāṃ*[9] *vakṣye / gṛhastho vā brahmacārī vā / gṛhastho gṛhyāgnau brahmacārī laukikāgnau / gṛhastheṣv iti caraṇena*[10] *paricaraṇe vā brahmacaryavicchinne*[11] *laukikāgnau prātarāhutipūrvakaṃ naimittikaṃ kāryam* / (*KauthGṛ* 1)
>
> Now, the penances. Now I shall speak of (?) the rites. A *gṛhastha* or a *brahmacārin* [should perform them]—the *gṛhastha* [doing so] in the *gṛhya* fire, the *brahmacārin* in ordinary fire. If [a *brahmacārin*] engages in misconduct or associates with *gṛhasthas*, [and] if *brahmacarya* is interrupted,[12] a special (*naimittika*) service should be performed in the ordinary fire, preceded by a morning *āhuti*-offering.

In a separate, poorly transmitted chapter (17) toward the end of this short Gṛhyasūtra, the topic of penances is raised again, ambiguously in relation to "*gṛhastha* [and?] *brahmacārin*" without throwing further light on why just these two statuses are juxtaposed here.[13] But we note that these two statuses seem to constitute here a binary division of potential ritual agents into celibate and non-celibate.

Baudhāyana-Gṛhya-Paribhāṣāsūtra

The *Baudhāyana Gṛhya Paribhāṣāsūtra* (*BGṛ* 5), an interesting older supplement to the *Baudhāyana Gṛhyasūtra*, opens by quoting a famous maxim from the *Taittirīya Saṃhitā* on the three congenital debts with which a man is born, the first of which, the debt to the Vedic sages, is repaid through celibate studentship (*brahmacarya*).[14] Taking the term *brahmacarya* in its metonymically wider sense of "sexual chastity," the author uses this as an opportunity to enumerate all the ways in which some form of sexual discipline should

9. Sūryakānta understands *karmaṇāṃ*.

10. Sūryakānta understands *aticaraṇe (na)*.

11. Sūryakānta understands *brahmacarye vicchinne*.

12. This translation reflects Sūryakānta's emendations of this apparently corrupt clause.

13. *athātaḥ prāyaścittānāṃ gṛhastho brahmacārī* . . . [a list of misdeeds in the accusative follows, ending with the words:] *prāyaścittaṃ vakṣyāmīti*.

14. This section expands on my comments on this passage in Lubin 2016.

be practiced. The period of studentship that ends with the rite of returning home is mentioned first, cross-referencing its treatment in the Gṛhyasūtra proper. The fact that this period of *brahmacarya* is described as an *āśrama* (1.1.3) indicates that the author accepts Manu's reformulation of the vocations as sequential (in contrast to the Dharmasūtras, for which juvenile studentship is merely preparatory to a choice of *āśrama*, and the *āśrama* of studentship is a lifelong status). But the celibacy of the student is only one way to observe the rule. We are next told of subsequent forms of marital *brahmacarya* that allow one to marry and beget sons and thus to discharge the debts to the gods and ancestors:

> *atha vai bhavati "jāyamāno vai brāhmaṇas tribhir ṛṇavā jāyate brahmacaryeṇa ṛṣibhyo yajñena devebhyaḥ prajayā pitṛbhyaḥ" iti* [*TS* 6.3.10.5] / *1* / *brahmacaryaṃ vyākhyāsyāmaḥ* / *2* / *ā samāvartanād evaitad bhavati "nācīrṇavrato brahmacārī bhavati" iti tad etad āśramaṃ vyākhyātam* / *3* / *ata ūrdhvaṃ brahmacaryaṃ yenānṛṇo bhavati* / *4* / *svadāra ity ekam* / *5* / *mantravatprayoga ity ekam* / *6* / *ṛtāv ity aparam* / *7* / *athādhi brahmacaryam vivāhe trirātram* / *8* / *ṛtau trirātram* / *9* / *amāvāsyāyāṃ paurṇamāsyāṃ śrāddhaṃ datvā bhuktvā caikarātram* / *10* / *parastrīṣu divā ca yāvajjīvam* / *11* / *agnyādheye dvādaśarātram* / *12* / *āgrayaṇeṣṭipaśubandhānām upavasatheṣv ekarātram* / *13* / *evam eva sarveṣu vedakarmasu* / *14* / *cāturmāsyeṣu saṃvatsaram* / *15* / *yathāprayogam anyeṣu yajñakratuṣv anyatra rtau dīrghasattreṣu dharmavrateṣu ca* / *16* / *tad etad dharmyaṃ puṇyaṃ putryam āyuṣyaṃ svargyaṃ yaśasyam ānṛṇyam iti vyākhyātaṃ brahmacaryam* / *17* /
>
> 1.1.1. Now there is [a *brāhmaṇa*]: "A Brahmin, as he is being born, is born endowed with three debts: to the sages [he pays] with *brahmacarya*; to the gods, with worship; to the ancestors, with progeny" [*TS* 6.3.10.5]. 2. We shall explain *brahmacarya*. 3. Now up until the *samāvartana*, there is this [*brāhmaṇa*]: "There can be no *brahmacārin* who does not follow the regimen [viz. *brahmacarya*]." This *āśrama* has been explained [in *BGṛ* proper]. 4. From that point onward, [there is a form of] *brahmacarya* by which one becomes debt-free. 5. "One's own wife [only]" is one [kind of *brahmacarya*]. 6. "Copulating[15] with the use of mantras" is [another] one. 7. [Chastity] "during [the menstrual] period" is another. 8. Now, concerning *brahmacarya*: At the wedding, [it lasts] three nights. 9. During the [menstrual] period, three nights. 10. At the

15. *Prayoga* for *samprayoga* as in 1.1.27.

new moon, at the full moon, and when one has given or eaten *śrāddha* offerings, one night. 11. With respect to women belonging to another, or during the day, [*brahmacarya* should last] as long as one lives. 12. At the "Laying of the Fires," twelve nights. 13. On the fast-days preceding the harvest and animal sacrifices, one night. 14. Likewise in all rites of the Veda (*vedakarmasu*). 15. In the Four-Monthly offerings, a year. 16. [It lasts] in accordance with [the normal] practice in other rites of worship; [it is observed] except during the [wife's] fertile period in the case of lengthy *sattras* and dharma-regimens. 17. This indeed confers dharma, merit, sons, long life, heaven, and glory, and pays off the debts: so *brahmacarya* is explained.

Regarding the debt to the gods, four modes of worship (*yajña*) are defined—*svādhyāyayajña, japayajña, karmayajña, and mānasa[yajña]*—which are then correlated with the four *āśramas*:

"yajñena devebhyaḥ" iti yajñaṃ vyākhyāsyāmaḥ | 18 | ekaviṃśatisaṃstho yajña ṛgyajuḥsāmātmakaś chandobhiś cito grāmyāraṇyapaśvoṣadhībhir haviṣmān dakṣiṇābhir āyuṣmān| 19 | sa caturdhā jñeya upāsyaś ca svādhyāyayajño japayajñaḥ karmayajño mānasaś ceti | 20 | teṣāṃ parasparād daśaguṇottaro vīryeṇa | 21 | brahmacāri-vanastha-gṛhastha[16]*-yatīnām aviśeṣeṇa pratyekaśaḥ | 22 | sarva evaite gṛhasthasyāpratiṣiddhāḥ kriyātmakatvāt | 23 | nākriyo brāhmaṇo nāsaṃskāro dvijo nāvidvān vipro naitair hīnaḥ śrotriyo nāśrotriyasya yajña iti | 24 |* (*BGPS* 1.1.18–24)

18. We shall explain *yajña* as it is mentioned in the phrase "to the gods, with worship" (1.1.1 above). 19. *Yajña* has twenty-one standard forms, consists of *ṛcs, yajuses,* and *sāmans,* is built up by meters, confers oblations by virtue of domestic and wild beasts and plants, and confers long life by virtue of the priests's fees. 20. It should be known and venerated as fourfold: *yajña* through private recitation, *yajña* through ritual mantra-repetition, *yajña* through ritual acts, and mental [*yajña*]. 21. Each one of these is ten times greater in strength than the one that precedes. 22. [They are to be performed] by the student, *vanastha, gṛhastha,* and *yati,* respectively without distinction. 23. But all of them

16. This sequence, which corresponds much better with the sequence of modes of *yajña* as listed, is found in some manuscripts and is probably original, though others, as well as the Mysore edition, place the *gṛhastha* before the *vanastha* (or *vānaprastha*), in deference to Manu's classical sequence; one modern manuscript further adjusts the sequence of *yajñas* to match.

> are not forbidden to the *gṛhastha*, since they all have the nature of ritual acts. 24. There is no Brahmin without ritual acts, no twice-born without a consecration, no *vipra* without wisdom, no *śrotriya* lacking these these, and no *yajña* without a *śrotriya*.

In any case, none of these practices is said to be forbidden to the householder, and in the following section, the *Baudhāyana Gṛhya Paribhāṣāsūtra* asserts that, because all *yajñas* are available to the *gṛhastha*, "therefore all these modes of worship belong to the *gṛhastha*; therefore it is said that the household is the better state" (*tasmāt gṛhasthasya sarva evaite yajñās tasmād gṛhāḥ śreya iti*, 1.2.9).

Here we find the *gṛhastha* first set on a par with other, less worldly religious vocations (*āśramas*), and then elevated above them by representing their distinctive forms of practice as nothing but other modes of ritual worship (*karmayajña*). Moreover, the *gṛhastha* is shown to practice several valid forms of *brahmacarya* while still fulfilling his other "debts" (to the gods and the ancestors) through ritual worship (*yajña*) and procreation.[17]

Conclusion

On the admittedly slender evidence collected here, the status of *gṛhastha* first appears by name in the Gṛhya literature only in a few passages that may well be contemporary with the older Dharmasūtras, or younger still. Thus, they presuppose the philosophical innovations of the dharma-theorists among the priestly authors. But their belated appearance in the Gṛhya canon does not render their testimony uninteresting. It is quite striking that the *gṛhastha* crops up in these later-added chapters only when the authors want to identify the model practitioner of Vedic Gṛhya piety as an object of veneration worthy to be considered beside the *snātaka* and various types of professional ascetic as recipient of the guest-reception ceremony (*atithikarma, argha*) and of feeding in the context of a *śrāddha*.

17. A few other Gṛhya-related instances, which derive from texts that certainly postdate the Dharmasūtras and may in fact be much younger, may be mentioned. *Hiraṇyakeśi Gṛhya Śeṣasūtra* 1.7, a discussion of proper *ācāra* and the importance of the sacred thread, specifies that whereas a *baṭu* (young student?) wears only a single *yajñopavīta*, "a *gṛhastha* or *araṇyavāsin* has two, or in the absence of an upper-garment, he should wear a third for that purpose; some say *yatis* should wear just one" (*baṭor ekam upavītam / gṛhasthāraṇyavāsinor dve / vastrābhāve tṛtīyam uttarīyārthaṃ dhāryam / ekam eva yatīnāṃ syād ity eke*). *Baudhāyana Gṛhya Śeṣasūtra* 4.10 and *Āgniveśya Gṛhyasūtra* 2.7.3 contain some instructions for when a *gṛhastha* takes a second wife. These references have no particular bearing on the questions raised here.

As Brereton and Olivelle argue in this volume, Aśoka applied the term *gahattha* to those associated with religious groups (*pāṣaṇḍas*) who "stayed at home" rather than "going forth" as a *pabbajita*. Brereton is inclined to what Olivelle calls the minimalist view, that Aśoka mentioned "religiously dedicated people" who "stay home" rather than "leave home" alongside *pāṣaṇḍas* ("religious groups"), while Olivelle advocates a maximalist reading, that any *pāṣaṇḍa* could include both types of member, and that the Buddhists had a special name for their stay-at-home affiliates: *upāsaka*. Whatever Aśoka may have meant, Brahmanical theorists appear to have taken a maximalist approach, formalizing a ritual and disciplinary (*vrata*-based) program to define *gṛhastha* status as an *āśrama* alongside the celibate and homeless professions. Against this background, the earliest mentions in the Gṛhya literature, probably contemporary with the Dharmasūtras, likewise insert the word *gṛhastha* only in a few places where the emphasis is on the householder as a religious professional, bound by the elaborate strictures of Gṛhya ritual practice—what the *Gobhila Gṛhyasūtra* 1.4.18 calls the "rule for those who sacrifice at home" (*gṛhamedhivrata*, referring to the obligations on the "master and mistress of the house" [*dampatī*] to sacrifice in the fire, make offerings to the ancestors, and offer *bali* from all food prepared, *GobhGṛ* 1.4.13–17), in contrast to those who undertake religious professions outside of married life.

The reclassification of the *gṛhamedhin* as *gṛhastha* would seem to coincide with the appearance of *pravrajita*-type religious professions in the Brahmanical discourse: the *yati* and the *araṇyavāsin* or *vanavāsin* as well—figures Aśoka would likely have called *pabajjitas*, though the edicts do not explicitly mention them. The point of the reclassification, then, is to emphasize that being a Brahmanical *gṛhamedhin* could itself be a religious vocation demanding discipline and imbuing one with charisma (in the Weberian sense), with the aim of making the *gṛhastha* equally worthy of public admiration. This is the idea behind the precepts that pious laymen should "feed Brahmins" on many occasions[18] and perform *argha* for guests (including *snātakas* and exemplary *gṛhasthas*): it justifies a Brahmanical practice of venerating and feeding Brahmin virtuosi in a manner parallel to laymen giving alms to Buddhist, Jainist, or Ājīvika mendicants. The land-grants to Brahmins (*brahmadeyas*) so well documented from the first millennium CE in copper-plate grants is another institutionalization of this practice.[19]

18. Sayers 2012 has noted the significance of this aspect of the *śrāddha* cult.

19. I first proposed this hypothesis about the original purpose of the ritual feeding of Brahmins and of early land-grants to Brahmins in a paper, "Feeding Monks, Feeding

The *gṛhastha* has inherited much of the special cachet of the *snātaka*, who also is a prime candidate for guest-reception. Indeed, according to *Baudhāyana Gṛhya Paribhāṣāsūtra* 1.15.10, a chapter on the different kinds of *snātakas*, the only difference between *snātakas* and *gṛhasthas* is marriage: "Up to their union with a wife, they are *snātakas*; they are *gṛhasthas* thereafter" (*ā jāyāsaṅgamāt snātakā bhavanty ata ūrdhvaṃ gṛhasthāḥ*). It is not so much that *gṛhasthas* are ex-*snātakas*, but that they are married *snātakas* with a new title. The codification of *gṛhastha* status as an "*āśrama*," a central innovation of the Brahmanical Dharmasūtras, in fact took the form of transferring many of the rules of the *snātaka* to the *gṛhastha*, as becomes evident in Manu (*MDh* 4.13–256) where they are embedded into the middle of the chapters on the *dharma* of the *gṛhastha* (books 3–5).[20]

Brahmins: Competing Idioms of Religious Semiotics in Early India," presented at the 45th Annual Conference on South Asia, Madison, Wisc., 20–23 October 2016.

20. I discussed the implications of this placement in Lubin 2011, updated in Lubin 2018b.

7

Gṛhastha, Āśrama, *and the Origin of Dharmaśāstra*

Patrick Olivelle

AT ABOUT THE same time as Aśoka was writing his inscriptions, two significant and innovative developments—the one institutional and the other literary—took place within the Brahmanical tradition. The former was the creation of the fourfold *āśrama* system, which, along with the parallel system of the four *varṇas* (social classes), became so central to Brahmanical religion and theology, to Brahmanical identity, that Brahmanism (and later Hinduism) came to define itself as *varṇāśramadharma*, the dharma of *varṇas* and *āśramas*. The system of *āśrama* appears for the first time in a brand-new genre of literature devoted to explicating the Brahmanical dharma, appropriately named Dharmaśāstra. This chapter explores the connection between the institutions of *pāṣaṇḍa, pravrajita,* and *gṛhastha* recorded for the first time in Aśoka's inscriptions, on the one hand, and the invention of the *āśrama* system and the creation of the genre of Dharmaśāstra, on the other.

The Āśrama *System*

A quarter century ago in my monograph on the *āśrama* system (Olivelle 1993: 94), commenting on its origin, I noted:

> Two common assumptions have prevailed among scholars regarding the authorship and intent of the *āśrama* system: it was created by conservative Brahmins with the intention of resisting the new religious movements and of safeguarding the Brāhmaṇical religion by

> incorporating the renunciatory life style into a scheme that would lessen its impact and reduce or eliminate the conflict between it and the life of the householder.

Rejecting this view, I attempted then to offer a new interpretation of its origins (Olivelle 1993: 96):

> A close reading of these early texts [Dharmasūtras] leads us to the conclusion that the *āśrama* system was created not by the conservative mainstream in order to encompass in a stifling embrace new ideas and institutions that it had failed to suppress but by Brahmins who shared those ideas and ideals and who sought exegetical loopholes to introduce these into the Brāhmaṇical mainstream. From our examination of the debate on the *āśrama* system within the Dharmasūtras we can draw the following conclusions with some confidence. (1) The authors of the system were Brahmins who were supporters of or sympathetic toward the ideals of celibacy and renunciation, and who belonged to what may be termed the "liberal" segments of the Brāhmaṇical community. (2) Their purpose in creating the system was to legitimize the modes of life different from that of the householder by providing a place for them within the sphere of *dharma*, thereby stretching this central concept in new directions.

Although the general direction of my conclusions was, I think, correct, yet I was then ignorant of a crucial set of data that was essential for a more comprehensive and accurate explanation of the origins of the *āśrama* system. My confidence in those conclusions was misplaced. The new data come from the Aśokan inscriptions and their presentation of the crucial categories of *pāṣaṇḍa*, *pravrajita*, and *gṛhastha*, which we have examined in previous chapters. In a special way, the newly discovered history of the term *gṛhastha* and its underlying mode of life as divergent from, yet related to, the *pravrajita* provides a new lens through which to explore the origins of the *āśrama* system.

Let us look briefly at the system as described in our earliest sources. Regarding the four *āśramas*—householder (*gṛhastha*), student (*brahmacārin*), wandering mendicant (*pravrajita*), hermit (*vānaprastha*)—we can make the following observations: (1) they are permanent and adult modes of life; (2) all of which are equally legitimate; (3) a person may freely choose one of them; (3) this choice is made after the temporary studentship following Vedic initiation. The creators of the system have neatly tied the four modes of life to the preparatory period following initiation, a period that ideally lasted about twelve years and that prepared the boy to undertake adult activities and responsibilities.

From Aśoka's writings we gather several significant bits of information regarding the Brahmanical community. Rather than being a *varṇa*, a demographically identified social group, contrasted with the three other *varṇas*, "*brāhmaṇa*" is presented as a religious group identified as *pāṣaṇḍa*. The groups the *brāhmaṇas* are contrasted to are not the other *varṇas* but the other *pāṣaṇḍas*, such as the Buddhists and Jains. Being a *pāṣaṇḍa*, the *brāhmaṇa* community had within it (at least?) two kinds of members: the "gone-forth" (*pravrajita*) and "stay-at-home" (*gṛhastha*). Now, this description of the Brahmanical community—that they constituted a *pāṣaṇḍa* and that they had *pravrajitas* and *gṛhasthas*—is applicable to that community as known to Aśoka, and his experience was derived probably from the state of *brāhmaṇas* in the eastern region of Magadha. Whether this was true of Brahmanical communities throughout India is unclear. The fact that the term *gṛhastha* becomes central within Brahmanical literature makes it probable that this division was present everywhere at least during and after the time of Aśoka.

Given the centrality of the *gṛhastha* and the *pravrajita* within the *āśrama* system, and given the centrality of the *gṛhastha* more generally within Brahmanism as depicted in the Dharmaśāstras, I think we can say with some confidence that the *āśrama* system was an institution that was created by theologians of the Brahmanical community identified as *pāṣaṇḍa* by Aśoka. This represents a specificity that was lacking in my previous assessment, where I concluded that the authors of the system were "Brahmins who were supporters of or sympathetic toward the ideals of celibacy and renunciation, and who belonged to what may be termed the 'liberal' segments of the Brāhmaṇical community." As a *pāṣaṇḍa* group the two modes of life—*pravrajita* and *gṛhastha*—were present within that Brahmanical community. As I will point out in the next section, the same Brahmanical community was responsible for the creation of the new genre of literature, the Dharmaśāstra, where the term *gṛhastha* appears for the first time in Sanskrit literature and in which the *gṛhastha* occupies the central role.

The distinction between the two theologies espoused by the proponents of the *āśrama* system, on the one hand, and by the early writers of Dharmasūtras, on the other, point to two divergent theological viewpoints within the Brahmanical *pāṣaṇḍa* group. The former was probably more wedded to the ideals of the *pravrajita* mode of life: the goal of liberation in some form (*mokṣa*), abandonment of ritual activities, and celibacy. It also sought to put the four modes of life represented by the *āśramas* on an equal footing: they were equally legitimate, and a young adult could choose one of them freely. The latter could be called a *gṛhastha*-theology propounding the centrality of the married householder engaging in ritual and sexual activities and procreating children. It brought together the older Vedic theology centered around the *gṛhapati*-householder and the newer *pāṣaṇḍa* theology focused on the *gṛhastha*-householder. The connection between the two is brought into focus by the only occurrence of the term *gṛhastha* in the second-century-BCE grammarian Patañjali. In explaining the rule of Pāṇini (4.1.33) on the formation of *patnī* (wife) from *pati* (husband), that is, a wife who takes part in her husband's sacrifices (*yajñasaṃyoge*), Patañjali introduces the term *gṛhastha* as a synonym of *pati* (i.e., *gṛhapati*) and points out the ritual obligations of a *gṛhastha*: "All *gṛhasthas* should offer the five great sacrifices" (*sarveṇa ca gṛhasthena pañca mahāyajñā nirvartyāḥ*).[1] The centrality of the so-called "five great sacrifices" is also pointed out in Manu's last verse on the *gṛhastha*: "In accordance with these rules, he should never neglect the five sacrifices; and, marrying a wife, he should live at home during the second quarter of his life"—*anena vidhinā nityaṃ pañca yajñān na hāpayet | dvitīyam āyuṣo bhagaṃ kṛtadāro gṛhe vaset ||* (*MDh* 5.169). Although *gṛhastha* theology found a secondary place for the ideals of ascetic life and the search for liberation, it existed in tension and conflict with the latter as can be seen in passages of the Dharmaśāstras that extol the householder.

Let us look at the first of these two theologies, the one directly connected with the *āśrama* system. Now, one may ask how the twofold division of Aśoka—namely, the *pravrajita* and the *gṛhastha*—corresponds to the fourfold division of the *āśramas*. If we look closely at the four *āśramas*, however, we find that they actually represent two institutions each subdivided into two. The man who chooses to "stay at home," the *gṛhastha*, is contrasted with the man who chooses to "go forth," the *pravrajita*. The former, however, includes the *brahmacārin*, that is the student of the Veda who chooses not to return to his natal home in order to get married and establish a new home (*gṛha*), but to stay on permanently at his teacher's home devoting himself to Vedic studies. Instead of creating a new household, one's own *gṛha* with wife and sacred fire, he remains part of his teacher's household, serving the teacher's wife, son, or fire after the teacher passes away.

More significantly, however, the man who chooses to "go forth" also has two options: he can become a *vānaprastha* or a wandering ascetic variously called *bhikṣu*, *parivrājaka*, *muni*, and *yati*. That the verb *pravrajati* applies to

1. These five great sacrifices are enumerated by Manu (*MDh* 3.70): "The sacrifice to the Veda is teaching; the sacrifice to ancestors is the quenching libation; the sacrifice to gods is the burnt offering; the sacrifice to beings is the Bali offering; and the sacrifice to humans is the honoring of guests."

both institutions is demonstrated by the way Āpastamba introduces the two institutions with identical phrases:

> *atha parivrājaḥ | ata eva brahmacaryavān pravrajati ||*
>
> Next, the wandering ascetic. From that very state (*brahmacārin*), remaining chaste, he goes forth. (*ĀpDh* 2.21.7–8)
>
> *atha vānaprasthaḥ | ata eva brahmacaryavān pravrajati ||*
>
> Next, the forest hermit. From that very state (*brahmacārin*), remaining chaste, he goes forth. (*ĀpDh* 2.21.18–19)

The conclusion that the wandering ascetic and the forest hermit belong to the category of *pravrajita* is also supported by an interesting statement in Kauṭilya's *Arthaśāstra*. In his discussion of the *janapada* or countryside (as opposed to the city or fort, *pura*), he lists people and groups who should be barred from entering or living in the *janapada*. In this context he states: *vānaprasthād anyaḥ pravrajitabhāvaḥ*—"any kind of *pravrajita* other than forest hermits" (*KAŚ* 2.1.32). Here *pravrajitabhāva*, the category of *pravrajita*, includes the *vānaprasthas*, who alone are permitted to reside in the *janapada*.

The list of the *āśramas* given by our oldest author, Āpastamba, further confirms this two-by-two view of the four: *catvāra āśramā gārhastyam ācāryakulaṃ maunaṃ vānaprastham iti*—"There are four *āśramas*: the householder's life, living at the teacher's family, the life of a sage, and the life of a *vānaprastha*" (*ĀpDh* 2.21.1). Here we have the householder placed ahead of the student and sage (*muni*) by which is meant the *parivrāja* (see *ĀpDh* 2.21.7), ahead of the *vānaprastha*, pointing to the latter two being variants of the former two. Thus, I think, the original formulation of the *āśrama* system found in the Dharmasūtras can be seen as an elaboration of the actual demography within the ancient *pāṣaṇḍa* groups as described by Aśoka, groups that according to him included the Brāhmaṇas. The expansion of Aśoka's two into four can be readily explained by the centrality that "four" played in Brahmanical thought: four Vedas, four *varṇas*, and so on. There is one element in the *āśrama* elaboration, however, that is crucial and significant.

Aśoka's discussion of *pāṣaṇḍa* assumes and, indeed, celebrates religious pluralism, or at least the pluralism of *pāṣaṇḍa* communities. They are many and on an equal footing, in spite of Aśoka's partiality to the Buddhist *saṅgha* (note that even in enumerating the *pāṣaṇḍas* in PE 7 he simply uses *saṅgha* for the Buddhists, while using other terms of identification, such as *ājīvaka* and *nirgrantha*, for other *pāṣaṇḍas*). The *āśrama* system, on the other hand, eliminates this pluralism, making Vedic initiation followed by Vedic studentship obligatory on all members of the three upper *varṇas* (Brahmin, Kṣatriya, and Vaiśya) and making the four *āśramas* the religious modes of life open to members of these three *varṇas*. Thus, the Śūdras and other lower classes of society are excluded from religious modes of life and relegated to the margins of society and religion. Brahmanical hegemony is thus imposed on the whole of society. Brahmins are not simply one *pāṣaṇḍa* among many. The system of *āśramas* makes both Brahmins and the other two upper classes part of a single system of religious living; it comprehends all the upper echelons of society. The term *pāṣaṇḍa* is given, *pari passu*, a pejorative meaning, referring to the "other," the excluded ascetic orders, who are equated with Śūdras by Manu.

A final note on the use of *gṛhastha* in the Dharmasūtras. As David Brick has noted in Ch. 8 of this volume, the term in used in the four extant Dharmasūtras *only* within the context of the *āśramas*. The term is not used in the sections on marriage and household life in Āpastamba and Baudhāyana. In Gautama, it is used at the beginning of the section on the householder, but this section comes immediately after the section on the *āśramas* and continues that discussion, because the householder was omitted within the discussion of the *āśramas*.

The larger question that we need to answer is whether *gṛhastha* in Aśoka and in early usage referred to *all* married males who were heads of households or only to special householders who lived a religious live within a *pāṣaṇḍa*. We have seen that the term *gṛhastha* in Aśoka was reserved for special individuals dedicated to the religious life but without actually going forth into the strictly ascetic mode of life. In this the *gṛhastha* is similar to or coincides with the Buddhist *upāsaka*. Thus we can assume that most ordinary people living in Aśoka's realm were householders without being technically *gṛhasthas*. It is this religious nature of the category that made it possible for it to be assumed into the *āśrama* system, which also envisages four *religious* modes of life. The Vedic *gṛhápati* has become the Dharmaśāstric *gṛhastha*.

The final issue I want to consider is what, if any, influence the new conception of *gṛhastha* as a member of a religious group parallel to *pravrajita* and its incorporation into the new institution of the four *āśramas* had on the creation of the new genre of literature called Dharmaśāstra. The last few centuries of the Common Era, as I will discuss below, were not kind to Brahmins; they were a beleaguered group. Through various strategies, especially the production of literature, they attempted to reverse their fortunes, and in this they were largely successful. The Dharmaśāstras constituted a primary literary vehicle in achieving this goal.

Let me here propose a hypothesis. The impetus for writing a *śāstra* on the dharma of a *gṛhastha*—which is what the Dharmaśāstras are, with some marginal comments on the *pravrajitas*—came, I think, from the hegemonizing effort by Brahmin intellectuals to encompass all of society within its fold through the *āśrama* system, which was the reason for the creation of the *āśrama* system in the first place. This dharma is not the diverse and contentious doctrines espoused by the various *pāṣaṇḍas* or the bland and wishy-washy dharma of Aśoka. It is the desire to distinguish the true, single, authentic dharma from these other diverse voices that made all the Dharmaśāstras—uniquely in the history of Brahmanical literature—begin with the epistemology of dharma. The epistemic source of this singular and true dharma is the Veda and/or the authoritative Brahmanical communities; note the conception of the practices (*ācāra*) of *śiṣṭas* (Brahmanical elite) and the *āryāvarta* (core Brahmanical geography).[2] The *āśrama* system enabled the Brahmins to introduce a new theological evaluation of the *gṛhastha* as a religious professional and this-worldly ascetic, and at the same time to elevate his status vis-à-vis the *pravrajita*. Note the repeated statements in the early Dharmasūtras that the *gṛhastha* is the only legitimate mode of life, the best mode of life, and the person on whom all others depend:

> *aikāśramyaṃ tv ācāryāḥ pratyakṣavidhānād gārhasthyasya* |
>
> There is, however, only a single *āśrama*, the Teachers maintain, because the *gṛhastha's* state alone is prescribed in express Vedic texts. (*GDh* 3.36)
>
> *aikāśramyaṃ tv ācāryā aprajanatvād itareṣām* |
>
> There is, however, only a single *āśrama*, the Teachers maintain, because no offspring is produced in the others. (*BDh* 2.11.27)

The connection of *gṛhastha* to ascetic holiness paralleling the *pravrajita* is found in the ways in which Dharmaśāstras speak of the *gṛhastha* as being almost the same as a *pravrajita*. One obvious area is celibacy, a hallmark of renunciatory asceticism. But by following the strict guidelines for having sex with one's wife, a *gṛhastha* can become a true celibate. Here is Yājñavalkya (*YDh* 1.78):[3] "A woman's season consists of sixteen nights. During that period he should lie with her on even nights; thus he remains a true celibate." Food is another area. He is asked to diminish his storage of food: "Let him be a man who stores grain sufficient to fill a granary or sufficient to fill a jar, a man

2. For an extensive discussion of the epistemology of dharma, see Olivelle 2017.

3. Although this is a text from the fourth or fifth century CE, I think it reflects a common view of the holiness of a *gṛhastha* in all Dharmaśāstras.

who has grain sufficient for three days, or a man who keeps nothing for the next day; or else, he may live by gleaning. Of these, each succeeding one is superior to each preceding" (*YDh* 1.127). With regard to becoming a vegetarian, Yājñavalkya (*YDh* 1.180) says: "By refraining from meat, a Brahmin obtains all his wishes, as well as the fruit of a horse sacrifice, and while still living at home he becomes a sage." And a *gṛhastha* can indeed aspire to *mokṣa* or liberation just as an ascetic: "Even a *gṛhastha* is liberated when he acquires wealth by lawful means, is firmly established in the knowledge of the truth, loves guests, performs ancestral offerings, and speaks the truth" (*YDh* 3.206).

So, we can draw a line from Aśoka's classification of *pāṣaṇḍas* to the creation of the hegemonic *āśrama* system, and further to the creation of the genre of literature devoted to dharma of the ways of life subsumed under the *āśramas* where the central position is occupied by the *gṛhastha*, the new *homo religiosus*. The Vedic *gṛhapati* recedes to the background and gradually vanishes from the scene.

The Origins of Dharmaśāstra

The investigation into the origins of Dharmaśāstra flows naturally from our study of the *āśrama* system. The central question is: Why is there Dharmaśāstra, rather than no Dharmaśāstra? This genre was not simply a continuation of the ritual texts, as earlier generation of scholars thought,[4] but constitutes a "conceptual discontinuity" with them. Who created the genre of Dharmaśāstra? What social, political, and religious factors were responsible for its emergence? These are questions that have rarely been seriously addressed in any of the extant "histories" of Dharmaśāstra, questions that need to be answered at least hypothetically if we are to understand the early history of this śāstric literature.

These are questions that I have attempted—inadequately, I now realize—to answer in my previous works.[5] I took as my starting point the theological centrality that the term *dharma* had attained by the third century BCE, especially

4. See Kane 1962–75, I: 19–20: "It seems that originally many, though not all, of the *dharmasūtras* formed part of the Kalpasūtras and were studied in distinct *sūtracaraṇas*. . . . The Dharmasūtras belonging to all sūtracaraṇas have not come down to us." Lingat (1973: 10–12), likewise, takes the Dharmasūtras to be compositions within the Vedic schools producing the Kalpasūtras: "Each school of the Veda should have, in addition to its *saṃhitā* and its *brāhmaṇa*, its threefold series (at least in theory) of the *kalpa-sūtra: śrauta, gṛhya*, and *dharma*."

5. See Olivelle 2006b, 2009b, and especially 2010. Some of the ideas presented here are also found in Olivelle 2018.

with its adoption by Aśoka in developing an imperial ideology. I wrote (Olivelle 2010: 31–32):

The hypothesis I want to propose is that once dharma had become a central concept in the religious discourse of Buddhism and once it had penetrated the general vocabulary of ethics especially through its adoption by the Maurya emperors, certainly by Aśoka and possibly also by his predecessors, in developing an imperial theology, Brahmanical theologians had little choice but to define their own religion, ethics, and way of life in term of dharma. Indeed, the scrutiny of the early meaning of dharma within its Dharmaśāstric use suggests that it was not the Veda but the "community standards" prevalent in different regions and communities that were taken to constitute dharma. The early texts on dharma speak of *deśadharma, jātidharma, kuladharma*—the dharma of regions, castes, and families/lineages. Clearly, these texts regard dharma as multiple and varied; each of these kinds of dharma can hardly be expected to be based on the Veda.

With the new insights into the history of *gṛhastha* and the *āśrama* system that we now possess, however, I think we can come up with more adequate answers to these central questions with regard to the origin of Dharmaśāstra.

There is also another historical reality during and after the Maurya empire that sets the social and economic background to the issues that we are about to consider. And that is the plight of the Brahmanical communities during this period, to which I have already made reference. In his recent book *How the Brahmins Won*, Johannes Bronkhorst (2016) has put into sharp focus both their plight and the multiple creative ways the Brahmin intellectuals responded to the situation they found themselves in. The gist of his argument is that Brahmins were faced with what he calls the "catastrophe" following the invasion of the northwestern regions of the subcontinent (the greater Gandhāra) by Alexander when Brahmins were slaughtered in large numbers and their position in emergent social and political structures was deeply undermined. There was a large-scale migration of Brahmins from that region to the north-central regions of India. The book is devoted to analyzing how the Brahmins ultimately won, especially through the judicious employment of literature ranging from grammar and politics to law and epics. Many texts that were viewed as pre-Mauryan, such as the Gṛhyasūtras, are shown to have been composed much later and as part of this Brahmanical response. And Bronkhorst (2016: 108) gives greater detail and texture to this general observation:

> The data considered in Part I suggest that during this period [the last few centuries BCE] Brahmanism revised and reinterpreted some of its traditions, furthermore introducing new elements that found expression

> in forms of literature that had not hitherto existed. Grammar had existed before Alexander, and received a new impetus from Patañjali's *Mahābhāṣya* after the collapse of the Maurya empire. . . . Our limited evidence allows us to surmise that the literature on domestic ritual and on Dharma, as well as epic literature, may have come into existence rather late, perhaps under the Mauryas or even later.

This Brahmanical response both in literature and in the reconceptualization of the Brahmanical mode of life created what we term "Brahmanism." It is this reconceptualization that we note especially within the theologies of *āśrama* and of *gṛhastha* propounded in the Dharmaśāstras. Even if one does not accept every argument of Bronkhorst, the major point to note for our own study in his analysis is that a socio-political context was created for the emergence of new theologies and new genres of literature. That, I think, is beyond doubt. These theologies and literatures placed the Brahmin at the very center of society and polity as the group that was indispensible to both king and subjects. During this period Brahmin intellectuals reinvented Brahmanism.

At some point during this period, and as part of that reinvention, probably in the third century BCE or a bit earlier, new theological developments appear to have taken place within the Brahmanical intellectual classes. One such development, as we have seen, was the *āśrama* system. This theological development alone, however, could not have been the catalyst for the creation of the new Dharmaśāstra genre of literature, at least in the form that we now have it. The reason is twofold. First, we have already seen that some early writers, such as Gautama and Baudhāyana, rejected the *āśrama* system as propounded by its advocates, proposing instead the "single-*āśrama*" (*aikāśramya*) theory: namely, there is only one *āśrama*, that of the *gṛhastha*.

> *aikāśramyaṃ tv ācāryāḥ pratyakṣavidhānād gārhastyasya* ||
>
> There is, however, a single *āśrama*, the Teachers say, because the state of *gṛhastha* is prescribed in express Vedic texts. (*GDh* 3.36)
>
> *aikāśramyaṃ tv ācāryā aprajanatvād itareṣām* ||
>
> There is, however, a single āśrama, the Teachers say, because no offspring is produced in the others. (*BDh* 2.11.27)[6]

6. Gautama's reason for upholding the *aikāśramya* theory is based on the fact that the *āśrama* of the *gṛhastha* is prescribed in explicit or visible Vedic texts, the kind of text referred to in Mīmāṃsā as *pratyakṣaśruti*. They are Vedic texts that we actually have and can examine are distinguished from the other category *anumitaśruti*, or Vedic texts whose existence has to be inferred on the basis of texts of recollection (*smṛti*), which are supposed to be based on the

According to this reasoning, the only legitimate mode of life for a young adult after he has completed his Vedic studentship is that of a *gṛhastha*. The young adult, after he returns home from his teacher's house, must get married, establish a household, and raise a family. Further, given that *āśramas* during this period are viewed as permanent modes of life—one cannot go from one *āśrama* to another—the choice of the *gṛhastha* life would preclude a person from becoming a *pravrajita*.

The second reason why the *āśrama* system could not have been the sole catalyst for the genesis of Dharmaśāstra is that none of the early dharma texts incorporates the system into the structure of their compositions. The sections on the *āśramas* even in texts such as Āpastamba's, who accepts the fourfold *āśrama* theory, give the appearance of being parenthetical or appendices to the main body of the works. It is the *gṛhastha*, now modeled after the Vedic householder and following a ritual cycle centered on the "five great sacrifices" (*pañcamahāyajña*), rules of purity and diet, and Vedic recitation, who occupies center stage.[7] Yet, the writers never use the old Vedic term *gṛhápati* but the novel *gṛhastha*, a term that, as we have seen, had no prehistory in the Vedic literature. So, the Dharmaśāstric writers, while rejecting or marginalizing the theology of four *āśramas*, nevertheless operated within the newly emerging conceptual world and its vocabulary. Further, the Dharmaśāstric *gṛhastha* is not simply a ritualist in the mold of the Vedic *gṛhapati*; the rules given in these texts promote virtuous and holy living often modeled after the celibate ascetic life. These texts present the dharma, in the sense of proper behavior called *ācāra*, to be followed by a *gṛhastha*. Below I will further explore these competing theological innovations to lay the groundwork for assessing the possible motives for creating this genre of literature.

Finally, even the opponents of the *āśrama* system, nevertheless, present the *gṛhastha* as the one and only legitimate *āśrama*, thus co-opting the term and its implied theology. A telling piece of evidence lies hidden at the very beginning of the fourth chapter of Gautama's Dharmasūtra, a chapter that follows

---

Veda. For theological discussions surround these two categories of Vedic texts, see Olivelle 2017: 31–33, 88–139. Baudhāyana's defense of the *aikāśramya* theory is based on the doctrine of the three debts with which a person is born: the debt to seers to be paid by the study of the Vedas, the debt to gods to be paid by offering sacrifices, and the debt to ancestors to be paid by making ancestral offerings. The fact that one marries and can legitimately produce offspring, especially sons, only in the *āśrama* of the *gṛhastha* makes it impossible for those in other *āśramas* to pay the debts to the gods (a wife is required to perform Vedic sacrifices) and to the ancestors (sons are required to continue the line and to make future ancestral offerings). See Olivelle 1993: 46–53.

7. See Patañjali's comment (on Pāṇini 4.1.33), cited above.

immediately after the one on the four *āśramas*. That chapter ended with the pronouncement of the "single *āśrama*" theory that we already saw. Gautama begins the next chapter with a statement about the *gṛhastha*:

> *gṛhasthaḥ sadṛśīṃ bhāryāṃ vindeta, ananyapūrvāṃ yavīyasīm ||*
>
> A *gṛhastha* should marry a wife who is similar to him [i.e., belongs to the same *varṇa*], who has not been with another man before, and who is younger than he. (*GDh* 4.1)

This is a curious statement. It is generally assumed that a person becomes a *gṛhastha* by getting married, but here a *gṛhastha* is told to get married. Even though it may well be that Gautama uses the term as a generic label, I think this statement reveals the original meaning of *gṛhastha* as a person who has decided to remain at home rather than go forth as an ascetic, while his married status is secondary at best.

Let me, then, present my hypothesis with regard to the reasons and motives behind the creation of the Dharmaśāstra genre of literature. I think there arose around the third or fourth century BCE within what Aśoka called the *brāhmaṇa pāṣaṇḍa* institution two kinds of theological sociologies based on a new definition of dharma. In their own way, they both sought to integrate the *pāṣaṇḍa* religious life and ideology, the *pāṣaṇḍa* dharma, into the older Vedic ritualism, modifying the latter drastically in the process. One was the theology of the four *āśramas*, which, as we have seen, presented a variety of lifestyles, especially the *gṛhastha* and the *pravrajita*, as alternative and equally legitimate religious paths for Brahmins, and possibly also for other classes of society. We should note that the notion of "twice-born" individuals would not come into being until a couple of centuries later (Olivelle 2012b). The proponents of the *āśrama* theology were probably thinkers who took the ascetic ideology and mode of life seriously and were probably partial to the new ideal of *mokṣa* or liberation.

Parallel to this, a new theology appears to have been constructed asserting the centrality of the *gṛhastha* and his ritual and domestic life, as well as the obligation to produce offspring, learn the Veda, and perform ancestral and divine rituals, an obligation already enshrined in the famous theology of the three debts. This *gṛhastha* theology, represented in the *aikāśramya*, or single-*āśrama*, doctrine, probably represented the mainstream of Brahmanical tradition.[8]

---

8. At this point, I am not confident enough to assert that this theology came from the *gṛhastha* members of the Brahmanical *pāṣaṇḍa*, or to speculate whether there were theological disputes between the *gṛhastha* and *pravrajita* demographics within it.

Yet this new theology was markedly different from the Vedic theology centered around Vedic rituals and represented, as Jamison (Ch. 1, this volume) puts it, "a conceptual discontinuity." It had a lot in common with the āśramic theology, and the two coexisted in some fashion—sometimes in conflict and sometimes in harmony, but always in tension—throughout Dharmaśāstric history. Its debt to the āśramic theology and śramaṇic vocabulary is evident not just in the adoption of the term *gṛhastha* for its central *homo religiosus*, but also in presenting the household life as an *āśrama*, indeed, as the only legitimate *āśrama* in the view of Gautama and Baudhāyana. I think it is the dialogue and disputes between these two Brahmanical theologies (and perhaps others that we cannot readily identify) that are captured in the texts of the Dharmaśāstric tradition, disputes that continue well into the medieval period. We see them articulated in the strong defense of the householder as the highest form of religious life. As Vasiṣṭha (*VaDh* 8.14–16) says:[9]

gṛhastha eva yajate gṛhasthas tapyate tapaḥ |
caturṇām āśramāṇāṃ tu gṛhasthas tu viśiṣyate ||
yathā nadīnadāḥ sarve samudre yānti saṃsthitim |
evam āśramiṇaḥ sarve gṛhasthe yānti saṃsthitim ||
yathā mātaram āśritya sarve jīvanti jantavaḥ |
evaṃ gṛhastham āśritya sarve jīvanti bhikṣukāḥ ||

A *gṛhastha* alone offers sacrifices, a *gṛhastha* performs austerities. Of all the four *āśramas*, the *gṛhastha* is the best.
As all rivers and rivulets ultimately end up in the ocean, so people of all the *āśramas* ultimately end up in the *gṛhastha*.
As all living beings live dependent on the mother, so all mendicants live dependent on the *gṛhastha*.[10]

On the other hand, with the emergence of the ideal of liberation (*mokṣa*) shared by Brahmanism and ascetical theologies such as Buddhism, the wandering mendicant (variously called *pravrajita, parivrājaka, śramaṇa, yati, muni,*

---

9. For a similar statement, see *MDh* 6.87–90.

10. The exact meaning and reference of the last two verses are not altogether clear. I think the first of the two with its reference to "ending up" (*yānti saṃstitim*) perhaps refers to the old doctrine of the five fires. According to this, humans after death at cremation rise up as smoke and finally find their way down to earth in the form of rains, and through food become semen of a man to complete the cycle of birth (see *Bṛhadāraṇyaka Upaniṣad* 6.2.9–13). So, in this cycle of births and deaths everyone in the other *āśramas* end up in the *gṛhastha*. The second verse is clearer; the reference is to the fact that all mendicants must receive their sustenance from the householders.

and *bhikṣu*) came to be seen as the figure most closely associated with that ideal. This is clearly revealed in the vocabulary of Manu, who calls it *mokṣāśrama*, the *āśrama* leading to liberation.[11]

It was this *gṛhastha* theology, then, that, in all likelihood, provided the impetus to the creation of the Dharmaśāstric genre of literature. This explains both the centrality given to the *gṛhastha*[12] and the appearance, often somewhat marginally, of the *āśrama* system within this literature—until the creation of the classical formulation of the system by Manu that transformed it into a life-cycle ritual system.

Yet, I think that the creation of this genre was not simply due to the interactions between these two Brahmanical theologies. Another major factor was what we may call "interreligious" debates on the concept of dharma between Brahmanical theologians and those representing the ascetic or *śramaṇa* ideologies, especially Buddhism, that I have referred to in my earlier writings on the subject.[13] The concept of dharma was very much a site of contention and debate. What is dharma? And how and where do you find it? In other words, the epistemology of dharma (*dharmaparmāṇa*) was a central theological issue, an issue that is addressed at the very opening of every Dharmaśāstra. Buddhist theologians had a clear position: *buddhavacana* (the words of the Buddha) is the sole epistemic source of dharma. Either proximately or ultimately all valid pronouncement on dharma must go back to the *ipsissima verba*, the very words, of the Buddha. This position is encapsulated in the opening words of every Buddhist scriptural statement: *evaṃ mayā śrutam* (Pāli: *evam me sutam*), "Thus have I heard." It thus comes as no surprise that all the early Dharmasūtras open with a discussion on the epistemology of dharma (Olivelle 2017). This feature of the texts on dharma stands in sharp contrast to other similar Brahmanical texts such as the Śrauta- and Gṛhyasūtras, which saw no need to state where they get their knowledge from, taking the epistemological issues as self-evident and non-controversial. In a much more direct manner than the Gṛhyasūtras, the texts on dharma aimed at providing guidance on how to live a holy life as a *gṛhastha*, and more broadly as a Vedic student, forest hermit, and wandering

11. For further details on Manu's use of the term *mokṣa* for renunciation, see Olivelle 2005: 243. Manu uses the term to refer to an ascetic also in *MDh* 6.35–37. Bronkhorst's (2016: 431–435) attempt to discount this interpretation is misplaced, given that he does not even consider the verses that gave rise to my interpretation (*MDh* 1.114, as well as 6.35–37).

12. See the reference to *gṛhasthadharma* in Aśvaghoṣa's *Buddhacarita*.

13. See above p. 113 and note 2, and Olivelle 2006b, 2009b, 2010.

mendicant, as well as kings and women. The dharma of Dharmaśāstras was all-encompassing and hegemonic.

We should also add to this mix the dire situation Brahmins found themselves during this period, as I have already noted. This was the period when "Brahmanism" was being reinvented to suit the new socio-political situation especially in northern India.

It is, then, from within this theological ferment that the genre of Dharmaśāstra was born. There is yet another significant element that, even if it may not have been a causal factor, shaped the structure and tenor of these texts. And that is the system of *varṇas*. It is clear that the *varṇa* system was not an objective and disinterested classification of ancient Indian society. It was from the start an ideologically driven enterprise designed to place the Brahmin at the top of a pyramidal social hierarchy, supporting the claim to power of the Kṣatriya class, and in a special way reducing the Śūdras and other lower classes to a marginal and oppressed status. This is clearly indicated in the foundational document on the *varṇas*, the *Puruṣasūkta* (*RV* 10.90), in which the vertical structure of the human body provides the basis for the hierarchical structure of the *varṇa* system. The Śūdra, born from the feet, is placed at the bottom. So, to uphold and to promote the *varṇa* system is at the same time to uphold the supremacy of the Brahmin class and its exceptional status.

This, I think, was a crucial element of the Dharmaśāstric project. One may question the need for Brahmanical theologians to aggressively assert the *varṇa* system; many scholars, after all, take the system to be not just old but also reflecting the social reality of the ancient Indian society. I think this is a mistake, because all the evidence presented for this claim comes from Brahmanical sources, which generally sought to shape rather than simply to reflect social reality. Aśokan inscriptions constitute one of the few independent sources, and they are completely silent on the *varṇas*; the very term is absent in them and so are terms for three of the four *varṇas*: Kṣatriya, Vaiśya, and Śūdra. Aśoka does mention the *brāhmaṇa* but, as we have seen in Chapters 2 and 3, not as a *varṇa* but as a religious group, first as a counterpart to the *śramaṇa* and second as one among the many *pāṣaṇḍas*. Further, the Aśokan reforms greatly undermined Brahmanical exceptionalism. The special relation between king and Brahmin advocated in the Vedic texts was eliminated. The need to assert and reassert the centrality of the *varṇa* system with the Brahmin at its apex was never more urgent. And the construction of the new theory of *dvija*, the "twice-born," toward the end of the second century BCE (Olivelle 2012b) further solidified Brahmanical hegemony by providing a structure within which Brahmins, Kṣatriyas, and Vaiśyas were constituted as a single "twice-born" group, and opposed to all the lower segments of society. The dharma of the Dharmaśāstras thus could be addressed to this newly formed constituency.

The dharma articulated in the Dharmaśāstras was thus not simply a narrowly religious one centered on the holy life of a *gṛhastha* or of those belonging to the four *āśramas*; it was also a socio-political blueprint for the proper management of society by the king. Even the early Dharmasūtras contain sections on family, civil and criminal law, and on governance by the king, however rudimentary these appear in comparison to the detailed treatments of these topics by later authors such as Manu and Yājñavalkya. In the socio-political ethic of the Dharmaśāstra, the *varṇa* system and Brahmanical exceptionalism are fundamental elements.

Such, I think, was the religious, social, and ideological background for the creation of the genre of literature known as Dharmaśāstra. But what was the actual institutional framework of inquiry and education that produced the early texts on dharma? We can look at the parallel literature, the ritual sūtras, for a model. These were produced within specific "schools" or *caraṇas* belonging to the various Vedic branches (*śākhā*). It is reasonable to assume that Dharmasūtras also were produced within the same kinds of educational settings. Looking at the extant works, we have two that are attached to precisely such *caraṇas* and are ascribed to their respective founders: the Dharmaśūtras of Baudhāyana and Āpastamba. The other two, those of Gautama and Vasiṣṭha, however, are independent of any *caraṇa*. It is fair to assume that there were educational and intellectual homes other than the *caraṇas* to engage in scholarly activities, as demonstrated by the composition of some Upaniṣads, the grammatical treatises, and the literary activities that gave rise to the Sanskrit epics.

In this context, I think we should extend Jamison's conclusion of "a conceptual discontinuity" from the notion of *gṛhastha* as such to the broader literary genre of Dharmaśāstra in which the *gṛhastha* occupies center stage. In other words, I think the theologians who composed these texts were operating with a different Weltanschauung than their ritual counterparts, even as they shared the Vedic ritual and mythological worlds. This Weltanschauung was very much molded by ascetic ideologies, values, and vocabularies, as we see most prominently in the term *gṛhastha* itself and in the value these texts place on sexual abstinence, fasting, and other ascetic practices. We need not assume that these new intellectuals shared a uniform theology; but they did share a broad vision of what it was to be a good and religious Brahmin.

The term and ideology associated with *gṛhastha* had an impact on literature beyond the Dharmaśāstra, literature on which those texts had an influence. Foremost among such authors is Aśvaghoṣa, the Buddhist monk who was probably an educated Brahmin prior to his conversion, who wrote two of the earliest epic poems (*kāvya*) in Sanskrit literature.[14] In his two epic poems, Aśvaghoṣa uses the term *gṛhastha* six times, often within the implicit context of the *āśrama* system and taking to renunciation in old age.[15] In *Saundarananda* (13.18–19) he explicitly contrasts the life of an ascetic or mendicant who has gone forth to that of a *gṛhastha*. Both the mendicant (*bhikṣu*) and the *gṛhastha* face different problems in sticking to the correct path of proper conduct (*ācāra, śīla*), but when this is lacking "there is neither the state of going forth (*pravrajyā*) nor the state of a *gṛhastha* (*gṛhasthatā*)." Aśvaghoṣa speaks of the *gṛhasthadharma* and *gṛhasthaveśa* (the attire of a *gṛhastha*), which the future Buddha discarded when he assumed the dress of an ascetic (*Buddhacarita* 5.33; 8.10).

After offering my hypothesis, let me finally confess that it will certainly have to be revisited and revised as we gather further data about this crucial but dark period of Indian history. I think we have only scratched the surface, and we will have to integrate the emergence of the Sanskrit epics also into this larger narrative.

---

14. For his knowledge of and interaction with Brahmanism, see Olivelle 2008; Hiltebeitel 2006.

15. *Saundarananda* 5.37; 13.18–19; *Buddhacarita* 5.33; 8.10; 9.19; 9.48.

8

The Householder in Early Dharmaśāstra Literature

David Brick

THIS CHAPTER PROVIDES a historical and philological analysis of the Brahmanical householder as he is portrayed in the early Dharmaśāstra literature, by which term I mean in particular the four early Dharmasūtras of Āpastamba, Gautama, Baudhāyana, and Vasiṣṭha and the later Smṛtis or Dharmaśāstras of Manu, Yājñavalkya, Nārada, and Viṣṇu. Specifically, this chapter will focus on the precise meanings, connotations, and usages of the various terms employed by these texts to denote a householder or married man. Although the absolute and relative dating of the early Dharmaśāstra works has long been controversial, this chapter assumes the relative and absolute dates assigned to them by Patrick Olivelle (2010), whose various arguments put forth in this regard are now generally accepted by scholars of classical Indian law. In addition to the early Dharmaśāstra literature itself, this chapter will also examine the use of terms for householder in one non-Dharmaśāstra text that can be confidently dated to the second century BCE, namely, the *Mahābhāṣya* of Patañjali, a famous early commentary on Pāṇini's *Aṣṭādhyāyī*. My primary reason for including an analysis of the *Mahābhāṣya* in this chapter is that it is, in all likelihood, roughly contemporaneous with the *Gautama* and *Baudhāyana Dharmasūtras* and appears to share broadly the same conservative Brahmanical worldview as these texts. An examination of the *Mahābhāṣya*, therefore, greatly helps to illuminate early Dharmaśāstra materials. The philological analysis of texts in this chapter will proceed in roughly chronological order.

Āpastamba Dharmasūtra

The *Āpastamba Dharmasūtra*, probably the very earliest surviving Dharmaśāstra text, differs markedly from even the somewhat later, but still early Dharmasūtras of Gautama, Baudhāyana, and Vasiṣṭha in the terminology that it uses to refer to a married man or householder. For whereas the three later Dharmasūtras almost exclusively use the classical Brahmanical term *gṛhastha* to denote a householder, Āpastamba uses the word only once (2.9.13) in his entire treatise and even then only in an independent verse that he is merely quoting. Instead, Āpastamba seemingly prefers to use the words *gṛhamedhin* and *kuṭumbin* to denote a Brahmanical householder, using each of these terms three times in his work.[1]

All three occurrences of the term *gṛhamedhin* within Āpastamba are in the dual, genitive (*gṛhamedhinoḥ*), where it undoubtedly denotes in every case a pious Brahmanical householder and his lawfully wedded wife. The reason for Āpastamba's apparent preference for the grammatical dual over the singular when referring to the Brahmanical householder is likely his fairly faithful adherence to the old Vedic view of the institution of marriage, according to which a husband and wife are principally conceived of as ritual partners and, therefore, as a single, inextricably linked, corporate household unit.[2] As Jamison (2006: 192–97) has shown, this feature of Āpastamba sets his work noticeably apart from all later works within the Dharmaśāstra tradition, which—in contrast to Āpastamba—tend to view wives as independent agents in need of male supervision.

The following line (2.1.1) constitutes the first place in Āpastamba's text where he uses the term *gṛhamedhin*:

> *pāṇigrahaṇād adhi gṛhamedhinor vratam* |
>
> Following marriage come the vows of a *gṛhamedhin* pair.

Significantly, this line immediately follows Āpastamba's discussion of the *snātaka* or "bath-graduate," that is, a twice-born man who has taken the ritual bath formally marking the successful completion of his Vedic studentship (1.30.6–32.29). Furthermore, it occurs at the very beginning of Āpastamba's treatment

1. For uses of *gṛhamedhin*, see *ĀpDh* 2.1.1, 2.1.15, 2.3.12. For uses of *kuṭumbin*, see *ĀpDh* 2.6.5, 2.7.1, 2.29.3.

2. On this, see Jamison 1996: 30–31, 253–56.

of a married householder's special duties. These, as described by Āpastamba, include the performance of various set rituals (2.1.10–15, etc.), the observance of assorted restrictions governing the consumption of food (2.1.2–7, etc.), and the proper engagement in and abstention from sexual intercourse (2.1.16–22, etc.). Therefore, if marriage is taken to be a defining characteristic of the twice-born householder, the line quoted above effectively constitutes Āpastamba's introduction to the topic. And this, in turn, suggests that *gṛhamedhin* is his preferred term of reference for a married householder or more precisely a pious, twice-born householder, who is the focus of much of his work.

Shortly after the previously quoted line, Āpastamba (2.1.15) repeats the phrase *gṛhamedhinor vratam* in a passage (2.1.15), where he enjoins a twice-born householder and his wife to keep their waterpots always filled with water (*nityam udadhānāny adbhir ariktāni syuḥ*) and, immediately thereafter, describes this practice as a "vow of a *gṛhamedhin* pair" (*gṛhamedhinor vratam*). The final passage where Āpastamba uses the term *gṛhamedhin* occurs a little bit later in the text. It (2.3.12) reads as follows:

> *gṛhamedhinor yad aśanīyasya homā balayaś ca svargapuṣṭisaṃyuktāḥ* |
>
> Oblations and *bali* offerings made with food that belongs to a *gṛhamedhin* pair lead to heaven and prosperity.

This passage nicely illustrates that, according to Āpastamba at least, a *gṛhamedhin* was expected not only to possess his own store of food, but also to use it in an assortment of ritual offerings together with his wife. Naturally, this feature of the *gṛhamedhin* marks him as a special sort of married man, distinguished from others by his commitment to a regimen of rituals, understood to bring about prosperity in this world and the next. However, it does not appear to distinguish a *gṛhamedhin* from a *gṛhastha*, the standard term for a pious Brahmanical householder in the later literature.

Of course, from an etymological point of view, it is entirely unsurprising that a *gṛhamedhin* would be intimately involved in ritual, for the term undoubtedly denotes a person connected with *gṛhamedha*, a compound clearly comprised of the common Sanskrit nouns *gṛha* ("house, home") and *medha* ("sacrifice"). Thus, a *gṛhamedhin* would seem to be by definition a man engaged in domestic ritual. Interestingly, however, when Āpastamba uses the term *gṛhamedha*, as he does three times in his work (1.2.7, 1.4.29, 2.25.7), he seemingly intends it to denote not any ritual or sacrifice in particular, but rather something notably broader, in my opinion, probably the way of life of a *gṛhamedhin* or married, twice-born man. In other words, for Āpastamba, *gṛhamedha* appears to be roughly synonymous with the abstract noun *gārhasthya* ("the state of being a *gṛhastha*").

In two of the three passages where Āpastamba uses the term *gṛhamedha*, the precise meaning intended is slightly ambiguous. In the first of these, Āpastamba (1.2.5) discusses the case of a man whose known ancestors failed to be initiated into Vedic studentship despite belonging to a twice-born social class. According to Āpastamba (1.2.6), such a man may spend more than ten years performing a series of expiatory observances, if he so wishes. Completion of such lengthy expiatory rites then entitles him to be taught *gṛhamedha* (*ĀpDh* 1.2.7: *atha gṛhamedhopadeśanam*), but not the Veda (*ĀpDh* 1.2.8: *nādhyāpanam*). From this we learn the interesting detail that *gṛhamedha* can be carried out, at least in some modified form, even without knowledge of the Veda. It is unclear, however, whether *gṛhamedha* in this passage refers specifically to domestic rituals or more generally to the set of rules governing a pious, twice-born man and his lawfully wedded wife. And, indeed, Āpastamba's commentator, Haradatta, explicitly mentions both possibilities.[3]

A second similarly ambiguous passage in Āpastamba involves the ritual duties of a king. It reads:

> *agnipūjā ca nityā yathā gṛhamedhe* |
>
> And the worship of sacred fires should be done daily, as in *gṛhamedha*. (2.25.7)

Although domestic ritual is perhaps a more natural interpretation of the term *gṛhamedha* in this passage, it is also entirely consistent with the contents of the passage and, therefore, plausible to interpret the term as denoting more generally the way of life of a pious, twice-born householder and his wife.

The final passage in which Āpastamba uses the compound *gṛhamedha* helps to clarify the term's precise meaning in his text. This passage (1.4.22–28) concerns a student who looks after his teacher in exemplary fashion. Āpastamba (1.4.29) describes the rewards that accrue to such a devoted student as follows:

> *sa ya evaṃ praṇihitātmā brahmacāry atraivāsya sarvāṇi karmāṇi phalavanty avāptāni bhavanti yāny api gṛhamedhe* |

3. Haradatta on *ĀpDh* 1.2.7: *gṛhamedho gṛhyaśāstraṃ gṛhasthadharmo vā* |

> A student who dedicates himself in this manner accomplishes in that very state all rites that bring rewards, even those which are within *gṛhamedha*.

Given that this passage apparently speaks of meritorious rites (*karmāṇi*) that are within *gṛhamedha* or perhaps pertain to *gṛhamedha* (*gṛhamedhe*), it is unlikely that the term here refers directly to domestic ritual itself, unless it refers to the overall system of domestic rituals rather than a single specific ritual. Moreover, Āpastamba here seems to use the locative *gṛhamedhe* in explicit contrast with the earlier phrase *atraiva* ("in that very state"), which is undoubtedly intended to refer to the state of being a student of the Veda. That is, the point of the passage appears to be that through faithful service to his teacher, a student can achieve even the rewards of being a married householder, while still a celibate student. Hence, it seems most natural to interpret *gṛhamedha* here and by extension elsewhere in Āpastamba's work as a term denoting the way of life or general set of rules governing a married twice-born man.[4]

Now, let us turn to the word *kuṭumbin*, which is the only other term besides *gṛhamedhin* that Āpastamba uses to denote a householder more than once in his text. Etymologically, a *kuṭumbin* must denote someone possessed of or somehow connected with a *kuṭumba*, which in Sanskrit most typically means "family," but in Āpastamba's text apparently denotes a house or home instead. Hence, within Āpastamba, the word *kuṭumbin* literally seems to denote a home-owner or perhaps the head of a household. Important evidence in support of this interpretation comes from the only passage (2.7.1–2) in his work, where Āpastamba uses the word *kuṭumba*:

> *sa eṣa prājāpatyaḥ kuṭumbino yajño nityapratataḥ / yo 'tithīnām agniḥ sa āhavanīyo yaḥ kuṭumbe sa gārhapatyo yasmin pacyate so 'nvāhāryapacanaḥ /*
>
> This [= hospitality] is a *kuṭumbin's* sacrifice to Prajāpati, which is constantly offered. The fire inside his guests is the Āhavanīya fire; that

4. Āpastamba's modern translators Bühler and Olivelle both appear to agree with my interpretation of the term *gṛhamedha* in *ĀpDh* 1.4.29. Bühler (1879: 18) renders the relevant phrase (*yāny api gṛhamedhe*) into English as "and also those which must be performed by a householder," while Olivelle (2000: 31) gives a similar translation "as well as those that pertain to a householder." Haradatta, for his part, glosses *gṛhamedha* in the passage as *gṛhyaśāstra* ("the science of domestic ritual"), confirming at least that the term cannot refer to domestic ritual itself.

within the home (*kuṭumba*) is the Gārhapatya fire; and that in which cooking is done is the Southern fire.

Here the word *kuṭumba* clearly cannot mean "family," as it typically does, but must instead mean "house" or "home."[5] Therefore, as I have said, a *kuṭumbin* would seem to be a home-owner or head of a household.

Furthermore, the usage of the term throughout Āpastamba seemingly supports this interpretation, for Āpastamba uses *kuṭumbin*—rather than *gṛhamedhin* or *gṛhastha*—exclusively within the context of the disposal of food and other property. Thus, in the above passage, he uses the word *kuṭumbin* to denote a householder who properly receives and feeds guests, thereby effectively performing a sacrifice to Prajāpati. Moreover, in a slightly earlier passage (2.6.5) similarly concerned with hospitality, Āpastamba defines a guest as a righteous and learned man who approaches a *kuṭumbin*:

> *svadharmayuktaṃ kuṭumbinam abhyāgacchati dharmapuraskāro nānyaprayojanaḥ so 'tithir bhavati* |
>
> When a man devoted to dharma and with no other motive approaches a *kuṭumbin* who is committed to his own dharma, he is a "guest."

Here again a *kuṭumbin* would seem to be the owner of a home or head of a household, who possesses the means and legal right to receive and offer food to guests. The final passage in which Āpastamba uses the word *kuṭumbin* is more secular in nature, but directly addresses the right to dispose of property. Specifically, it lays down the general legal rule that the two *kuṭumbins*—undoubtedly meaning the male head of a household and his lawfully wedded wife—jointly have control over their wealth (*ĀpDh* 2.29.3: *kuṭumbinau dhanasyeśāte*).

Therefore, the evidence from Āpastamba suggests that although there is a general semantic overlap between the terms *kuṭumbin* and *gṛhamedhin*, they also appear to have slightly different meanings or at least different connotations. On the one hand, a *gṛhamedhin* is in essence a performer of domestic sacrifices. As such, he is necessarily a married, twice-born man who lives by a strict set of rules governing especially his dietary, sexual, and ritual activities. A married man who is not of twice-born status or not committed to the appropriate lifestyle cannot properly be called a *gṛhamedhin*. Beyond this, a *gṛhamedhin* may not necessarily have been a home-owner. It is possible,

5. Significantly, Haradatta agrees, glossing *kuṭumbe* in *ĀpDh* 2.7.2 as *gṛhe*.

for instance, that in Āpastamba's mind, the term could have been applied to certain married men still living under their fathers' roofs. A *kuṭumbin*, by contrast, appears simply to be a home-owner of any type. Context may often lead us to understand that the *kuṭumbin* mentioned in a given passage is twice-born or associated with Vedic ritual (as at *ĀpDh* 2.7.1), but this is not inherent to the word *kuṭumbin* itself. Moreover, even the possibility of an unmarried *kuṭumbin* (e.g., a widower) cannot be ruled out and may explain why Āpastamba twice (2.6.5, 2.7.1) uses the word in the singular rather than the dual.

Finally, before moving on from Āpastamba, let us turn to the term *gṛhastha*, which is the standard term for a twice-born householder throughout the later dharma literature. Despite its preponderance in later literature, however, the word occurs only once in Āpastamba's text (2.9.13) in the following floating verse maxim, which he cites in order to establish that a householder must not seriously deprive himself of food:

> *aṣṭau grāsā muner bhakṣaḥ ṣoḍaśāraṇyavāsinaḥ* |
> *dvātriṃśataṃ gṛhasthasyāparimitaṃ brahmacāriṇaḥ* ||
>
> Food for a sage is eight mouthfuls, for a forest-dweller sixteen, for a householder thirty-two, and for a student unlimited.

Here the term *gṛhastha*, like the term *gṛhamedhin* elsewhere, is seemingly used to refer to a special type of austere householder, since his daily food intake is restricted to only thirty-two mouthfuls. More importantly, the term *gṛhastha* is obviously used within the context of the four standard Brahmanical *āśramas* or orders of life, given that this verse explicitly compares him to a sage (*muni*), a forest-dweller (*araṇyavāsin*), and a student (*brahmacārin*) in that order. This fact is striking in Āpastamba, where the so-called *āśrama* system plays only a rather marginal role.

Moreover, Āpastamba (2.21.1) uses the abstract noun *gārhasthya*—derived from *gṛhastha*—once in his text, specifically when listing the four orders of life at the beginning of his discussion of the *āśrama* system.[6] Significantly, Āpastamba makes no explicit mention of the *gṛhastha's* duties within the context of the *āśrama* system itself, but instead lays down only the special rules governing the lifelong student, sage, and forest-dweller. This omission constitutes strong evidence that he understands the *gṛhastha* of this system

6. See *ĀpDh* 2.21.1: *catvāra āśramā gārhasthyam ācāryakulaṃ maunaṃ vānaprasthyam iti* | ("There are four orders of life: living as a householder, staying with one's teacher's family, living as a sage, and dwelling in the forest.")

to be identical with the *gṛhamedhin* and *kuṭumbin*, whose duties he lays down earlier in his work (2.1.1–20.23). Thus, it seems that *gṛhastha* is Āpastamba's preferred term of reference for a householder within the context of the *āśrama* system, but only within that context. And this, in turn, suggests that the term entered the Dharmaśāstra tradition specifically in connection with the notion of the *āśramas*, which all four of the early Dharmasūtras discuss, but interestingly only the youngest, the *Vasiṣṭha Dharmasūtra*, fully incorporates into its organizational structure.[7] For his part, Āpastamba (2.21.1–24.14) seems not to reject the *āśrama* system per se, but rather merely the claim that the celibate *āśramas* are superior to that of the married householder.[8]

As has been explained elsewhere,[9] etymologically the term *gṛhastha* must literally denote someone who stays at home. Hence, there would seem to be either an implicit or an explicit contrast between a *gṛhastha* and other sorts of persons who leave home, such as particularly itinerant ascetics and forest-dwelling hermits. And within the Dharmasūtras, discussions of the *āśrama* system are the only places where such a contrast is of much importance. With this in mind, it is easy to understand why Āpastamba uses the word *gṛhastha* (literally "stay-at-home") only within the context of the four *āśramas* and elsewhere in his text prefers to use terms for a Brahmanical householder that emphasize certain of his more positive qualities, such as the performance of domestic rituals (*gṛhamedhin*) and his role as the head of a household (*kuṭumbin*). Furthermore, *gṛhastha* appears to have been a relatively recent coinage in Āpastamba's time, perhaps one largely associated with heterodox groups,[10] whereas the word *gṛhamedhin* has a long history of use in Vedic literature, going back at least as far the *Maitrāyaṇī Saṃhitā*.[11] Thus, Āpastamba may well have preferred *gṛhamedhin* as a term for householder,

---

7. See *ĀpDh* 2.21.1–24.14; *GDh* 3.1–36; *BDh* 2.11.9–34; and *VaDh* 7.1–10.31. For a discussion of the views of the *āśramas* expressed in these texts, see Olivelle (1993: 73–94). See Olivelle (Ch. 7, present volume) for further analysis of the householder within the *āśrama* system.

8. The clearest textual indication of this is Āpastamba's concluding statement (2.24.14) regarding the *āśramas: syāt tu karmāvayavena tapasā vā kaścit saśarīro 'ntavantaṃ lokaṃ jayati saṃkalpasiddhiś ca syān na tu taj jyaiṣṭhyam āśramāṇām* | ("It might be the case that through a portion of his karma or through austerities, some person might win a finite world, while still embodied, and accomplish things through mere thought. However, this does not establish the superiority of certain *āśramas* over others.")

9. See Jamison (Ch. 1, present volume).

10. See Jamison and Olivelle (Ch. 1 and Ch. 7, present volume).

11. See, e.g., *Maitrāyaṇī Saṃhitā* 1.6.3, where it is explained that people call a *gṛhamedhin* a *purīṣin* ("possessor of soil"), because he establishes his sacred fire after first scattering soil from a molehill. The term *gṛhamedhin* in the sense of "domestic sacrificer" also occurs at

because it connected his innovative treatment of that figure in a new class of Brahmanical texts on dharma with the preceding Vedic tradition. By contrast, the term *gṛhastha* may have been rather off-putting to a contemporaneous Brahmanical audience.

However, although Āpastamba apparently prefers the Vedic term *gṛhamedhin* as a way of denoting a Brahmanical householder, he does break from Vedic tradition by consistently using it in the grammatical dual, for dual forms of *gṛhamedhin* seem to be entirely absent from all earlier Vedic works. Of course, as I have argued above, Āpastamba's habit of using terms for householder in the dual likely stems from his commitment to the traditional Vedic view of a married couple as more of a joint corporate entity than two distinct people. Nevertheless, it is noteworthy that this linguistic usage of Āpastamba is rather innovative, even if its aim is merely to promote an older idea. Moreover, it brings to light a telling difference between the terms *gṛhamedhin* and *gṛhastha*: the former term can be used in the dual to denote a husband and wife, whereas the latter is used only in the singular and plural to refer exclusively to a married men. Relatedly, the word *gṛhastha* seems to have no feminine form whatsoever, whereas the feminine form *gṛhamedhinī* occurs in at least one later passage (*VaDh* 21.14). The reason that *gṛhastha* is exclusively masculine in gender and never dual in number is most likely that the term itself implies a contrast with individual men who have left home and taken up one or another celibate lifestyle. In other words, there would be a disturbing asymmetry, if the dharma tradition spoke of *gṛhasthas* in the dual, but students, forest-dwellers, and itinerant ascetics in the singular.

Gautama, Baudhāyana, *and* Vasiṣṭha Dharmasūtras

Unlike Āpastamba, the three later Dharmasūtras of Gautama, Baudhāyana, and Vasiṣṭha all strongly favor using the word *gṛhastha* to denote a married man or householder. In fact, aside from a single passage of Vasiṣṭha (11.11), these three works invariably refer to a householder as a *gṛhastha* in the masculine, singular or occasionally plural, and consistently use the abstract noun *gārhasthya* to denote the state of being a householder. The term *kuṭumbin*, used three times by Āpastamba, is completely absent from these texts; and the term *gṛhamedhin*, seemingly favored by Āpastamba, is practically absent,

Śatapatha Brāhmaṇa 13.4.3.3 among other places. Interestingly, the earliest occurrence of the term *kuṭumbin* seems to be the relatively late Vedic *Sāmavidhāna Brāhmaṇa* (2.5.5).

occurring only once in a verse within the *Vasiṣṭha Dharmasūtra*, where it takes the feminine gender and must denote something like a pious wife.[12] Thus, a marked shift in the terminology used within the dharma tradition to refer to a householder seems to have taken place between the time of Āpastamba and that of the three later Dharmasūtras.

Gautama uses the word *gṛhastha* four times in his text (3.2–3, 4.1, 9.1) and the abstract noun *gārhasthya* once (3.36). In all but one of these passages, the context is clearly a discussion of the four *āśramas*.[13] The remaining passage, however, is far removed from any mention of the other three *āśramas* and, thus, appears not to be directly related to the *āśrama* system as such.[14] Baudhāyana likewise uses the word *gṛhastha* four times in his text,[15] but never uses the abstract noun *gārhasthya*. Interestingly, two of the passages in which Baudhāyana uses the word *gṛhastha* (2.13.7, 2.18.13) are identical to the floating verse maxim cited by Āpastamba (2.9.13), which I have discussed above and which contains Āpastamba's sole usage of the term *gṛhastha*. These passages, therefore, obviously assume the basic framework of the *āśrama* system. Another passage of Baudhāyana (2.11.12) simply lists the occupants of the four standard *āśramas* or Brahmanical orders of life, including the *gṛhastha*. However, the final passage in which Baudhāyana uses the word *gṛhastha*—another floating verse—does not explicitly invoke the framework of the four *āśramas*. Instead, it essentially warns of the great sin that students of the Veda and twice-born householders commit, if they fail to eat properly in the pursuit of ascetic practices.[16]

Thus, in Gautama and Baudhāyana, unlike Āpastamba, the standard term for a householder is undoubtedly *gṛhastha*. Certainly the absence of other terms

---

12. See *VaDh* 21.14: *pativratānāṃ gṛhamedhinīnāṃ satyavratānāṃ ca śucivratānām / tāsāṃ tu lokāḥ patibhiḥ samānā gomāyulokā vyabhicāriṇīnām //* ("Pious wives who are devoted to their husbands and sworn to honesty and purity attain the same worlds as their husbands, but those who are unfaithful attain the worlds of jackals.")

13. *Gautama Dharmasūtra* 3.2–3 and 3.36 clearly fall within Gautama's discussion of the *āśramas* (3.1–36). Moreover, *GDh* 4.1, which lays down that a *gṛhastha* should marry a woman of the same class (*gṛhasthaḥ sadṛśīṃ bhāryāṃ vindeta*), immediately follows this discussion.

14. See *GDh* 9.1: *sa vidhipūrvakaṃ snātvā bhāryām adhigamya yathoktān gṛhasthadharmān prayuñjāna imāni vratāny anukarṣet /* ("A man who has completed his studies should bathe according to the prescribed rules; take a wife; and, observing the rules for a householder as laid down, carry out these vows.")

15. See *BDh* 2.11.12, 2.13.7, 2.13.9, 2.18.13.

16. See *BDh* 2.13.9: *gṛhastho brahmacārī vā yo 'naśnaṃs tu tapaś caret / prāṇāgnihotralopena avakīrṇī bhavet tu saḥ //* ("If a householder or student performs austerities, neglecting to eat, he becomes a student who has broken his vow of chastity through failing to perform the Agnihotra to his breaths.")

for householder within these texts strongly supports this conclusion. And further support comes from those passages in these texts that use the word *gṛhastha* outside of the explicit framework of the *āśramas*, for these passages show that usage of the term was no longer restricted to one specific context, but instead viewed as generally appropriate. As we have seen, however, within Gautama and Baudhāyana most occurrences of the term *gṛhastha*, as well as the sole occurrence of the abstract noun *gārhasthya*, do take place within the explicit framework of the *āśrama* system. And, even aside from the fact that the term seems to have originally entered the dharma tradition in connection with the *āśramas*, it is easy to understand why this would be the case: explicit mention of the householder would seem most necessary within the context of a discussion of the four *āśramas*, where he is directly contrasted with men who have adopted alternative and invariably celibate lifestyles. Elsewhere in their texts, context makes it sufficiently obvious when Gautama and Baudhāyana are addressing the twice-born householder.

Nevertheless, from a certain perspective, the apparent preference for the term *gṛhastha* within Gautama and Baudhāyana is puzzling, for these authors, in contrast to Āpastamba, apparently reject the *āśrama* system outright and recognize the lifestyle of the householder as the sole legitimate one for a twice-born man who has studied the Vedas.[17] Thus, if the *āśrama* system is the original context within which Dharmaśāstra adopts the term *gṛhastha*, its preponderance in Gautama and Baudhāyana reflects a peculiar development. Perhaps, despite these authors' objections, the *āśrama* system had become so popular and influential during their time that its term for a householder simply developed into the standard designation.

Unlike Gautama and Baudhāyana, Vasiṣṭha—the author of the youngest extant Dharmasūtra—clearly accepts the basic legitimacy of all four *āśramas*, although he apparently takes pains to defend the pious householder as being in no way inferior to those individuals who have taken up one of the three celibate orders of life.[18] Like his predecessors, Vasiṣṭha largely uses the term *gṛhastha* within the explicit framework of the four *āśramas*.[19] However, there

17. See *GDh* 3.36 and *BDh* 2.11.27–34. For a discussion of this, see Olivelle (1993: 83–91).

18. See *VaDh* 8.14–16, which comprises verses extolling the greatness of the householder in relation to the other *āśramas*. Also see Olivelle (1993: 93–94) for a discussion of Vasiṣṭha's view of the *āśrama* system.

19. Vasiṣṭha discusses the *āśramas* at 7.1–10.31 and, in the course of this discussion, uses the term *gṛhastha* five times (7.2, 8.1, 8.14–16). He also uses the term slightly earlier at 6.19, which is a verse explaining how the rules of personal purification apply to each *āśrama*, and at 6.20, which is identical to *ĀpDh* 2.9.13/*BDh* 2.13.7, 2.18.13 (see above).

is one passage where he uses it outside of such a context.[20] Furthermore, Vasiṣṭha uses the abstract noun *gārhasthya* twice, both times outside of any discussion or mention of the other *āśramas*.[21] Hence, in his clear preference for *gṛhastha* over other terms for householder even outside the framework of the *āśramas*, Vasiṣṭha appears to be fundamentally the same as Gautama and Baudhāyana.

It is noteworthy, however, that there is a single passage where Vasiṣṭha employs a term other than *gṛhastha* to denote a householder. The passage in question uses the term *dampati* in the dual rather than the singular and instructs that, after feeding an assortment of deities, persons, and animals (*VaDh* 11.3–10), the master and mistress of a house should eat what remains (*VaDh* 11.11: *śeṣaṃ dampatī bhuñjīyātām*). Vasiṣṭha's reason for using *dampati* (literally "lord of a home") here instead of his more usual *gṛhastha* is likely that he explicitly intends his statement to apply to both a householder and his wife. Consequently, he uses the noun *dampati*, which seems to occur exclusively in the dual within the literature, where it invariably denotes a husband and wife. By contrast, as discussed above, works of Dharmaśāstra use the noun *gṛhastha* exclusively in the singular and less often in the plural, but tellingly never in the dual.

Patañjali's Mahābhāṣya

Although by no means a work of Dharmaśāstra, the *Mahābhāṣya*—Patañjali's great commentary on Pāṇini's foundational Sanskrit grammar, the *Aṣṭādhyāyī*—has been included here for the reasons stated at the beginning of this chapter: it is likely roughly contemporaneous with the *Gautama* and *Baudhāyana Dharmasūtras* (ca. second century BCE) and appears to share broadly the same conservative Brahmanical worldview as these and other Dharmaśāstra works. Interestingly, Patañjali seems to mention householders in only two passages. One of these is his commentary on *Aṣṭādhyāyī* 4.4.90 (*gṛhapatinā saṃyukte ñyaḥ*), which accounts for the nominal form *gārhapatya*—a term that is used as the name of one of the three sacred fires in solemn Vedic rites and that literally indicates association with a *gṛhapati*, an old Vedic word for householder. Hence, this passage addresses a term fundamentally

20. VaDh 11.17 lists virtuous householders (*gṛhasthān sādhūn*) among the individuals that a man should feed at ancestral rites.

21. Vasiṣṭha instructs a king to appoint a priest to carry out his ritual observances as a householder (*VaDh* 19.3: *gārhasthyanaiyamikeṣu purohitaṃ dadhyāt*), while *VaDh* 19.12 allows a king to damage fruit- and flower-bearing trees to provide components necessary to fulfil his duties as a householder (*gārhasthyasyāṅge*).

embedded in the old Vedic ritual system and Patañjali uses the word *gṛhapati* in it, simply because Pāṇini does.

However, the other passage in which Patañjali speaks of householders is considerably more illuminating for present purposes. This comprises his commentary on *Aṣṭādhyāyī* 4.1.33 (*patyur no yajñasaṃyoge*), which prescribes the form *patnī* ("wife") as the feminine equivalent of *pati* ("husband, lord"), when there is a connection with sacrifice. In other words, this rule of Pāṇini lays down that one should use the word *patnī* ("wife") only in cases where there is some connection to or relationship with sacrifice. Patañjali comments on this sūtra as follows:

> *yajñsaṃyoga iti ucyate / tatra idaṃ na sidhyati / iyam asya patnī / kva tarhi syāt / patnīsaṃyāja iti yatra yajñasaṃyogaḥ / naiṣa doṣaḥ / patiśabdo 'yam aiśvaryavācī / sarveṇa ca gṛhasthena pañca mahāyajñā nirvartyāḥ / yac cādaḥ sāyaṃprātarhomacarupuroḍāśān nirvapati tasyāsāv īṣṭe / evam api tuṣajakasya patnīti na sidhyati / upamānāt siddham / patnī iva patnī iti /*
>
> [Objection:] The sūtra says "when there is a connection with sacrifice." This being the case, it is not established that one might say, "This is his *patnī* ('wife')." To what expressions then does this sūtra apply?
>
> [Author:] To the expression *patnīsaṃyāja* ("wife-offering"), where there is a connection with sacrifice.[22] There is also no error in the example sentence given. The word *pati* ("husband") expresses lordship. And every householder (*gṛhastha*) must carry out the five great sacrifices and he is lord of whatever he ritually offers: evening and morning oblations, *caru* porridge, and *puroḍāśa* cakes.
>
> [Objection:] Even so, it is not established that one might speak of "Tuṣajaka's *patnī* ('wife')."[23]
>
> [Author:] This is established on account of analogy. The word *patnī* in such expressions means that a woman is like a *patnī*.

Before discussing what Patañjali has to say about this particular sūtra of Pāṇini, it is worth noting that the above passage is the only one in Patañjali where he uses the word *gṛhastha*. And, significantly, here it is clearly his choice

22. The *patnīsaṃyājas* are a series of ritual offerings made to the wives of the gods in certain Vedic rituals. For a discussion of these, see Jamison (1996: 50–51) and Kane (1962–75, II: 1076–77).

23. Within the *Mahābhāṣya*, Tuṣajaka is the archetypal name of a Śūdra man.

of a term for householder rather than Pāṇini's. Moreover, Patañjali does not mention *gṛhasthas* within the context of the *āśrama* system—a theological construct that he, in fact, never refers to in his text.

As we can see, Patañjali begins the above passage with the hypothetical question: if the word *patnī* can only be used when there is a connection with sacrifice, as Pāṇini prescribes, how can one call a man's wife his *patnī* in an ordinary context? Patañjali answers that this is possible, because the word *pati* ("husband, lord") indicates lordship and every *gṛhastha* must faithfully perform the five so-called "great sacrifices" (*mahāyajña*), well-known from Dharmaśāstra sources.[24] Consequently, as the performer of these rites, a *gṛhastha* is lord over whatever he offers at them. Hence, his female counterpart—his wife and ritual partner—is similarly connected with sacrificial offerings and can, thus, rightly be called his *patnī*. This then raises another question: how can one say that Tuṣajaka—a man whose name clearly marks him as a Śūdra—has a *patnī* ("wife")? Patañjali replies that such usage of the term *patnī* is based upon analogy with a true *patnī* and, thus, effectively metaphorical.

For the purpose of this chapter, this passage of Patañjali is especially illuminating, because it explicitly shows that the term *gṛhastha* could only be applied to a twice-born man engaged in a regimen of prescribed ritual observances. Married Śūdra men and married twice-born men who were neglectful of their religious duties were not considered *gṛhasthas*, at least not by Patañjali. And this is important, because the etymology of the term *gṛhastha*, which literally means "stay-at-home," does not obviously lead to this conclusion. Furthermore, its usage within the Dharmasūtras is similarly inconclusive. It is true, of course, that when these texts speak of *gṛhasthas*, they invariably mean twice-born men engaged in various prescribed rituals. These characteristics of a *gṛhastha*, however, could be the result of textual context rather than the meaning of the term itself. After all, the Dharmasūtras simply do not concern themselves to any significant degree with married men lacking twice-born pedigree. Therefore, the above passage of Patañjali is significant in that it clarifies that *gṛhastha* is not simply a generic word for householder or married man, but rather a somewhat technical term that refers specifically and exclusively to a married, twice-born man committed to the faithful execution of his religious duties. In other words, the term *gṛhastha* appears to

24. These are: *devayajña* (ritual offerings to the gods); *pitṛyajña* (ritual offerings to the ancestors); *bhūtayajña* (offerings of food to living beings); *manuṣyayajña* (feeding Brahmin guests); and *brahmayajña* (reciting the Veda). See, e.g., *ĀpDh* 1.12.13–13.1, *GDh* 8.16, and *BDh* 2.11.1–6. For a discussion, see Kane (1962–75, II: 697–700).

be essentially equivalent to the older term *gṛhamedhin* ("domestic sacrificer"), favored by Āpastamba.

Mānava Dharmaśāstra

Like his immediate predecessors within the dharma tradition, Manu clearly prefers *gṛhastha* as a term of reference for Brahmanical householders, for he uses it in his work as many times as he does all other words for householder combined. And like his predecessors, Manu invariably uses the word *gṛhastha* to refer to a man who is married, twice-born, and engaged in a fairly austere religious lifestyle in which ritual plays a central role. Moreover, like the authors of the earlier Dharmasūtras, he employs the word *gṛhastha* primarily within the explicit context of the *āśrama* system,[25] but by no means exclusively so.[26] Hence, in its preference for and use of the term *gṛhastha*, the *Mānava Dharmaśāstra* appears to be essentially the same as the earlier Dharmasūtras of Gautama, Baudhāyana, and Vasiṣṭha.

Unlike these works, however, the *Mānava Dharmaśāstra* does employ words other than *gṛhastha* to refer to householders with some frequency. For instance, in a single passage that is virtually identical to and, thus, clearly dependent upon an earlier passage of Vasiṣṭha (11.11), which has been discussed above, Manu uses the word *dampati* ("lord of a home") in the grammatical dual.[27] And in another passage (3.80), he uses the word *kuṭumbin* ("head of a household"), which had been absent from the extant Dharmaśāstra literature since Āpastamba. In contrast to Āpastamba, however, Manu does not use the word specifically within the context of the disposal of property or the offering of hospitality to guests. Instead, he essentially states that a *kuṭumbin* should

---

25. See *MDh* 3.2 (which speaks of the *gṛhasthāśrama* or "householder's order of life"), 3.77–78 (which proclaim the householder to be the basis of all other *āśramas*), 5.137 (which lays down the differing rules of purification for members of the four *āśramas*), 6.2 (which prescribes the transition from householder to forest-dwelling hermit), 6.87 (same as 3.77–78), and 6.89–90 (same as 3.77–78, 6.87).

26. See *MDh* 3.68 (which explains why householders must perform the five *mahāyajñas* or "great sacrifices"), 3.104 (which warns householders against becoming too attached to food cooked by others), 3.117 (which concerns the five *mahāyajñas*), 4.259 (which concludes a discussion of Brahmin householders), 6.30 (which instructs forest-dwellers to perform the religious observances carried out by seers and Brahmin householders), and 9.334 (which enjoins Śūdras to serve Brahmin householders).

27. Compare *VaDh* 11.11 (*śeṣaṃ dampatī bhuñjīyātām*) with *MDh* 3.116: *bhuñjīyātāṃ tataḥ paścād avaśiṣṭaṃ tu dampatī* | ("Then, afterward, the master and mistress of the house should eat what is left.")

carry out the five so-called "great sacrifices" (*mahāyajña*).[28] Hence, Manu seemingly employs the term simply as a metrically convenient synonym for *gṛhastha*, his preferred way of referring to a twice-born householder.

In addition, Manu uses the masculine noun *gṛhamedhin*—favored by Āpastamba, yet absent from the later Dharmasūtras—six times in his text, although never in the dual, as it exclusively occurs in Āpastamba. And like Āpastmaba, Manu clearly understands the terms *gṛhamedhin* and *gṛhastha* to be effectively synonymous. Strong evidence of this can be found in the following passage (MDh 3.68–69):

> *pañca sūnā gṛhasthasya cullī peṣaṇy upaskaraḥ |*
> *kaṇḍanī codakumbhaś ca badhyate yās tu vāhayan ||*
> *tāsāṃ krameṇa sarvāsāṃ niṣkṛtyarthaṃ maharṣibhiḥ |*
> *pañca kḷptā mahāyajñāḥ pratyahaṃ gṛhamedhinām ||*
>
> A householder (*gṛhastha*) has five slaughterhouses, through employing which he is bound: fireplace, millstone, broom, pestle and mortar, and waterpot. To atone for all these in order, the great seers devised for householders (*gṛhamedhin*) the five great sacrifices that they must perform daily.

As one can see, the first verse of this passage lists the five "slaughterhouses" (*sunā*)—meaning sites of violence—that hinder a *gṛhastha's* progress in the hereafter. And the following verse then explains that the five *mahāyajñas* or "great sacrifices" were devised so that *gṛhamedhins* might expiate the sin resulting from their use of these slaughterhouses. Hence, in this passage, one is presumably supposed to identify the *gṛhamedhins* in the second verse with the *gṛhastha* mentioned in the first. Moreover, it is likely that Manu uses *gṛhamedhin* instead of *gṛhastha* both here and elsewhere in his text, merely because it is a metrically convenient term. Certainly the fact that in five of its six occurrences, the word *gṛhamedhin* occupies the concluding cadence of an *anuṣṭubh* line supports this interpretation.[29] Furthermore, although Manu never uses *gṛhamedhin* within the explicit context of the *āśrama* system, the passages in which he employs the term generally depict a *gṛhamedhin* as being engaged in the sorts of activities associated with a *gṛhastha*. For example,

28. See *MDh* 3.80: *ṛṣayaḥ pitaro devā bhūtāny atithayas tathā | āśāsate kuṭumbibhyas tebhyaḥ kāryaṃ vijānatā ||* ("Seers, ancestors, gods, living beings, and guests expect things from householders. A wise man should grant these to them."). On the *mahāyajñas*, see n. 24.

29. See *MDh* 3.69, 3.105, 4.8, and 4.31–32. The sole exception to this pattern is *MDh* 6.27 (see below).

Manu states that a *gṛhamedhin* should never turn away a guest (3.105); should avoid accumulating too large a store of grain (4.8); should be honored at rites to the gods and ancestors (4.31); and should feed those who do not cook for themselves (4.32).

There is, however, a single passage of Manu that uses the term *gṛhamedhin* in a markedly different context than all other passages in the early Dharmaśāstra literature. This difficult and ambiguous passage issues an instruction for a sort of advanced-stage *vānaprastha* or forest-dwelling ascetic. As explained by Manu, upon undertaking the forest-dweller's order of life, a man is supposed to maintain a sedentary lifestyle in the forest and continue to observe the same domestic rites that he did as a householder, but using only uncultivated foods (6.4–5). Then, at a later stage, while still considered a *vānaprastha*, he may abandon the outward performance of sacrificial rites, placing his sacred fires within himself, and take up an itinerant lifestyle within the forest (6.25–26). Manu (6.27) explains that such a wandering *vānaprastha* should acquire food as follows:

> *tāpaseṣv eva vipreṣu yātrikaṃ bhaikṣam āharet |*
> *gṛhamedhiṣu cānyeṣu dvijeṣu vanavāsiṣu ||*
>
> He should collect almsfood merely sufficient to sustain his life only from Brahmin ascetics (*tāpasa*) and from other twice-born *gṛhamedhins* residing in the forest.

The surprising feature of this verse for present purposes is that it apparently speaks of *gṛhamedhins* who live in the forest—a notably different picture of the *gṛhamedhin* than is seen anywhere else in the dharma literature.[30] This then raises the question: What are these *gṛhamedhins* doing residing in the forest? One possible answer, offered by the commentator Sarvajñanārāyaṇa, is that even certain householders were understood to take up residence in the forest due to their extreme virtuousness.[31] Such an answer, however, leads to another question: Why then does Manu refer to them as "other *gṛhamedhins*" (*gṛhamedhiṣu cānyeṣu*)? For this implies that there are two sets of *gṛhamedhins*

30. The most natural way to read this verse is to construe the second line as referring to a single class of people ("other twice-born *gṛhamedhins* residing in the forest"). And Manu's commentators all construe the verse in this way. It is possible, however, to interpret the second line as referring to two separate classes of people: *gṛhamedhins* (i.e., householders) and other twice-born forest-dwellers. But such an interpretation has the disadvantage of being rather forced syntactically, requiring one to construe the word *anyeṣu* ("other") across metrical boundaries and to ignore the placement of the single *ca* ("and") in the third *pāda*.

31. Sarvajñanārāyaṇa on *MDh* 6.27: *ekāntaśīlatayā gṛhasthasyāpi vanavāso darśitaḥ |*

mentioned in the verse. And the need to explain this puzzling fact compels Sarvajñanārāyaṇa to gloss the word *anyeṣu* ("other") rather unconvincingly as *asaṃbandhiṣu* ("unrelated").

An alternative—and perhaps more satisfactory—answer requires a careful consideration of the precise meanings of the words *tāpasa* and *gṛhamedhin* in *Mānava Dharmaśāstra* 6.27. Manu only uses the word *tāpasa* two other times in his text. One of these passages (12.48) merely lists *tāpasas* alongside world-renouncers (*yati*), Brahmins, Daityas, and others as comprising the first "path of goodness" (*sāttvikī gatiḥ*). Hence, it does little to clarify the term's precise meaning other than to indicate that the terms *tāpasa* and *yati* are not entirely synonymous. The other passage (6.51) prohibits a world-renouncer from visiting a home crowded with *tāpasas*, Brahmins, crows, dogs, and other beggars. It, therefore, portrays a *tāpasa* as a sort of itinerant ascetic beggar. However, the *tāpasas* mentioned in 6.27 seem notably different from such a person for several reasons. First, they are clearly presented as a class of people from whom one might reasonably beg rather than as beggars themselves. Second, they appear to be inhabitants of the forest rather mendicants living largely on the outskirts of towns and villages. And, third, given that the second line speaks of "other *gṛhamedhins*," they would appear to be *gṛhamedhins* themselves in some sense of that term. Thus, the *tāpasas* in 6.27 and 6.51 seem to be rather different characters. In order to come to a satisfactory understanding of who the *tāpasas* in the former verse are, it is useful to note that in Kālidāsa's famous play, the *Abhijñānaśākuntala*, *tāpasa* is the standard term used to denote the forest-dwelling ascetics encountered by Duṣyanta in the play's first act—sedentary ascetics who are portrayed as living with their families and engaged in the performance of various rites.[32] And, in this regard, it is noteworthy that several of Manu's commentators gloss *tāpasa* in *Mānava Dharmaśāstra* 6.27 as *vānaprastha*, a term that one might reasonably apply to the ascetics in Kālidāsa's play. Bearing this in mind, one can see how the *tāpasas* in 6.27 might be regarded as *gṛhamedhins*. This requires, first, that the term *tāpasa* is used to the denote essentially the same sorts of ascetics that it is used to denote in the *Abhijñānaśākuntala*, which importantly are people that one might plausibly beg from. And, second, it requires that the term *gṛhamedhin* not refer specifically to the *gṛhastha* of the classical *āśrama* system, but instead to any man who lives a settled life and performs the rites prescribed for Brahmanical householders. In these senses of these terms, a *tāpasa* might be described as a *gṛhamedhin*. Therefore, *Mānava Dharmaśāstra*

---

32. See in particular *Abhijñānaśākuntala* 1.45 and the surrounding dialogue.

6.27 might effectively lay down that a *vānaprastha* should beg for almsfood from Brahmin ascetics who live in the forest, performing rituals, as well as from other twice-born men (i.e., Kṣatriyas and Vaiśyas), who similarly live in the forest and perform domestic rites.

Finally, although Manu largely refers to householders using terms found in earlier Dharmaśāstra texts and, like his immediate predecessors, has a special preference for the word *gṛhastha*, he also introduces one new word for householder into the vocabulary of the dharma tradition. This word is *gṛhin*, which literally denotes a home-owner and, thus, could reasonably be used to refer to a householder of any type and not necessarily a pious, twice-born one. However, Manu generally prescribes for a *gṛhin* the same sorts of activities that he prescribes for a *gṛhastha* or *gṛhamedhin*. For instance, he states that a *gṛhin* should faithfully serve his father, mother, and teacher, who are equated with the three sacred fires (2.232); perform various rites and his daily cooking in his nuptial fire (3.67); practice alms-giving (3.95); and avoid quarreling with such people as his priests and teachers (4.179–81). This suggests that for Manu, the word *gṛhin* is simply a synonym for *gṛhastha*, meaning a pious, twice-born householder. And the following verse (3.78), which clearly uses the terms *gṛhastha* and *gṛhin* to refer to the same class of person at different places, strongly supports this conclusion:

> *yasmāt trayo 'py āśramiṇo jñānenānnena cānvaham |*
> *gṛhasthair eva dhāryante tasmāj jyeṣṭhāśramo gṛhī ||*
>
> Since *gṛhasthas* alone daily sustain members of the other three orders of life with knowledge and with food, the *gṛhin*, therefore, constitutes the highest order of life.

However, the following verse of Manu (8.62) seemingly indicates that, unlike a *gṛhastha*, a *gṛhin* could also be a Śūdra:

> *gṛhiṇaḥ putriṇo maulāḥ kṣatraviṭśūdrayonayaḥ |*
> *arthyuktāḥ sākṣyam arhanti na ye ke cid anāpadi ||*
>
> Men who are householders (*gṛhin*), possessed of sons, natives of the region, and of Kṣatriya, Vaiśya, or Śūdra origin, when called upon by a plaintiff, are fit to act as witnesses, not just anyone except in cases of emergency.

Hence, although Manu normally seems to use *gṛhin* as a synonym for *gṛhastha*, perhaps mainly for metrical reasons, he at least once appears to use it as a generic word for a home-owner or married man—a usage befitting the word's etymology.[33]

Later Dharmaśāstras

Finally, let us turn to the three youngest surviving Dharmaśāstras, which are those ascribed to the mythological figures Yājñavalkya, Nārada, and Viṣṇu. The selection and use of terms for householder within these texts are rather eclectic but provide little new information. Consequently, the discussion of each of these texts will be kept fairly brief.

Probably due to a combination of its metrical form and its obvious aspiration to be highly aphoristic, the *Yājñavalkya Dharmaśāstra* uses a variety of established Brahmanical terms for householder without seeming to favor any particular one. Thus, it uses the word *gṛhastha* only twice; and in neither of these cases is the text dealing directly with the classical Brahmanical system of the four *āśramas*. Instead, in the first passage (1.111), Yājñavalkya explains that both a traveler and a learned Brahmin who has mastered the Vedas should be regarded as guests and instructs a *gṛhastha* to honor them both.[34] And in the second (3.205), he states that even a *gṛhastha* can attain liberation, if he lawfully acquires his wealth, dedicates himself to right knowledge, devotes himself to guests, performs Śrāddha rites, and speaks only the truth. Hence, like all earlier authors of Dharmaśāstra texts, Yājñavalkya apparently uses the term *gṛhastha* to denote specifically a pious householder of understood twice-born social class. In addition, like Manu, Yājñavalkya uses the term *gṛhin* to denote precisely such a householder, employing the word twice in his text. In one verse (1.97), he enjoins a *gṛhin* to perform the rites laid down by the Smṛtis on a daily basis in his nuptial fire. And in another passage (1.157–58), which is clearly dependent upon an earlier statement of Manu (4.179–81), he says that a *gṛhin* should avoid quarreling with such people as his priests and teachers. Furthermore, the word *gṛhamedhin* occurs in a single verse of the *Yājñavalkya Dharmaśāstra* (3.186), where it describes a group of eighty-eight

33. Interestingly, in contrast with Manu and most other Dharmaśāstra sources, early Pāli texts never seem to use the word *gihin* (Skt. *gṛhin*), which appears to have the negative connotation of inferiority vis-à-vis itinerant ascetics, with reference to a Brahmin. On this, see Freiberger (Ch. 4, present volume).

34. The *Mitākṣarā* offers a slightly different interpretation of this verse. According to it, *YDh* 1.111 explains that anyone set out on a path should be considered a guest and that a *gṛhastha* should, therefore, regard both a learned Brahmin and a Brahmin who has mastered the Vedas as guests.

thousand sages who are destined to return to this world at a future time in order to restore dharma on earth. Yājñavalkya likely describes these sages as *gṛhamedhins* in order to indicate that they will not remain celibate, but rather produce lines of earthly descendants.

Yājñavalkya also uses the term *dampati* ("lord of a home") four times in his work, which is surprisingly more than any other term for householder. In three of these occurrences, the term is in the dual, genitive (*dampatyoḥ*) and undoubtedly denotes a married couple. In two of these three, the dual of *dampati* clearly refers to a husband and wife who are both twice-born and generally committed to the religious lifestyle of the *gṛhastha*.[35] However, the other passage of Yājñavalkya (2.52) containing the dual, genitive of *dampati* deals with the general adjudication of lawsuits and prohibits a husband and wife from acting as legal sureties for one another, owing debts to one another, and serving as witnesses for one another. Hence, it likely uses the term *dampati* to refer generically to any married couple and not necessarily a twice-born one. In the sole passage of Yājñavalkya where the word *dampati* is used, but not in the dual, genitive, it is part of a long *dvandva* compound and undoubtedly denotes a married couple.[36] Specifically, the passage issues a fine for any husband who abandons his wife without her losing caste and any wife who abandons her husband without him losing caste.

The final passage of Yājñavalkya to discuss (2.45) is a bit more informative than the aforementioned ones and contains the sole occurrence of the word *kuṭumbin* within his text:

> *avibhaktaiḥ kuṭumbārthe yad ṛṇaṃ tu kṛtaṃ bhavet |*
> *dadyus tad rikthinaḥ prete proṣite vā kuṭumbini ||*
>
> When jointly living co-heirs incur a debt for the sake of their family, the inheritors must pay it off if the head of the family (*kuṭumbin*) dies or goes abroad.

---

35. See *YDh* 1.74 (which states that the three goals of human life—dharma, worldly gain, and sensual pleasure—flourish when a husband and wife get along well) and *YDh* 1.105 (which is clearly dependent upon *VaDh* 11.11 and *MDh* 3.116 and instructs the master and mistress of a home to eat what remains after first feeding a variety of other people).

36. See *YDh* 2.237: *pitṛputrasvasṛbhrātṛdampatyācāryaśiṣyakāḥ | eṣām apatitānyonyatyāgī ca śatadaṇḍabhāk ||* ("Father and son, sister and brother, husband and wife, and teacher and student—when one of these abandons the other without that person losing caste, he receives a fine of 100 *paṇas*.")

In order to make sense of this passage, it is more or less necessary to assume that the *kuṭumbin* referred to in it is specifically the head of a joint family or household and not simply any married man. This is significant, because this meaning of *kuṭumbin* corresponds rather closely to the way that, centuries earlier, Āpastamba seems to use the word, that is, as a term specifically for a home-owner or head of a household within the context of the disposal of property (typically for the purpose of offering hospitality to guests).

Furthermore, there is also a passage in the *Nārada Smṛti* (1.10), where *kuṭumbin* seems to have precisely this meaning:

> *śiṣyāntevāsidāsastrīvaiyāvṛttyakaraiś ca yat* /
> *kuṭumbahetor utkṣiptaṃ voḍhavyaṃ tat kuṭumbinā* //
>
> The head of the family (*kuṭumbin*) must bear any (debt) incurred for the sake of his family by his students, apprentices, servants, and women, as well as those he has commissioned.

Here again the word *kuṭumbin* must denote specifically the head of a family or household, who alone is personally responsible for repaying any debts incurred by his dependents or underlings on his family's behalf. However, in the only other verse of Nārada where the word *kuṭumbin* occurs, it is not definite that the term likewise refers explicitly to the head of a household.[37] But, interestingly, it is clear that both times Nārada uses the word *gṛhin* in his work (1.28, 1.30), he intends it to denote precisely such a person, for in both cases he lists a *gṛhin* as a rare example of a free or independent (*svatantra*) individual. Moreover, in one of these two passages (1.28), he explicitly states that a *gṛhin* of every social class is independent within his own home, indicating that the term could be applied to Śūdras as well as twice-born men. Hence, Nārada's usage of the term *gṛhin* differs slightly from that of Manu, who typically treats it as a synonym for *gṛhastha* in the sense of pious, twice-born householder. Aside from the passages just mentioned, Nārada only speaks directly of householders once in his text, in an unremarkable passage (12.89) where he uses *dampati* in the dual to refer to a husband and wife and prohibits them from bringing before their kinsmen or king any quarrel between them arising out of jealousy or the like.

---

37. See *NSm* 11.37: *gṛhaṃ kṣetraṃ ca vijñeyaṃ vāsahetuḥ kuṭumbinām / tasmāt tan nākṣiped rājā tad dhi mūlaṃ kuṭumbinām //* ("House and field should be known as the foundation of householders' dwellings. Therefore, a king should not disturb them, for they are the root of householders.")

For the purposes of the present chapter, probably the most interesting feature of Nārada is that he nowhere uses the word *gṛhamedhin*, favored by Āpastamba, or the word *gṛhastha*, favored by essentially all later authors within the dharma tradition. But the absence of these terms from Nārada's work becomes considerably less surprising, when one notes that, unlike all of his predecessors, he deals only with the adjudication of lawsuits and not the many other topics with which Dharmaśāstra literature concerns itself. Hence, it is entirely understandable that when Nārada speaks of householders or married men, he has no desire to imply their twice-born status or commitment to a particular religious lifestyle and, thus, avoids terms carrying such implications (i.e., *gṛhamedhin* and *gṛhastha*).

Lastly, let us turn to the *Vaiṣṇava Dharmaśāstra*, which uses a number of words to denote a householder. Significantly, in every case within his text where Viṣṇu refers to a householder, this householder is unambiguously a man of twice-born status, committed to an orthodox Brahmanical lifestyle. Thus, references to married men or householders in general are entirely absent from Viṣṇu's work. In a single verse (59.29), virtually identical to an earlier verse of Manu (3.80), Viṣṇu uses the word *kuṭumbin*. And in another verse (67.41), completely identical to an earlier verse of Manu (3.116), he uses the word *dampati*. In addition, Viṣṇu employs the term *gṛhin* in three passages, always to denote a pious, twice-born householder.[38] Two of these passage (59.30, 67.44) are in verse; and it is, therefore, possible that here metrical exigencies determined Viṣṇu's choice of words. The third passage (94.1), however, is in prose; and, unfortunately, it is unclear to me why Viṣṇu chose the term *gṛhin* in this case over other words for householder. Whatever the reason may be, evidence suggests that, like most other Dharmaśāstra writers, Viṣṇu prefers *gṛhastha* as a term of reference for a Brahmanical householder, for he uses it seven times in his work, more than any other single term.[39]

---

38. Verse 59.30 is an *upajāti* stanza, which states that through performing such typical twice-born activities as reciting the Vedas and satiating his ancestors, a *gṛhin* will reach the realm of Indra. Verse 67.44 is an *anuṣṭubh* stanza, which states that a *gṛhin* attains greater rewards through honoring guests than he does through reciting the Vedas, performing sacrifices, and engaging in austerities. And *ViDh* 94.1 lays down that a *gṛhin* should take up the forest-dweller's order of life when he sees that he has wrinkles and grey hair. It is highly reminiscent of *MDh* 6.2, which uses the word *gṛhastha*.

39. See *ViDh* 59.19 (on the five "slaughterhouses" of a *gṛhastha*, which he must expiate through the five great sacrifices), 59.27–28 (on others' dependence on and the superiority of the *gṛhastha*), 60.26 (on the rules of purification for each *āśrama*; same as *VaDh* 6.19), 67.31 (on a guest being a *gṛhastha's* lord), 67.33 (on the bad consequences that result from a *gṛhastha* failing to satisfy a guest), and 67.42 (which states that a *gṛhastha* should eat what remains after feeding gods, ancestors, guests, and dependents).

Although Viṣṇu uses a number of established words for householder in his work, he also seems to have introduced a new one into the dharma tradition: *gṛhāśramin* ("inhabitant of the household order of life").[40] He uses this term five times in his text, always as a synonym for *gṛhastha*. The synonymy of the terms *gṛhāśramin* and *gṛhastha* is especially apparent in the following verse (59.28), where the *gṛhastha* mentioned in the first three *pādas* must undoubtedly be identified with the *gṛhāśramin* mentioned in the fourth:

> *gṛhastha eva yajate gṛhasthas tapyate tapaḥ |*
> *pradadāti gṛhasthaś ca tasmāc chreṣṭho gṛhāśramī ||*
>
> A *gṛhastha* alone offers sacrifices; a *gṛhastha* alone performs austerities; and a *gṛhastha* alone gives gifts. Therefore, the *gṛhāśramin* is the greatest.

Given that Viṣṇu employs the word *gṛhāśramin* in prose more often than in verse,[41] metrical exigencies seem insufficient to account for the term's development. Whatever the precise reason for its coinage may be (if, indeed, there is a precise reason), it is noteworthy that Manu once refers to the householder's order of life as *gṛhāśrama* (6.1), as does the *Mahābhārata* in a handful of passages.[42] This usage would seem to foreshadow the development of *gṛhāśramin* as a term for Brahmanical householder in Viṣṇu and also in the *Śāntiparvan*, a text that likely predates this Dharmaśāstra and employs the word twice.[43]

Conclusion

We are now in a position to list the various terms for householder used by early Dharmaśāstra texts in their probable order of introduction to the dharma tradition; to present succinctly the precise meanings or range of meanings

40. See *ViDh* 33.2 (which states that due to his attachment to possessions, a *gṛhāśramin* is especially susceptible to lust, anger, and greed), 58.1 (which explains the three kinds of wealth that a *gṛhāśramin* may use in funerary rites), 59.1 (which states that a *gṛhāśramin* should perform sacrifices in his nuptial fire), and 59.28–29 (on the superiority of the *gṛhāśramin*).

41. While *ViDh* 33.2, 58.1, and 59.1 are in prose, *ViDh* 59.28–29 comprises a pair of verses.

42. See *MBh* 1.3.83, 3.2.50, 3.2.59, 12.61.4, 12.66.18, 12.184.1, 12.184.17, 13.2.90.

43. See *MBh* 12.61.12 (which defines a *gṛhāśramin* as a virtuous giver of food and performer of rites) and 12.142.26 (which explains the negative consequences for a *gṛhāśramin*, if he fails to perform the five *mahāyajñas*).

of these words; and to provide brief histories of their usage within early Dharmaśāstra.

Gṛhamedhin: This seems to be Āpastamba's preferred term of reference for a married, twice-born man committed to an orthodox Brahmanical way of life. The word *gṛhamedhin* is, thus, apparently the standard term for a Brahmanical householder in the earliest period of Dharmaśāstra literature. And such usage of the term by the dharma tradition to refer specifically and exclusively to married, twice-born men makes sense, given that it literally denotes someone engaged in domestic sacrifice and that numerous Vedic texts use it with precisely this meaning. Āpastamba—rather innovatively—uses the word only in the dual, where it denotes a pious, twice-born man and his wife. After Āpastamba, however, the term temporarily disappears from the dharma tradition only to reappear occasionally as a convenient synonym for a twice-born householder in the metrical works of Manu and Yājñavalkya, where the word never appears in the dual. Moreover, in a single puzzling verse (6.27), Manu speaks of *gṛhamedhins* who live in the forest, perhaps using the term to refer to performers of domestic rites rather than householders per se.

Kuṭumbin: Āpastamba seems to use this term to denote a home-owner, who is in charge of a certain estate or property, rather than a married man per se. Unlike *gṛhamedhin*, the term appears to be applicable to a person of any social class, provided that he is the owner of a home or head of a household. The other Dharmasūtras after Āpastamba never use the word *kuṭumbin*, but Manu (3.80) and Viṣṇu (59.29) both use it once in virtually identical passages to refer to a man who performs the five *mahāyajñas* ("great sacrifices") and, thus, seemingly as just a convenient synonym for *gṛhastha*. However, Yājñavalkya (2.45) and Nārada (1.10) both clearly employ the term to refer specifically to the head of a joint family and, thus, in a manner strikingly similar to Āpastamba.

Gṛhastha: All of the early Dharmaśāstra literature uses this term exclusively to denote a married man of twice-born social class who is actively committed to an orthodox Brahmanical way of life, including especially the performance of rituals. The grammarian Patañjali usefully clarifies that the term cannot properly be applied to a married man of any other type (i.e., a Śūdra or a man neglectful of his religious duties). Moreover, it is clear that Āpastamba regards the terms *gṛhastha* and *gṛhamedhin* as essentially synonymous and employs the former term only within the context of the four *āśramas*. This suggests that the word *gṛhastha* entered the dharma tradition in connection with the notion of the classical Brahmanical *āśramas*; and this makes sense, given that it literally means "stay-at-home" and, thus, implies a contrast with other men who have left home, such as itinerant and forest-dwelling ascetics. Beginning with Gautama, *gṛhastha* becomes the standard term for a Brahmanical householder throughout Dharmaśāstra literature and appears to be Patañjali's preferred term of reference as well. The seemingly rapid popularization of the term *gṛhastha* after Āpastamba is puzzling, considering that both Gautama and Baudhāyana explicitly reject the notion of the four *āśramas*. The fact that proponents of the *āśrama* system were able to set the terms of discourse even for their opponents suggests their considerable intellectual and social influence at the time.

Dampati: This term enters the dharma tradition with Vasiṣṭha (11.11) and appears occasionally thereafter. Throughout the literature, it is used exclusively in the dual to denote a husband and wife and, after Āpastamba at least, seems to be the preferred way of referring to a married couple, regardless of their social status.

Gṛhin: Manu introduces this term, which literally means "home-owner," into the dharma tradition. As used by Manu and later authors, *gṛhin* is seemingly a generic word for a householder or married man. Thus, depending upon context, it can function either as a synonym for *gṛhastha* in the sense of "pious, twice-born householder" or as a way of referring simply to a home-owner, regardless of social class. The combination of metrical exigencies and the need for a malleable term for householder may account for its coinage.

Gṛhāśramin: This is a late term for a Brahmanical householder within the dharma tradition, used exclusively by Viṣṇu. Evidence strongly suggests that the term (meaning literally "one who occupies the household order of life") is entirely synonymous with *gṛhastha*. The reasons for its coinage are unclear.

9

Householders, Holy and Otherwise, in the Nīti *and* Kāma *Literature*

Mark McClish

THIS ESSAY EXPLORES the use of terms for the "householder" in the extant *nīti* (statecraft) and *kāma* (erotics) texts of the classical period. Of the *nīti* literature, I look at the *Arthaśāstra* of Kauṭilya, the *Nītisāra* of Kāmandaki, and the *Rājadharmaparvan* of the *Mahābhārata*. Of the *kāma* literature, I look at the *Kāmasūtra* of Vātsyāyana. In them, I examine the use of the word *gṛhastha* ("householder"), its synonyms *gṛhamedhin*, *gṛhāśramin*, and *gṛhin*, and its derivative *gārhasthya* ("householdership"). I look also at three other words for the "householder," namely *gṛhapatika*, *gṛhasvāmin*, and *kuṭumbin*, which among these texts occur only in the *Arthaśāstra* of Kauṭilya.

All of these texts were written or redacted after the emergence of both the "original" and "classical" formulations of the *āśrama* system (Olivelle 1993: 131–34), and references in them to the *gṛhastha* (or *gṛhamedhin*, et al.) generally occur in the context of the other *āśramas*.[1] Such discussions serve either to signal adherence to the theology of *varṇāśramadharma*, in which the concepts of *gṛhastha* and *āśrama* had already long been embedded, or, as is sometimes the case in the *Rājadharmaparvan*, to argue for the superiority of the *gṛhastha* to the other *āśramas*. Nearly all references to the *gṛhastha* in these texts conform to how he appears in the dharma texts: the married

1. Some depictions of the *āśrama* system in these texts preserve what Olivelle defines as a key feature of the "original" system, namely that the *āśramas* are not "temporary stages of a person's life but . . . four alternate and permanent modes of life open to an individual" (1993: 74). See, e.g., *KAŚ* 1.3.9–12, *MBh* 12.61.1–21, and, arguably, *MBh* 12.12.7–11. On these "survivals" of the original system, see Olivelle 1993: 151–4.

twice-born who performs the dharmas or karmas of his *varṇa*. Only in the *Kāmasūtra* is the presentation of *gārhasthya* inflected otherwise. All the same, the category of *gṛhastha* is not itself central to the technical focus of either tradition, and references to the householder in the context of state policy or sex and seduction often see him from a perspective other than that of the *āśramas*.

In what follows I look at each of the four texts individually, focusing on the terms for "householder" found therein. I pay particular attention to how the concept of the householder relates to the technical focus of each genre. In keeping with the larger issues explored in this volume, I also examine the possibility of whether the *gṛhastha* is conceived as a kind of "stay at home" ascetic.

The Arthaśāstra

Gṛhastha: The term *gṛhastha* occurs only twice in the *Arthaśāstra* (*KAŚ* 1.3.9; 1.4.12), both times in the discussion of the four *vidyās* ("Sciences" or "Knowledge Systems") that begins the text (*KAŚ* 1.2.1–1.5.1) and both times in the context of the other *āśramas*. The discussion of the *vidyās* presents the four fundamental areas of human knowledge—*ānvīkṣikī* ("Critical Inquiry"), *trayī* ("the Triple [Veda]"), *vārttā* ("Economics"), and *daṇḍanīti* ("Governance"). This enumeration serves a few different purposes. First, it delineates each of these domains as independent and irreducible areas of human learning, whether based in theory or in practice. Second, it establishes all four as constituting the proper curriculum for the education of princes. Third, it identifies what is beneficial about each. Finally, it argues for the priority of Governance (*daṇḍanīti*) over the other three, whose "enterprise and security" (*yogakṣema*; see Olivelle 2013: 657) depend upon it.

Although the *Arthaśāstra* argues that the requirements of Governance should come before those of the Triple Veda, it is *trayī* that in fact receives the most attention in this passage. I have argued elsewhere that the *Arthaśāstra* was redacted by an editor who was congenial to the authority of sacred writ,[2] and that this created a dissonance in the ideological commitments of the extant text that shows up in this discussion of the *vidyās*. At any rate, the received text argues that the Triple Veda is beneficial (*aupakārika*) because "this dharma of the Triple Veda . . . establishes the *svadharma* of the four *varṇas* and *āśramas*" (*KAŚ* 1.3.4). Thereupon follows a concise presentation

2. See Olivelle 2013: 6–25 and McClish forthcoming.

of *varṇāśramadharma* (*KAŚ* 1.3.5–15),[3] which serves here, as elsewhere, as an epitome of the teachings of the Dharmaśāstra tradition (Olivelle 1993: 3). The Triple Veda is beneficial, in other words, because it teaches the precepts of Dharmaśāstra.

Because the *gṛhastha* is presented in the context of *varṇāśramadharma*, we can understand the usage here to conform generally with conceptions of the householder that predominated within the Brahmanism of Dharmaśāstra in the centuries around the beginning of the first millennium CE. By this time, the system of *varṇa*s and *āśrama*s had been fully systematized and the tradition of Dharmaśāstra had come to emphasize the conduct and practices of the married householder as the archetypal mode of religiosity, a shift in emphasis away from the earlier focus on the Vedic sacrifice itself. This shift is evident in the redacted *Arthaśāstra*, where *trayīdharma* ("Veda-*dharma*") essentially substitutes the teachings of Dharmaśāstra for the Triple Veda itself and the authority of the latter is projected onto the former by means of the legal fiction of *vedamūlatva* ("rootedness in the Veda").

Like the earlier Dharmasūtra of Āpastamba, the *Arthaśāstra* lists the *gṛhastha* as the first of the *āśramas*. And like all of the *varṇas* and *āśramas* presented in the *Arthaśāstra*, the *gṛhastha* is defined by his *svadharma* ("individual duty"):

> *gṛhasthasya svadharmājīvas tulyair asamānarṣibhir vaivāhyam ṛtugāmitvaṃ devapitratithipūjā bhṛtyeṣu tyāgaḥ śeṣabhojanaṃ ca |*

3. *eṣa trayīdharmaś caturṇāṃ varṇānām āśramāṇāṃ ca svadharmasthāpanād aupakārikaḥ* | 1.3.4
svadharmo brāhmaṇasyādhyayanam adhyāpanaṃ yajanaṃ yājanaṃ dānaṃ pratigrahaś ca | 1.3.5
kṣatriyasyādhyayanaṃ yajanaṃ dānaṃ śastrājīvo bhūtarakṣaṇaṃ ca | 1.3.6
vaiśyasyādhyayanaṃ yajanaṃ dānaṃ kṛṣipāśupālye vaṇijyā ca | 1.3.7
śūdrasya dvijātiśuśrūṣā vārttā kārukuśīlavakarma ca | 1.3.8
gṛhasthasya svadharmājīvas tulyair asamānarṣibhir vaivāhyam ṛtugāmitvaṃ devapitratithipūjā bhṛtyeṣu tyāgaḥ śeṣabhojanaṃ ca | 1.3.9
brahmacāriṇaḥ svādhyāyo agnikāryābhiṣekau bhaikṣavratitvam ācārye prāṇāntikī vṛttis tadabhāve guruputre sabrahmacāriṇi vā | 1.3.10
vānaprasthasya brahmacaryaṃ bhūmau śayyā jaṭājinadhāraṇam agnihotrābhiṣekau devatāpitratithipūjā vanyaś cāhāraḥ | 1.3.11
parivrājakasya jitendriyatvam anārambho niṣkiṃcanatvaṃ saṅgatyāgo bhaikṣavratam anekatrāraṇye ca vāso bāhyābhyantaraṃ ca śaucam | 1.3.12
sarveṣām ahiṃsā satyaṃ śaucam anasūyānṛśaṃsyaṃ kṣamā ca | 1.3.13
svadharmaḥ svargāyānantyāya ca | 1.3.14
tasyātikrame lokaḥ saṃkarād ucchidyeta | 1.3.15

> [The *svadharma*] of a *gṛhastha* is to live according to his [*varṇa*]*svadharma*, matrimony with equals of a different lineage, having sex with his wife in her season, worship of the gods, ancestors, and guests, generosity to servants, and eating the remainder. (*KAŚ* 1.3.9)

The *gṛhastha* here is the married householder observing the *svadharma* of his *varṇa*, whose other religious obligations are largely expressed through the duty of *devapitratithipūjā*, "worship of the gods, ancestors, and guests," and *śeṣabhojana*, "eating the remainder." This is a more restricted formulation of the *gṛhastha's* religious obligations than found in the dharma texts, even when those texts give them in brief. In the Dharmasūtra of Gautama, for example, a précis of the duties of the householder (*GDh* 5.3–9) includes *devapitṛmanuṣyabhūtarṣipūjaka*, "worshiping gods, ancestors, men, beings, and sages" and *devapitṛmanuṣyayajña*, "sacrifices to the gods, ancestors, and men," but to these are added both Vedic recitation (*svādhyaya*) and Bali offerings (*balikarma*). There is, however, no reason to think that the *Arthaśāstra's* concise enumeration of the *gṛhastha's* religious duties is out of keeping with the more expansive instructions of Dharmaśāstra texts. One potentially significant difference between the two, however, is that *gṛhastha* of the *Arthaśāstra* is not explicitly limited to the twice-born *varṇas* (i.e., Brahmin, Kṣatriya, and Vaiśya). It is possible that this should be implied at 1.3.9 (insofar as Śūdras are not reckoned as having descended from a *ṛṣi*), but the absence of an explicit prohibition calls to mind the *Arthaśāstra's* inclusion of Śūdras among the Ārya elsewhere (*KAŚ* 3.13.1), something universally rejected in the Dharmaśāstra literature.

The second occurrence of the term *gṛhastha* comes later in the same discussion of the *vidyās*, this time in the extended discussion of Governance (*daṇḍanīti*). The term *daṇḍanīti* literally means "leading with" or "administering" (*nīti; praṇīti*) "the staff" (*daṇḍa*), in reference to the constructive use of king's capacity for violence. The appropriate use of this coercive power is discussed (again in a passage added during the redaction) by means of one of the text's characteristic debates between Kauṭilya and the "earlier teachers" (*pūrvācāryas*) of the statecraft tradition. The prima facie view (*pūrvapakṣa*) is provided by the earlier teachers, and the proper view is ascribed to Kauṭilya. Whereas the teachers argue that the king should strike a consistently threatening posture, Kauṭilya demurs and invokes the *gṛhastha* as well as the two renouncer *āśramas* to explain his position:

> *tasmāl lokayātrārthī nityam udyatadaṇḍaḥ syāt | na hy evaṃvidhaṃ vaśopanayanam asti bhūtānāṃ yathā daṇḍaḥ ity ācāryāḥ | neti kauṭilyaḥ | tīkṣṇadaṇḍo hi bhūtānām udvejanīyo bhavati | mṛdudaṇḍaḥ paribhūyate | yathārhadaṇḍaḥ pūjyate | suvijñātapraṇīto hi daṇḍaḥ prajā dharmārthakāmair yojayati | duṣpraṇītaḥ kāmakrodhābhyām avajñānād vā vānaprasthaparivrājakān api kopayati, kim aṅga punar gṛhasthān | apraṇītas tu mātsyanyāyam udbhāvayati | balīyān abalaṃ hi grasate daṇḍadharābhāve | sa tena guptaḥ prabhavatīti |*
>
> "Therefore, one who seeks the proper way of the world should always have his staff raised to strike. For, there is nothing like the staff for bringing beings under his power," thus say the teachers.
>
> "No," says Kauṭilya. "For, one rash with the staff is fearsome to creatures. One meek with the staff is disregarded. One who uses the staff justly is honored. For, applied wisely, the staff endows his subjects with *dharma*, *artha*, and *kāma*. Wrongly applied because of desire or anger or out of contempt, it provokes even *vānaprasthas* and *parivrājakas*. How much more *gṛhasthas*? Not applied at all, it gives rise to the law of the fishes. For, the stronger eats the weak when the staff-bearer is absent. Protected by him, the weak prevails." (*KAŚ* 1.4.5–15)

Kauṭilya imagines the example of a king who applies punishment badly, essentially doing so for personal reasons that are harmful to justice. The actions of such a king are outrageous even to the renouncer *āśramas*, who are disengaged from worldly affairs and have presumably attained a greater degree of control over their own passions. If even such dispassionate and withdrawn individuals are angered by a king who punishes improperly, then how much more will it anger *gṛhasthas*, men of the world who are fully engaged in society? It is unclear which factor—lesser control of one's emotions or greater engagement with the world—is meant to account for the *gṛhastha's* increased liability to outrage in this illustration, but either relies on an understanding of the householder as being more invested in the regnant political order. The *gṛhastha* is not presented simply as a home-bound version of either of these types of renouncers, but instead as an individual by nature more engaged with the world. As much would suggest that, at least in this instance, the *gṛhastha* is something other than a domestic renouncer.

These two examples provide the only references to *gṛhastha* in the entire *Arthaśāstra*. The first gives us a rather generic impression of the *gṛhastha* as a married twice-born who observes the occupations ascribed to his *varṇa*, discharges his ritual obligations, and shows generosity to his dependents. The second relies on his intrinsic engagement with worldly affairs, something lacking in the other three *āśramas*. Both references date to the redaction of the *Arthaśāstra* around the third century CE. This means that the earlier version of the *Arthaśāstra*, which I would date to around the first century BCE, possessed no references whatsoever to the *gṛhastha*. Its total absence in the early text and limited use in the redacted text point to two conclusions. First, the *gṛhastha* delineated a sociological category of no use to the earlier *Arthaśāstra* with respect to state policy. Whereas Aśoka mentions the *gṛhastha* as part of his attempt to demonstrate his comprehensive support for all types of religious practitioners (see Ch. 3 of this volume), the interests and strategies of the earlier *Arthaśāstra* lay elsewhere. Second, the presence of the *gṛhastha* in the redacted text should be recognized as part of the shadow that Dharmaśāstra comes to throw across the statecraft tradition.[4] This conclusion will be reinforced in the *Nītisāra* and *Mahābhārata*, two texts even more extensively influenced by dharmaśāstric thought than the *Arthaśāstra*.

Gṛhapatika: More common in the *Arthaśāstra*, although not much more common, is the term *gṛhapatika*[5] (literally, "master of the house"), which occurs seven times in the extant text.[6] It is always found in the compound *gṛhapatikavyañjana*, referring to a spy "in the guise of a *gṛhapatika*." The clandestine cohort of this spy are collectively called the *saṃsthās* (literally, "stations"). They include, along with the *gṛhapatikavyañjana*, the spies called *kāpaṭika* ("student") and *udāsthita* ("apostate ascetic") as well as the *vaidehakavyañjana* ("in the guise of a merchant") and *tāpasavyañjana* ("in the guise of an ascetic").[7] The *saṃsthā* agents are different from other kinds of spies because they continue to fulfill their public social roles while working as informants for and agents of the king.[8] Their chief common characteristic, therefore, is that they operate in plain sight, using their manifest social identity as cover for espionage. They pass the intelligence that they gather to the "mobile agents" (*saṃcāras*), who transmit it back to the king himself, his

4. Further, in the early text, *āśrama* and *āśramin* only refer to "hermitage" and "hermit" and never to one living according to the rules of one of the orthodox *āśramas*. This confirms the sense that all mention of the *āśrama* system date to the redaction of the text and are, in that sense, foreign to the concerns of the original treatise. Those late uses include *KAŚ* 1.3.4; 1.3.17; 1.4.16; 3.1.38; 3.16.33; 13.4.62; and 15.1.9.

5. It does not appear that the suffix *-ka* changes the meaning of *gṛhapati* in this instance. See Jamison 2009.

6. See *KAŚ* 1.1.4; 1.11.1; 1.11.9; 2.35.8; 5.3.22; 12.4.1; 13.3.45.

7. See *KAŚ* 1.11.

8. See Scharfe 1993: 209–212.

"Counselor-Chaplain" (*mantripurohita*),[9] or an official called the "Collector" (*samāhartṛ*).

The three *vyañjana* spies—householder, merchant, ascetic—seem to represent sociological "ideal types" in the Weberian sense. They are described, respectively, as a *karṣaka* ("farmer") (*KAŚ* 1.11.9), a *vāṇijaka* ("merchant") (*KAŚ* 1.11.11), and a *muṇḍa* ("shaved ascetic") or *jaṭila* ("matted-hair ascetic") (*KAŚ* 1.11.13). It might be that these three groups possessed a particular categorical prominence in popular imagination, where they represented important social types that had means, influence, or status, but were not already associated directly with the king (like the royal family, soldiers, ministers, and royal officials). It is noteworthy, however, that the *gṛhapatika* is to be found in the *Arthaśāstra* only with regard to the spy of this type, and never otherwise as the subject of any specific royal policies. This is not so for the *vaidehaka* and *tāpasa*, regarding both of whom specific rules can be found. Perhaps the category of *gṛhapatika* was too internally diverse to make an effective subject of policy.

The *gṛhapatikavyañjana* is defined by Kauṭilya at 1.11.9 as a *karṣako vṛttikṣīṇaḥ prajñāśaucayukta*, "a farmer with a diminished livelihood, smart and honest." The instructions for his recruitment are based on those given in previous passages for the recruitment of the *kāpaṭika* ("student") and *udāsthita* ("apostate ascetic"). I supply here the implied concepts and phrases:

> *sa kṛṣikarmapradiṣṭāyāṃ bhūmau . . . [prabhūtahiraṇyāntevāsī karma kārayet | karmaphalāc ca sarvapravrajitānāṃ grāsācchādanāvasathān pratividadhyāt | vṛttikāmāṃś copajapet – 'etenaiva veṣeṇa rājārthaś caritavyo bhaktavetanakāle copasthātavyam' iti | sarvapravrajitāś ca svaṃ svaṃ vargam evam upajapeyuḥ |]*
>
> In a place assigned to him for agriculture [and supplied with plenty of money and assistants, he should have the work carried out. From the profits of his work, moreover, he should provide food, clothing, and shelter to all renouncers. And he should instigate those who are looking for a livelihood: "Wearing this same outfit, you should work for the benefit of the king and come here at the time for rations and wages." All renouncers, furthermore, should similarly instigate their respective groups.] (*KAŚ* 1.11.10; tr. Olivelle 2013)

9. On this official, see Olivelle 2013: 474.

It is unlikely that the *gṛhapatika* is meant, like the *udāsthita*, to work among renouncers (*pravrajitas*). We should probably understand mutatis mutandi that he works among other agriculturalists. The *gṛhapatika* is described as a farmer (*karṣaka*), but he has rights to land access, whether through ownership or not, as well as wealth and assistants. It is likely, therefore, that the *gṛhapatika* is not merely a field laborer, to which the term *karṣaka* can also refer, but rather someone of higher status in the community. Whatever the case, the *gṛhapatika* is defined by vocation and not religious practice.

We can divine something more about the *gṛhapatika* by examining the activities assigned to the *gṛhapatikavyañjana*. In their work for the Collector, the *gṛhapatikavyañjanas* are instructed to "learn the sum of fields, homes, and families in the villages to which they are assigned" (*KAŚ* 2.35.8).[10] That *gṛhapatikas* were active in villages conforms to their identification as farmers. Because the Collector's official duties focus primarily on the countryside, however, this passage provides less decisive testimony of their social geography than it might otherwise. In what is probably a late passage (*KAŚ* 12.4.1), the *gṛhapatikavyañjana* is again said to carry out his activity in villages, this time the villages of the enemy king. By comparison, *vaidehakavyañjanas* are said there to be deployed within the enemy's fortified city, while *gorakṣakatāpasavyañjanas* (spies "in the guise of herders and ascetics") work on the borders of the enemy's country.[11] Presumably all of these agents are recruited from among the enemy's subjects. A final bit of context is provided by instructions for a ruse meant to give the king's army access to the enemy's fortress. The specifics of the plan are somewhat unclear in the text, but it begins with soldiers entering the enemy's fortified city disguised as "artisans, craftsmen, monks, performers, and merchants" (*kāruśilpipāṣaṇḍakuśīlavavaidehakavyañjana; KAŚ* 13.3.44). The use of these identities as disguises for soldiers, however, undermines the earlier description of such spies as actual members of their respective social groups. So, when the next passage instructs *gṛhapatikavyañjanas* to smuggle them "weapons and armor in carts conveying wood, grass, grain, and goods or in flags and images of gods" (*KAŚ* 13.3.45), it is not clear whether these are truly *gṛhapatikas* or soldiers disguised as them.[12] Either way, the strategy relies on the assumption

---

10. . . . *yeṣu grāmeṣu praṇihitās teṣāṃ grāmāṇāṃ kṣetragṛhakulāgraṃ vidyuḥ* . . .

11. *ye cāsya durgeṣu vaidehakavyañjanāḥ, grāmeṣu gṛhapatikavyañjanāḥ, janapadasaṃdhiṣu gorakṣakatāpasavyañjanāḥ, te sāmantāṭavikatatkulīnāparuddhānāṃ paṇyāgārapūrvaṃ preṣayeyuḥ 'ayaṃ deśo hāryaḥ' iti* |

12. *teṣāṃ gṛhapatikavyañjanāḥ kāṣṭhatṛṇadhānyapaṇyaśakaṭaiḥ praharaṇāvaraṇāny abhihareyuḥ, devadhvajapratimābhir vā* |

that *gṛhapatikas* bringing agricultural goods and wares into the fortified city were commonplace. We might imagine the rural farmer bringing his produce and cottage manufactures to sell in the markets of the city.

A verse added to the *Arthaśāstra* during its redaction discusses the use of some of the *saṃsthās* among one's enemies and replaces the *gṛhapatika* with *karṣaka*, whose domain is described as the countryside. This verse also adds another sociological type to the group, the *vrajavāsin* ("herdsman"):

> *durgeṣu vaṇijaḥ saṃsthā durgānte siddhatāpasāḥ |*
> *karṣakodāsthitā rāṣṭre rāṣṭrānte vrajavāsinaḥ ||*
>
> The *saṃsthās* in the fortified city are the merchants, on the edge of the fortified city are the *siddhatāpasas*,
> in the countryside, the *karṣakas* and *udāsthitas*, and at the edge of the country, the *vrajavāsins*. (*KAŚ* 1.12.22)

The substitution of *gṛhapatika* with *karṣaka* here, in light of his earlier description by the same term, reinforces a degree of identity between the two categories, so that characteristics of the *karṣaka*, such as his residence in the rural countryside, might reasonably considered to help confirm the geography of the *gṛhapatika* (*KAŚ* 3.9.11; 3.10.35).

At the same time, the *karṣaka* is commonly found throughout the text in distinct, if related, sociological contexts. He appears alongside the *gorakṣaka/gopālaka* ("cowherd"), *vaidehaka*, and sometimes other groups (*KAŚ* 2.35.4; 2.35.13; 3.9.11; 3.13.28; 3.15.5), all of whom appear to constitute what we might think of as the productive classes. At 5.2.2–16, *karṣakas* are the objects of royal exploitation when a king in dire straits is in need of wealth. At 6.1.8, the *karṣaka* is described as having a master (*svāmin*), although the identity of this master is not clear. This conflicts with the seeming independence of the *gṛhapatika*. Finally, at 7.11.21, the same three groups—*karṣaka, gorakṣaka,* and *vaidehaka*—are identified as comprising *avaravarṇa*, "the lower *varṇa*." The term *karṣaka* probably had relatively broader semantic range than *gṛhapatika*, so I would hesitate to ascribe the former's lack of independence and low status to the latter as a class.[13]

Gṛhasvāmin/kuṭumbin: The words *gṛhasvāmin* and *kuṭumbin* are used four and three times in the *Arthaśāstra*, respectively. Both refer to the "head of household" understood as the individual who is the authorized and legally

13. One possibility that deserves further investigation is whether some of this terminological variation can be explained by different layers or sources within the complex compositional history of the *Arthaśāstra*.

liable representative of a household. The term *gṛhasvāmin* (literally, "master of the house") occurs three times in the final chapter of the second of book and once in the legal code of the third book. Two of these passages identify the *gṛhasvāmin* as a liable party in case of misconduct:

> *cikitsakaḥ pracchannavraṇapratīkārakārayitāram apathyakāriṇaṃ ca gṛhasvāmī ca nivedya gopasthānikayor mucyeta, anyathā tulyadoṣaḥ syāt | prasthitāgatau ca nivedayet, anyathā rātridoṣaṃ bhajeta |*
>
> A physician who informs the Revenue Officer or the County Supervisor about a man who has made him treat a wound secretly or has done something pernicious is to be released—and so would a head of household; otherwise he becomes guilty of the same crime. He should also inform on anyone who departs or arrives; otherwise he becomes guilty of a night offense; on secure nights, he should pay three Paṇas. (*KAŚ* 2.36.10–11; tr. Olivelle 2013)
>
> *pradīptam anabhidhāvato gṛhasvāmino dvādaśapaṇo daṇḍaḥ, ṣaṭpaṇo 'vakrayiṇaḥ |*
>
> If the head of a household does not run to a house on fire, he is fined 12 Paṇas; a tenant, six Paṇas. (*KAŚ* 2.36.23; tr. Olivelle 2013)

In both cases, the *gṛhasvāmin* bears a legal responsibility presumably not shared by others in the household. The second example, in contrasting him with a tenant, emphasizes that the *gṛhasvāmin* is a "homeowner" specifically. The third occurrence recognizes the *gṛhasvāmin's* right to speak on behalf of his household in negotiations with neighbors on building requirements:

> *sambhūya vā gṛhasvāmino yatheṣṭaṃ kārayeyuḥ, aniṣṭaṃ vārayeyuḥ |*
>
> Alternatively, the heads of household may come together and jointly get them constructed as they like and prevent what they do not like. (*KAŚ* 3.8.18; tr. Olivelle 2013)

All of these passages infer that the *gṛhasvāmin* is a homeowner. In the first passage, the *gṛhasvāmin's* house is presumably the site where the wounded man received secret treatment and/or was harbored. The second case refers to a burning house, probably a building near the householder's home. In the third passage, it is the *gṛhasvāmin* as a local home-owner who confers with his peers on acceptable building codes for their dwellings. This is confirmed in a fourth occurrence, *KAŚ* 2.36.21, which refers to a *gṛhasvāmin*'s "own home" (*svagṛha*).

The term *kuṭumbin* (literally, "one who has a family") is also used in legal contexts in which the rights and responsibilities of householders are discussed:

> *karmāntakṣetravaśena kuṭumbināṃ sīmānaṃ sthāpayet* |
>
> [In the capitol] he should establish the boundaries of householders in conformity to the land for their manufactories. (*KAŚ* 2.4.24)
>
> *kuṭumbinaḥ kṛtyeṣu śvetasurām, auṣadhārthaṃ vāriṣṭam, anyad vā kartuṃ labheran* |
>
> Householders should be permitted to produce white Surā-liquor during festive occasions, and for medicinal purposes Ariṣṭa or other kinds. (*KAŚ* 2.25.35; tr. Olivelle 2013)
>
> *sūnādhyakṣaḥ pradiṣṭābhayānām abhayavanavāsināṃ ca mṛgapaśupakṣimatsyānāṃ bandhavadhahiṃsāyām uttamaṃ daṇḍaṃ kārayet, kuṭumbinām abhayavanaparigraheṣu madhyamam* |
>
> The director of abattoirs should levy the highest fine for the binding, killing, or harming deer, wild animals, birds, or fish that have been proclaimed to be protected or dwell in sanctuaries, the middle fine for householders in sanctuary enclosures. (*KAŚ* 2.26.1)

The physical house is directly invoked in the first example and implied in the second. The third is unclear: it could refer to householders whose homes are in sanctuary enclosures. Whatever the case, the term *kuṭumbin* seems to have a slightly broader semantic range under the law than *gṛhasvāmin* under the law. It is quite possible, for instance, that a *kuṭumbin* is not conceived as necessarily owning a house, as is certainly the case with the *gṛhasvāmin* and presumably also with the *gṛhapatika*. In none of the examples are the *gṛhasvāmin* or *kuṭumbin* associated specifically with agriculture or village life.

In conclusion, the extant *Arthaśāstra* discusses the householder in three distinct registers. The first, chronologically later than the other two, involves the *gṛhastha āśrama*. The *gṛhastha* is present in the text only as part of the late and secondary influence of Dharmaśāstra. He never features as the subject of state policies. The second register invokes the *gṛhapatika* as a spy. He is closely related to the *karṣaka* insofar as he derives his income from agricultural lands, but he does not appear to be identical to him. There is some evidence to suggest that the *gṛhapatika* possesses land and means and is a person of some standing in the community. For reasons that are not clear in the text, however, discussion of the *gṛhapatika* is limited to espionage. Finally, the terms *gṛhasvāmin* and *kuṭumbin* are used when the legal rights and obligations of home-owners and heads of families are discussed.

Nītisāra

Gṛhamedhin: It is well known that Kāmandaki presents his work as being abridged (*saṃkṣipta*) from the *Arthaśāstra* (*KNS* 1.7–8), even though he does include material from other sources. Like Kauṭilya, he refers to the *āśramas* (*KNS* 2.10, 23, 24, 35; see also 14.41) and the householder (*gṛhamedhin; KNS* 2.25–26) in the context of the four *vidyās* and the importance of proper *daṇḍanīti*. He is somewhat more fulsome in his description of the duties of the *gṛhamedhin*:

> *agnihotropacaraṇaṃ jīvanaṃ ca svakarmabhiḥ |*
> *dharmadāreṣu kalyeṣu parvavarjaṃ ratikriyā ||*
> *devapitratithibhyaś ca pūjā dīnānukampanam |*
> *śrutismṛtyarthasaṃsthānaṃ dharmo 'yaṃ gṛhamedhinaḥ ||*
>
> Attending to the *agnihotra* sacrifice and making a living according to his prescribed activities,
> sex with his lawful, healthy wife except during the days of the changes of the moon;
> worship of gods, ancestors, and guests, compassion for the poor,
> obedience to the meaning of *śruti* and *smṛti*: this is the dharma of a *gṛhamedhin*. (*KNS* 2.25–26)

The correlation between the instructions for the *gṛhamedhin*/*gṛhastha* in the two texts is extensive, with Kāmandaki's only substantive addition being an explicit requirement to observe the precepts of *śruti* and *smṛti*. As in the *Arthaśāstra*, the presentation of the *āśrama* system serves here to signal the adherence of Kāmandaki's instructions to the orthodox social order propounded in the Dharmaśāstra tradition. Likewise, the *gṛhamedhin* is never the subject of state policies in the *Nītisāra*. Kāmandaki's presentation of the ascetics called *vanavāsin* (=*vānaprastha; KNS* 2.27–28) and *parivrāj* (=*parivrājaka; KNS* 2.29–31) make clear that he does not conceive of the *gṛhamedhin* as some kind of home-bound ascetic.

The only other use of *gṛhamedhin* in the *Nītisāra* goes beyond the application of the concept in the *Arthaśāstra*. Kāmandaki uses a trope that we will see again in the *Rājadharmaparvan*, namely that the king himself is a *gṛhamedhin*.

His third chapter, which deals with the topic of *ācāravyavasthāpana* ("The Establishment of Good Conduct"), dilates on commendable behavior and gives the following two verses before its conclusion at *KNS* 3.40:

> *sanātane vartmaṇi sādhu tiṣṭhatām ayaṃ hi panthā gṛhamedhināṃ mataḥ |*
> *anena gacchan niyataṃ mahātmanām imam ca lokaṃ paramaṃ ca vindati ||*
> *iti pathi viniveśitātmano ripur api gacchati sādhumitratām |*
> *tad avanipati matsarād ṛte vinayaguṇena jagad vaśaṃ nayet ||*
>
> This is considered to be the path of householders who are firmly established in the eternal way.
> Always going by this, the way of the great-souled, he obtains this world and the highest world.
> For him who is devoted to this path, even an enemy becomes a dear friend.
> Thus, a king, because of his zeal for what is right, brings the world under his power through the quality of his discipline. (*KNS* 3.38–39)

In the first of these verses, the elements of good conduct praised in the prior passage are connected with the path of the householder (*gṛhamedhin*). Observing them brings about good results in this world and the next. In the second verse, the same elements of good conduct are operationalized as a political strategy based on their capacity to win over even the enemies of the king. The substitution of the king for the *gṛhamedhin* relies on a degree of identity between the two, although Kāmandaki says nothing further about it. These verses, read in the context of the passages that proceed them, rule out the possibility that the *gṛhastha*/*gṛhamedhin* might refer here to a "stay at home" ascetic of any kind.

There are no references to the *gṛhapati(ka)* in the *Nītisāra*, nor are there any other terms for "householder" used. With respect to spies in the guise of everyday people, Kāmandaki mentions *tapasvivyañjanas* ("in the guise of ascetics"; *KNS* 13.14) and, later, *tapasviliṅgins* (agents "dressed like ascetics") along with *dhūrtas* ("rogues"), *śilpins* ("aristans"), and *paṇyopajīvins* ("merchants"; *KNS* 13.27). Among the *saṃsthā* spies, however, he lists: *vaṇij* ("merchant"), *kṛṣīvala* ("farmer"), *liṅgin* ("ascetic"), *bhikṣuka* ("monk"), and *adhyāpaka* ("teacher") (*KNS* 13.36). Here, *kṛṣīvala* appears to stand in for the *gṛhapatikavyañjana* from the *Arthaśāstra*.

Rājadharmaparvan (Mahābhārata *12.1–12.128*)

The *gṛhastha* and the *āśrama* system are far more prominent in the *Rājadharmaparvan* of the *Mahābhārata* than in either the *Arthaśāstra* or *Nītisāra*.[14] A search reveals that the term *gṛhastha* occurs there fourteen times and *gārhasthya* thirteen times. The term *gṛhamedhin* is found once, *gṛhāśrama/in* three times, and *gṛhin* twice. There are no references to the *gṛhapati, gṛhasvāmin*, or the *kuṭumbin*, all terms of art in the *Arthaśāstra*. This suggests from the outset that the *Rājadharmaparvan's* conceptualization of the householder conforms with that of the *āśrama* system.

The *Rājadharmaparvan* is heterogeneous text, likely with a complex compositional history, which deserves much fuller exploration (Fitzgerald 2004: 145–52). Fitzgerald has proposed "an original core of a course of *rājadharma* instruction" (Fitzgerald 2004: 152), *Mahābhārata* 12.67–90, to which various other texts were prepended or postpended. Significantly, there is only one reference to the householder (*gṛhin*) in this core tract:

> *naikāntavinipātena vicacāreha kaścana |*
> *dharmī gṛhī vā rājā vā brahmacāry atha vā punaḥ ||*
>
> If he has been observant of dharma, one who erred in this world does not go to complete ruin,
> Be he a householder, king, or *brahmacārin*. (*MBh* 12.76.28)

The reference to the *brahmacārin* suggests that the *gṛhin* here is someone in the *gṛhastha āśrama*. Unlike in other passages, examined below, the king is differentiated from the *gṛhin*. This verse does not, however, establish any policy of the state with special reference to the householder, even though it is found in Fitzgerald's "original core" of the *Rājadharmaparvan*. If we isolate the technical *nīti* passages in the *Rājadharmaparvan*, those concerned with practical matters of statecraft,[15] we find no references to the householder whatsoever.

---

14. Occurrences of householder terms in the Kyōto e-text (http://www.cc.kyoto-su.ac.jp/~yanom/sanskrit/mahabharata/m12.2.e), which follows the numbering of the Poona critical edition: *gṛhastha* (12.1.5; 12.12.11; 12.12.21–22 (2x); 12.15.12; 12.18.27–28 (3x); 12.23.2–3 (2x); 12.37.27–28 (2x); 12.61.16; 12.63.2); *gārhasthya* (12.11.20; 12.11.27; 12.12.21; 12.23.2–3; 12.61.2; 12.61.10; 12.61.16; 12.66.15–17 (3x); 12.66.19; 12.66.29); *gṛhamedhin* (12.37.26); *gṛhāśrama/in* (12.61.4; 12.61.12; 12.66.18); *gṛhin* (12.23.5; 12.76.28).

15. For example, all or parts of 12.69; 12.72; 12.80–81; 12.84–89; 12.96–97. The coherence of this *nīti* instructions, and whether they represent a root text around which Fitzgerald's "core course" was constructed, requires further investigation.

Other than 12.76.28, all references to householders in the *Rājadharmaparvan* come either in its first part (*MBh* 12.1–55), which frame Bhīṣma's direct instruction to Yudhiṣṭhira (Fitzgerald 2004: 146), or in the eleven chapters "prepended" to the "original core" (*MBh* 12.56–66; Fitzgerald 2004: 152). This reinforces what we have observed in both the *Arthaśāstra* and *Nītisāra*, which is that the *gṛhastha* and *āśrama* are external to state policy as the technical focus of the *nīti* tradition. It is only with respect to the ideology of kingship, and then only insofar as that is influenced by Dharmaśāstra, that either becomes relevant in the extant literature. The comparatively rich number of references to *gṛhastha/gārhasthya/gṛhamedhin/gṛhin* in the *Rājadharmaparvan* should be read, therefore, as an index of the extent to which the *Mahābhārata* as we have it participates more fully and intentionally in the project of presenting kingship and statecraft within the framework of Brahmanical theology.

The *Rājadharmaparvan* does, in this way, provide the most thorough view of the *gṛhastha* in the political literature of the period. In it, we find no significant distinction in the religious practices implied for the *gṛhastha, gṛhamedhin, gṛhāśramin,* and *gṛhin*, all of which appear to be fully synonymous and refer to the married twice-born who fulfills the *svadharma* of his *varṇa* (see, e.g., 12.63.2).[16] Most occurrences come in the first part of the *Rājadharmaparvan* in passages in which various interlocutors attempt to persuade Yudhiṣṭhira from renunciation by arguing for the superiority of the *gṛhastha āśrama* to that of the renouncer.[17] Often these arguments claim that the *gṛhastha,* and not the renouncer, is actually the true or highest ascetic. This should not, however, be understood to indicate an invariable association of kings with householders. We have already seen a verse in which the two are distinguished from one another (*MBh* 12.76.28), and we find another passage in which different *āśrama*s are prescribed to the king based on his specific activities (*MBh* 12.61). Despite the ready association of the king with the *gṛhastha*, the *āśrama* system could be and was applied to kingship in different ways.

In the chapters prepended to Fitzgerald's "original core," Bhīṣma is asked for and gives an overview of the *āśramṇs* (*MBh* 12.61.1–21). He says the following of the householder:

16. For example, these terms appear to be used interchangeably at *MBh* 12.37.26–28 and 12.66.15–19.

17. See, e.g., *MBh* 12.11.1–28 12.12.11–22, 12.18.27–28, and 12.23.2–5. See also *MBh* 12.1.5, 12.15.12, and 12.37.27–8.

adhītya vedān kṛtasarvakṛtyaḥ saṃtānam utpādya sukhāni bhuktvā |
samāhitaḥ pracared duścaram tam gārhasthyadharmam munidharmadṛṣṭam ||
svadāratuṣṭa ṛtukālagāmī niyogasevī naśaṭho najihmaḥ |
mitāśano devaparaḥ kṛtajñaḥ satyo mṛduś cānṛśaṃsaḥ kṣamāvān ||
dānto vidheyo havyakavye 'pramatto annasya dātā satatam dvijebhyaḥ |
amatsarī sarvaliṅgipradātā vaitānanityaś ca gṛhāśramī syāt ||

By studying the Veda, fulfilling all of his duties, begetting progeny, and enjoying pleasures, a steadfast man may discharge the dharma of the householder, which is difficult to follow and seen as the same as the dharma of an ascetic.[18]

Someone who observes the *aśrama* of the house should be satisfied with his own wife, should have sex with her in her season, observe levirate, and should be neither false nor dishonest. He should be measured in what eats, pious to the gods, grateful, honest, mild, benevolent, and patient. He should be restrained, compliant, and attentive in his offerings to the gods and his ancestors. He should always give food to Brahmins. He should be liberal and generous to people of all religious groups. And he should never neglect the Vedic sacrifices. (*MBh* 12.61.10–12)

Thereupon follow a few verses praising *gārhasthya* along lines already established earlier in the *Rājadharmaparvan*: it involves an exceeding measure of *tapas* (*MBh* 12.61.13) and is the best of the *āśrama*s for the good (*MBh* 12.61.15). As mentioned above, *gārhasthya* is often presented as a kind of asceticism in the *Rājadharmaparvan*:

devān pitṝn manuṣyāmś ca munīn gṛhyāś ca devatāḥ |
pūjayitvā tataḥ paścād gṛhastho bhoktum arhati ||
yathā pravrajito bhikṣur gṛhasthaḥ svagṛhe vaset |
evaṃvṛttaḥ priyair dāraiḥ samvasan dharmam āpnuyāt ||

The gods, the ancestors, men, sages, and the household deities:
Only after worshiping these may a *gṛhastha* eat.
Just as a monk who has gone forth, so should the *gṛhastha* dwell in his own home.

18. It appears that the gerunds in *MBh* 12.61.10ab should be understood as causal rather than denoting prior completed actions.

Living thus and dwelling with his beloved wife, he shall obtain dharma. (*MBh* 12.37.26c–28)

This example shows how readily the vocation of the *gṛhastha* is interpreted as a kind of domestic asceticism in the *Rājadharmaparvan*. For the most part, such interpretations appear to be a secondary development in which the *gṛhastha* is homologized with the ascetic for the purpose of enhancing his prestige. There is no hint that the *gṛhastha* represented a kind of domestic religiosity more esteemed than and distinct from typical, unmarked householders.

In all, the *Rājadharmaparvan* confirms what has already been observed in both the *Arthaśāstra* and *Nītisāra*, namely that the *gṛhastha* was not a subject of state policy in the statecraft literature. Confined to ideological discussions of kingship, the *gṛhastha* is most pertinent in the *Rājadharmaparvan* in arguments tendered against Yudhiṣṭhira's renunciation.

Kāmasūtra

Gārhasthya/gārhapatya: We can conclude, then, with a look at the only surviving classical text from the expert tradition on erotics, the *Kāmasūtra* of Vātsyāyana. Much like the *nīti* texts, the *Kāmasūtra* signals its adherence to Brāhmaṇical orthodoxy by recognizing the validity of *varṇa* and *āśrama* (*KS* 1.2.25). There is, however, little integration of the *āśramas* into the teaching of the text, with one possible exception, explored below. Instead, Vātsyāyana divides human life into three phases: *bālya* ("childhood"); *yauvana* ("youth"); and *sthāvira* ("old age"). He distributes across these the four *puruṣārthas* ("benefits to man") and *vidyā* ("learning"):

> *bālye vidyāgrahaṇādīn arthān | kāmaṃ ca yauvane | sthāvire dharmaṃ mokṣaṃ ca |*[19]
>
> In childhood he should devote himself to material gains (*artha*), such as getting an education. In youth, he should devote himself to *kāma*. In old age, he should devote himself to *dharma* and *mokṣa*. (*KS* 1.2.2–4)[20]

19. At least one manuscript reads *balye vidyāgrahaṇādīn | arthaṃ kāmaṃ ca yauvane* (Durgaprasād 1900: 11n), thus assigning *artha* also to the period of youth. This is not supported, however, by the commentary of Yaśodhara (Durgaprasād 1900: 11–12; Shastri 1929: 11.

20. In his comment on this passage, Yaśodhara cites a verse "in another text" that divides life into three phases: *bāla*, up to age 16; *madhyama*, from there to age 70; and *vṛddha*, "beyond that."

It is not clear how much the *āśramas* should be read into these three phases. Rocher (1985: 524) has argued that the three stages do map onto the *āśramas* (*bālya=brahmacarya; yauvana=gṛhastha; sthāvira=vānaprastha* and *parivrajaka*).[21] It is true that two lines later Vātsyāyana does equate *brahmacarya* with *bālya*, saying *brahmacaryam eva tv ā vidyāgrahaṇāt* ("And celibacy until the completion of study"; *KS* 1.2.6). In this line, *brahmacarya* refers specifically to celibacy, which is the hallmark of the first of *āśrama*. Vātsyāyana's intent is to prohibit the pursuit of *kāma* by children. Even so, understanding these three life stages in terms of *āśrama*, as Rocher suggests, leaves us with the uncomfortable equation of dharma not with the *gṛhastha*, who is the chief subject of Dharmaśāstra texts and defined by his observance of the *svadharma* of his *varṇa*, but with the forest-dwelling *vānaprastha* and the wandering *parivrajaka*, both of whom have retreated from the full observance of their *varṇadharma*.

The tension between Vātsyāyana's view and that of the *āśramas* is further evident in his only reference to the *gṛhastha*, which comes in the form of the abstract noun *gārhasthya*, "householdership."[22] The protagonist of the *Kāmasūtra*, who is called the *nāgaraka* or "man-about-town," is said to occupy the state of *gārhasthya* (*KS* 1.4.1). The instructions for the *nāgaraka* begin thus:

> *gṛhītavidyaḥ pratigrahajayakrayanirveśādhigatair arthair anvayāgatair ubhayair vā gārhasthyam adhigamya nāgarakavṛttaṃ varteta | nagare pattane kharvaṭe mahati vā sajjanāśraye sthānam | yātrāvaśād vā | tatra bhavanam āsannodakaṃ vṛkṣavāṭikāvad vibhaktakarmakakṣaṃ dvivāsagṛhaṃ kārayet |*
>
> When his education is complete, a man should become a householder by means of wealth obtained as a gift, through conquest, through purchase, or wages, or obtained from his family, or both, and he should follow the conduct of a man-about-town. His abode is in the company of good people, whether in a city, town, or large market-town, or where his livelihood may allow. There he should establish his residence near water, with an orchard, apportioned into areas for different activities, and provided with two bedchambers. (*KS* 1.4.1–3)

---

21. On these phases of life, see Olivelle 1993: 132–33.

22. Interestingly, Rocher renders this *gārhapatya* in his 1985 article. The edition of the *Kāmasūtra* that he cites (Shastri 1929), however, reads *gārhasthya*, as does Yaśodhara's commentary thereupon. I am yet to find the source of this reading, although it would strengthen my general argument here.

The first words of this passage, *gṛhītavidya*, indicate clearly that the phase of *gārhasthya* begins after the completion of the education, which was assigned earlier to the period of *bālya*. To this extent we can imply a relationship between *bālya*/*brahmacarya* and *yauvana*/*gārhasthya*.

Vātsyāyana's use of *gārhasthya* exhibits certain differences with the Dharmaśāstra texts, however. He says that one "goes to" or "acquires" (*adhi* + *gam*) *gārhasthya* "by means of wealth" (*arthaiḥ*), which emphasizes the material aspects of becoming a householder. The subsequent passages discuss the establishment of his residence specifically as well as his mode of habitation and his social behavior. They say nothing about getting married and establishing the domestic fire, which are the most important elements of becoming a *gṛhastha* in the dharma literature.[23] Even more interesting, Vātsyāyana is clearly invoking the four *varṇas* when he identifies the various means of income (gifts=Brahmins; conquest=Kṣatriyas; purchase=Vaiśyas; wages=Śūdras), meaning that he sees *gārhasthya* as a state open also to Śūdras, as may also be the case in the *Arthaśāstra* (Cf. *Arthaśāstra*). This underlines the extent to which the *Kāmasūtra* discusses *gārhasthya* in social/material terms, in sharp distinction to the ritual/religious terms of Dharmaśāstra. For Vātsyāyana, being a *gṛhastha* means having one's own dwelling, an independent social life, and access to sex. Even as he links this state to *varṇa* and *āśrama*, he appears to rely on a conceptualization of *gārhasthya* somewhat distinct from the orthodox perspective.

Ultimately, our estimation of the relationship between Vātsyāyana's *gārhasthya* and that of the Dharmaśāstra depends on the extent to which we presume an a priori adherence of the former to the latter. As Rocher (1985) has pointed out, Vātstyāyana goes to great lengths to harmonize his instructions on *kāma* within the broader normative framework of orthodox Brahmanism, but he sometimes runs counter to it. Hence, we cannot deny that Vātsyāyana is aware of and writing in the context of Dharmaśāstra. And yet, there is a critical gap or tension between the two. Certainly, Vātsyāyana knew of the *āśramas* and had these terms at his disposal. That he did not use them as a means of apportioning the *puruṣārthas* to the phases of human life would therefore seem significant. Moreover, it is not entirely correct, as I have shown, to say

23. The commentator Yaśodhara explains that Vātsyāyana has used the term *gṛhastha* precisely to imply that a *nāgaraka* must be married, which he says is a necessary condition for "living the life of a *nāgaraka*." But this fails to account for the instrumental role played by wealth in Vātsyāyana's connection with becoming a *gārhasthya*. Hence, it cannot simply refer to the married state. Yaśodhara instead construes marriage and wealth as distinct necessary preconditions, but this hardly seems to be Vātsyāyana's intention.

that Vātstyāyana's presentation is made "plainly within the framework of the *āśramas* established by the *dharma* texts" (Rocher 1985: 524). A more accurate explanation would seem to be that Vātstyāyana was trying to demonstrate the conformity of a certain way of life (that of the *nāgaraka*) to dharmaśāstric precepts, but did not fully resolve differences between the two. Whether he was adapting the dharmaśāstric concept of *gārhasthya* to the *nāgaraka*'s way of life or drawing on a distinct, if related, conceptualization thereof, remains uncertain.

Conclusion

In the classical *nīti* and *kāma* literature, the *gṛhastha*, as the holy householder depicted in the *āśrama* system, sits on the margins of each as a technical tradition. He is pertinent only to what we might consider the ideological framework in which the technique of each tradition is embedded. In all of these texts, discussion of the *gṛhastha* comes as part of an effort to signal adherence to Brahmanical orthodoxy, but in none of them does the category penetrate the specialized instructions of their respective traditions. This is true even for the *Kāmasūtra*. The *nāgaraka* is described as occupying the state of *gārhasthya*, but few to none of the characteristics that define the *gṛhastha* in the Dharmaśāstra bear on the details of the text's instructions on sex and erotics.

With the possible exception of the *Kāmasūtra*, the *gṛhastha* is presented in all of these texts just as he is in Dharmaśāstra: a married twice-born man who performs the activities ascribed to his *varṇa*. In both the *Nītisāra* and *Rājadharmaparvan*, there is an emphasis on the householder as embodying specific moral virtues. Much of this praise is bound up in efforts to extol the virtues of *gṛhastha* to the king. In the *Rājadharmaparvan*, such praise often comes in claims that the householder mode of life, which would allow Yudhiṣṭhira to remain on the throne, is superior to that of renunciation. Certain passages there go so far as to argue that the householder is the true renouncer and, in doing so, depict him as a kind of "stay-at-home" ascetic. These seem to be rhetorical efforts used to elevate the *gṛhastha* rather than the survival of an older conceptualization of the *gṛhastha* as a form of domestic religiosity distinct from other modes of domestic religious life available to Brahmins or the twice-born in general.

The *gṛhastha*, it would seem, is a denizen of the ideological precincts of these four texts. All of the *nīti* texts avoid making the *gṛhastha* a subject of state policy, for which purpose the *Arthaśāstra* prefers the use the terms *gṛhapatika*, *gṛhasvāmin*, and *kuṭumbin*. The *gṛhapatika* appears to be understood as an agriculturalist enjoying a certain amount of wealth and standing in the community.

He inhabits the rural countryside whose various relationships and resources position him well as a node in the king's information-gathering activities. He appears to be distinct from more common farmhands and is only discussed in the context of espionage. When the householder is discussed in legal contexts, with respect to liability or rights, the *Arthaśāstra* uses *gṛhasvāmin* or *kuṭumbin*. Of these, the former seems to be preferred in instances when the physical house (*gṛha*) itself is the focus of discussion. The preference of the *Arthaśāstra* for these terms further underlines the extent to which the *gṛhastha* was largely invisible to the state from the perspective of policy.

PART III

Epic and Kāvya Literature

10

The Gṛhastha *in the* Mahābhārata

Adam Bowles

Introduction

The present chapter offers a survey of terms and concepts relating to the "householder" in the *Mahābhārata* (*MBh*). The two most significant terms for this survey are *gṛhastha* and its derivative *gārhasthya*, but others fall within its ambit as well, such as the roughly coterminous *gṛhāśrama*, *gṛhin*, and *kuṭumbin*, and the sometimes synonymous *gṛhamedhin* ("performer of the domestic sacrifices"). In many cases these terms are used interchangeably, though by far the most common is *gṛhastha*, as we shall see below. The *gṛhapati* (literally, "lord of the house") is relevant too, though its register is by now quite distinct from the other terms.

Surveys of words or concepts in the *Mahābhārata* are beset by certain well-known problems. Leaving aside the epic's vast size, its complex history of composition, redaction, and transmission—much of which remains unclear, despite recent, often brilliant, attempts to resolve such issues[1]—bedevil simplistic approaches to the narrative, and the ideological and sociological imperatives, and the temporality of these imperatives, underlying the text "as we have received it." The cautionary quotation marks serve to flag that "we" scholars "receive" the *Mahābhārata* in most cases through the great scholarly enterprise that produced its "Critical Edition," published

1. Of most significance recently is the work of Mahadevan (2008), who has advanced a complex theory regarding the transmission of the *MBh* to the south of India, thereby providing a *terminus ante quem* for the *MBh* taken to be approximately "recovered" in the constituted text of the Critical Edition.

by the Bhandarkar Oriental Research Institute in Pune between 1927 and 1966.[2] The present survey, as with most such studies, will by and large be concerned with the "constituted" text of the Critical Edition—that which appears "above the line" in the printed corpus. Nevertheless, the Critical Edition is not just that text, but also all those elements that appear "below the line," as variations from the constituted text,[3] and those that appear in the appendixes, being large text fragments not meeting the criteria for being included in the constituted text of the Critical Edition.[4] Yet, even a focus on just the constituted text of the Critical Edition does not relieve us of the problems of composition, redaction, and transmission. When was it composed? In whose interests? Does it represent a unitary voice (that of a community, or a "time," or a set of identifiable "interests")? If not, what can we infer from such a conclusion for the history of the *Mahābhārata*'s composition, redaction, and transmission? These questions could continue ad infinitum, and often lend themselves to circularity. Variable ideas in the text become evidence for temporal conclusions; but the evidence for the variability of ideas is often the very same text itself. Temporal clarity requires evidence external to the text; even then, we must be wary of uniformity as a governing principle of composition. We shall return to such issues in the conclusion.

The starting point for this chapter is two key insights provided by Stephanie Jamison, first in her recent contribution to a volume on Hindu Law (Jamison 2018a: 125–27), and now in her contribution to this volume (Ch. 1). First, the term *gṛhastha* appears for the first time in Sanskrit sources in the Dharmasūtras, and gradually comes to take over the semantic terrain of,

2. I leave out here the *Harivaṃśa*, regarded as an "appendix" (*khila*) of the *MBh*, but which is also of undoubted interest for the development of terms such as those being discussed here.

3. The constituted text represents to a significant degree a "consensus" between the major recensions of the North and South. Nevertheless, the constituted text is not necessarily the majoritarian view reconstructed from the manuscripts. In principle the editors of the Critical Edition adopted the Śāradā-script Kashmir recension as its *textus simplicior*. In practice, the constituted text not infrequently varies from the Śāradā codex. Other editorial principles, such as *lectio difficilior melior est*, dictate that the constituted text may vary from the consensus. This study, like many others of a similar nature, have been considerably expedited by the availability of a digital corpus of the *MBh*, first made available by Muneo Tokunaga, then revised by John Smith, which includes the constituted text and the more substantial additions (some minor, some more substantial and found in the appendixes), but excluding the word-for-word variations that populate much of the "below the line" Critical Edition. See http://gretil.sub.uni-goettingen.de/#MBh.

4. Two of these larger text fragments are not without interest for the terms surveyed here, even if they will be only tangentially referred to.

especially, the term *gṛhapati*, which had been used in a comparable manner in the Gṛhyasūtras and as far back as the *Atharva Veda* (see Ch. 1). And, second, that the evidence from Middle Indo-Aryan (MIA) exemplars, most especially the edicts of Aśoka, is that the *gṛhastha* of Brahmanical discourse has a Middle Indo-Aryan cognate in *gahattha* (or similar forms) appearing in a contrastive pairing as the "stay-at-home" layman opposed to the "gone-forth" ascetic *pravrajita* (RE 12, PE 7) or the "striving" ascetic *śramaṇa* (RE 13). Such data leads Jamison to conclude that the *gṛhastha* "is actually a coinage of and a borrowing from śramaṇic discourse, which discourse, at this period, was conducted in various forms of Middle Indo-Aryan" (See Ch. 1 and 3, this volume).

In viewing the problem of the *gṛhastha* from the viewpoint offered by the *Mahābhārata*, the following contribution will first briefly outline the statistical data of the term's occurrence, along with other semantically comparable terms, such as the *gṛhamedhin* and *gṛhapati*. It will offer an account of the *gṛhastha's* predominant occurrences, especially in terms of the "stay-at-home" and "gone-forth" contrastive pair and its appearance in varying forms of "*āśrama* systems." It will become evident that many accounts of *āśrama* systems emerge from the basic problem posed by the existence of the binary. Some consideration will also be given to social registers of the *gṛhastha*, particularly the number of accounts that posit the king as the model *gṛhastha*, in which his capacity to redistribute capital to dependents is central. The good *gṛhastha* is above all a paragon of generosity, sustaining familial and societal dependents. Finally, some consideration will be given to the implications of the findings in relation to the problems of the composition, redaction, and transmission of the *Mahābhārata*.

The Data

Table 10.1 shows the *parvan* by *parvan* occurrence of the terms *gṛhastha*, *gārhasth-*, *gṛhāśrama*, *gṛhamedhin*, and *gṛhapati* in the *Mahābhārata*, distinguishing those appearing in the constituted text of the Pune Critical Edition from those appearing in appendices and "star passages" by means of italicization.

The general frequency of such terms in the *Mahābhārata* stands in stark contrast to the other great Sanskrit epic, the *Rāmāyaṇa*, which contains only one instance of *gārhasthya* (2.98.58—"the best of the four *āśramas*"), none of *gṛhastha*, *gṛhāśrama*, or *gṛhapati*, and only two of *gṛhamedhin* (2.42.3 and 6.62.7). Such a difference accords with the well-acknowledged differences between the two epics, the *Rāmāyaṇa* generally showing less interest in a comprehensive account of society and culture in light of Brahmanical norms,

Table 10.1 Distribution of terms for householder in the *Mahābhārata*

Parvan	*gṛhastha*	*gārhasth-*	*gṛhāśrama*	*gṛhamedhin*	*gṛhapati*
1	3, *7*	1, *1*	1	1	2
2				4	
3	3	2	2	4	1
4				2	
5	1, *1*				
8	1				
9		3			
12	46, *3*	27, *2*	6	6, *1*	2
13	27, *17*	6, *5*	1, *7*	9, *5*	1
14	4, *7*	4, *1*		*1*	*1*
18	*1*				
Total	**85, *36* (121)**	**43, *9* (52)**	**10, *7* (17)**	**24, *9* (33)**	**6, *1* (7)**

Note: Of the terms in the table (or, rather, the first three) falling outside of the constituted text ("above the line") of the Critical Edition, a significant percentage occur in just two texts: the Southern recension version of the *Umāmaheśvarasaṃvādaḥ* appearing in Book 13; and the *Viṣṇudharma* appended to the end of Book 14 (the *Āśvamedhikaparvan*) of the Telugu and Grantha manuscript traditions, as well as three Malayalam (M2–4) manuscripts, of the Southern recension (see the Critical Edition Appendix 1 No.4). In the case of the *Viṣṇudharma*, this accounts for all such instances of *gṛhastha*, and the single instances respectively of *gārhasthya*, *gṛhamedhin*, and *gṛhapati*. The *Umāmaheśvarasaṃvādaḥ* appears at 13.126–34 in the Critical Edition; the Southern recension "substitute" is found in Appendix 1 No.15. Of the seventeen instances of *gṛhastha* appearing in star passages or appendixes of the *Anuśāsanaparvan*, twelve of these are in this reconstituted Southern recension; while this passage also accounts for all such instances of *gārhasthya* (5), *gṛhāśrama* (7) and four of the five instances of *gṛhamedhin*. As Hiltebeitel has pointed out (2018), the decision by the Critical Edition's editor of the *Anuśāsanaparvan* to present two versions of the *Umāma heśvarasaṃvādaḥ*, the northern and southern, obscures the fact that the two versions have much in common, the substantially longer southern introducing passages between shared sections. Some of the instances indicated in the italicized numbers in the table are from these shared sections; consequently, these numbers do not accurately reflect the instances of these terms extra to those found in the constituted text of the Critical Edition. Further on the *Viṣṇudharma*, see Grünendahl (1984: 51–54).

and therefore fewer connections with the genre of Dharmaśāstra (Goldman 1984: 19; Brockington 1998: 425–40, esp. 428, 440); on the other hand, this may well corroborate arguments for an early date for the *Rāmāyaṇa* (Olivelle 1993: 103). However, as is evident, much of the data from the *Mahābhārata* are concentrated in the two *parvans* showing perhaps the greatest departure from the *Rāmāyaṇa*, since these *parvans*—often referred to as "didactic" by scholars—show a tendency for discourses responding to ethical concerns that entertain questions of right conduct interwoven with anxieties over ultimate ends, and, in doing so, reference the traditions embodied in Dharmaśāstra and Arthaśāstra.

A few general points can be made on the basis of the table's data. First, clearly for the *Mahābhārata* the term *gṛhastha* and its derivatives (mainly *gārhasthya*; occasionally *gārhastha*) have become the predominant terms marking the duties, lifestyles and "religious" obligations of the domestic life, most particularly in the case of Brahmins. The older term, *gṛhapati*, which Jamison has shown to be prominent in the Gṛhyasūtras, has fallen almost totally into disuse (see Ch. 6). Of its six appearances in the constituted text of the Critical Edition, two refer to its archaic meaning of Agni, the hypostasized ritual fire (3.212.4, 12.260.26),[5] and three refer to the head of a *satra* sacrifice, a meaning that can be traced back to the Vedic Brāhmaṇa literature (Ch. 1). *Gṛhapati* in this sense is found at 1.4.11 in reference to Śaunaka at the head of the *sadasya* and *ṛtvij* priests attending his twelve-year *satra* at which the bard Ugraśravas recites to them the *Mahābhārata*;[6] at 1.50.13 in reference to King Janamejaya in Āstīka's praise of the *sarpasatra* of which the king is patron; and at 13.85.25 where Varuṇa describes himself as the *gṛhapati* at his own *satra*. The one remaining occurrence, 12.235.27, introduces the human subjects—the "forest-dwelling (*vanaukas*) *gṛhapatis*"—of the third *āśrama*, which is subsequently described in 12.236, where such people are referred to as *vānaprasthas*. In the *Mahābhārata*, therefore, leaving aside one instance in the aforementioned *Viṣṇudharma* passage of the *Mahābhārata*,[7] the *gṛhapati* does not refer to the ideological construct of the householder, but rather, where its referent is a human, marks a ritual participant of high status, indeed, in most cases, a ritual leader.

The term *gṛhamedhin*, the "domestic ritualist," has a different pattern of usage. Appearing as early as the *Atharvaveda Saṃhitā*, where it is found alongside *gṛhapati* (8.10.2; 19.31.13; see also Ch. 1), the term has a sporadic life in the Brāhmaṇas (e.g., *Gopatha Brāhmaṇa* 1.2.4; *Pañcaviṃśa Brāhmaṇa* 17.14.1;

5. Jamison (Ch. 1, p. 8): "*gṛhápati*- in the *Rig Veda* is almost never used of the human householder, but always of the god Agni, in his capacity as the fire lodged in the household."

6. Van Buitenen translates *gṛhapati* here as "family chieftain," presumably taking it as a synonym for *kulapati*, which occurs in the same passage in reference to Śaunaka at 1.4.1 and 5. The term *kulapati* has its own curious history, appearing only four times in the *MBh* (twice here in reference to Śaunaka, and twice in 13.10), and never (as far as I have been able to establish) in the Vedas or the dharma literature.

7. Line 2585 in Appendix 1 No.4 of the *Āśvamedhikaparvan* defines the *gṛhapti* as *gṛhyakarmavaho yasmāt tasmād gṛhapatis tu saḥ*.

Śatapatha Brāhmaṇa 13.4.3.3) and *Vedāṅgas* (*Āśvalāyana Śrautasūtra* 10.7.1; *Śāṅkhāyana Śrautasūtra* 16.2.2 [both = *Śatapatha Brāhmaṇa* 13.4.3.3]; *Jaimini Gṛhyasūtra* 1.11; *Śaṅkhāyana Gṛhyasūtra* 16.2.2; *Gobhila Gṛhyasūtra* 1.4.18). The *Āpastamba Dharmasūtra* adopts it (and *gṛhamedha*) as one of its key terms—if not the key term—for the householder, it appearing in this sense on five occasions (1.2.7; 1.4.29; 2.1.1; 2.1.15; 2.3.12), compared to single occurrences each of *gṛhastha* (2.9.13) and *gārhasthya* (2.21.1).[8] But this prominence would seem to be short-lived; the remaining Dharmasūtras do not use it at all, seemingly having resolved upon *gṛhastha* and its derivatives for its technical terminology (see Brick in Ch. 8, this volume). However, *gṛhamedhin* reappears in the *Mānava Dharmaśāstra* (6 times: 3.69, 3.105, 4.8, 4.31–32 [cf. *MBh* 12.235.8], 6.27) and the *Mahābhārata*, where it seems to be more or less synonymous with *gṛhastha*.

In the *Mahābhārata*, *gṛhamedhin* occurs both independently of and in proximity to *gṛhastha*, *gārhasthya*, and *gṛhāśrama*. When in proximity to these terms (3.2.51; 12.37.26; 12.234.29; 12.235.1, 4, 10; 12.284.19, 13.27.20; 13.128.43, 13.131.55), one might expect some subtle gradations of meaning to explain its co-occurrence with other words for the householder, but if this is the case, then it is not obvious. For example, in one cluster of four instances appearing at 12.234.29–235.10, a passage on the *āśrama* system showing clear parallels to the *Mānava Dharmaśāstra*, it is used interchangeably with *gṛhastha*.[9] On those occasions where *gṛhamedhin* appears independently of references to *gṛhastha*, it still displays a range of contexts and contrasts that are comparable to those occurring for the latter word, with perhaps a tendency for stressing the piety or the social status of the household ritualist. As with other terms for householders, sometimes it is used as the contrastive term to one or another kind of mendicant (*vanecara* at 2.59.9 and 3.252.3, the same phrase; and *yati* at 3.28.16). *Gṛhamedhins* are reported to have been at the court of Indra (2.7.6); Duryodhana jealousy complains of the eighty-eight thousand *snātaka gṛhamedhins* supported by Yudhiṣṭhira as evidence of the latter's wealth (2.45.17 and 2.48.39),[10] and, later, Draupadī (3.28.16) ruefully reflects on Yudhiṣṭhira's inability to do so in exile, though she also lauds Yudhiṣṭhira's generosity in

8. *Kuṭumbin*, another term meaning householder, appears three times: 2.6.5, 2.7.1, 2.29.3.

9. Compare Manu 4.31–32 with *MBh* 12.235.8–10. Similarly, *MBh* 3.2.51, in which Yudhiṣṭhira describes himself as a *gṛhamedhin*, is the same as 12.235.10. *Mahābhārata* 12.234.9cd and 235.1ab show a clear relationship to Manu 4.1ab and 5.169cd, though the former pair use *gṛhamedhin*, and the latter pair *kṛtadāra*.

10. Also in star passage 360, inserted after 4.17.20 in a significant number of Northern-recension manuscripts.

the same words as Duryodhana in her dialogue with Kṛṣṇa's wife Satyabhāmā (3.222.41).[11] Elsewhere the *gṛhamedhin* is an emblem of pious poverty, living by gleaning (13.27.20) or "like a pigeon" (13.32.19). In a cluster of references, he is the pious ritualist performing the domestic rites (13.102.2; 13.103.4, 36)[12] or Vedic recitation and *dāna* (13.104.21).

The term *gṛhāśrama*, the "order of life pertaining to the house[-holder]," which may well be a contraction of *gṛhasthāśrama*, is not problematic, being used synonymously with *gṛhastha*. It is noteworthy, however, that the compound is entirely absent from the dharma literature until Manu, in which it appears just once (6.1), though it is rather more frequent in the Purāṇas and the significantly later *Vaiṣṇava Dharmaśāstra*.[13] Though I have not included them in the table, *kuṭumbin* (e.g., 12.308.41)[14] and *gṛhin* (e.g., 12.23.5) also occasionally appear, though not with statistical significance; they are certainly not ideologically significant in the ways in which the other terms are.

Table 10.2 organizes the data in such a way as to identify the textual portions in which the terms under consideration appear in clusters, or in which the idea of the householder (as marked by one of these terms) is given focused discussion. Even though isolated references are not included in this table, they are not without significance, and shall occasionally be referred to in the course of the discussion. The table indicates the textual location, provides a useful designation for the unit culled from the manuscript colophons collected at the end of each chapter in the Critical Edition, and quantifies the appearance of each term. In this case, only material from the constituted text of the Critical Edition has been included.

Again, the significance of the *Mahābhārata's Śāntiparvan* (book 12) and the *Anuśāsanaparvan* (book 13)—especially the former—for discussions of the householder stands out. If we were to parse these *parvans* into their

11. Indicating the interchangeability of the terms, in 12.1.5 *snātaka gṛhasthas* visit Yudhiṣṭhira after he has performed the obsequial rites following the war.

12. These three instances notably include references to *pūjā* with *puṣpa* (flowers), *dhūpa* (incense), and *dīpa* (lamps), otherwise absent as a collocation in the *MBh*, and possibly reflecting a later configuration of domestic ritual procedure; according to Einoo (1996), such offerings are mentioned only sporadically in the Gṛhyasūtras, and do not "seem to belong to the mainstream of the *Gṛhya* tradition" (1996: 79). In the Gupta period, these become part of the standard offerings in temple *pūjās*; see Willis 2008. In 13.128.43, among the duties of the *gṛhamedhin*, here clearly a synonym for *gṛhastha* (13.128.43, 45), is the "constant offering of flowers and *balis* to the domestic deities" (*gṛhyāṇāṃ caiva devānāṃ nityaṃ puṣpabalikriyā*).

13. The *ViDh* is assigned to the eighth century by Olivelle 2009a.

14. The term *kuṭumba* is often used to refer to the "household" as a familial and economic unit.

Table 10.2 ***Mahābhārata*** **passages containing concentrations of terms for "householder"**

Location	Title	*gṛhastha*	*gārhasth-*	*gṛhāśrama*	*gṛhamedhin*
1.86.1–7[a]	*Uttarayāyātam, Caturāśramavarṇanam*	2			
1.87.1–4	*Uttarayāyātam*	1			
3.2	*Śaunakavākyam*			2	1
9.49	*Asitadevalajaigīṣavyasaṃvādaḥ*		3		
12.11	*Arjunavākyam*		2		
12.12	*Nakulavākyam*	3	1		
12.18	*Arjunavākyam, Janakopākhyānam*	3			
12.23	*Vyāsavākyam, Gṛhasthāśramastutiḥ*	2	2		
12.37	*Bhakṣyābhakṣyavidhiḥ*	2			1
12.61	*Caturāśramadharmaḥ*	1	3	2	
12.63	*Kṣatriyadharmakathanam*	1			
12.66	*Cāturāśramyavidhiḥ*		5	1	
12.142	*Kapotalubdhakasaṃvādaḥ*	2		1	
12.184	*Bhṛgubharadvājasaṃvādaḥ*	2	2	1	
12.226	*Śukānupraśnaḥ* (224–247)	1			
12.234–36	*Śukānupraśnaḥ* (224–247)[b]	9			4
12.260–62	*Gokapilasaṃvādaḥ*	7	3		
12.277	*Sagarāriṣṭanemisaṃvādaḥ*		1		
12.284	*Parāśaragītā* (279–87), *Tapaḥpraśaṃsā*	5			1
12.308	*Sulabhājanakasaṃvādaḥ*	1	4		

12.309, 311, 313	*Yāvakādhyāyaḥ* (309)	1	2		
	Śukajanakasaṃvādaḥ (310–320)[c]				
12.321	*Nārāyaṇīyam, Nārāyaṇanāradasaṃvādaḥ*	1	1		
12.342	*Uñchavṛttyupākhyānam* (340–353)[d]	1	1		
13.2	*Sudarśanopākhyānam*	12		1	
13.62	*Annadānapraśaṃsā*	2			
13.100	*Balipradānavidhiḥ, Vāsudevapṛthivīsaṃvādaḥ*	2	3		
13.102–3	*Agastyabhṛgusaṃvādaḥ*				3
13.128–131	*Umāmaheśvarasaṃvādaḥ* (126–34)	4	4		2
14.35	*Anugītā* (16–50), *Guruśiṣyasaṃvādaḥ* (35–50)		2		
14.45–46	*Anugītā* (16–50), *Guruśiṣyasaṃvādaḥ* (35–50)	3	1		

Notes: [a] While this and the next passage are part of the longer *Uttarayāyātam*, I have treated them separately, since each of Aṣṭaka's questions to Yayāti lead to distinct, if related, 'texts'. 1.87.1–4 could possibly be read with 1.86.8–17.

[b] While the *Śukānupraśnaḥ* runs from 12.224 to 12.247, the terms relating to the householder appear in chapters devoted to a discussion of the *āśramas*, the most sustained account of which starts at 234 and concludes at 237 with a description of the *yativṛtta*. However, there is some discussion of the *gṛhastha* and the *āśramas* in 12.226 also, in which Vyāsa explains to Śuka the duties of a good Brahmin. I have kept 12.226 and 234–237 separate because they are somewhat different, as discussed below.

[c] I have included the *Yāvakādhyayaḥ* ("the chapter on barley-gruel") with the *Śukajanakasaṃvādaḥ* because the former serves as a preamble for the latter, providing an explanation for why Śuka pursues *mokṣa*, a tale then told in the subsequent *saṃvāda*. Some manuscript colophons call this chapter the *Śukānuśāsanam*. While the references to the householder are scant, they are not without significance.

[d] *Gṛhastha* also occurs at 12.347.7 in the *Uñchavṛttyupākhyānam*.

sub-*parvans*, then it becomes apparent that the treatment of the householder in each substantially follows the lead of the broad topic indicated by the sub-*parvan* title. Thus passages found in the early *Rājadharmaparvan* (12.11, 12, 18, and 23) in which Yudhiṣṭhira's brothers and wife question his solution for his own post-war ethical crisis, the passages of Bhīṣma's royal instructions in the *Rājadharmaparvan* and *Āpaddharmaparvan* (12.56–167), Bhīṣma's instructions on "freedom" in the *Mokṣadharmaparvan* (12.168–353), and, finally, the instructions peculiar to the *Dānadharmaparvan* of the *Anuśāsana* (13.1–152), show a tendency to reflect the broad concerns of the corpus in which they are incorporated. Such differences will become apparent in the subsequent analysis.

It is rather pointless to expect a uniform statement regarding the householder in the *Mahābhārata*. The polyvocality of the *Mahābhārata*—which must in part reflect the complicated nature of its composition, redaction, and transmission—allows for multiple perspectives and treatments of themes. Nevertheless, arguably, the *Mahābhārata's* householder reflects the struggles of a fuzzily bounded yet roughly singular cultural system coming to terms with the multiplicity of lifestyles, institutions, and religious vocations available to the denizens of the complex society to which the epic is self-consciously addressed. Consequently, one aspect of the *Mahābhārata's* treatment of the householder is that it is not uniform, but rather responds to the varied discursive contexts in which it appears. This is just one of many complicating factors when considering whatever evidence the *Mahābhārata* might evince for the history of ideas.

The following analysis will highlight what I see to be the key themes of the data on the householder in the *Mahābhārata*. It will become evident that these themes overlap. Not surprisingly given the relatively well-known data from the Dharmaśāstra tradition, a considerable quantity of the instances of the householder occur within the context of varying iterations of "*āśrama*" systems, in which "religious" vocations are given some kind of systematic treatment relative to other members of the same system.

The Binary

As discussed already, both Stephanie Jamison and Patrick Olivelle have argued that Middle Indo-Aryan sources are likely to be the earliest contexts in which the term *gṛhastha* is introduced. The key data in this case are derived from the corpus of the Aśokan inscriptions, which deploy *gahattha* (and cognates reflecting the dialectical diversity of the inscriptions) on three occasions. In each of these cases the householder appears with one of two contrastive terms (*pravrajita* and *śramaṇa*) that establish the fundamental binary of the "stay-at-home" householder and the "gone-forth" renouncer. This basic binary informs much of the data from the *Mahābhārata*.

We shall begin, therefore, with a consideration of ways in which the basic binary is presented in the *Mahābhārata*. But we shall see, too, that this binary also informs many of the discursive treatments of *āśrama* systems.[15] It is perhaps worth noting at the outset that in the vast majority of cases where the householder appears—certainly in developed treatments—it is in a context referencing either the binary or the *āśramas* (in whatever shape). This indicates that conceptually the institution of the householder gains its meaning within a relatively small set of vocational contrasts. We can see this even in slight references, where the householder-contrasted-to-mendicant as a culturally meaningful unit serves as a ready metaphor. For example, Śalya when criticizing Karṇa's haughtiness in thinking he could best Arjuna, compares Karṇa to a dog "in his own lair" (*svagṛhastha*) daring to speak to a tiger "inhabiting the forest" (*vanagata*). Lying behind the simile is the trope of householder and forest mendicant. When Vidura reproaches Duryodhana for provoking the Pāṇḍavas in his treatment of Draupadī (2.59.9), and (perhaps ironically) Draupadī reproaches Jarāsaṃdha for denigrating her husbands (3.252.3), both cite the same stanza that warns against calling wretched (*pāpa*) someone laudable (*īḍya*) because he's full of *tapas* and knowledge (*tapasvinaṃ saṃparipūrṇavidyaṃ*), "whether he be wandering in the forest or a domestic ritualist" (*vanecaraṃ vā gṛhamedhinaṃ vā*). In each case Vidura and Draupadī use the binary as a kind of natural set that encapsulates a breadth of possible laudable types.[16] In the dialogue (*saṃvāda*) between Cyavana and Kuśika in the *Anuśāsanaparvan*, the food enjoyed by householders (*gṛhastha*) and forest-dwellers (*vanavāsin*) serves as a summation of the various foods King Kuśika presents to the seer Cyavana (13.53.19), while in Nārada's laud to gifting food—a primary obligation of a householder—the assertion that *bhikṣus* and *gṛhasthas* depend on food (13.62.8) metonymically underscores that people of all types rely on food to live (cf. 12.18.27).

Some, generally more extensive, passages engage the binary in order to evaluate the relative merits of each of its members. In such cases the context and the participants in the dialogues and narratives frequently reflect the side of the binary being emphasized. In 9.49, during Baladeva's *tīrthayātra*, a story is told of Asita Devala who, living in his ashram at the *Āditya tīrtha*, is

15. See also Olivelle in Ch. 7, this volume.

16. Van Buitenen translates this differently—though I think incorrectly—in each case.

both celibate (*brahmacarya*, 9.49.4) and pursuing the law of the householder (*gārhasthyaṃ dharmam*, 9.49.1). But then a mendicant (*bhikṣuka*), the *muni* Jaigīṣavya, comes and impresses him with his yoga powers, in particular his ability to appear in any place at will, and his transcending of various divine realms, otherwise acquired through ritual performance, to a higher realm altogether, the eternal (*śāśvata*), undecaying (*avyaya*) world of Brahmā. Asita Devala, suitably impressed, wants to accomplish this *mokṣadharma* as well (9.49.52). Jaigīṣavya teaches him the method (*vidhi*) of yoga and initiates him as a renouncer (9.49.53–54). But, the living beings (*bhūtas*) and ancestors (*pitṛs*) panic, concerned that they will miss out on their share that would have otherwise been distributed to them through Asita Devala's ritual performances. Consequently, Asita resolves to give up *mokṣa* (*mokṣaṃ tyaktum mano dadhe*). But now it is the turn of the various plant forms—presumably those used in rituals—to panic, worried that Asita would return to cutting them down, for, though he has "granted safety to all beings," a standard ascetic formula, he has not understood it (9.49.58). Asita then reflects on which is more conducive to prosperity (*śreyaskara*), *mokṣa* or *gārhasthyadharma*, and resolves upon the former (9.49.59–60).

A somewhat different outcome to a similar weighing up the two sides of the binary appears in a number of passages in the early chapters of the *Śāntiparvan*, in which Yudhiṣṭhira's brothers and wife try to convince him to not renounce the kingdom, as he wishes to do in remorse at the destruction of the war. There are two particular features to note in these speeches. On the one hand they argue for the primacy of the ritual life embodied in the householder, in which case, by implication, the king is the maximal householder (see further below). And on the other, they take a behavior that otherwise might be associated with renouncers (the other side of the binary) and argue that the householder is the best exponent of that behavior. In *Mahābhārata* 12.11, Arjuna recounts the old *itihāsa* of Indra's conversation with some ascetics (*tāpasa*). The latter, "fool" (*manda*) Brahmins whose beards have yet to grow, nevertheless practice celibacy and leave behind their homes and ancestors, wandering the forest. Indra, in the guise of a golden bird, praises to them the *vighasāśins*, the "eaters of the leftovers."[17] The ascetics think he's referring to them, but Indra sets them straight (12.11.7):

nāhaṃ yuṣmān praśaṃsāmi paṅkadigdhān rajasvalān |
ucchiṣṭabhojino mandān anye vai vighasāśinaḥ ||

17. On which see Wezler 1977–78.

> I don't praise you, smeared as you are in mud and covered in dust, fools eating the leftovers (*ucchiṣṭabhojin*). Others are the real leftover-eaters (*vighaśāsin*)!

Asked to explain, Indra praises the rites of the Veda, which are conducive to heaven and constitute the highest path, and denounces those men who revile ritual and follow the wrong path (12.13–16), indeed, the non-Vedic path (*aśrutīpatham*). He enjoins them to "give" (12.11.18) and proposes to explain the "difficult to do" austerity (*tapas*) that pertains to the householder (*gārhasthya*). Such an austerity is free of envy and dualities; the forest in comparison is just a "middling" austerity (12.11.22). The *vighasāśins* go to the place difficult to reach. A definition follows (12.11.24):

> *dattvātithibhyo devebhyaḥ pitṛbhyaḥ svajanasya ca |*
> *avaśiṣṭāni ye 'śnanti tān āhur vighasāśinaḥ ||*
>
> Those who eat the leftovers after having given to the guests, gods, and ancestors, and to their own people, they say they are the *vighasāśins* (eaters of the leftovers).

We now understand that the eaters of the leftovers are those good householders who only eat after having performed their domestic rituals and fed the recipients of these ritual offerings before they themselves eat. These are not the leftovers the mendicant consumes in his peripatetic wanderings, the ritual-leftovers distributed *from* the house rather than *within* the house, a contrast captured by the difference between *ucchiṣṭabhojin* (eating someone else's leftovers) and *vighasāśin* (eating the leftovers of offerings) in 12.11.7. Upon hearing Indra's counsel, the Brahmin youths, premature mendicants, leave behind their heretic path (*nāstikagati*), and come to be devoted to the law of the householder (*gārhasthyaṃ dharmam*; 12.11.27). Yudhiṣṭhira is urged to seize this eternal foundation (*dhairya*) and rule the earth (12.11.28).

Nakula then takes up the cudgel to convince Yudhiṣṭhira to "stay at home." He too lauds the Veda and the rites it entails, and reviles the extreme heretics (*bhṛśanāstika*) who reject them (12.12.3–6). The householder, Nakula argues, is the genuine "renouncer" (*tyāgin*),[18] who "examines profit, desire, and heaven" and determines that that is the "path of the great seers, the way of those who know the worlds" (*ayaṃ panthā maharṣīṇām iyaṃ lokavidāṃ gatiḥ*, 12.12.12), not the one who "like a fool goes to the forest after leaving behind his house" (*na yaḥ*

---

18. Nakula offers a typology of renouncers at 12.12.7–10.

parityajya gṛhān vanam eti vimūḍhavat, 12.12.13). "Renunciation" is the "giving" (*dāna*) associated with the householder, and, for Nakula, the model householder is the king, performing the large state rituals, providing shelter to his people, and being generous to Brahmins (12.12.27–33). Yudhiṣṭhira's refusal to give away his wealth in sacrifices (*makheṣv anabhisaṃtyajya*), because he plans to formally renounce, is tantamount to advocating heterodoxy (*nāstikya*, 12.12.25). Nakula has taken a behavioral norm, *tyāga*, "renouncing," which in some contexts is definitive for the renouncer, the *tyāgin*, and turns it into the central norm pursued by the royal householder. The preeminent form of "renouncing" here is not "leaving behind" (*parityaj-*) or "setting out from" (*pravraj-*) the home, but the renouncing of one's wealth in the pious activities of the stay-at-home householder.

A similar type of inversion deploying the binary is found in another of Arjuna's speeches directed at Yudhiṣṭhira in 12.18. On this occasion Arjuna recounts an old *itihāsa*, the conversation between King Janaka and his wife. Janaka in this instance is an obvious mirror for Yudhiṣṭhira, since he's made up his mind to leave his realm and take up mendicancy (*bhaikṣa*). The king, again, represents a maximal householder; he's at once a provider and a ritualist. Janaka, however, has given up such things, and adopted baldness (*mauṇḍya*), begging, and the livelihood (*vṛtti*) of the "skull-bearers" (*kāpālī*).[19] Consequently, he fails to now support the usual beneficiaries of the householder, guests, gods, seers, and ancestors, and they in turn have abandoned him (12.18.9–10). The essential failure Janaka's wife charges him with is that, in avoiding his ritual obligations (*niṣkriya*), Janaka has turned away from being a "maintainer" (*bhartṛ*) to one who now wishes to be maintained by others (*anyair bhṛtim icchet*, 12.18.11). The binary is understood here in the straightforward terms of the giver and the receiver (12.18.23):

> *yo 'tyantaṃ pratigṛhṇīyād yaś ca dadyāt sadaiva hi |*
> *tayos tvam antaraṃ viddhi śreyāṃs tābhyāṃ ka ucyate ||*
> Who perpetually takes and who always gives—of these two you must know the difference. Who is said to be the better of these two?

The *dāna*, "giving," of the householder establishes his centrality, though others deny the importance of householders (12.18.28):

> *gṛhasthebhyo 'bhinirvṛttā gṛhasthān eva saṃśritāḥ |*
> *prabhavaṃ ca pratiṣṭhāṃ ca dāntā nindanta āsate ||*

19. The latter term represents a form of asceticism sometimes reviled in the *MBh*; see 5.131.23, 12.18.7, 12.105.49 (=5.131.23).

> Those proceeding from householders, depend entirely on householders;
> though restrained, they lay about reviling their origin and their support.

True mendicants (*bhikṣuka*) are not known on account of their renunciation (*tyāga*), baldness (*mauṇḍya*), or soliciting (*yācana*), but rather due to their abandoning (*tyaj*) wealth (12.18.29). Conversely, those who adopt the trappings of the renouncer's life—baldness, red robes, wandering—do so for wealth (*dhānārtha, īhārtha*), posturing their piety (12.18.31–33).

The Binary and the Āśramas

The significance of the binary of the householder and the mendicant, in whatever form the latter manifests, is evident also in treatments of *āśrama* systems in the *Mahābhārata*, of which there are numerous. In simple terms, the *āśrama* system is a way of structuring four different lifestyles as religious vocations—the celibate student learning his ritual obligations (*brahmacārin*), the householder (*gṛhastha*), the forest-dweller (*vānaprastha*) and the renouncer (*parivrājaka, bhikṣu, yati*). The seminal work of Olivelle (1974; 1993) established that an early model in the Dharmasūtras treating these four vocations as alternative options (*vikalpa*) was subsequently developed into a sequential model (*samuccaya*), as evidenced by, especially, the *Mānava Dharmaśāstra*. The latter model came to be normative. In the *āśrama* system—whether in its *vikalpa* or *samuccaya* forms, both of which appear in the *Mahābhārata*—the householder appears in binaries of two different forms. One of these structures the householder as the supporter (*bhartṛ*) in complementary opposition to the other three members of the system, members of which require support (*bhṛtya*). We shall discuss this further later. The binary being accounted for now sees the whole *āśrama* system as growing out of, and perhaps responding to, the essential opposition between householder and mendicant. Frequently, where the binary is explicitly raised, the context is evaluative.

I will start with a passage from the *Mokṣadharmaparvan* found in the *Śukānupraśnaḥ* (12.224–47), in which a confused Śuka asks his father Vyāsa about the difference between two vocations prescribed in the Veda (12.234.3):

> *vede vacanam uktaṃ tu kuru karma tyajeti ca |*
> *katham etad vijānīyāṃ tac ca vyākhyātum arhasi ||*

> But the words uttered in the Veda: "Perform deeds!" and "Renounce!"
> How is this to be understood? Please explain this.

This way of describing the basic binary appears on three other occasions in the *Mahābhārata*. Each of the four occasions has a distinctly worded resolution to the problem provoked by the seeming Vedic contradiction between performing deeds entailing, above all, ritual procedures, and renouncing, above all, rites. This distinction finds a ready foothold in the Vedas, in the ritual prescriptions of the Saṃhitās and Brāhmaṇas on the one hand, and on the other hand in the Upaniṣads, which both adapt and pose problems for the antecedent ritual paradigm. The first of the *Mahābhārata* instances occurs at 3.2.70, where the explanation follows an Upaniṣadic distinction between the ritualistic "way of the fathers" (*pitṛyāna*), and a path of individual restraint, the "way of the gods" (*devayāna*), two terms that appear in the two earliest Upaniṣads (*Bṛhadāraṇyaka Upaniṣad* 6.2.15 and *Chāndogya Upaniṣad* 5.10) as defining a distinction between (by then) two Vedic paths with two distinct goals.[20] The second instance occurs at 12.19.1, just after the second of Arjuna's speeches discussed above, in which Yudhiṣṭhira counters Arjuna's concerns raised across a number of early chapters in the *Śāntiparvan*.[21] Yudhiṣṭhira uses the formula to establish that he knows of the varying religious vocations, and later describes a number of them that expand on the binary, including forest-dwellers who reach heaven by reciting the Veda, *āryas* who control their senses and reach the worlds of the renouncers (*tyāga*) via the "northern course" (*uttareṇa panthānam*), those who go via the "southern course" (*dakṣiṇena . . . panthānam*) to the world of ritualists, and finally those following the inscrutable path of the liberated (*mokṣin*), the renunciation regarded as the best (12.19.11–15).[22] In the third instance, the chapter immediately preceding the one from which the stanza above is cited, Śuka posits the apparent problem to his father, Vyāsa, who proceeds to explain the "two paths founded on the Veda" (12.233.66), the "law marked by *pravṛtti*," the active life of the social and ritual participant, and the "inactive" (*nivṛtti*) life of the one who

20. The *MBh* passage couples these together as one "eightfold path of the law" (*dharmasyāṣṭavidha*). The passage then introduces another eight-limbed (*aṣṭāṅga*) path (*mārga*) involving (among other things) giving up rites (*karmopasaṃnyāsa*) and the ceasing of thought (*cittanirodhana*), which leads the practitioner to defeating transmigration (*saṃsāra*). This latter is either an expansion of the *devayāna*, or a new path altogether. Van Buitenen's translation opts for the former, though he introduces a conjunction between the two hemistichs of 3.2.73 that is missing in the text. See further Bailey (forthcoming).

21. I follow here the amendments to the dialogic structure of this passage suggested by Fitzgerald (2004).

22. See further Fitzgerald's excellent notes to this passage.

avoids such things. All of these passages represent attempts to resolve the tension between two broad lifestyles evoking distinct (but increasingly complementary) religious pursuits. The coupling of *pravrtti* and *nivṛtti dharmas* as in 12.233, and the formal articulation of the *āśramas* as a sequential system as in 12.234, together with the *karmayoga* theory espoused by the *Bhagavadgītā*, perhaps come to be the most widely circulated ways of resolving this fundamental tension. The four chapters of the *Śukānupraśnaḥ*, 12.234–37, represent a good example of how the *āśrama* system, which in this case is described as sequential "life-stages," is used to respond to the fundamental tension of the binary. After a brief précis of the four stages (12.234.5–9), a chapter is devoted to each in turn—the celibate student (*brahmacarya*), the householder (*gṛhastha, gṛhamedhin*), forest-dweller (*vānaprastha*), and the mendicant (*bhikṣu*).[23] In this model, the final stage is regarded as not only the best, but also as the culmination of the previous stages. Consequently, a potentially dichotomous understanding of the binary, which Śuka seems to think it is in 12.234.3, is diffused through the four sequential stages of the *āśramas* in a manner that establishes the complementarity of the vocations underlying the binary in the individual's cultivation of his religious well-being, culminating in his emancipation in the fourth *āśrama*.

The *Mokṣadharmaparvan* is especially fond of posing the problem of the binary, with varying conclusions, and with varying degrees of reference to the *āśrama* system. The *Gokapilasaṃvādaḥ* in 12.260–62 is told in response to Yudhiṣṭhira asking which is best, the dharma of the householder or of renunciation (*tyāga*). Both have merit, Bhīṣma says, and then tells the story of the *yati* Kapila,[24] who, seeing a cow about to be sacrificed, plaintively exclaims "I regret that truth has become feeble. O Vedas!" (*smarāmi śithilaṃ satyaṃ vedā ity . . .*). Kapila's unease leads a *ṛṣi*, Syūmaraśmi, to possess the cow and engage the ascetic in a debate about the validity of the Veda and the performance of sacrifice. Kapila, however, denies he has a problem with the Vedas, and suggests that both acting and not are grounded in the sacred tradition

23. There is some confusion in the presentation of, and transition between, the third and fourth stages in 12.236–37. The treatment of the *āśramas* here shows clear parallels with the *Mānava Dharmaśāstra*, including the formula that each life-stage consumes a quarter of a life.

24. Houben (1999: 502) considers that the name Kapila (a name often associated with the foundation of Sāṃkhya) lends credence to this text being evidence for an association between nonviolence, asceticism, and Sāṃkhya. This has been questioned by Jacobsen (2008: 16–17, 27). For this passage, see also Olivelle 1993: 99.

(12.260.12–16). Yet he does have a preference for *ahiṃsā* (12.260.17),[25] and, given the supreme course (*gatiṃ parāṃ*) acquired by *yatis*, can't really see the point of the householder option.[26] Syūmaraśmi, on the other hand, views the householder as the necessary foundation of the other *āśramas*, in part because it is the only one that allows for procreation (12.261.5–8).[27] Kapila, however, gets the final say. Householders are good, but they don't obtain the bliss of renunciation (*tyāgasukha*; 12.262.33). They are limited to ritual, which is good for "cleansing the body" (*śarīrapakti*), but knowledge is the supreme course (*paramā gatiḥ*; 12.262.36).

In 12.308, Yudhiṣṭhira again evokes the binary when he asks who it was who obtained *mokṣa* without giving up being a householder (12.308.1–2), to which Bhīṣma responds with the *Sulabhājanakasaṃvādaḥ* (Fitzgerald 2002). Janaka was a king of Mithilā enjoying the "fruits of renunciation" (*saṃnyāsaphalika*), while remaining in his royal office. A *bhikṣuṇī*, Sulabhā, hears of this renouncer king and has her doubts. During the long dialogue between the two, which takes place within Janaka's mind since Sulabhā enters his body by means of her yoga, Janaka maintains that he can act within the world without attachments, and thereby fulfill his royal office while being liberated. Indeed, he questions that someone passing from the householder stage to the next really gives up attachments at all (12.308.44). Sulabhā, in some depth, demonstrates that he is a fraud; indeed (12.308.175),

> *sa gārhasthyāc cyutaś ca tvaṃ mokṣaṃ nāvāpya durvidam |*
> *ubhayor antarāle ca vartase mokṣavātikaḥ ||*

> You've fallen from the householder mode of life and haven't acquired the freedom that's hard to understand. You exist in between them, prattling of freedom.[28]

Sulabhā's critique of Janaka argues, therefore, that one must leave behind one lifestyle in order to accomplish the goal of another, which, from the point of view of the *āśrama* system (whether *samuccaya* or *vikalpa*), is perfectly orthodox.

---

25. In 12.261.19, Kapila doesn't object to the *darśa* (new moon), *paurnamāsa* (full moon), *agnihotra*, and *cāturmāsya* (four-monthly) sacrifices, since, as *iṣṭi* rites, they do not involve the offerings of animals.

26. See further below, p. 193.

27. Compare *BDh* 2.11.27 and Olivelle, Ch. 7, p. 113 of this volume.

28. Modified from Fitzgerald 2002: 667.

Not surprisingly, more than half of the passages identified in Table 10.2 discuss the householder with some reference to the *āśramas*, though the *āśramas* and "*āśrama* systems" are presented in some variety, and, occasionally, the idea of *āśrama* is put to quite innovative use. Olivelle (1993: 149) has counted some 160 occurrences of the term *āśrama* in the *Mahābhārata*, many of which, not surprisingly, co-occur with instances of *gṛhastha*. As Olivelle notes (1993: 148–51, 153–55), the *Mahābhārata* includes instances of both the "classical" sequential (*samuccaya*) system and the earlier ("original") system based on "choice" (*vikalpa*) between life-long options, though in the latter case this conclusion is often based on an inference from the basic data.[29] The longest account of the sequential *āśrama* system is that of 12.234–37, in the *Śukānupraśnaḥ* discussed above.[30] In the *Sulabhājanakasaṃvādaḥ*, Janaka, in his ultimately unsuccessful justification of being a *mokṣin* while also a royal *gṛhastha*, appears to refer to the sequential system at 12.308.44. There are clear indications of the latter in 14.35.30, in a passage in the *Anugītā* attributed to Brahmā. In the *Śukajanakasaṃvādaḥ* (12.310–20), a Janaka responds to Śuka's doubts over *pravṛtti* and *nivṛtti* (313.11) with an account of the sequential *āśramas* (313.14–19). Śuka, however, is rather impatient, and wants to know if all the *āśramas* are necessary (313.20).[31] Before answering, Janaka affirms the importance of a clear insight into knowledge (*jñānavijñāna*) and a teacher (*ācārya*), and explains the function of the four *āśramas* (313.24)

> *anucchedāya lokānām anucchedāya karmaṇām |*
> *pūrvair ācarito dharmaś cāturāśramyasaṃkathaḥ ||*
>
> In order not to destroy the worlds, and in order not to destroy actions, people of old practiced the law consistent with the four orders of life.

With the destruction of karma, both good and bad, through many lifetimes, *mokṣa* is indeed possible from the first *āśrama* (313.25–26). The subsequent narrative describes Śuka's ascension through the solar path to emancipation, never having become a *gṛhastha*. Though this story suggests the *gṛhastha* is unnecessary, it nevertheless appears to presuppose that the sequential system

---

29. For the hermeneutics underlying these alternate accounts, see Olivelle 1993: 134–36.

30. See pp. 178 and 189.

31. *kim avaśyaṃ nivastavyam āśrameṣu vaneṣu ca* | "Is it necessary to live in the *āśramas* and the forests?" The reading *vaneṣu ca* is marked as uncertain in the Critical Edition. The Śāradā codex and three other Kashmiri manuscripts instead have *na vā nṛpa*, while a substantial number of other Northern-recension manuscripts read *bhavet triṣu*.

is normative; it is not, in other words, a reflection of the *vikalpa* system, but, rather, a modification or critique of the *samuccaya* system.

On other occasions, however, the evidence is either ambiguous, or suggests the earlier *āśrama* model of choice between life-long options of religious vocation. Olivelle (1993: 153–55) employs a number of criteria to determine that an instance of the *āśrama* system follows the *vikalpa* mode: the absence of reference to passage between the members of the system, an order of presentation of the four modes that prevents their being treated as a sequence, and after-death rewards (often the same) being presented for each *āśrama* (implying, therefore, that one dies in that *āśrama*). In the story of Yayāti's fall from heaven, in a passage which does not use the word *āśrama*, but which clearly indicates some such system, the royal seer Aṣṭaka asks Yayāti (1.86.1):

> *caran gṛhasthaḥ katham eti devān; kathaṃ bhikṣuḥ katham ācāryakarmā |*
> *vānaprasthaḥ satpathe saṃniviṣṭo; bahūny asmin saṃprati vedayanti ||*
>
> Acting in what way does a householder go to the gods? Or a mendicant? Or [the student] obligated towards his teacher? Or the forest-dweller focused on the path of the good? People now hold many views on this.

Yayāti responds with a brief account of each, which follows the usual order, unlike the question. In this case, on account of Yayāti not mentioning passage from one to the next, and the question indicating that the goal is the same for each (they go to the gods), Olivelle suggests these are permanent rather than sequential states.

Nakula's typology of different *tyāgins* at 12.12.7–10 evokes religious vocations reflecting the ideals of the *āśramas*.[32] The order defies understanding them as sequential, and therefore they seem to represent life-long options. Similarly, in the dialogue between Bhṛgu and Bharadvāja at 12.184–85—a prose, Dharmasūtra-like passage[33]—Bhṛgu describes each of the *āśramas* with their after-life consequences, suggesting again that they are whole-of-life vocations. Early in the *Śukānupraśnaḥ*, Vyāsa, in contradiction to his later exposition,[34] explains to Śuka the conduct of a Brahmin, and very clearly indicates that each

---

32. The stanzas either side of this passage, 12.12.6 and 12.12.11, establish that the context is the *āśramas*, even if the language describing them in 7–10 is somewhat unusual. The purpose of the passage is to elevate the ritualist embodied in the householder, as 12.12.11 makes clear, though 12.12.6 suggests that the ritualist transcends (*ati*) all the *āśramas*.

33. See Olivelle (1993: 154), citing Deussen (1909: 131).

34. Discussed above, p. 189.

āśrama should be practiced "until the relinquishing of the body" (*ā vimokṣāc charīrasya*; 12.226.4). In 12.260.12–14 of the *Gokapilasaṃvādaḥ*,[35] Kapila also appears to describe four options, all of which "have the same goal" (*ekārtha*) and are "regarded as the four eternal paths leading to god" (*devayānā hi panthānaś catvāraḥ śāśvatā matāḥ*).[36]

The passage from 12.60 to 12.66 has a number of different approaches to the *āśrama* system and the householder. After Yudhiṣṭhira questions Bhīṣma on various matters in 12.60.1–5, including the four *āśramas*, the *varṇas*, and aspects of kingship, chapter 61 is the first to consider the *āśramas*, which Bhīṣma lists in 61.2 in an order suggesting they are not sequential. The subsequent passage presents a kind of hybrid system. While 12.61.2–5 says that after going through various life-cycle rituals to reach the householder stage, the householder can then progress to the *vānaprastha* stage, wherein, his obligations done, he can reach a "state of absorption in the undecaying" (*akṣarasātamatā*), the subsequent verses (61.6–9) indicate that a person living as a celibate student (*brahmacarya*) has the right to live by begging (*bhaikṣacaryā*) and seek *mokṣa*.[37] He, too, having obtained the *āśrama* of "tranquility" (*kṣema*), is absorbed in the undecaying (*akṣara*). In this case, we have some suggestion of progression from one stage to the next, but also of permanence, and, in the cases of the *vānaprastha* and the mendicant *mokṣa* seeker, the same reward. The life-long option of the householder is then described in 61.10–17, which is equated with the "law of sages" (61.10) and which involves humility, piety, ritual dutifulness, and generosity. The reward is heaven. And, finally, the chapter closes with a description of the life-long option of the celibate student (61.18–21).

The next chapter, however, appears to unequivocally require that a Brahmin should treat all four *āśramas* as a unit to be progressed through (the *samuccaya* model) in order to win the "undecaying" (*akṣara*) worlds (12.62.6–7).[38] All the *āśramas* are again commended for a Brahmin in 12.63.7. The same chapter contemplates the non-Brahmin *varṇas* in relation to the

---

35. See further above, p. 189–90.

36. Compare 12.262.19–21. At 12.262.34–35 Syūmaraśmi contrasts the knowledge-focused types like Kapila with the householders focused on ritual (*karman*), and then queries how all the *āśramas*, despite their differences, are said to be the same "in the end" (*niṣṭhā*; the end being, perhaps, the death of the practitioner). Kapila, however, declares a preference for Veda-grounded knowledge (*jñāna*), in which ritual is at best preparatory to that knowledge. See above, p. 190.

37. While this is reminiscent of Śuka's quest to skip over the *gṛhastha* stage at 12.313.20, the context in that case, as I have suggested above, is that the sequential system is normative, and Śuka's preference represents a modification to that system.

38. See also Fitzgerald's note on 12.62.6 (2004: 730).

āśramas (12.63.12–22), in which case the passages provoke some conundrums, to which we shall turn shortly. It nevertheless also seems to propose a sequential model of the *āśramas*.[39] Chapters 12.64–65 set out to establish the primacy of the *kṣatradharma* for the maintenance of other dharmas, including those of the *āśramas*, through the conversation between Indra and King Māndhātṛ. Among a number of interesting statements regarding the *āśramas* is the following uttered by Indra when explaining what happens when a king no longer maintains order (12.65.25):

> *asaṃkhyātā bhaviṣyanti bhikṣavo liṅginas tathā |*
> *āśramāṇāṃ vikalpāś ca nivṛtte 'smin kṛte yuge ||*
>
> There will be innumerable mendicants and ascetics and there will be choices of the *āśramas* when the Kṛta age has passed.

If *vikalpa* here refers to the notion of there being alternative choices between the *āśramas* as life-long options—in other words, what Olivelle refers to as the "original" system—then this passage identifies it with a dystopic age, and therefore presumably implies that the sequential (*samuccaya*) model is both prior and utopian.

This passage on the *āśramas* culminates in 12.66 with a novel take on the idea of the *āśramas*. The point would appear to be that the king, at the time he virtuously performs his various royal activities, resides in an *āśrama* said to correspond to such activities and receives its rewards. Ultimately, he receives the benefits of all the *āśramas*, and the passage thereby charts a course for the virtuous king's salvation in *brahman* (66.32–37), and as such represents another argument for Yudhiṣṭhira to assume the royal office rather than renounce (see, especially, 66.35–36). However, the terminology of the passage is largely unique, with *bhaikṣāśrama* (the *āśrama* of mendicancy), *kṣemāśrama* (the *āśrama* of peace or security), *dīkṣāśrama* (the *āśrama* of consecration), *vanyāśrama* (the *āśrama* of the forest) and *brahmāśrama* (the *āśrama* of *brahman*, the Veda) substituting for the more familiar terms.[40] Of the standard

---

39. See especially *āśramamaṇḍala* (the "cycle of *āśramas*") in 63.15 and *ānupūrvyāśrama* (the "*āśramas* in succession") in 12.63.21.

40. See 12.66.5–12. The terms *bhaikṣāśrama* and *dīkṣāśrama* are unique to this passage; *kṣemāśrama* appears at 12.61.9, where it refers to a stage of tranquility achieved by a mendicant either before or simultaneously to reaching the "undecaying"; *vanyāśrama* and *brahmāśrama* are the terms used by Janaka in the *Śukajanakasaṃvādah* in his description of the sequential *āśramas* for the third and fourth stages respectively (12.313.18–19; see above, p. 191). By way of contrast to the latter case, the types of activities associated with *brahmāśrama* in the present passage (12.66.10–11) bring it more closely into alignment with those of the *brahmacarya*.

āśrama terms, the passage uses only those pertaining to the householder (*gārhasthya* and *gṛhāśrama*) in five stanzas (66.15–19) that highlight aspects of protection, guest worship, attitudes to household dependents and generosity. Indeed, the householder *āśrama* seems to hold a premier position among the others (66.29) for royal types, perhaps especially because it models the king's protective obligations (66.33–37).

While these differences between the householder and types of ascetics, either within the context of the binary or the *āśramas*, provide much fodder for debating the relative merits of each in relation, especially, to their attendant post-death outcomes, such differences tend to collapse in devotional contexts. Thus in the *Gaṅgāmāhātyam* in 13.27 a Siddha tells a gleaner that all the *āśramas* honor Gaṅgā; and in the *Nārāyaṇīyam*, in response to Yudhiṣṭhira's query as to which deity each of the four *āśramas* should make offerings, it is, of course, Nārāyaṇa.[41]

Who Is the Gṛhastha*? Brahmins, Kings, and Others*

As should already be evident, in the *Mahābhārata* the institution of the *gṛhastha* does not always apply merely to the Brahmin. Though characters referred to as *gṛhasthas* are frequently Brahmins, and though also on many occasions the Brahmin—so often the unmarked term in Brahmanical apologetics—is probably the implied subject of rules where none is explicitly stated, some passages in the *Mahābhārata* evidently reflect a broader application, especially in respect to the king. In 12.63.12–22 Kṣatriyas, Vaiśyas, and even Śūdras could aspire to progress through the *āśramas*. This section initially states that all the *āśramas*—bar that based on "desirelessness" (*nirāśis*)—are prescribed for a Śūdra who has only a short while to live and who has completed his ordinary duties, in other words, once he has completed what appear to be householder-like duties, but apparently not those of the formal *gṛhastha āśrama* (12.63.12–13). This is then extended to the Vaiśya and the Rājaputra, again stipulating that it does not include the "life of begging" (*bhaikṣacaryā*; 63.14). This appears to be immediately contradicted in the subsequent verses (63.15–22), which recommend that a Vaiśya (15), and then a king (16–22), may go through all the *āśramas*, again once their householder-like obligations are out of the way. As

41. Lines 32–33 of Appendix 1 No. 13 in the *Anuśāsanaparvan*, which appears in the Southern recension after 13.124, say that all four *āśramas* fail to reach the highest path if they give up worshiping Keśava (Kṛṣṇa Nārāyaṇa).

Fitzgerald notes (2004: 730–31), this passage suggests that the householder-like activities such a Vaiśya or king are to undertake before entering the *āśramas* are distinct from the *gṛhastha āśrama* as a formal religious obligation. This presents something of a conundrum, since it is not entirely clear what the difference is; it nevertheless evidently entails a view that their own householder activities are not considered sufficient for the particular religious vocation encapsulated by the term *gṛhastha*.

Much later in the *Mahābhārata*, in the *Umāmaheśvarasaṃvādaḥ* (13.126–34), to Umā's question regarding the characteristics of dharma (13.128.23) Maheśvara (Śiva) responds in general terms regarding the best dharma of the *gṛhastha* (128.25–27). Umā wants more detail about the four *varṇas* (128.28–29; 34), which Maheśvara then describes in turn. After beginning with a Brahmin's celibate studentship, Maheśvara describes the Brahmin's responsibilities as a *gṛhastha* (128.39–45), using householder terms four times and focusing particularly on ritual and the care of dependents. Subsequently Maheśvara describes the laws of Kṣatriyas (128.46–52), Vaiśyas (128.53–55) and Śūdras (128.56–58). These accounts contain many elements typical of the specificity of each *varṇa's* occupations, but they also contain many householder-like elements that seem typical for *gṛhasthas*; unlike in the case of Brahmins, however, technical householder terms do not occur in these contexts. It is tempting to view such passages as reflecting a restriction of *gṛhastha* as a technical term for a vocation and its rewards peculiar to Brahmins. However, later on Umā asks Maheśvara in 13.131 how members of the various *varṇas* may reach the state of other *varṇas* (whether "up" or "down"). Maheśvara explains how a Śūdra might become a Brahmin through successive lives of virtue, which involves first becoming a Vaiśya and then a Kṣatriya. Interestingly, among the many things a virtuous Vaiśya must do to become a Kṣatriya is to abide by the vow of the *gṛhastha* (13.131.31). In the *Anugītā* of the *Āśvamedhikaparvan*, Kṛṣṇa relates the god Brahmā's response to questions put to him by some eminent seers.[42] Brahmā's sermon includes a description of the four *āśramas* (seemingly sequential, see above p. 191), not long after which he restricts the *vānaprastha* mode to the three twice-born *varṇas* (14.35.32), while declaring that *gṛhastha* is for all the *varṇas* (14.35.33).

While these are quite meager and hardly consistent views with regard to the *gṛhastha* and the non-Brahmin *varṇas*, it is another case altogether when it comes to the king, for whom the references are rather more frequent.

42. In fact, Kṛṣṇa is relating a guru's response to his disciple's questions, which defers to Brahmā's response to the seers' similar questions. This is the *Guruśiṣyasaṃvādah*.

Indeed, the king may be understood as a hyper-realized *gṛhastha*, manifesting in maximal form the householder's fundamental attributes of protection, the supporting of dependents, generosity, and ritual propriety, all of which are mutually constitutive. A number of stories dramatize the connection between the king and the vocation of the *gṛhastha*. As we have already seen, the *Sulabhājanakasaṃvādaḥ* tells the story of King Janaka as a critique of the possibility of combining the *gṛhastha* vocation with the methods and accomplishments of the pursuit of *mukta*. The *bhikṣunī* Sulabhā (a kṣatriyā) demonstrates that he is a fraud, and therefore is both not liberated and a poor *gṛhastha*. The problem for Janaka and householders more generally is that the royal and domestic lives involve so many attachments. But it is not necessarily all bad news for kings who desire the ultimate rewards of *mokṣa*. In 12.277.1 Yudhiṣṭhira asks Bhīṣma how a king "like myself" (*asmadvidha*) can wander the earth liberated, "freed from the noose of attachments" (*saṅgapāśād vimucyate*), to which Bhīṣma responds with what the seer Ariṣṭanemi told King Sagara. Ariṣṭanemi confirms that the "noose of affection" (*snehapāśa*) renders a man incapable of *mokṣa* (12.277.5–7), and recommends that once Sagara's children have become adults, he should leave them and his wife and pursue freedom (12.277.8–9). Ariṣṭanemi then goes on to explain *mokṣa* at length, an explanation that boils down to the problems posed by feelings and attachments, especially as these are embodied in kin; the household (*kuṭumba*), he says in 12.277.43, is a place of "misery" (*duḥkha*). But seemingly having suggested that one must leave the house and its attachments behind in order to pursue freedom, he closes with (12.277.46–47):

> *etac chrutvā mama vaco bhavāṃś caratu muktavat /*
> *gārhasthye yadi te mokṣe kṛtā buddhir aviklavā //*
> *tat tasya vacanaṃ śrutvā samyak sa pṛthivīpatiḥ /*
> *mokṣajaiś ca guṇair yuktaḥ pālayām āsa ca prajāḥ //*
>
> "Once you've listened to these words of mine, sir, you must act as if freed. If you're in the state of the householder, focus your intellect unwaveringly on freedom." Having duly heard his speech, the king, yoked to qualities born of freedom (*mokṣa*), protected his people.

Ariṣṭanemi therefore appears to propose two solutions to Yudhiṣṭhira's question. On the one hand, the pursuit of freedom can be pursued in retirement from the domestic life, not unlike the sequential *āśrama* system, and on the other hand, disciplined non-attachment ("freedom") can be attained during the householder or royal career, contradicting, therefore, the primary message of the *Sulabhājanakasaṃvādaḥ*.

That Yudhiṣṭhira is the audience for these stories underscores their significance as "mirror texts"[43] for Yudhiṣṭhira's own dilemmas, since he repeatedly expresses conflict over the compromises of the royal life and the appeal of the moral absolutes of the ascetic life, especially in reflecting on the events of the war in the early chapters of the *Śāntiparvan*, as we have already seen. Indeed, in these contexts Yudhiṣṭhira becomes the *Mahābhārata's* principal means through which to promote the king as *gṛhastha*, primarily in order to argue that the royal life has ethical merit, and therefore to convince Yudhiṣṭhira that it is a worthwhile vocation for him to pursue. It is in fact Yudhiṣṭhira who first aligns himself with the *gṛhastha āśrama* in the second chapter of the *Āraṇyakaparvan*, when the Pāṇḍavas are heading off for their period of exile in the forest. Yudhiṣṭhira wants the Brahmins following them to turn back, since he can't afford to feed them. They refuse, and one of their leaders, Śaunaka, delivers a homily (which he attributes to a Janaka) on anguish (*duḥkha*), desire (*tṛṣṇā*), and their link to wealth (*artha*) (3.2.20–48). Yudhiṣṭhira is quick to protest; his desire for wealth is not for himself, but in order to support Brahmins, which he cites as a fundamental duty of one like himself (*asmadvidha*) who is in the *gṛhāśrama* (3.2.49–50). He proceeds to give a more extensive account of the duties of the householder (3.2.51–59), in which performing domestic rituals and sustaining dependents (which, again, are mutually constitutive) are paramount.

This initial statement would have Yudhiṣṭhira in agreement with his brothers and elders in the early chapters of the *Śāntiparvan*. But by then Yudhiṣṭhira seems to have absorbed the teachings of Śaunaka and, in reflecting on his role in the war, decided to give up the royal office and renounce. As we have seen above, a key plank of the brothers' arguments (Arjuna in 12.11 and 12.18; Nakula in 12.12) is that as king Yudhiṣṭhira ought to be a model *gṛhastha*, who is, indeed, superior in the attributes of ascetics than are ascetics themselves. Vyāsa takes up and provides a summative point to the same line of reasoning in his praise (*stuti*) of the *gṛhasthāśrama* in 12.23, which is regarded as the highest *āśrama* (12.23.2; 23.5). This is Yudhiṣṭhira's *svadharma*, not going to the forest as he currently wishes (23.3). Vyāsa stresses the economic and ritual centrality of the householder; not only do "gods, ancestors, seers and dependents (*bhṛtya*)" rely on him, but so do "birds, animals, and living things (*bhūta*)" (23.4–5). Of the four *āśramas*, it is the most difficult to do (23.6). Vyāsa then turns to the difference between Brahmins and royal Kṣatriyas, which ought not to be confused. A king must wield the rod of punishment, his

43. On this notion, see Biardeau (2002, I: 412–13), pursued further by Bowles (2016).

pathway to perfection, as previously achieved by King Sudyumna (23.8–16), a story told in the subsequent chapter.

The king is the maximal householder because he maximally replicates the primary ritual and economic obligations of the householder. Through the performance of domestic rites (and, in the case of the king, the larger public rites), the economically productive householder distributes his wealth to gods, ancestors, dependents, Brahmins, mendicants, and guests. As such, kings and householders are the redistributive hubs of a ritualized exchange system that sustains not merely social order, but the heavenly realms as well. It is for his ritual, economic, and procreative centrality that the *gṛhastha* is configured as one side of another binary, in which all of the remaining *āśramas*—and, indeed, other dependent types, especially family members—are construed as being wholly dependent on the householder; frequently in such situations the *gṛhastha* is referred to as their "foundation" (*mūla*) or the best among them.[44]

While the ritually redistributive aspect of the *gṛhastha* is stressed in many passages, it is particularly a feature of descriptions of the householder in the *Dānadharmaparvan*, which constitutes almost all of the *Anuśāsanaparvan* and which gives itself over to matters of "generosity" (*dāna*), frequently combining ritual humility with forms of distribution. We see this already in the second chapter of this collection, where Yudhiṣṭhira asks Bhīṣma how a householder can defeat death. Bhīṣma responds with the tale of Sudarśana, the son of Agni and a king's daughter, who does so by he and his wife taking *atithipūjana*, the "worship of guests," to an extreme: his wife lies with a Brahmin guest, who happens to be Dharma in disguise.[45] The couple's piety is rewarded. Bhīṣma summarily states that a householder has no divinity other than a guest (13.2.90). In 13.62, Yudhiṣṭhira asks Bhīṣma what kings should give Brahmins, to which Bhīṣma defers to Nārada, who praises food (*anna*) and the giver of food (*annada*), in which case the latter is clearly a householder. And in 13.100, Yudhiṣṭhira asks about the law of the *gṛhastha*, and Bhīṣma recounts the conversation between Kṛṣṇa Vāsudeva and the Earth. The Earth explains to Kṛṣṇa the various offerings to gods, ancestors, Brahmin seers and guests; the

44. See, for example, 12.12.11; 12.142; 12.184.10; 12.226.5; 12.261.5–8; 12.311.27; 12.321.25; 13.128.46; 14.45.13.

45. On this story, one of many in which rites of hospitality place women in jeopardy, see Jamison (1996: 153–55).

householder should always be an "eater of the leftovers" (*śiṣṭāśin*; 13.100.20), a refrain, as we have seen, found elsewhere in relation to the householder.[46]

Concluding Remarks

While the *Mahābhārata* witnesses the consolidation of the idea of the householder in Indic discourse, it also bears witness to the shifting terrain underpinning its development, especially in respect to the *āśramas* and aspects of class. This reflects the *Mahābhārata's* polyvocality. In the two *parvans* that contain the overwhelming majority of householder terms, the *Śānti-* and *Anuśāsanaparvans*, the way in which the *gṛhastha* (and the *āśramas* generally) is handled reflects in large part the topic that governs the *parvan*. Thus those passages that appear in the *Rājadharmaparvan* (and, to a lesser extent, the *Āpaddharmaparvan*[47]) focus on the king in relation to the *gṛhastha*, sometimes in respect to issues of governance (e.g., 12.15.12), but, perhaps surprisingly, more so in respect to the king modeling good *gṛhastha* behavior.[48] In the *Mokṣadharmaparvan*, the key passages tend to focus on issues pertaining to ideas of liberation, and the householder's orientation in respect to those. Finally, in the *Anuśāsanaparvan*, which has as its premier topic the law of giving (*dānadharma*), the focus of householder passages is on the giving that occurs in domestic rituals.

Nevertheless, given that there is clear evidence external to the *Mahābhārata* of historical developments both in the very appearance of the term *gṛhastha* and in the relational contexts in which the *gṛhastha* appears—from the binary in the Aśokan inscriptions, to the *vikalpa āśrama* model in the Dharmasūtras, to the sequential *samuccaya* model of the *āśramas* in the *Mānava Dharmaśāstra*—historical questions regarding the *Mahābhārata's* polyvocality inevitably arise. Are we able to determine layers of historical development in the *Mahābhārata* itself on the basis of the *gṛhastha*? We must

46. See, e.g., 3.2.58, 12.11 (discussed above, p. 184–85), 12.235.11 and 13.128.39–42, where the term is *vighasāśin*, and 14.45.17 where it is *śiṣṭāśin*. Compare also 12.37.27. The very similar passages 12.214 and 13.93 discuss the *vighasāśin* in the same type of context, but where the only householder term is *kuṭumbika* (12.214.6 and 13.93.6). See also *ĀpDh* 2.7.3 and *MDh* 3.285 (= *MBh* 3.2.58 and 12.235.11).

47. For the key passage in this case, see Bowles (2007: 295–306 and 2016: 334–47).

48. Such considerations appear to be rare in the dharma literature, at least in respect to technical "householder" terminology. The *VaDh* (19.3–6) gives it some thought, when it advises that the king should hand over his "householder duties" to his appointed personal priest (*purohita*), because it is too difficult to govern and observe his obligatory household (*gārhasthya*) rituals. Compare also *ĀpDh* 2.25.6–9 and *MDh* 7.78.

be cautious here in a number of ways. First, given the fundamental significance of the binary between the householder and the mendicant for the *gṛhastha* in most contexts, we should not assume that instances of this binary alone represent a necessarily earlier instantiation of the *gṛhastha*. Second, we should be wary of over determining the extent to which such a large text as the *Mahābhārata*—in which many minds may have participated in its composition, redaction, and transmission—will represent a linear development of ideas. Once new ways of thinking about problems arise, older ways of thinking might still persist, sometimes side by side with the new ways, perhaps championed by individuals or communities involved in the creation of the *Mahābhārata*. Indeed, the *Mahābhārata* in some instances is self-conscious of such differences. Though the *Mahābhārata* in my view represents, as I have earlier said, a fuzzily bounded yet approximately singular cultural system, this does not mean that ideological uniformity was a governing principle of its composition and redaction. The *Mahābhārata*, whether by design or by accident, reflects the diversity of its communities of interest. Third, we must consider what it is that the *Mahābhārata* represents. If the "*Mahābhārata*" is a creation that consciously drew upon antecedent elements—whether in respect to aspects of the "narrative," or those sections regarded as "didactic"—would we be uncovering historical moments in the creation of the antecedent elements, or of the creation of the *Mahābhārata*?

There are also some glaring distribution problems that require further thought. As Tables 10.1 and 10.2 demonstrate, householder terms are overwhelmingly concentrated (more than 80%) in the *Śānti-* and *Anuśāsanaparvans*, regarded by scholars as "didactic" (and, by many, as relatively late), though the "didacticism" of the *Śāntiparvan's* early chapters, which include a significant number of instances of *gṛhastha*, is rather crucial for the development of the narrative. Does this reflect generic properties? Or historical processes? Or a mix of both? There are some striking anomalies. In the constituted text of the Critical Edition, there are no householder terms in *parvans* 4, 6, 7, 10, 11, and 15–18. Similarly, the *Sabhāparvan* (*parvan* 2) only has four, and in each case the term is *gṛhamedhin*, even though given the courtly context we might have expected more (as might also have been expected in the courtly *Virāṭaparvan*). The large *Āraṇyaka-* and *Udyogaparvans* have only eight and one instance respectively,[49] even though both have much in the way of "didactic" material. Even the remaining *parvans* outside of the *Śānti-* and *Āraṇyakaparvans* are

49. In the case of the *Udyogaparvan*, not including one further instance excised from the Critical Edition.

hardly verbose on the *gṛhastha*. Perhaps the most glaring anomaly is the complete absence of householder terms in the *Bhagavadgītā* (*MBh* 6.23–40),[50] even though it attempts in part to resolve the essential problem of the binary in which the householder participates, and even though the syntactic structure of the *vibhūtiyoga* (*MBh* 6.33) would have invited the deployment of the fourfold *āśramas* with a pronouncement as to which is best among them.[51] The absence of *gṛhastha* in the *Bhagavadgītā*, which most scholars have regarded as a relatively late inclusion in the *Mahābhārata*, serves as a caution to those who might quickly jump to temporal conclusions on the basis of the presence or absence of such terms.[52]

In spite of these fairly substantial reasons for caution, I do think some limited temporal conclusions can be drawn, at least for the householder passages. Since there appear to be good reasons to suppose that the term *gṛhastha* appears first in Middle Indo-Aryan contexts, then it would seem the *Mahābhārata* material comes later, though the *Mahābhārata* must also have had a role, alongside the Dharmasūtras, in making such a category "Brahmanical." Given that a considerable amount of the material surveyed above presents the *vikalpa* ("alternative choice") system of *āśramas*, or hybrid forms in which some consideration appears to be being given to how different *āśramas* might cohere as a singular system for an individual, I think it is safe to conclude that such material reflects the period spanning the Dharmasūtras. Again, the *Mahābhārata* should be regarded as a co-traveler with these texts in establishing the normativity of the *gṛhastha*. However, in regard to the most extensive account of the *samuccaya āśrama* system in the *Śukānupraśnaḥ*, I think this is most likely a derivative of the very similar (but more coherent) system presented in the *Mānava Dharmaśāstra*. Since there is an earlier reference to the *vikalpa* system in the same (fairly long) story, the *Mānava*-derivative account may represent an amendment introduced by a *samuccaya* enthusiast. Further, the term *gṛhāśrama*, which appears once in the *Mānava Dharmaśāstra*, but not before, is a possible *Mahābhārata* coining. The occurrences of *gṛhamedhin* in the *Mahābhārata* and *Mānava Dharmaśāstra*, after its neglect in the three Dharmasūtras after the *Āpastamba*

---

50. Compare Olivelle (1993: 103–6) in respect also to the absence of *āśrama* from the *Bhagavadgītā*.

51. Precisely such a syntactic structure is found in 13.14.155, but in relation to Śiva. Vāsudeva, who once had a *darśana* of Śiva (13.14.11), recites a *stotra* to him, describing Śiva in 155 as the *gṛhastha* among the *āśramas*.

52. Is the absence of the terms in the *Rāmāyaṇa* (see Ch. 11, this volume) due to the period of its composition, generic considerations, or the choices of its authors?

Dharmasūtra, reflect a revitalizing of that term. Interestingly, the instances of the *gṛhamedhin* (and no other householder term) in the *Agastyabhṛgusaṃvādaḥ* in 13.102–3, in which Yudhiṣṭhira has asked about the fruit of offering incense (*dhūpa*) and lamps (*dīpa*) with the *bali* offerings, may bear witness to the reconfiguration of the domestic ritual.[53]

53. See above, n. 13.

11

Gṛhasthas *Don't Belong in the* Rāmāyaṇa

Aaron Sherraden

IN HIS SEMINAL work *The Āśrama System*, Olivelle notes with surprise that the critical edition of the *Rāmāyaṇa* contains exactly one clear reference to a systematized and codified institution of *āśramas* while the *Mahābhārata* has more than 160.[1] Why should the two major epics of classical India diverge so starkly on an institution that seems so integral to classical Hindu thought? The singular passage in the *Rāmāyaṇa* reads, "Those who know dharma—and you are one who knows dharma—say that of the four *āśramas*, that of the householder is best. How, then, can you abandon it?"[2] Olivelle fairly concludes, "the author of the *Rāmāyaṇa* was either ignorant of the *āśrama* system or could choose to ignore it because it had not gained the prominence that it did in later times."[3] Any attempt to further investigate the author's apparent lack of knowledge or support of the *āśrama* system would likely result in speculation, but it is possible to clarify the

I thank Donald R. Davis, Jr. for all his contributions throughout the preparation of this article. His guidance and comments provided me with the necessary foundation to articulate the ideas presented here, which are, in actuality, the product of our mutual conversations.

1. Olivelle 1993: 103.

2. *caturṇām āśramāṇāṃ hi gārhasthyaṃ śreṣṭham āśramam / āhur dharmajña dharmajñās taṃ kathaṃ tyaktum arhasi* // 2.98.58

3. Olivelle 1993: 103.

Rāmāyaṇa's portrayal of its various characters as they conduct their lives and assume a gamut of social roles—their "life-modes." Such a clarification allows us to contrast the life-modes as depicted in the *Rāmāyaṇa* with the *āśramas*, which must be understood as life-modes participating in an overarching system of social and religious obligations. This system of *āśramas*, explored unremittingly in the dharma literature, itself underwent significant developments over time. In it original formulation (i.e., as described in the early Dharmasūtras), one elected an *āśrama*—studentship, householdership, retirement to the forest, or full-fledged renunciation—as their permanent mode of life after an initial period of studentship. Later, in the classical formulation (i.e., as described in the later dharma texts starting especially with the *Mānava Dharmaśāstra* [*MDh*]), these *āśramas* stopped being optional and became connected elements in a progressive sequence. One started as a student, then became a householder, later retired to the forest, and finally became a renouncer.[4] Whatever relationship the author of the *Rāmāyaṇa* may have had with the *āśrama* system, the fact remains that it did not make its way into the epic in any formulation, and the glaring absence of any description of such a system certainly has considerable consequences when explaining the equally glaring absence of system's main player and the quintessential social role in the classical Hindu socio-religious worldview: the *gṛhastha*.

The *Rāmāyaṇa* is precisely as silent on the *gṛhastha* as it is on the *āśrama* system in general. The same passage cited above is the text's only reference to the *gṛhastha*, or rather to *gārhasthya* (ritual householdership). With this chapter, I venture down the troubling road of trying to detail the presence of life-modes but the absence of *āśramas* in the *Rāmāyaṇa*. In doing so, I hope to illuminate why it was possible to entirely leave out the *gṛhastha*, a figure we have come to accept as essential to classical Hinduism in many other contexts. I will first properly contextualize the single reference to the *gṛhastha* institution in the text and then outline how the *Rāmāyaṇa* depicts the various life-modes to show that they do not align with a system of *āśramas*. It should become clear after such an investigation that the *Rāmāyaṇa* establishes no narrative or social need to mention the *gṛhastha*.

4. See Olivelle 1993 and 2018.

A Closer Look at Rāmāyaṇa *2.98.58*

Rāma's path to the throne of Ayodhyā provides the entire gravity around which the *Rāmāyaṇa's* plot rotates. His coronation is the foundation for the epic's conflicts and the last condition for the full resolution of those conflicts.[5] The focus of the *Rāmāyaṇa* never drifts far from Rāma or the steadfast nature of his moral compass. Even in the *Sundarakāṇḍa*, a book where Rāma is largely absent, Hanumān incessantly praises his hero when he finds Sītā in Rāvaṇa's Aśoka Grove. Stated simply, the *Rāmāyaṇa* is about Rāma, the next in line in a lineage of kings that is tormented by a tragic lapse in proper succession. It is about the standard of conduct by which Rāma lives as this tragedy unfolds and is ultimately resolved. I begin the investigation into the missing *gṛhastha* by setting the *Rāmāyaṇa's* singular reference to this institution in its proper context. In addition to considering the reference as a legitimate part of the narrative, I also begin to draw attention to the jagged edges left exposed by the *gṛhastha's* imprecise fit in the passage, which will hopefully help us start to see the inability of the *gṛhastha* to meld into the ethos of the text as a whole.

By the end of the *Ayodhyākāṇḍa*, where the mention of *gārhasthya* occurs, Rāma, Sītā, and Lakṣmaṇa have established their humble residence in the Daṇḍaka Forest, not long after Rāma's impending coronation as king of Ayodhyā was sabotaged by the two boons given to Kaikeyī, the most beautiful wife of King Daśaratha. Kaikeyī's son, Bharata, is now to be given the throne, but he does not want it, for he loves Rāma and knows him to be the rightful heir. In a desperate attempt to set things right, Bharata rushes to the forest after Rāma to plead with him to accept the kingdom.

It is in this context that Bharata uses a number of arguments to persuade Rāma that his decision to accept Daśaratha's coerced command was unnecessary and wrong. Bharata starts his argumentation in *sarga* 95 by suggesting that Rāma's status as the eldest brother necessitates his coronation as king (2.95.2). Bharata's line of thinking becomes stronger starting in *sarga* 97. Here, Bharata explains that Daśaratha was wrong to act under the sway of Kaikeyī and Rāma's succession is the right course. Rāma responds with a single stream of rebuttal that applies in two different ways. He cannot disobey an

---

5. This point is even more poignant when one considers the first and seventh books, the *Bālakāṇḍa* and *Uttarakāṇḍa* respectively, to be later interpolations. One could easily argue that the *Uttarakāṇḍa* presents an entirely new set of conflicts, but the disruption of Rāma's coronation—arguably the *Rāmāyaṇa's* main concern—is ultimately resolved by the end of the *Yuddhakāṇḍa*. For more on the addition of the *Uttarakāṇḍa*, see the introduction to Goldman and Sutherland Goldman 2017.

order given by Daśaratha as it is an order given by his father (2.97.19) and his king (2.97.21). What his father, the king, bids him to do is the most suitable for him, not the kingship (2.97.24). Bharata then attempts to bestow the throne on Rāma as an act of a king (2.98.4). Rejecting this offer as being outside his fate, Rāma maintains that he must follow his father's order and implores Bharata to do the same (2.98.37–39). Growing increasingly disheartened with Rāma's consistent reasoning (which has thus far spanned three *sargas*), Bharata blasts his mother for putting him in this position and unleashes a flurry of arguments for Rāma's legitimate claim to the throne in quick succession (2.98.51–61). Bharata's brief mention of the *gṛhastha* institution in 2.98.58 comes in the midst of these impassioned pleas to Rāma.

In the immediate lead-up to this verse valorizing the *gṛhastha*, Bharata contrasts the ascetic life in the wilderness with the duty of Kṣatriyas and the matted hair of ascetics with ruling the kingdom. He then pleads with Rāma not to do such a despicable thing as to follow a path not meant for him (2.98.56). "If you want to lead a life of hardship," he continues, "then please do so by taking on the hardship of protecting the four *varṇas* in accordance with dharma."[6] As the culmination of this line of thought, Bharata then refers to the opinion of those who know dharma as holding that the *gṛhastha* mode of life is superior to all others.

> Those who know dharma—and you are one who knows dharma—say that of the four *āśramas*, that of the householder is best. How, then, can you abandon it? (2.98.58)[7]

The thrust of Bharata's argument in 2.98.56–58 is that asceticism is inappropriate for Rāma, who is instead destined for the throne. He appeals to a simply summarized description of what the appropriate dharma for a king is, namely, to protect his subjects and to establish the four *varṇas* in their appropriate dharmas. Rather than leaving it at that, Bharata then seems compelled

---

6. *atha kleśajam eva tvaṃ dharmaṃ caritum icchasi | dharmeṇa caturo varṇān pālayan kleśam āpnuhi ||* 2.98.57

7. See n. 2 above for the Sanskrit as found in the Baroda Critical Edition. There are a number of variations in the manuscripts listed in the Critical Edition, but they are mostly just minor semantic variations (e.g., *hātum* in place of *tyaktum* or *icchasi* instead of *arhasi*). One variation worth mentioning in particular comes with the seventeenth-century Devanāgarī manuscript (D2, Baroda Oriental Institute No. 12864) representing the NW Recension. Taking note of the *caturvarṇāśramāṇāṃ* ("of the four *varṇas* and *āśramas*") in the first *pāda*, 2.98.58 as it appears in this manuscript is: *caturvarṇāśramāṇāṃ hi gārhasthyaṃ śreṣṭham āśramam | āhur dharmajña dharmajñās taṃ kathaṃ hātum icchasi ||*

to supplement his plea for the protection of the *varṇas* with his mention of the *āśramas* and praise of the *gṛhastha*. Such a compulsion is symptomatic of the trend in later dharma literature to frequently place the *varṇas* and *āśramas* side-by-side and place the proper governance of these institutions (representative of the totality of Brahmanical dharma) within the scope of a king's duties.[8]

Having brought the *āśramas* up very briefly in this passage, neither Bharata nor Rāma return to the subject. Rāma does not acknowledge or refute Bharata's argument about a king's role in upholding *varṇāśramadharma*, even obliquely (perhaps a reason to look at 2.98.58 with suspicion). Instead, the text tells us that Rāma, "true to himself, remained firm in his decision not to leave, fixed as he was on his promise to his father."[9] And we would expect nothing less given the preceding *sargas*' demonstration of Rāma's refusal to entertain anything short of following Daśaratha's order. Though the people were disappointed that he would not return to Ayodhyā, they nevertheless delighted in his amazing resilience and commitment to his word (*sthirapratijñatva*, 2.98.70).

After Bharata's flood of arguments is met with Rāma's resolve, Jābāli and Vasiṣṭha both try to convince to Rāma of his right to Ayodhyā's throne. Jābāli makes a concerted effort to downplay—among other things—the importance of Rāma's relationship to his father (2.100.2–7), dharma (2.100.12), and even the ascetic and sacrificial prescriptions of texts composed by intellectuals (2.100.15). This is met with a dramatic rejection by Rāma where we find his most clearly stated philosophy stressing proper conduct (*cāritra*, 2.101.4) and his duty to the truth (2.101.12). Here, we also find his explicit rejection of the Kṣatriya code in the service of his personal dharma (2.101.19–20).[10]

---

8. Olivelle 1993: 201–204. This pairing is, in and of itself, perhaps a clue to this verse being an interpolation, as the *Rāmāyaṇa* as a whole seems rather unaware of—or at least unconcerned with—a unified concept of *varṇāśramadharma* while 2.98.57–58 refers to it in its fully developed form (to be discussed below)

9. *na caiva cakre gamanāya sattvavān matiṃ pitus tadvacane pratiṣṭhitaḥ* || 2.98.69 c–d.

10. Compare 2.18.36: *tad enāṃ visṛjānāryāṃ kṣatradharmāśritāṃ matim / dharmam āśraya mā taikṣṇyaṃ madbuddhir anugamyatām* || "Give up this ignoble thought based on a Kṣatriya's dharma. Do not resort to that cruel dharma. Follow my way of thinking." This earlier statement by Rāma to Lakṣmaṇa demonstrates a similar disdain for a Kṣatriya's dharma. Lakṣmaṇa's ignoble thought is his threat of violence against any citizen of Ayodhyā who backs the kingship of Bharata at Kaikeyī's bidding (2.18.10–11). When Rāma asks Lakṣmaṇa to follow "my way of thinking" (*madbuddhi*), he is referring to the same philosophy that would later inform his rejection of Bharata's pleas in the Daṇḍaka wilderness—i.e., that not following his father's command would be contrary to his dharma (2.18.32–35).

Following Jābāli, Vasiṣṭha tries a number of methods to convince Rāma of his claim to Ayodhyā's throne. He explains the origins of the world and Rāma's genealogical connection to it, thereby placing Rāma—Daśaratha's eldest son—into an ages-old tradition of royal succession (2.102.1–31). He also demonstrates that of the three gurus in Rāma's life (his father, his mother, and Vasiṣṭha himself), both his mother and teacher are calling for his return to Ayodhyā, thereby arguing that coming back to Ayodhyā would not be straying from a path of good conduct (2.103.2–4). Still, Rāma maintains that his word to his father is of utmost importance to him (2.103.11).

In short, it is clear that the *Rāmāyaṇa's* one mention of the *gṛhastha* institution is a single attempt among many that Bharata and company use to try to persuade Rāma. And like all other attempts, 2.98.58 fails. Even if we accept this verse as a genuine part of the narrative, Rāma's rejection of this argument based in *varṇāśramadharma* establishes a king's obligations to this Dharmaśāstric code of ethics—and, by way of collateral damage, the *gṛhastha*—as being outside Rāma's scope of concern. Rāma's claim to the throne has been disrupted, drastically shifting his dharmic priorities. Given his obligation of keeping his father a man true to his word, Rāma is now unconcerned with any sort of canonic Kṣatriya code or the duties of a king, which includes the proper maintenance of the *āśramas*, foremost of which, we are told, is the *gṛhastha*. His new dharma is releasing his father from his debts and committing himself to upholding his own word. Rāma makes this clear throughout his debate with Bharata. *Kṣatradharma* used to be the clearest code of conduct by which Rāma should live as he progressed toward being Ayodhyā's king, but the applicability of a generalized dharma for kings or Kṣatriyas could not hold up in the face of Rāma's obligations to his father, his king, and the truth. When *kṣatradharma* could be an instrument of discharging these obligations, Rāma would gladly follow its tenets. When it became an obstacle, however, he was quick to dismiss it.[11] The new circumstances of life in the forest brought Rāma away from the landed concerns of the *gṛhastha* and into the world of forest-dwelling ascetics, where *gṛhastha*-ness had little purchase. Together with the rest of Bharata, Jābāli, and Vasiṣṭha's arguments, it serves as a tradition inapplicable to Rāma's personal circumstances. Bharata's mention of the *gṛhastha* is an intellectual project diluted in a barrage of appeals to which Rāma responds with blatant and total rejection.

11. See n. 10.

Missed Opportunities: The Absence of Āśrama *in the* Rāmāyaṇa

Rāma's unwillingness to acknowledge any obligation toward the four *varṇas* and *āśramas* certainly makes for compelling narrative, but this does not wholly account for the *Rāmāyaṇa's* silence on the *āśramas* in general or the *gṛhastha* specifically. There are scores of other figures in the epic who could have embodied the ideals of the *āśrama* system and perhaps shed some light on the *gṛhastha*. To this end, Olivelle observes that the author of the *Rāmāyaṇa* had every opportunity to expound on the duties of the various *āśramas*, especially given the "frequent and lengthy accounts of forest hermits and itinerant mendicants."[12] But we are let down as "[h]ermits and renouncers are never introduced as belonging to a particular *āśrama*. Their duties and practices are never presented as *āśramadharma*."[13] There is actually one instance that appears to outline a forest hermit's duties, at least in an abbreviated form (3.11.24, see below), but the *Rāmāyaṇa* otherwise does keep curiously silent on the technical duties of the various life-modes. While the novelty of narrative allows us to understand and perhaps even admire Rāma's reasons for dismissing the *āśramas*, its harder to make a narrative-based argument for the proclivity of entire cast of the *Rāmāyaṇa* to appear unconcerned with the *āśramas* and their role in society. To evaluate the place of life-modes in the *Rāmāyaṇa*, I'll have to instead resort to a bit of close reading. This section surveys a number of instances where the text alludes to these life-modes in order to narrow down where the *Rāmāyaṇa* sits ideologically in relation to the *āśrama* system. Understanding the *Rāmāyaṇa's* general position with regard to the *āśramas* in this way helps explain the absence of the *gṛhastha* and even helps substantiate the claim that 2.98.58 is a late addition to the text.

I begin with the term *brahmacarya*, which, in the context of the *āśrama* system, signifies a period of celibate Vedic study. When free of technical meaning, however, it can simply mean "celibacy."[14] The first occurrence of *brahmacarya* in the *Rāmāyaṇa* is in 1.8.9, when the charioteer, Sumantra, is describing the sage Ṛśyaśṛṅga to Daśaratha. When translating this and other

12. Olivelle 1993: 103.

13. Olivelle 1993: 103.

14. Lubin 2018a: 107.

verses dealing with *brahmacarya*, I have left technical terms untranslated in order to facilitate further discussion on their potential meanings.

> That great man's *brahmacarya* will be disrupted, O king, making him famous throughout the world and forever talked about by the Brahmins. (1.8.9)[15]

The disruption to Ṛśyaśṛṅga's *brahmacarya* is likely a disruption to his celibacy given the long narration of the Ṛśyaśṛṅga legend following this reference, describing the isolated sage's first encounters with women and his eventual marriage to King Romapāda's daughter, Śāntā, as a reward for ending a terrible drought in the king's realm.[16]

In 2.24.10, Sītā commits herself to be a *brahmacāriṇī*, following Rāma into the forest. The implications of *brahmacāriṇī* here clearly point toward a meaning of Sītā's willingness to be a celibate companion to Rāma during their time in exile, devoid of any connotations of studentship.

> I will tend to you always and practice restraint as a *brahmacāriṇī*. I will be happy with you, my hero, in the sweetly scented forests. (2.24.10)[17]

The association of *brahmacarya* with celibacy is also evident in 5.33.12, when Hanumān is describing Rāma to Sītā while she is held captive in Rāvaṇa's Aśoka Grove. At this point in the epic, Rāma has long since graduated, clearly emphasizing the connotations of celibacy in *brahmacarya*. Also, *brahmacarya* is even suffixed with *vrata* ("vow"), making this association even stronger.

---

15. *dvaividhyaṃ brahmacaryasya bhaviṣyati mahātmanaḥ | lokeṣu prathitaṃ rājan vipraiś ca kathitaṃ sadā ||* By taking *dvaividhyaṃ brahmacaryasya* to mean that the *brahmacarya* is "disrupted," I rely on Goldman's note on this unclear phrase. Though not accepting this in his own translation, Goldman also notes that Govindarāja's commentary explains that *dvaividhyam* implies that "chastity is of two kinds, that of the celibate and that of the householder who engages in sexual activity only at the times prescribed by the law texts" (1984: 293). Govindarāja never uses the word *gṛhastha*, however. We are to read the *gṛhastha* between the lines when he says the Brahmin teachers note (*vipraiḥ smartṛbhiḥ kathitam*) that *brahmacarya* can mean "approaching [one's wife] during the [fertile] period" (*ṛtugamanalakṣaṇam*). See also n. 18.

16. There is some room to suggest that it is a disruption to his studentship. Compare *Rāmāyaṇa* 1.9.3, which describes Ṛśyaśṛṅga as being intent on his austerities and self-study (*tapaḥsvādhyāyane rataḥ*).

17. *śuśrūṣamāṇā te nityaṃ niyatā brahmacāriṇī | saha raṃsye tvayā vīra vaneṣu madhugandhiṣu ||*

> [Rāma is] magnificent and greatly revered; firm in his vow of *brahmacarya*, he understands how to serve the virtuous and properly conduct rituals. (5.33.12)[18]

The appearances of *brahmacarya* in 2.46.10 and 2.76.10 can each be taken as "studentship," but in both cases, they are paired with other terms that undoubtedly have implications of study. Both of these instances happen after Rāma finds out about his impending banishment. In the first, the charioteer Sumantra bids farewell to Rāma, wondering how such a horrible thing could happen to him.

> I suppose there is no reward for *brahmacarya* or *svadhīta*, kindness or sincerity, if such a misfortune could happen to you. (2.46.10)[19]

Both *brahmacarya* and *svadhīta* can carry a meaning of Vedic studentship, though I find it to be an unnecessary recapitulation in meaning to take them both as studentship when placed side-by-side in this verse. That being so, I tend to favor reading *brahmacarya* in this verse with stronger connotations of celibacy. A stronger indication of *brahmacarya* in its technical sense of an *āśrama* of studentship occurs in 2.76.10, when Bharata laments about how the kingdom could be given to him instead of a more qualified Rāma.

> How could someone like me take the kingdom away from that wise *vidyāsnāta* who is dedicated to dharma and has completed *brahmacarya*? (2.76.10)[20]

Bharata here refers to Rāma as both *caritabrahmacarya* and *vidyāsnāta*. The former can mean one who has undergone a period of studentship and/or

---

18. *arciṣmān arcito 'tyarthaṃ brahmacaryavrate sthitaḥ | sādhūnām upakārajñaḥ pracārajñaś ca karmaṇām ||* Goldman and Sutherland Goldman observe in their notes to this verse that the commentators push for Rāma's continence here being the continence prescribed for a householder, thus effectively identifying Rāma as a householder. See Goldman and Sutherland Goldman 1996: 438. The *Tilaka* commentary of Rāma (i.e., Nāgeśabhaṭṭa), for example, describes this *vrata* as approaching one's wife for intercourse only at times deemed appropriate for a *gṛhastha* (*brahmacaryavrate gṛhasthocitaparvādivarjanapūrvakam ṛtugamanalakṣaṇe sthitaḥ*). See also n. 15.

19. *na manye brahmacarye 'sti svadhīte vā phalodayaḥ | mārdavārjavayor vāpi tvāṃ ced vyasanam āgatam ||*

20. *caritabrahmacaryasya vidyāsnātasya dhīmataḥ | dharme prayatamānasya ko rājyaṃ madvidho haret ||*

celibacy. The latter, however, clearly refers to Rāma having completed his studentship.[21] The reference to *vidyāsnāta* has strong connotations of Vedic studentship and provides a contextual framework that weighs heavily on how we are to read *brahmacarya*, namely as a period of studentship.[22]

According to a progressive sequence of *āśramas* in the classical formulation, *gārhasthya* would follow studentship. It must be admitted that this is indeed suggested in the *Rāmāyaṇa*. Daśaratha's sons are born in 1.17.6–9, they graduate (*jñānasaṃpannāḥ*) in 1.17.21, and Daśaratha right away begins thinking of their marriages (*dārakriyā*) in 1.17.22. Where the *Rāmāyaṇa* falls short is in defining these eventual marriages in terms of the ritualized *gṛhastha* institution. It is not long after Rāma and Sītā's marriage, for instance, that we learn that they are to be sent into exile. The few cantos in between are filled with descriptions of Rāma's virtuous conduct in royal matters, Daśaratha's decision to crown him prince-regent, and Mantharā's scheming with Kaikeyī. There are no significant discussions of Rāma's duties as a *gṛhastha*; all discussions revolve around a regal image of Rāma as the future king of Ayodhyā.

As we might expect, the *Rāmāyaṇa* places most of its focus on the ascetic modes of life in the forest.[23] Brockington notes that the terms *ṛṣi* and *muni* account for most of the references to ascetics in the epic, with *tapasvin* and *tāpasa* occurring less frequently (and in specific reference to the practicing of *tapas*), and the terms with the potential to denote adherence to an ascetic *āśrama* (e.g., *parivrājika, bhikṣu, yati, śramaṇa*, and even *vānaprastha*) occur only rarely.[24] As a general note at the outset, then, the semantic preference for terms like *ṛṣi* and *muni*—which do little to orient us toward the *āśrama* system—detracts from the ability to detect any semblance of the *āśramas* in the *Rāmāyaṇa*.

The majority of the epic occurs in the wilderness, and Rāma is meant to live his life as an ascetic while he is away from Ayodhyā. Also important

21. See also *Vālmīki Rāmāyaṇa* 6.80.52 for a similar connotation of *snāta*: *vedavidyāvratasnātaḥ svadharmanirataḥ sadā / striyāḥ kasmād vadhaṃ vīra manyase rākṣaseśvara //*

22. For more on the *snātaka*, see Lubin 2018b: 113–24.

23. Brockington comes to a similar conclusion that other than a few references to studentship, "all other references [to the various life-modes] are to individuals becoming ascetics or to those who already are." Brockington 1984: 159.

24. Brockington 1984: 205. For a note on the appearances of the term *vaikhānasa* in the *Rāmāyaṇa*, see ibid., 204. Another common term for a forest-dweller, *vanavāsin*, occurs on numerous occasions but, because most of the *Rāmāyaṇa's* cast lives in the forest and the term is used descriptively without any technical meaning, it is not particularly helpful in determining how the life-modes are treated in the text.

is the fact that a great number of the characters he interacts with in the epic are ascetics of various kinds. The forest is the predominant cultural milieu depicted in the *Rāmāyaṇa*, and this greatly disrupts the balance of treatment given to the range of life-modes. Given the wealth of opportunities we are given to witness how the lives of forest-bound ascetics are conceived of in the text, the ascetic modes of life are key to demonstrating how any potential semblance of an *āśrama* system in any formulation ultimately breaks down. What we see in the *Rāmāyaṇa* is that the adherence to a life of asceticism as depicted in the text is a fluid commitment. In my study here, I will focus especially on the terms *vānaprastha* and *pravrajita* as a window into how these life-modes (which carry clear technical connotations when used in the context of the *āśrama* system) are treated in the *Rāmāyaṇa*.

Relatively rare though it may be, the *vānaprastha* receives a few interesting moments of attention in the epic. The first occurs in *Ayodhyākāṇḍa* 58.20 as Daśaratha is pondering the consequences of his past deeds and tells Kausalyā about the ascetic he shot in the forest some years ago (2.57.8–39). At various moments while narrating the story to Kausalyā, Daśaratha conflates ascetic (*tapasvin, tāpasa*), seer (*ṛṣi*), and forest hermit (*vānaprastha*), using them all to refer to the same person either in his own terms (2.57.27; 2.58.14; 2.58.20) or as reported speech (2.57.18, 20; 2.58.7). This same passage provides some clue as to the *vānaprastha's* place within a system of *āśramas*. In 2.57.32, Daśaratha reports the dying man as saying, "clearly there is no reward for austerities or study," suggesting that he had previously gone through a period of studentship and now lives as a *vānaprastha*.[25] This could signify an example of the original formulation of the *āśrama* system wherein one chooses a life-long *āśrama* after an initial period of studentship. But because the dying ascetic does not give any descriptions of his dharma as a *vānaprastha*, nor does he mention a life-long commitment to being a *vānaprastha*, it cannot be said for certain that he is acting in accordance with an *āśrama* system. Whatever the case may be, the dying ascetic makes no reference to a marriage or time living as a *gṛhastha*, thus making it unlikely that he is participating in the progressive *āśrama* system of the classical formulation.

It is also notable that in Daśaratha's memory of the event, the boy explicitly states that he is not a Brahmin but is instead the son of a Vaiśya father and Śūdra mother (2.57.37). While the *Rāmāyaṇa* apparently does permit

25. *na nūnaṃ tapaso vāsti phalayogaḥ śrutasya vā |*

non-Brahmins to be called *vānaprasthas*, it mentions Brahmin forest hermits in two instances, both in the *Araṇyakāṇḍa*. The first is when a group of forest hermits approaches Rāma for help in vanquishing the terrorizing Rākṣasas.

> This large group of defenseless *vānaprasthas*—most of them Brahmins—are being violently slain by the Rākṣasas. You, Rāma, are their defender. (3.5.14)[26]

Again, it is noteworthy that the *vānaprasthas* here are only mostly Brahmins (*brāhmaṇabhūyiṣṭha*), implying that there are some non-Brahmins in the group. In 3.11.24, however, *vānaprastha* is clearly referring to a single Brahmin, Agastya. The following instance of the term occurs when Agastya welcomes Rāma, Lakṣmaṇa, and Sītā in his hermitage.

> After presenting an oblation to the fire, making an offering of welcome-water, and honoring his guest[s], he [Agastya] gave them food according to a *vānaprastha's* dharma. (3.11.24)[27]

This is the clearest expression of *vānaprastha* as an *āśrama* in that it uses the term in a context commenting on a forest hermit's duties.[28] Unfortunately, in its isolation and brevity, the reference provides us with only minor insights into the *Rāmāyaṇa's* conception of the *vānaprastha's* code of conduct and give us no sense of the *vānaprastha's* place in relation to a broader system of *āśramas*.

The last appearance of *vānaprastha* in the *Rāmāyaṇa* seems like a deliberate choice. This occurs in the *Sundarakāṇḍa* when Hanumān, frustrated that he has not yet been able to locate Sītā, threatens to become a forest hermit.

---

26. *so 'yaṃ brāhmaṇabhūyiṣṭho vānaprasthagaṇo mahān / tvannātho 'nāthavad rāma rākṣasair vadhyate bhṛśam //*

27. *agniṃ hutvā pradāyārghyam atithiṃ pratipūjya ca / vānaprasthena dharmeṇa sa teṣāṃ bhojanaṃ dadau //*

28. Perhaps troubling for my arguments, this conduct appears, at least in part, to be in line with *MDh*, a classical Dharmaśāstra text. Note *MDh* 6.7–8: "He [i.e., the forest hermit] should give Bali offerings and almsfood to the best of his ability with whatever food he eats and honor those who visit his hermitage with water, roots, fruits, and almsfood. He should be always diligent in his vedic recitation; remain controlled, friendly, and collected; be always a giver and never a receiver of gifts; be compassionate towards all creatures." (tr. Olivelle 2005: 148).

> If I cannot find the daughter of Janaka, I will become a *vānaprastha*, living on what I can take with my hands and mouth living at the base of a tree, controlling the senses. (5.11.40)[29]

Instead of conceiving of the *vānaprastha* as either one *āśrama* in a progression of several or as a choice in permanent lifestyle, Hanumān considers life as a *vānaprastha* to be a self-imposed punishment should he not live up to the expectations of those who sent him on the mission to find Sītā. What's more, Hanumān's ideas of begging and living at the foot of a tree bears a closer resemblance to the renunciant life-mode than that of the forest hermit.[30]

Considering the *vānaprastha*, then, the *Rāmāyaṇa* does have a couple of instances that potentially hint toward the *vānaprastha* as an *āśrama*, but the code by which one leads this life is not strongly defined and is, at times, even confused with renunciation. What's clear, however, is that the references to the *vānaprastha* are not clearly associated with an institution of old age as we would expect in the original formulation of the *āśrama* system, nor do these references do anything to identify a progressive sequence of *āśramas* wherein life as a *vānaprastha* would come after life as a *gṛhastha* as a person takes on new sets of social and religious responsibilities in life.[31]

The renunciant life-mode also has a complicated presentation in the *Rāmāyaṇa*. For the purposes of this study, I am limiting myself to the term *pravrajita*, which provides a good sampling of different ways the *Rāmāyaṇa* envisions renunciation. As noted above, other terms that can signify the renunciant *āśrama* do occur in the *Rāmāyaṇa*, but they are infrequent and often not very useful for the exploration at hand. The term *bhikṣu*, for instance, only occurs a few times and it most often refers to the beggar form that Rāvaṇa and Hanumān assume as a disguise.[32] The same is true of the term *parivrājaka*, which is only used to describe Rāvaṇa's mendicant appearance as he approaches Sītā.[33] The superficial nature of these references

29. *hastādāno mukhādāno niyato vṛkṣamūlikaḥ / vānaprastho bhaviṣyāmi adṛṣṭvā janakātmajām //*

30. Compare *MDh* 6.5–28, 6.42–85.

31. See Olivelle 1993: 114–122 (for accounts of old-age life-modes in the *āśrama* system's original formulation) and 161–182 (for the classification of *āśramas* in the classical formulation).

32. See 3.44.8 and 3.47.6, which describe Rāvaṇa as respectively assuming and abandoning the form of a beggar when he approaches Sītā. Similarly, 4.3.3 and 4.3.21 describe Hanumān assuming the form of a beggar as he approaches Rāma and Lakṣmaṇa. In 4.5.14, he gives up that form.

33. Compare 3.44.2–3, 3.45.1, 3.47.8, and 5.32.15.

thus offers no insights into identifying renunciation as an *āśrama*. Another common term for renouncer, *saṃnyāsin*, does not occur at all in the *Rāmāyaṇa* except in its form *saṃnyāsa*, which can mean either "entrusting" or "renunciation." Both uses of *saṃnyāsa*—in 2.107.14 and 2.107.17—are clearly to be taken in the former meaning, as they occur in the context of Rāma entrusting the kingdom to Bharata.[34] In contrast, the term *pravrajita* provides some more useful contexts of interpretation.

Nearly all mentions of *pravrajita* (or other terms stemming from the root *pra*√*vraj*) in the *Rāmāyaṇa* are in a context describing Rāma's specific circumstances—namely, that he has been banished from Ayodhyā in accordance with the boons Kaikeyī demanded from Daśaratha in 2.10.27–28.[35] During his fourteen-year exile, Rāma is meant to "dwell in the Daṇḍaka Forest" (*daṇḍakāraṇyam āśritaḥ*) as an ascetic (*tāpasaḥ*) "donning clothes of bark and animal hide and wearing matted hair" (*cīrājinajaṭādhārī*). In light of the terms of Rāma's time in the forest, the question becomes whether or not he is a renouncer in conformity with any form of the *āśrama* system. Using both the *Rāmāyaṇa* and the *Mahābhārata* as examples, Olivelle states in a discussion of the changes that led to the classical *āśrama* system that, "[i]t appears that an ascetic life was required of any person exiled from society and not just of those who retire in old age."[36] Kaikeyī's demands in 2.10.27–28 illustrate this clearly.[37] Rāma's departure is often described using the verb *pra*√*vraj*. The real question is how often this term truly refers to renunciation and—if and when it does—how often could it possibly signify an *āśrama*?

Rāma's actual adherence to an ascetic life during his exile is scrutinized at a number of moments throughout the *Rāmāyaṇa*. One interesting moment to this end occurs in the *Araṇyakāṇḍa* wherein Sītā voices her concern about

---

34. 2.107.14: *etad rājyaṃ mama bhrātrā dattaṃ saṃnyāsavat svayam / yogakṣemavahe ceme pāduke hemabhūṣite //* 2.107.17: *rāghavāya ca saṃnyāsaṃ dattveme varapāduke / rājyaṃ cedam ayodhyāṃ ca dhūtapāpo bhavāmi ca //* There is also 5.53.8, where Hanumān contemplates giving up his life (*prāṇasaṃnyāsa*). Clearly this does not refer to a renunciant lifestyle but an abandonment of life itself.

35. See 2.19.12; 2.42.22; 2.45.12; 2.57.3; 2.71.6; 3.35.10; 3.45.13; 3.45.17; 5.29.7; 6.23.25; 6.70.40; 6.114.5. Olivelle has a different list of uses of *pra*√*vraj*, which excludes some of those I have mentioned here and includes some of the verb's causative forms such as *pravrājita*, which I have not included given the clear meaning of "banished." See Olivelle 1993: 117n.16.

36. Olivelle 1993: 117.

37. The *Rāmāyaṇa* also portrays the more standard retirement to the forest in old age. Consider, for example, 1.70.14, wherein Janaka recites his lineage to Daśaratha prior to giving Sītā away to Rāma. He describes his father as going to the forest (*vanaṃ gataḥ*) after consecrating Janaka, the eldest son, as king.

Rāma's ability to control any unprovoked violence against the creatures of the forest, Rākṣasas included (3.8.1–29). This violence against innocent creatures is a grave sin and a sin to which Sītā feels Rāma is prone. Armed with a bow and committed to a promise of killing the Rākṣasas in a battle context, Sītā is worried about Rāma's ability to abstain from undue violence. She implores Rāma to save the Kṣatriya lifestyle for his return to Ayodhyā and advocates for a lapse in *kṣatradharma* so long as Rāma is living as an ascetic. Interestingly, Sītā's concerns as expressed in 3.8.23–24 bear a strong resemblance to Bharata's argumentation in 2.98.56–58 where he tries to demonstrate that life in the forest is not meant for Rāma.[38] Also similar is Rāma's response to Sītā, wherein he cites a promise he has made to the sages to protect them from the Rākṣasas of the forest (3.9.16–18).

The Rākṣasas are undoubtedly the most overt critics of Rāma's life as a renouncer. There are two occasions where Rākṣasas refer to Rāma as a "false renouncer," adding the prefix *mithyā-* to the term *pravrajita*. The first is spoken by Rāvaṇa in the *Sundarakāṇḍa* as he scolds Sītā following her rejection of his advances.

> For this reason [i.e., Rāvaṇa's attraction to Sītā], lovely-faced woman, I do not kill you, though you, devoted to that false renouncer, deserve death and humiliation. (5.20.5)[39]

The second is spoken by Indrajit in the *Yuddhakāṇḍa*, when Rāvaṇa instructs him to kill the false renouncers, Rāma and Lakṣmaṇa.

> I will give my father, Rāvaṇa, a glorious victory by killing those two false forest renouncers during battle today. (6.67.16)[40]

---

38. Sītā's plea in 3.8.23–24: *kva ca śastraṃ kva ca vanaṃ kva ca kṣātraṃ tapaḥ kva ca / vyāviddham idam asmābhir deśadharmas tu pūjyatām // tad āryakaluṣā buddhir jāyate śastrasevanāt / punar gatvā tv ayodhyāyāṃ kṣatradharmaṃ cariṣyasi //* Bharata's plea in 2.98.56–58: *kva cāraṇyaṃ kva ca kṣātraṃ kva jaṭāḥ kva ca pālanam / īdṛśaṃ vyāhataṃ karma na bhavān kartum arhati // atha kleśajam eva tvaṃ dharmaṃ caritum icchasi / dharmeṇa caturo varṇān pālayan kleśam āpnuhi // caturṇām āśramāṇāṃ hi gārhasthyaṃ śreṣṭham āśramam / āhur dharmajña dharmajñās taṃ kathaṃ tyaktum arhasi //*

39. *etasmāt kāraṇān na tvāṃ ghatayāmi varānane / vadhārhām avamānārhāṃ mithyāpravrajite ratām //*

40. *adya hatvāhave yau tau mithyāpravrajitau vane / jayaṃ pitre pradāsyāmi rāvaṇāya raṇādhikam //*

In order for the Rākṣasas to claim that Rāma and Lakṣmaṇa are "false renouncers," they must have a conception of what a proper renouncer should be, perhaps suggesting a common conception of a renunciant institution. The question arises, then, as to what about the renunciation of Rāma and Lakṣmaṇa is patently "false" in the minds of the Rākṣasas. This is never made explicit, though there are a couple of potential inferences that can be made. The fact that Rāma's time in the forest comes with an expiration date is rampant throughout the text. There are scores of times when Rāma's exile is described as being fourteen years and the entire conversation between Bharata and Rāma at the end of the *Ayodhyākāṇḍa* culminates with Rāma consoling Bharata by promising that he will return to Ayodhyā after his exile to reclaim the throne. If considered in the context of the *āśrama* system, renunciation is either a life-long identity (in the case of the original formulation) or it is the last stage of life in one's final years (in the classical formulation). Rāma and Lakṣmaṇa's intention of returning to worldly life post-exile disqualifies them from being part of the renunciant *āśrama*, leaving room to label them as *mithyāpravrajita*. But one must also consider, of course, that Rāma and Lakṣmaṇa are waging war with the Rākṣasas—a deed that is somewhat unbecoming of a renouncer. This later consideration does not have much force in using the Rākṣasas' views of a *pravrajita* to identify an *āśrama* system in the text; the two brothers might just be bad ascetics, not necessarily participating in a codified system of *āśramas*. With the ambiguity, then, we are no closer to proving beyond a reasonable doubt that the *pravrajita*—or any other life-mode explored above—can be understood as an *āśrama* in the *Rāmāyaṇa*.

No Space for the Gṛhastha *in the* Rāmāyaṇa

The survey above makes it clear that, in addition to not mentioning the *āśrama* system by name (with the exception of 2.98.58), the *Rāmāyaṇa* offers no solid ideological alignment with the *āśrama* system in any formulation, especially in its classical progressive form. With only rare exception, the life-modes surveyed above are not described in relation to one another. When they are (e.g., 2.57.32), it is done indirectly, without many detailed insights into the customs of that life-mode, and always while ignoring the *gṛhastha*. Considering the specific case of Rāma, by depicting his progression through the *āśramas* as starting with studentship, followed by renunciation, culminating in coronation, the *Rāmāyaṇa's* entire narrative would be a clear example of a *prātilomya* ("against the grain") navigation of life-modes, which would be unacceptable in a classical formulation of the *āśrama* system.[41] That the *Rāmāyaṇa* does not reflect a clearly defined classical *āśrama* system contributes to the absence of *varṇāśramadharma* throughout the text, leaving the lone reference to this concept and the *gṛhastha* in 2.98.57–58 a likely contender for a late interpolation. The ideology of a full-formed *varṇāśramadharma* in these verses is anachronistic to—or at the very least ideologically incompatible with—the rest of the text.

Even when considering the *āśrama* system in its original formulation, the *Rāmāyaṇa* presents no detailed accounts of what would be expected of someone committed to a particular *āśrama*. At a few points, the *Rāmāyaṇa* even illustrates the possibility for a person to move between life-modes, making it impossible to say that a person in the *Rāmāyaṇa's* social world would necessarily commit to a particular life-mode for the duration of their life. Instead, the *Rāmāyaṇa* portrays of a web of lifestyles that never figure into any kind of legally ordained system and thus cannot be considered *āśramas*.[42] This has serious consequences for any hope for the *gṛhastha* to show up in the text. If the narrative does not warrant mention of the *gṛhastha* and there is no mention of a social system that might make such mention obligatory, it is entirely reasonable to leave out the *gṛhastha* altogether. And this is precisely what happened.

The *Rāmāyaṇa* is about a particular family and the tribulations they endure under the circumstances comprising the plot. The conflicts in the epic stem from a disruption in the proper succession of kings and the resolution of that disruption leaves no room for the concerns of a *gṛhastha*. The work tracks Rāma's trajectory to the throne, not his path through the *āśramas*. In fact, any potential for depicting Rāma as a *gṛhastha* between his graduation and exile was overshadowed by descriptions of his suitability in the role of a king. What's more, during Rāma's exile—a vast majority of the epic—his interactions with other characters were limited to forest dwellers of various kinds, not *gṛhasthas*. All of this being the case, the *gṛhastha* does not show up in the *Rāmāyaṇa* and it is not even possible to confidently assert that the author of the text had imagined the *gṛhastha* to be a vital part of a person's

---

41. See Olivelle 1993: 133–34.

42. While the *āśramas* receive effectively no attention in the epic, their close partners, the *varṇas*, do. A prominent example of a strictly enforced *varṇadharma* in the *Rāmāyaṇa* comes with the *Uttarakāṇḍa's* Śambūka episode (7.64–67). While the principles of *varṇa* are presented didactically in this episode, they are never related to the *āśramas*. Considering the eventual close relationship between *varṇa* and *āśrama* as the basis of an all-encompassing dharma in the legal literature, the failure to connect these two ideological institutions even in an addition to the *Rāmāyaṇa* as late as the Śambūka story is instructive when trying (in vain) to locate any semblance of either *varṇāśramadharma* or the *āśrama* system in general.

progress through life—it certainly was not in Rāma's case. Given the text's plot concerns in combination with its author's understanding of the *āśramas*, there was no narrative space for the *gṛhastha* and no tradition of preeminence surrounding the *gṛhastha* that may have incited the author of the *Rāmāyaṇa* to include this institution in his text.

12

Householders and Housewives in Early Kāvya *Literature*

Csaba Dezső

THIS CHAPTER[1] IS going to study references to *gṛhasthas, gṛhapatis,* and *gṛhiṇīs* in early *kāvya* literature. It will certainly not be an exhaustive study, but the material we find in Aśvaghoṣa's epics, the *Jātakamālās,* early Prakrit poetry, and Kālidāsa's works is already so rich that adding more would have made the chapter even unwieldier. Looking into the representations of household life in *kāvya* is a rewarding task, and the present study can and hopefully will be enhanced in the future.

The Works of Aśvaghoṣa

In the *Buddhacarita* when Siddhārtha wants to renounce the world to escape from the cycle of repeated birth and death (*pravivrajiṣāmi mokṣahetoḥ,* 5:28) and asks his father's permission to leave the palace, the king reminds him of his responsibilities as crown prince and the right time of renunciation: first the prince should devote himself to the duties of a householder, and enter the forest only after enjoying the pleasures suited to his age (5:33). Siddhārtha, however, is unbending and when he reaches the forest he sends his householder's garb (*gṛhasthaveśa*) back to the palace with his groom

1. The research behind this article was supported by the ERC Synergy Project *Beyond Boundaries: Religion, Region, Language and the State.* I am grateful to Peter Bisschop, Joel Brereton, and Patrick Olivelle for their comments on an earlier draft of this paper. All the remaining shortcomings are mine. All translations are mine unless otherwise indicated.

Chandaka (8:10): discarding his worldly clothes makes his separation from worldly life complete.

The king sends his royal chaplain (*purohita*) and counselor (*mantrin*) after the prince to persuade him to return to the world. The *purohita* presents to Siddhārtha the examples of legendary kings who strove for the greatest good while remaining householders (9:21). But the Bodhisattva is not impressed. He says it would be a foolish thing to expose himself to the same dangers he has already managed to escape (9:47), and those legends about householders reaching liberation are simply not true, for such a lifestyle is fundamentally incompatible with quietude (*śama*, 9:48).

We read, however, in the *Saundarananda* that it is possible to live the life of a householder and at the same time make at least the first steps on the path of dharma. When the Ikṣvāku princes founded Kapilavastu they settled "respectable householders (*kuṭumbinaḥ*) of wealth and good character, who were modest, far-sighted, brave and industrious" (*cāritradhansaṃpannān salajjān dīrghadarśinaḥ | arhato 'tiṣṭhipan yatra śūrān dakṣān kuṭumbinaḥ* || 1:46 ||, tr. Covill 2007). Of the Śākyas whom the Buddha converted many became renouncers (*pravavrajuḥ*, 3:28), but even those who remained in their homes set foot on the path of dharma:

> *vijahus tu ye 'pi na gṛhāṇi tanayapitṛmātrapekṣayā |*
> *te 'pi niyamavidhim ā maraṇāj jagṛhuś ca yuktamanasaś ca dadhrire* ||
> 3:29 ||
>
> Even those who stayed at home out of consideration for their children or parents accepted the restraints of the precepts until death, and they kept them assiduously. (tr. Covill 2007)
>
> *akathaṃkathā gṛhiṇa eva paramapariśuddhadṛṣṭayaḥ |*
> *strotasi hi vavṛtire bahavo rajasas tanutvam api cakrire pare* || 3:39 ||
>
> Even the householders (*gṛhiṇaḥ*) were free from doubt, and their views were lofty and pure; for many were stream-entrants,[2] while others had minimized their passions. (tr. Covill 2007)

The Buddha sets these Śākyas as models to follow when he admonishes Nanda: some have followed him in renouncing the world (*anupravrajiteṣu*, 5:37), and even those who have stayed at home observe vows (*vratino gṛhasthān*, ibid.). Why does Nanda still show regard for his fleeting loves when so many

2. Compare Freiberger (Ch. 4, pp. 67, 71) on Pāli sources mentioning *sotāpanna gahapatis*.

kings and householders (*kuṭumbinaḥ*) have already renounced their relatives and possessions and gone forth, and just as many will do so in the future (5:43)?

Renouncers and householders are mentioned again side by side by the Buddha in the context of purity, *śuddhi*. A householder is influenced by various views, which makes it difficult for him to have a pure worldview. Similarly, a monk depends on other people's charity, he has no independent livelihood, therefore it is hard for him to maintain a pure living (13:18). *Śīla*, "moral conduct," is essential for both ways of life, thus being a true householder, just as being a true renouncer, requires integrity (13:19).

In the *Buddhacarita* the emphasis is on the incompatibility of household life and tranquillity, the latter being a necessary condition of realizing liberation. Once the Bodhisattva has renounced the world it is inconceivable for him to return to the householder state. Iṇ the *Saundarananda*, however, those *gṛhasthas* who live an exemplary life are said to be able to make at least the first steps on the path ultimately leading to *mokṣa*. Renunciation is still considered to be the better option, but those householders who for some reason cannot make it are not condemned en masse, and the most virtuous ones are even set as examples for their fellow *gṛhasthas*. Integrity, *śīla*, is a requirement that is essential for fulfilling both renunciatory and household life.

The Jātakamālā *of Ārya Śūra*

Ārya Śūra's *Jātakamālā*, written probably in the fourth century CE, is the first fully developed example of the *campū* genre in Sanskrit literature.[3] Thirty out of the thirty-four Jātakas have parallels in Pāli, but, as Khoroche observed, "[t]he condemnation of wordly ties and preoccupations . . . receives greater emphasis in the *Jātakamālā* than in the Pāli *jātakas*."[4]

In the *Vyāghrījātaka*, the Bodhisattva is a merchant who shakes off the householder state as if it were an illness and becomes a forest hermit (*gārhasthyam asvāsthyam ivāvadhūya kaṃ cid vanaprastham alaṃcakāra*, 1:6). In the *Agastyajātaka*, *gārhasthya* and *pravrajyā* are contrasted in detail (7, prose after verse 2):

3. Compare Khoroche 1989: xiii. Ratnaśrījñāna in his commentary on *Kāvyādarśa* 1:31cd classified Ārya Śūra's *Jātakamālā* as *campū* (see Hahn 2007: 40).

4. Khoroche 1989: xviii.

> *atha sa mahātmā kukāryavyāsaṅgadoṣasaṃbādhaṃ pramādāspadabhūtaṃ dhanārjanarakṣaṇaprasaṅgavyākulam upaśamavirodhi vyasanaśaraśatalakṣyabhūtam aparyantakarmāntān uṣṭhānapariśramam atṛptijanakaṃ kṛśāsvādaṃ gārhasthyam avetya taddoṣaviviktasukhāṃ ca dharmapratipattyanukūlāṃ mokṣadharmā rambhādhiṣṭhānabhūtāṃ pravrajyām anupaśyan mahatīm api tāṃ dhanasamṛddhim aparikleśādhigatāṃ lokasaṃnatimanoharāṃ tṛṇavad apāsya tāpasapravrajyāvinayaniyamaparo babhūva.*
>
> The Great One, however, came to perceive the householder life (*gārhasthya*) as unsatisfying and unsavory. Full of wicked attachments to vice, life as a householder was based on recklessness and involved an unruly addiction to acquiring and conserving wealth. A hindrance to tranquility (*upaśama*), it was the target of hundreds of arrows of woe, while the endless tasks one had to perform made it exhausting. Renunciation (*pravrajyā*), on the other hand, offered a happiness that was free from such faults. Conducive toward the practice of morality (*dharma*), it formed the basis for undertaking the teaching of liberation (*mokṣa*). Despite the magnitude of his riches, he therefore discarded, as though it were chaff, the wealth that he had acquired without trouble and that had the attractive quality of humbling the world, and instead became intent on the disciplines and restraints of ascetic renunciation (*tāpasapravrajyā*). (tr. Meiland 2009, Vol. 1)

The major problem with being a householder is that one is constantly occupied with securing material pleasures, and this exhausting fluster leaves no scope for calmness, *upaśama*. The renouncer, on the other hand, has got rid of all possessions and worldly attachments, and thanks to his quiet life he can apply himself wholly to pursuing *mokṣa*.

The irreconcilability of calmness and worldly life is repeatedly emphasized in Ārya Śūra's work: "the household life teems with qualities that conflict with virtue and serenity" (*śīlapraśamapratipakṣasaṃbādhaṃ gārhasthyam*, 18, prose before verse 1, tr. Meiland 2009); "home consists in dreadful troubles" (*asatparikleśamayaṃ . . . geham*, 20:12); and so on. Living in a household is again and again contrasted with life in the forest. As it is expressed eloquently in the *Ayogṛhajātaka* (32:45–46):

> *vikṛṣyamāṇo bahubhiḥ kukarmabhiḥ parigrahopārjanarakṣaṇākulaḥ |*
> *aśāntacetā vyasanodayāgamaiḥ kadā gṛhasthaḥ śamamārgam eṣyati ||*

> *vane tu saṃtyaktakukāryavistaraḥ parigrahakleśavivarjitaḥ sukhī |*
> *śamaikakāryaḥ parituṣṭamānasaḥ sukhaṃ ca dharmaṃ ca yaśāṃsi cārcchati ||*
>
> Distracted by various evil activities, householders fret over gaining and keeping possessions. Arisen or imminent disasters make them uncalm. When can one find peace (*śama*) if living in a house? In the forest one rejects this array of evil acts. Free from the toil of possessions, one is happy. Content at heart, tranquility (*śama*) one's sole task, one acquires happiness, virtue, and fame. (tr. Meiland 2009, Vol 2)

Jātakas 18–20 form a thematically connected group in Ārya Śūra's collection: they are centered around the evils of household life and the blessings of living in a forest. The *Bisajātaka* (No. 19) corresponds closely to the Pāli *Bhisajātaka* (Fausbøll and Andersen 1877–99, IV: No. 488, pp. 304–314), while the *Aputrajātaka* (Ārya Śūra, *Jātakamālā* No. 18) has no Pāli parallel and the *Śreṣṭhijātaka* (No. 20) is much more elaborate than its Pāli counterpart, the *Kalyāṇadhammajātaka* (Fausbøll and Andersen 1877–99, II: No. 171, pp. 63–65).

In the *Aputrajātaka* we read that the Bodhisattva was once born in a wealthy, respectable, and benevolent family, yet he realized that a householder always has to worry about gaining more, which militates against dharma, while real happiness is found in ascetic groves.[5] When his parents died, he distributed his wealth and renounced the world.[6] After wandering about for some time he finally settled at a *vanaprastha*, "forest plateau (?)," near a town and lived there a solitary, contemplative life, surviving on alms. One day he was visited by a friend of his father, who tried to convince him that he had committed a rash act (*cāpala*) when he renounced the world, without caring about his lineage (*anavekṣya kulavaṃśam*, 18, prose after verse 4), for "people of good conduct can accomplish this religiosity both in a house and in the forest" (*ārādhyate satpratipattimadbhir dharmo yadāyaṃ bhavane vane vā*, 18:5). Therefore he should return home and fulfil there both dharma and the wish for a good son (*satputramanorathaṃ*, 18:8).

But the Bodhisattva's thoughts have been pervaded by the bliss of solitude that tastes like nectar, and he has realized the difference between living at home and living in a forest (*pravivekasukhāmṛtarasaparibhāvitamatis . . .*

---

5. 18:3: *paryeṣṭiduḥkhānugatāṃ viditvā gṛhasthatāṃ dharmavirodhinīṃ ca | sukhodayatvaṃ ca tapovanānāṃ na gehasaukhyeṣu manaḥ sasañje ||*

6. The term *pravavrāja* is used in Kern's edition, though the Nepalese and the Tokyo manuscripts have *parivavrāja*, "he became a wandering mendicant"; see Meiland 2009, I: 495.

samupalabdhaviśeṣo gṛhavanavāsayoḥ, 18, prose after verse 9). He refers to home as a prison (*gṛhacāraka*, 18:10), and asserts that the householder's life is not a healthy, sound way of life: for the rich because they want to preserve what they have, and for the poor because they always fuss about securing possessions.[7] True, a *gṛhastha* can practice dharma, but only with extreme difficulty, because household life is full of obstacles to dharma and it is mostly stressful.[8] Living at home entails desires, lies, violence, and harming others (18:13). Home, therefore, is ultimately not compatible with dharma, because "the sole essence of the path of dharma is tranquility" (*praśamaikaraso hi dharmamārgo*), while "leading a successful household life involves constant struggle" (*gṛhasiddhiś ca parākramakrameṇa*, 18:14). To say that living in a household is pleasant appears to the Bodhisattva as "wishful thinking" (*śraddhāgamyaṃ*, 18, prose after verse 16, tr. Khoroche 1989). At home, peace has no chance:

> *prāyaḥ samṛddhyā madam eti gehe*
> *mānaṃ kulenāpi balena darpam* |
> *duḥkhena roṣaṃ vyasanena dainyaṃ*
> *tasmin kadā syāt praśamāvakāśaḥ* || 18:19 ||
>
> In the household life, people are arrogant if rich, proud if from a noble family, and insolent if strong. Suffering brings anger and misfortune brings sorrow. When is there a chance for tranquility (*praśama*) in such a life? (tr. Meiland 2009, Vol. 1)
>
> *madamānamohabhujagopalayaṃ*
> *praśamābhirāmasukhavipralayam* |
> *ka ivāśrayed abhimukhaṃ vilayaṃ*
> *bahutīvraduḥkhanilayaṃ nilayam* || 18:20 ||
>
> Inhabited by the snakes of arrogance, pride, and delusion, a house destroys the delightful joys of tranquility (*praśama*). Who then would set up home in this source of ruin, this abode of numerous bitter sufferings? (tr. Meiland 2009, Vol. 1)

The forest, however, is a place of content, where one can enjoy the happy state of solitude, and where "the mind becomes serene" (*prasīdati cetaḥ*, 18:21).

---

7. *gārhasthyaṃ mahad asvāsthyaṃ sadhanasyādhanasya ca* | *ekasya rakṣaṇāyāsād itarasyārjanaśramāt* || 18:11 ||

8. *yad api ceṣṭaṃ gṛhasthenāpi śakyo 'yam ārādhayituṃ dharma iti kāmam evam etat. atiduṣkaraṃ tu me pratibhāti dharmapratipakṣasaṃbādhatvāc chramabāhulyāc ca gṛhasya* (18, prose after verse 11).

With these arguments the Bodhisattva convinced the friend of his father, who expressed his appreciation with special acts of respect (*satkāraprayogaviśeṣas*).

According to the *Bisajātaka* (No. 19), the Bodhisattva was once born in a Brahmin family, and as a young man he lived an exemplary life at home (*gṛham āvasati sma*, 19, prose before verse 1), studying the Vedas, looking after his parents and teaching his younger brothers. Just as in the *Aputrajātaka*, it was the death of his parents that turned the Bodhisattva towards renunciation. His brothers and his sister did not want to lose him, so they all "renounced the world by ascetic renunciation" (*tāpasapravrajyayā pravrajitāḥ*, 19, prose after 7) and settled at a lake in a forest. They lived in separate huts, ate, meditated, and practiced asceticism separately, meeting only to listen to the Bodhisattva's sermons on the blessings of solitude and tranquility. After some time Śakra decided to put them to the test. Every day the servant woman of the brothers placed on the shore of the lake some lotus stalks, which the brothers took one by one and ate each in his own hut. One day Śakra stole the first portion, which had usually been taken by the Bodhisattva, who, not finding his share, returned empty-handed to his hut, without saying anything. After some days his brothers noticed the frail condition of the Bodhisattva, who finally told them what happened. Then the brothers and the sister, one after the other, uttered curses upon the thief, but very strange curses: one wished that he may have a rich home with wife and children (19:11), another wished that he may become a "family man" (*kuṭumbin*) who earns wealth by farming and takes pleasure in his home and children (19:13). Others wished that he may become a powerful king, or a royal chaplain, or a honorable Vedic teacher (19:14–16), or that the king may give him a rich village (19:17), or that he may become a village headman (*grāmaṇī*, 19:18). Finally the Bodhisattva cursed the one who claimed falsely that the lotus-portion had disappeared, saying, "may he die in the state of a householder" (*upaitu gehāśrita eva mṛtyum*, 19:24, tr. Meiland 2009). Then Śakra revealed himself to be the "thief" and asked the Bodhisattva why he and his brothers had uttered such strange curses. The Bodhisattva replied: *anantādīnavāḥ kāmāḥ*, "pleasures entail endless miseries" (19, prose after verse 25). For a renouncer nothing could be more cursed than the life of a householder.[9]

9. The Pāli *Bhisajātaka* (Fausbøll and Andersen 1877–99: IV, No. 488, pp. 304–314) is quite close to Ārya Śūra's version. There the Bodhisattva's parents want to get him married so that he can set up his own household (*gharāvāsaṃ saṇṭhapehi*), but the Bodhisattva is longing for renunciation (*nekkhamma*). When their parents die the Bodhisattva and his siblings perform the "great departure" (*mahābhinikkhamanaṃ nikkhamitvā*); they go to the Himalayas where they set up an *assama*. From here the story is very close to Ārya Śūra's version, including the strange curses (*agāramajjhe maraṇam upetu* being the last one, uttered by the Bodhisattva).

In the *Śreṣṭhijātaka* (No. 20), the Bodhisattva is the *śreṣṭhin*, financier of the king, a learned, noble, modest, generous, and respected man, who is held in high regard as the *gṛhapatiratna*, "burgher-jewel," one of the valuable assets of a mighty ruler.[10] One day his slightly deaf mother-in-law mishears her daughter's words and forms a false idea that his son-in-law has become a renouncer (*pravrajita*, 20, prose after verse 1). The old woman starts bewailing the rash act of the *śreṣṭhin*: he is still young, why does he want to live in the forest (20:2)? He has not been treated badly by his family, so why has he abandoned his wife and transgressed dharma (20:2–6)? Gradually her daughter, too, becomes convinced that her husband has really left her to live in the forest, and they manage to embroil the whole city: Brahmins and wealthy citizens (*brāhmaṇagṛhapatayaḥ*) come and question the *śreṣṭhin* about his motives for renouncing the world. The Bodhisattva is first surprised, but then he thinks that if people considered him capable of renouncement, if they have such a high opinion (*saṃbhāvanā*) of him, he shouldn't disappoint them. So he makes a vow: "I shall abandon my home, with all its evil distractions, out of love for a hermit's life in the forest" (*asatparikleśamayaṃ vimuñcaṃs tapovanapremaguṇena geham*, 20:12, tr. Khoroche 1989). He asks the king's permission and confirms that there is nothing "wrong" (*duḥkha*) with him, he just cannot ignore the people's opinion and wants to live in a solitary forest (*vijaneṣu vaneṣu*, 20:16), after giving up his possessions that only cause conflict (*parivarjayantaṃ . . . parigrahān vigrahahetubhūtān*, 20:21). Various people try to dissuade him from becoming a renouncer; some argue on the basis of the Vedas and reasoning that the status of the householder is the purest of all,[11] others describe to him the difficulties of living in a *tapovana*. The Bodhisattva is puzzled by their naiveté and cannot imagine how people of healthy thinking could possibly prefer home to the forest.[12] The *jātaka* ends with the reflections of the Bodhisattva about how weak and chicken-hearted people are when it comes to renouncing their homes and worldly pleasures (the Pāli *Kalyāṇadhammajātaka* is much shorter and it lacks these ruminations).

Beside this group of three Jātakas, the opening of the *Kṣāntivādijātaka* (No. 28) also offers an elaborate juxtaposition of household life and renouncement:

---

10. See Freiberger (Ch. 4, pp. 69–70).

11. *gṛhāśrama eva puṇyatama ity enam anye śrutiyuktisaṃgrathitaṃ grāhayitum īhāṃ cakrire* (20, prose after verse 22). Cf. *VaDh* 8:14–16, quoted by Olivelle (Ch. 7, p. 119).

12. *vanād gṛhaṃ śreya idaṃ tv amīṣāṃ svastheṣu citteṣu kathaṃ nu rūḍham?* (20:24cd)

> *bodhisattvaḥ kilānekadoṣavyasanopasṛṣṭam arthakāmapradhānatvād anaupaśamikaṃ rāgadveṣamohāmarṣasaṃrambhamadamānamatsa rādidoṣarajasām āpātaṃ pātanaṃ hrīdharmaparigrahasyāyatanaṃ lobhāsadgrāhasya kukāryasaṃbādhatvāt kṛśāvakāśaṃ dharmasyāvetya gṛhavāsaṃ parigrahaviṣayaparivarjanāc ca taddoṣavivekasukhāṃ pravrajyām anupaśyan śīlaśrutapraśamavinayaniyatamānasas tāpaso babhūva.*
>
> The Bodhisattva is said to have once become an ascetic after he realized that the household life (*gṛhavāsa*) offered meager opportunities for virtue because it thronged with vice. Afflicted by numerous faults and calamities, the household life was devoid of tranquility (*anaupaśamika*) due to its emphasis on profit and desire. It was a meeting place for wicked taints such as passion, hatred, delusion, intolerance, violence, infatuation, pride, and selfishness. Destroying a person's sense of shame and morality, it was an arena for greed and evil. He saw the renunciate life (*pravrajyā*), on the other hand, as providing a happiness that was removed from these vices, since it shunned possessions and desires. So it was that he became an ascetic, his mind rigorously intent on virtue, learning, tranquility, and discipline. (tr. Meiland 2009, Vol. 2)

Many motifs of this description might sound already familiar: a householder can never find peace, and his constant struggle for profit and pleasure entangles him in a net of vices.

The path of the renouncer is the path of the few, even though once the Bodhisattva has chosen this path he can no longer understand why anyone wants to remain at home. The householder's life is portrayed as the inferior one in the stories outlined above, a life that cannot lead to liberation. It makes one greedy, arrogant, miserable, jealous, envious, stressed and violent. There is also, however, a more forbearing view in certain Jātakas, according to which it is possible to live a commendable, virtuous life as a householder. In the *Bisajātaka* when the Bodhisattva decides to renounce the world, he tries to convince his brothers to "dwell at home in a proper way" (*samyag gṛham adhyāvastavyam*, 19, prose after verse 2). This "proper way" entails mutual love and respect, integrity, honesty, good behavior, the study of the Vedas, indulging friends, guests, and relatives, and dedication to dharma.[13] Being an ideal householder has moral and religious connotations:

---

13. *parasparasnehagauravābhimukhaiḥ śīlaśaucācāreṣv aśithilādarair Vedādhyayanatatparair mitrātithisvajanapraṇayavatsalair dharmaparāyaṇair bhūtvā* (19, prose after verse 2)

vinayaślāghibhir nityaṃ svādhyāyādhyayanodyataiḥ |
pradānābhirataiḥ samyak paripālyo gṛhāśramaḥ || 19:3 ||

Ever proud of your discipline, intent on studying your own Veda, you should take delight in giving and properly guard the householder state (*gṛhāśrama*). (tr. Meiland 2009, Vol 1, modified)

The results of such a life, though they do not include liberation, are still worth striving for: fame, religious merit, and wealth will accumulate, and the next life will be easy to plunge into.[14] Before turning into a renouncer, the Bodhisattva often already lives such a superior life at home: in the *Aputrajātaka*, he is a learned and virtuous member of a rich family, which is a generous patron of artists and beggars. In the *Mahābodhijātaka*, "while still in the state of a householder," he mastered the various recognized sciences and was curious to know the arts.[15]

We have seen that in the *Śreṣṭhijātaka* the Bodhisattva is a *gṛhapatiratna*, a "burgher-jewel" (20, prose before verse one). The term *gṛhapati* occurs in several stories: in Jātakas 4 and 5 the Bodhisattva is a rich merchant (*śreṣṭhin*), also addressed as *gṛhapati*. In the *Unmādayantījātaka* (No. 13), a prominent citizen, *pauramukhya*, is referred to as *gṛhapati*. In the *Śreṣṭhijātaka* when the news spreads that the king's financier has renounced the world, all his acquaintances flock to his home to condole, among them "Brahmins and burghers," *brāhmaṇagṛhapatayaḥ* (20, prose after verse 7), a compound familiar from Pāli texts.[16] In the *Mahābodhijātaka* we read that the Bodhisattva, as a mendicant (*parivrājaka*), "was worthy of approach and respect for the learned and for kings who favoured the learned, for ministers, Brahmins and burghers, as well as for renouncers belonging to other sects."[17] In these Jātakas the *gṛhapati* appears to be a wealthy citizen, a merchant or other kind of businessman, whose services are used by the king and who is a respected member of the society.

---

14. *evaṃ hi vaḥ syād yaśasaḥ samṛddhir dharmasya cārthasya sukhāspadasya* | *sukhāvagāhaś ca paro 'pi lokas tad apramattā gṛham āvaseta* ||19:4 ||

15. *gṛhasthabhāva eva parividitakramaprayāmo lokābhimatānāṃ vidyāsthānānāṃ kṛtajñānakautūhalaś citrāsu ca kalāsu* (23, prose before verse 1).

16. *brāhmaṇagahapatikā*; cf. Freiberger (Ch. 4, p. 68])

17. *viduṣāṃ vidvatpriyāṇāṃ ca rājñāṃ rājamātrāṇāṃ brāhmaṇagṛhapatīnām anyatīrthikānāṃ ca pravrajitānām abhigamanīyo bhāvanīyaś ca babhūva* (23, prose before verse 1, tr. Meiland 2009).

The Jātakamālā *of Haribhaṭṭa*

Haribhaṭṭa wrote his *Jātakamālā* probably in the early fifth century CE, perhaps in Kashmir. He probably used other sources than Ārya Śūra, and his style also differs from that of his great predecessor, mostly in his elaborate descriptions full of minute, realistic details[18] (in this he is a forerunner of Bāṇa and the poets of the Kanauj school). The antagonism between household life and renunciation, though perhaps not so emphatic as in Ārya Śūra's work, also appears in Haribhaṭṭa's Jātakas, and we find in them the familiar denouncements of *gārhasthya*, too, for instance in the *Jājvalījātaka* (No. 26), the story about the *yogin* in whose matted hair a dove nested and hatched her eggs. The context is also familiar: Jājvalin, a learned and pious Brahmin, lived an exemplary household life, yet he came to recognize its downside:

> *vibhave sati jāyate madaḥ sati tasmin praśamaḥ kuto bhavet* |
> *asati praśame gatatrapo malinaṃ karma samīhate janaḥ* || 26:2 ||
> *muhur apriyasaṃprayogaduḥkhaṃ muhur ādhiḥ priyaviprayogakāle* |
> *draviṇārjanakhinnamānasānāṃ yadi vāñchā viphalā tato viṣādaḥ* || 26:3 ||

> Wealth gives rise to arrogance and once that happens how can one be calm? Lack of calm (*praśama*) makes a man brash and then he is ready for any foul deed. At one moment the misery of keeping company with those one dislikes, at another the pain of parting from those one does like, and then the despondency in hearts weary of making money, when hopes are frustrated. (tr. Khoroche 2017)

Constantly worrying about something, one cannot find happiness at home (*tanur apy asti na nirvṛtir gṛheṣu*, 26:4d). So Jājvalin decides to quit this prison called home (*gṛhasaṃjñakam . . . bandhanam*) and leaves for the forest, the place of tranquility (*praśamasthānam*, 26, prose after verse 4).

In the *Śaśajātaka* (No. 4), the Bodhisattva, who was born as a hare, tries to persuade his hermit friend not to return home at the time of a great famine. He compares the hermit to an elephant who has once escaped to the forest and yet wants to go back to his former tormentors (4:12). "It is a gross error to suppose," argues the hare, "that once a person's thoughts have been purified he can be content with worldly life (*gṛhasthatā*)."[19] He describes the beauties

18. Compare Khoroche 2017: 7.

19. *gṛhasthatāyāṃ ramayanti yan manoviśuddhasattvās tad asāṃpratam mahat* (4:16cd, tr. Khoroche 2017)

of living in a forest, which is not the isolated ascetic life we saw in Ārya Śūra's Jātakas, but a life that offers the pleasures of gardening and having children playing around, much like in Kaṇva's ashram in the *Abhijñānaśākuntala*. So it is not simply having a family that is dangerous in household life, but the many evils or vices it entails (*bahuvyasanadoṣaṃ . . . gārhasthyam*), while renunciation leads to peace and shows the way to liberation (*śamānukūlāṃ vimuktimārgapr akāśinīṃ pravrajyāṃ*, 4, prose after verse 21). Household life will create many obstacles to renouncing it again, the major obstacle being women's seduction (4:22, 27). The hermit concedes: "It is true: worldly existence (*gṛhavāsaḥ*, literally 'living at home') is a target for countless arrows of reproach and humiliation. But, once their minds are beguiled by even the smallest taste of pleasure, people find it impossible to renounce it."[20]

Though the state of a householder never appears in a favorable light, living in a forest is not always contrasted to it as the only path to be taken. In the *Dharmakāmajātaka*, the Bodhisattva is born in a model Brahmin family: upstanding, learned, caring, reciting the Veda and performing sacrifices, teaching pupils (3, prose before verse 1). The Bodhisattva is very fond of wise sayings, and when a jealous Brahmin wants to destroy him, he performs a miracle. Then he delivers a sermon (*dharmyā kathā*) to his friends and relatives, "urging upon them generosity, moral awareness, and the other prime virtues" (*dānaśīlādisamuttejanāya*, 3, prose after verse 41, tr. Khoroche 2017). In this sermon he warns his audience about the dangers of household life:

> *bahucchalaṃ pālayatā gṛhāśramaṃ na dhīmatā viśvasanīyam aṇv api* |
> *na yujyate svaptum anāhitāṅkuśapracaṇḍamattadviradādhirohiṇaḥ* || 3:47 ||
> *sutapralāpā bhavanaṃ samṛddhimad vilāsalāvaṇyavibhūṣitāḥ striyaḥ* |
> *prasaṅgināṃ sarvam amedhasām idaṃ śamānukūlasya nirodhakaṃ pathaḥ* || 3:48 ||

The wise man, while still at the stage of worldly life (*gṛhāśrama*), should put not an atom of trust in it, since it is full of deception. He who mounts a furious rutting elephant that does not respond to the hook had better not doze off. Children's prattle, a luxurious home, flirtatious and beautiful women—for those stupid people who are attached to

20. *satyam anekeṣāṃ paribhavādīnāṃ doṣaśarāṇāṃ śaravyabhūto gṛhavāsaḥ sukhalavāsvādamohitātmabhir na śakyate parityaktum* (4, prose after verse 27, tr. Khoroche 2017).

> them all these are an obstacle along the path that leads to tranquility (*śama*). (tr. Khoroche 2017)

These are all familiar accusations about *gārhasthya*, but what makes this Jātaka different is that at the end of his sermon, after admonishing everyone to turn away from sensual pleasures, the Bodhisattva "entered the house together with his friends" (*sasuhṛjjano gṛhaṃ praviveśa*, 3, prose after verse 55). He did not become a *pravrajita*, and he did not urge others to renounce the world.

So it seems staying at home might be an alternative to moving to the forest, but only if one remains vigilant and, as we are told in the *Mṛgajātaka*, if one listens to wise people:

> *saṃsāre bhramato mahāndhatamase saṃtiṣṭhamānasya vā*
> *sādhoḥ sādhuphale nitāntamahatī dve eva te māṃ prati* |
> *yatra projjhya gṛhaṃ tapovanam abhiprasthīyate śreyase*
> *yasmin vā kriyate vivekapaṭubhiḥ sākaṃ kathā sūribhiḥ* || 11.41 ||
>
> For a good man straying through the profound darkness of transmigration, or simply remaining stationary in it, there are, in my opinion, only two courses of action, whose consequences are of real import: one is to leave home and retire in a forest for a life of austerity leading to final bliss, the other is to converse with wise men of true judgement. (tr. Khoroche 2017)

Since this is the sermon (*dharmadeśanā*) of the Bodhisattva to a king, it also teaches how to be a king, a special case of *gārhasthya*.

One of the most remarkable Jātakas in Haribhaṭṭa's collection is perhaps the *Rūpyāvatījātaka* (No. 6), in which the Bodhisattva (born as a woman) offers her own breasts as food to a starving young woman who has recently given birth and is ready to eat her own child. The realistic description of famine shows Haribhaṭṭa at the height of his poetic powers, and in two verses the figure of the despairing housewife (*gṛhiṇī*), familiar from the *Sattasaī* and later *muktaka*-poetry, also appears:

> *upalipya mṛdā gṛhāntarālaṃ śiśave paryuṣitaṃ pradāya bhojyam* |
> *gṛhiṇī na tathātmanānutepe gṛhiṇaṃ vīkṣya yathā kṣudhāvasannam* || 6:6 ||
>
> Smearing clay on the inside of her house and offering stale food to her baby, the housewife did not feel as sorry for herself as she did for her husband when she saw him listless with hunger. (tr. Khoroche 2017)

mṛtavatsatayā nirastacārīkavalavyāhṛtikampamānasāsnā |
gṛhiṇīṃ gṛham āgatā vanād gaur adhikaṃ sāśruvilocanāṃ cakāra || 6:7 ||

Now that her calf lay dead, the cow dropped her mouthful of grass, left the wild, and came to the house, lowing so that her dewlap shook. This made the housewife even more tearful. (tr. Khoroche 2017)

Early Prakrit Kāvya

While the term *gṛhastha* or *gārhasthya*, that is its possible Prakrit equivalents (*gihattha, gihaṇāha, gihi, gehia, gharattha, gihaliṃgi, gehālu, gihāvaṭṭa, gihavāsa, gihāsama/gehāsama*, etc.), do not seem to appear in the *Sattasaī*,[21] housewives (*ghariṇī*, Skt. *gṛhiṇī*), desperate or otherwise, are met with frequently in this collection of Prakrit (Mahārāṣṭrī) couplets, the core of which possibly dates from the first centuries of the Common Era and from the royal court of the Sātavāhanas (though it is difficult to say what belongs to this "core" out of the more than nine hundred verses found in all recensions).[22] Even when we read about married couples, the focus falls more often on the wife than on the husband. Verses about the poor wife portray women trying to save the face of their indigent spouse: she gets angry when their relatives try to help them with rich presents (W 38, *Bh* 39), or just asks for some water when she is asked about her pregnancy cravings (W 472, *Bh* 473).[23] We also hear about the lot of the first wife (*paḍhamaghariṇī*, Skt. *prathamagṛhiṇī*): her jealous sighs and sweating when she sees the plump breasts of the new, younger wife (W 382, *Bh* 385), and her sexual neglect by her husband when he is preoccupied with his approaching new wedding (W 479, *Bh* 507). In another verse the husband, who has been weakened by constant lovemaking with his new wife, pretends to be strong enough to stretch his bow so that his first wife may not suspect the truth and he can preserve her love (W 122, *Bh* 131). The wife of the traveler (*pahiaghariṇī*, Skt. *pathikagṛhiṇī*) is also a recurring figure: when she sees the

21. The *gharasāmi*, "master of the house," mostly occurs as the husband of the *ghariṇī* (Skt. *gṛhiṇī*, housewife).

22. I do not wish to enter here into the debate around the dating of the *Sattasaī*. The collection exists in several recensions (sharing many verses but also having many unique ones), and poems might have been added to it until the seventh-eighth century (e.g. the verses attributed to Vākpatirāja). For more on this subject see Ollett 2017, p. 56ff.

23. Similar stanzas are also found in the Sanskrit *subhāṣita*-collections, e.g., *Subhāṣitaratkanośa* 1310–14, 1316–17.

rising clouds, she gives up all hopes of living and looks at her little son with tears on her face (W 539, *Bh* 496; in Bhuvanapāla's version she catches sight of her husband). Or she bends over her little son to protect him from the water dripping from the roof, not noticing that she is soaking him with her tears (W 623, *Bh* 606). In another verse the traveler writes no message in his letter and asks nothing about things at home; he just fills the leaf with the letters of his wife's name (W 833, only in the Telinga recension).

Housewives often appear as mothers in sometimes humorous, sometimes tragic verses. In an amusing example of the former kind, the cheating husband falls at the feet of his wife to conciliate her: a scene that is familiar from *kāvya*, but here it is given a comical twist (W 11 = *Bh* 13 [quoted from *Bh*]):

> *pāyavaḍiassa païṇo paṭṭhiṃ putte samāruhaṃtammi* |
> *daḍhamaṇṇudūmiyāĕ vi hāso ghariṇīi ṇikkaṃto* ||

> As their son climbed on the back of her husband who had fallen at her feet, the housewife couldn't help giggling, though she was burnt by fierce anger.

In another delightful vignette we see a mother running after her little son who has fled from the barber, while she is trying to hold her slipping coiffure together (W 291, where the subject of the sentence is named as *ghariṇī; Bh* 275, where we find the variant *jaṇaṇī*, "mother," as the subject). Maternal and marital emotions coexisting in a housewife are described beautifully in another verse: sitting between her son and her husband, one of her breasts oozes milk while the other one, sporting nail marks, is covered in goose bumps (W 409).

Many verses show us scenes from marriages, and fidelity (or the lack of it) is a central topic. A cunning wife introduces her lover as a man seeking shelter to her husband (addressed as *gahavaï*, Skt. *gṛhapati*) who has unexpectedly returned home (W 401). Another unfaithful woman has taught her dog to welcome her lover and to bark at her husband (*gharasāmi*, Skt. *gṛhasvāmī*; W 664). Another wife (*ghariṇī*) washes the feet of her husband (*gharasāmia*) in the evening without hurry, making him smile, for he understands (so the commentary explains) that she tries to keep him at home with such a ruse (W 130, *Bh* 139). Another housewife cries out bitterly (W 736 = *Bh* 651 [quoted from *Bh*]):

> *chaṇapāhuṇiya tti kiṇo ajja vi ṇaṃ bhaṇaha saṃgayasahāvaṃ* |
> *jāyā amhagharillayaguṇeṇa gharasāmiṇī ceya* ||

"Her nature is to have affairs, why do you still refer to her as a guest for the festival? She has become the mistress of the house thanks to the virtue of my husband (*gharillaa*)."

Another verse paints a simple, blissful moment of wedded life: the husband laughs at his wife's face, which she has touched with her sooty hand, which has made it look like the moon with its spot (W 14, *Bh* 382). And then there is also a verse that praises a woman who has remained faithful against all odds (W 36 = *Bh* 37 [quoted from *Bh*]):

caccaraghariṇī piyadaṃsaṇā ya taruṇī paütthavaïyā ya |
asaī sayajjhiyā duggayā ya ṇa ya khaṃḍiyaṃ sīlaṃ ||

She lives in a house at the chowk, she looks lovely, she is young, her husband is away, her neighbor is an unchaste woman, and she is poor, yet she has not violated her virtue.

Of course these verses are open to different interpretations, and the above *āryā* might be about something else than what it appears to say: the commentator Gaṅgādharabhaṭṭa puts these words in the mouth of an *asatī*, an adulteress, who tries to conceal her own crime by citing the example of the good who remain virtuous even in adverse circumstances.

Another character we often meet in the *Sattasaī* is the *gahavaï* (Skt. *gṛhapati*). The word can simply mean "husband" (e.g., in W 401), but in most of the cases it refers to a rich farmer or a landowner who also owns livestock.[24] We read about a *gahavaï* who carried the bell-string of his dead buffalo cow with himself, inspected hundreds of herds to find a new buffalo, but finally tied the string up in the temple of the Goddess (W 172, *Bh* 372).[25] Another verse indicates the local power of these landowners: the villagers, when they notice that thieves select their loot on the basis of the names branded on the cattle, start marking their own cattle with the name of the *gahavaï* (W 793 [Jain recension], *Bh* 673).

The landowner's son (*gahavaïsua*, Skt. *gṛhapatisuta*) is depicted as an attractive young man: his young wife (or possibly someone else's wife?) lingers on the cotton field stroking the plants with her sweating hand even after he

24. This often seems to be the meaning of *gāhāvaī* in the Śvetāmbara Jain Canon (beside the general meaning "householder"); cf. More 2014: 116n44.

25. According to Gaṅgādharabhaṭṭa, this verse is spoken by a woman to her friend, whose man now wants to give her ornament to another woman. The speaker points out that her own husband is devoted even to a female animal, not to speak about his own wife.

has already plucked the cotton (W 359, *Bh* 310). Another verse in the same vein (W 107, *Bh* 114 [quoted from W]):

> *golāaḍaṭṭhiaṃ pecchiūṇa gahavaïsuaṃ haliasoṇhā |*
> *āḍhattā uttariuṃ dukkhuttārāi paavīe ||*
>
> When the farmer's daughter-in-law saw the landowner's son standing on the bank of the Golā, she started to climb up on a path that was hard to climb.

As the commentator Bhuvanapāla explains, she is trying to make the man help her, so that she can enjoy the touch of his hand.[26] Relationship between people of different social status is also the theme of W 602, but this time the genders are swapped:

> *maṃdaṃ pi ṇa āṇaï haliaṇaṃdaṇo iha hi ḍaḍḍhagāmammi |*
> *gahavaïsuā vivajjaï avejjae kassa sāhāmo ||*
>
> The ploughman's son in this damned village
> Hasn't a clue.
> The landowner's daughter is dying
> But with no doctor at hand.
> Whom to tell? (tr. Khoroche and Tieken, 2009)

Her illness might well be lovesickness caused by her separation from the farmer's son, as it is suggested by Gaṅgādharabhaṭṭa in his commentary.[27] Another verse (W 407) describes how the landowner's daughter (*gahavaïdhūā*, Skt. *gṛhapatiduhitṛ*) extinguishes the flames of her husband's funeral pyre (we

---

26. Tieken thinks this verse shows that when a farmer's daughter marries a landowner's son, she "encounters problems in her new environment": because she does not know anything about coquetry, she chooses a very clumsy way of attracting her husband's attraction (Tieken 1983: 147–48). This interpretation certainly fits Tieken's general idea that a class-based condescending tone can be heard almost everywhere in the *Sattasaī*. But to arrive at this interpretation he has to understand *soṇhā* as "daughter," not as "daughter-in-law." If we take the word in the latter, usual meaning, the woman who is trying to get the attention of the landowner's son is not his wife, but the wife of the farmer's son, flirting with a handsome, young, and rich man in a way whose awkwardness is also not that evident from the verse.

27. Tieken seems to think that this verse is about a married couple: this time the landowner's daughter married below her status and now she is dying in a village where there is no doctor and her boorish husband is completely ignorant (Tieken 1983: 147). But, again, nothing suggests that the characters are married.

have a case of *anumaraṇa* here), because her body is sweating profusely from the joy of embracing her beloved.[28]

In other verses the landowner's daughter appears as a kind of femme fatale: she turns everyone in the village into a god, because they stare at her with unblinking eyes (W 593, *Bh* 586; here the Jain recension has *dhūyā gahavaissa*, while other recensions read *gāmaṇidhūā*). A traveler is warned that if he wants to see his beloved again, he should avoid the village where the *gahavaïdhūā* lives, for she is an inescapable snare (W 957). Another verse seems to say she is a rich source of revenue for some people (W 785, *Bh* 662, [quoted from *Bh*]):

> *diyahe-diyahe ṇivaḍaï gahavaïdhūyāmiseṇa māucchā |*
> *saṃgahaṇaïttavāuyavasuhārā khujjasahayāre ||*
>
> O aunt, every day under this bent mango tree, a stream of wealth in the guise of the landowner's daughter pours down on the official (*vyāpṛta*, possibly the *grāmaṇī*) who is entitled to collect fines (?, *saṃgrahaṇavat*).

As Pathwardan suggests, probably men are fined because of unlawful lovemaking with the *gavahaïdhūā* under the mango tree.[29]

If we take a brief look at other Prakrit *kāvyas* possibly dating from a period before or around the fifth century CE, we see that both in the *Vasudevahiṇḍi* and in the *Paümacariya* the *gahavaï* is a rich man engaged in trade, agriculture, or cattle-breeding.[30] This tallies with the instructions of the *Arthaśāstra* concerning agents who work undercover as *gṛhapatikas*: they are agriculturalists (*karṣaka*) who have gone bankrupt and are employed by the state as spies (*KAŚ* 1.11.9) and are assigned to villages (*KAŚ* 2.35.8).[31]

In the *Vasudevahiṇḍi* we read about certain ascetics, *tāpasas*, who live in the forest with their wives and children.[32] They are said to perform *agnihotra* and other *yajñas*.[33] In the *Paümacariya* we meet a certain Brahmaruci who follows *tāvasadhamma* (Skt. *tāpasadharma*) together with his wife at a dwelling

28. I fail to see in this verse any sarcasm or condescension, even as a suggested meaning. Tieken, however, thinks this shows that the landowner's daughter could not fulfill the ambitions of her husband, the village chief or gendarme (*gāmaṇī*, though it is nowhere explicitly stated that her husband was a *gāmaṇī*). See Tieken 1983: 156n18.

29. Patwardhan 1988: 238, note ad 662.

30. *Vasudevahiṇḍi-prathamakhaṇḍa* pp. 56, 86, 283; *Paümacariya* 48:79.

31. See also Olivelle's translation of these passages.

32. *Vasudevahiṇḍi-prathamakhaṇḍa* pp. 216, 292.

33. *Vasudevahiṇḍi-prathamakhaṇḍa* pp. 293, 353.

of ascetics (*tāvasanilaya*, Skt. *tāpasanilaya*). When his wife becomes pregnant, a *sādhu* scolds him for not being able to renounce sex completely, for one who has once given up food that is not to be eaten should not eat it again (11:51–57). When we consider the lifestyle of these hermits we can understand that it was not impossible to regard them as *gṛhasthas* who live in the forest. This view was made explicit later by Murāri in his *Anargharāghava* (around 900 CE) where Viśvāmitra refers to the way of life of the sages in his ashram as *gārhasthyam ṛṣīṇām* (Act 2, prose after verse 41). He describes his hermitage to Rāma in the following verse:

> *paśyaite paśubandhavedivalayair audumbarīdanturair*
> *nityavyañjitagṛhyatantravidhayaḥ ramyāḥ gṛhasthāśramāḥ* |
> *yatrāmī gṛhamedhinaḥ pracalitasvārājyasiṃhāsanāḥ*
> *vaitāneṣu kṛpīṭayoniṣu puroḍāśam vaṣaṭkurvate* || 2:17 ||
>
> "Look, here are some *udumbara* wood sticks on the round altars of the animal sacrifice, making them uneven. All of this shows that in this wonderful hermitage of householders (*gṛhasthāśrama*) the domestic sacrificial duties are regularly observed. Here these householders (*gṛhamedhinaḥ*) make the throne of the heavenly kingdom shake by their constant offering of rice in the sacrificial fires." (tr. Törzsök 2006)

Rāma thinks that a great sage like Viśvāmitra cannot follow the householder's lifestyle entirely seriously. He says to Lakṣmaṇa:

> *prajñātabrahmatattvo 'pi svargīyair eṣa khelati* |
> *gṛhasthasamayācāraprakrāntaiḥ saptatantubhiḥ* || 2:35 ||
> Although he [Viśvāmitra] knows the true nature of *Brahman*, he amuses himself with sacrifices undertaken according to the rules laid down for householders (*gṛhastha*), in order to obtain heaven. (tr. Törzsök 2006)

What makes these hermits householders is in the first place the ritual regimen they follow. They also have families, they live together with their wives and children, and the term *gṛhamedhin* that is used for them in verse 2:17 is also interpreted traditionally as "married man."[34]

---

34. Compare Rucipati's commentary *ad loc.*: *gṛhamedhina iti gṛhā dārāḥ. na gṛhaṃ gṛham ity āhur, gṛhiṇī gṛham ucyate, teṣāṃ medhaḥ saṃgamaḥ . . . sa eṣām astīti gṛhamedhinaḥ.*

The Works of Kālidāsa

The word *gṛhamedhin* is also used by Kālidāsa in the meaning of "householder," or more precisely perhaps "married man." In the *Kumārasambhava* Himālaya tells his daughter that now that she is given to Śiva in marriage, he, her father, has "obtained the fruit of [being a] *gṛhamedhin*" (*prāptaṃ gṛhamedhiphalaṃ mayā*, 6:87). The commentator Vallabhadeva glosses *gṛhamedhin* as *gṛhastha*, and explains it as follows: *gṛhaṃ veśma dārāś ca, tair medhate saṃgacchanta iti gṛhamedhino gṛhasthāḥ*, "*gṛha* means 'house' and 'wife,' who unite with those are the *gṛhamedhins*, that is *gṛhasthas*." In the *Raghuvaṃśa* the scions of the Solar Dynasty are said to be "*gṛhamedhins* for the sake of progeny" (*prajāyai gṛhamedhinām*, 1:7). Here too the interpretation of *gṛha* as "wife" seems to be in place, as it is shown by Vallabhadeva's commentary: *santataye na rāgād dāraiḥ saṃgacchante ye teṣām; pitṝn anivāraṇārthaṃ gṛhasthānām*, "of those who unite with their wives for the sake of progeny, not because of passion; of them who are *gṛhasthas* in order to clear their debt to the ancestors."[35]

The word *gṛha* is used twice as a synonym of *gṛhāśrama* in the *Raghuvaṃśa*. In the Fifth Canto Kautsa, a young Brahmin who has just completed his studies, approaches Raghu in the hope of obtaining from the king the exorbitant *gurudakṣinā* his teacher has asked for. Raghu asks the polite questions one is supposed to ask from a Vedic graduate (*snātaka*), among which is the following:

> *api prasannena maharṣiṇā tvaṃ samyag vinīyānumato gṛhāya* |
> *kālo hy ayaṃ saṃkramituṃ dvitīyaṃ sarvopakārakṣamam āśramaṃ te* || 5:10 ||
>
> Has the great sage, satisfied after instructing you in the proper way, given you permission for household life (*gṛhāya*)? For this is the time for you to enter the second stage of life, which is capable of benefitting all.

The idea that *gārhasthya*, the second *āśrama*, is the one that can be resorted to by others for help appears in Dharmaśāstra texts.[36] The irony of the verse is

35. Mallinātha comments on this verse in a similar vein: *prajāyai santānāya gṛhamedhināṃ dāraparigrahāṇām. na tu kāmopabhogāya*. Both Śrīnātha and Vaidyaśrīgarbha, whose commentaries survive in Nepalese manuscripts, take *gṛhamedha* to mean *vivāha*, "marriage," and therefore *gṛhamedhin* to mean "married man."

36. Cf. Olivelle (Ch. 7, p. 119]), quoting *VaDh* 8.14–16 and referring to *MDh* 6.87–90. Nārāyaṇapaṇḍita, a Keralan commentator of the *Raghuvaṃśa*, actually quotes *VaDh* 6.16 in his commentary to this verse, with an interesting variant in the second line: *vartante gṛhiṇaṃ tadvad āśrityetara āśramāḥ*, making the members of all other life stages dependent on the *gṛhastha*, not just mendicants.

that Raghu has just distributed all his wealth and thus he cannot help Kautsa, even though as the richest and most powerful *gṛhastha* in the kingdom he should be someone to rely on. But the king certainly rises to the challenge and sets off to extract wealth from Kubera himself.

In Canto Seven we see the same Raghu preparing for retirement:

> *prathamaparigatārthas taṃ Raghuḥ saṃnivṛttaṃ*
> *vijayinam abhinandya ślāghyajāyāsametam* |
> *tadupahitakuṭumbaś cīram ādātum aicchan* [37]
> *na hi sati kuladhurye sūryavaṃśyā gṛhāya* || 7:71 ||
>
> Raghu, who had previously learnt all that had happened, shared Aja's joy when he returned victorious in the company of his admirable wife. He handed over to him the cares of the household (*kuṭumba*) and was eager to put on bark garments; for, when there is someone among them to support the family (*kula*), those of the solar line don't stay at home (*na gṛhāya*).

Kālidāsa uses the same expression here as in Canto Five, *gṛha* in the dative case, explained by Vallabhadeva as "they never stay at home," or "they do not strive to sustain the household" (*gṛhe na kadā cid āsate ity arthaḥ. gṛhaṃ poṣayituṃ na yatante iti yāvat*).

Ascetics and householders are juxtaposed by Kālidāsa in a verse in the *Abhijñānaśākuntala*, where Kaṇva muses on his distress produced by the separation from his adopted daughter: if he, a forest-dwelling hermit, is so devastated, how much more the householders (*gṛhiṇaḥ*) must be tormented when they part from their daughters?[38] While the *Jātakamālās* emphasize the radical difference between household life and the life of a renouncer in the forest, the latter being a life of tranquility and the former being under the pressure of constant worries, Kālidāsa rather points to a similarity between these two life styles, saying that even hermits are not immune to perturbation caused by their attachment to the members of their family.

37. This is the reading of Vallabhadeva. Mallinātha reads here *śāntimārgotsuko 'bhūt*. The question whether Raghu became a *vānaprastha* or a *saṃnyāsin* is a complicated one and there are many interesting variants in the description of his ascetic life at the beginning of Canto Eight. I am planning to devote a separate article to this problem.

38. *Abhijñānaśākuntala* 4:6: *vaiklavyaṃ mama tāvad īdṛśam idaṃ snehād araṇyaukasaḥ pīḍyante gṛhiṇaḥ kathaṃ nu tanayāviśleṣaduḥkhair navaiḥ?*

The *gṛhiṇī* or housewife also appears in Kālidāsa's works. In the context of the Himālaya giving Pārvatī to Śiva in marriage, we are told that "family men usually use their wives as eyes to look at matters concerning their daughters" (*prāyeṇa gṛhiṇīnetrāḥ kanyārthe hi kuṭumbinaḥ, Kumārasambhava* 6:85). Of course, as the next verse tells us, in a good marriage "devoted wives do not deviate from their husbands' wishes" (*bhavanty avyabhicāriṇyo bhartur iṣṭe pativratāḥ,* 6:86). When Kaṇva takes leave of Śakuntalā, he prepares her in a few words for the life that awaits her in the palace:

śuśrūṣasva gurūn kuru priyasakhīvṛttiṃ sapatnījane
bhartur viprakṛtāpi roṣaṇatayā mā sma pratīpaṃ gamaḥ |
bhūyiṣṭhaṃ bhava dakṣiṇā parijane bhāgyeṣv anutsekinī
yānty evaṃ gṛhiṇīpadaṃ yuvatayo vāmāḥ kulasyādhayaḥ || 4:18 ||

Obey your elders, be a fair friend to your fellow wives; though slighted by your husband do not reciprocate with anger; always be polite to servants, do not be arrogant in your prosperity; in this way young girls become the matron of the family (*gṛhiṇī*); those who act contrary are the misfortune of the family. (tr. Vasudeva 2006)

abhijanavato bhartuḥ ślāghye sthitā gṛhiṇīpade
vibhavagurubhiḥ kṛtyais tasya pratikṣaṇam ākulā |
tanayam acirāt prācīvārkaṃ prasūya ca pāvanam
mama virahajāṃ na tvaṃ vatse śucaṃ gaṇayiṣyasi || 4:19 ||

Assuming the celebrated status of matron (*gṛhiṇī*) to a husband of worthy family, involved every minute in his affairs, important because of his status, soon giving birth to a son who will fulfill you just as the east gives birth to the sun, you will count for nothing the grief of separation from me. (tr. Vasudeva 2006)

In the king's household she will be only one of his wives, and to survive first and then to rise in prestige she should avoid conflicts and make friends. Her status as *gṛhiṇī* will become strong and stable when she gives birth to a heir to the throne.

Conclusions

For a ruler, as we saw in the *Raghuvaṃśa,* the time of renouncement came when his son was suitable to take over the burden of kingship. The ruling king was expected to fulfill his duties as a model householder, doing good and benefitting all. Renouncing the householder state as a young man is disapproved by Siddhārtha's father in the *Buddhacarita*, and in the *Aputrajātaka* too we find the (prima facie) view expressed that one should not disregard one's family lineage and renounce the world without having offspring. In fact, having progeny is said to be the goal of being a married man in the *Raghuvaṃśa* (1:7: *prajāyai gṛhamedhinām*), and in the *Kumārasaṃbhava* Himālaya says that he has reaped the fruit of being a family man (*kuṭumbin*) when his daughter got married.

The Bodhisattva, however, does not feel himself bound by such considerations, either in the *Buddhacarita* or in the *Jātakamālās*. In the Jātakas it is often the death of his parents that spurs the Bodhisattva into making a decision not to take upon himself the burden of his family, not to continue the lineage or the family business, but to withdraw to the solitude of the forest.

In Buddhist *kāvya*, the life of the householder (*gṛhastha*) is presented as fundamentally irreconcilable with *śama*, quietude, which is an essential prerequisite for any mental exercise leading to enlightenment, and which is provided by solitary life in the forest. Constant worries for his loved ones, greed and parsimony, and the bewilderment caused by many conflicting worldviews make the householder's mind befuddled. Household life is never satisfying. It entangles one in a net of vices, and it is condemned as an illness to be shaken off, or a prison to be escaped from. Its pleasures are illusory and lead to sorrow in the end. Living as a family man and dying as a householder are the most abominable things that could happen to anyone.

The life of a forest hermit is mostly described as a solitary life in the *Jātakamālās*, though in Haribhaṭṭa's *Śaśajātaka* the ashram is reminiscent of the hermitage where Śakuntalā grew up, where hermits live in a community together with their wives and children, growing plants and keeping animals. Such *tāpasas*, who are described as performing Vedic fire rituals, could be regarded as *gṛhasthas* on the basis of their lifestyle, as Murāri's play shows. That there is still something slightly awkward about ascetics having wives is alluded to in the *Kumārasambhava*, when the Seven Sages are positively relieved of the embarrassment they feel as married men when they learn that Śiva, the foremost ascetic, is about to get married himself (6:34). One could say that the goal of the gods' project in the *Kumārasambhava* is to make the ascetic Śiva a householder again, which project succeeds only because of Pārvatī's devoted and selfless asceticism.

Housewives (*gharinī*) in early Prakrit *kāvya* stand by their men in dire straits, are neglected by their husbands when they bring a new, younger wife into the house, sometimes cheat on their husbands, sometimes try to prevent themselves from being cheated on. We see them as mothers sharing their affections between sons and spouses. Some of the most moving verses in Prakrit and Sanskrit poetry are about housewives and mothers who are trying hard to keep the household together. As the king is the model householder, his queen should be a model housewife: adaptable, accommodating, even obliging, unobtrusively involved in her husband's affairs, and giving birth to an heir to the throne, thereby stabilizing her own position in the royal family—at least this is how things should be from the viewpoint of the ascetic Kaṇva in the *Abhijñānaśākuntala.*

We have seen in the Jātakas that one can remain at home and yet at least make the first steps on the path of dharma ultimately leading to liberation. This is, however, an extremely arduous journey; it requires constant vigilance and the guidance of the wise, because the life of a *gṛhastha* entails constant stress and struggle, greed and violence, arrogance and selfishness. Still, it is not impossible to be a householder and live a religious and virtuous life founded on love, respect, generosity, and integrity (*śīla*), keeping passions at a minimum and observing vows. Such exemplary householders often appear as *gṛhapatis* in Buddhist texts, rich, respected, and magnanimous citizens, whose services are used by the king. When such a rich *gṛhapati* is considered to be capable of renouncing worldly life, this assumption is thought to be an expression of the greatest esteem, an expectation that should be lived up to. Being a model householder is only the second best option. In Buddhist *kāvya*, quitting society and living as an ascetic in the forest is presented as ultimately superior to the life of a householder, no matter how virtuous he might be. In Kālidāsa's works renunciation has its well-appointed time in the life of a householder, and the values of asceticism and family life can be reconciled.

Bibliography

Ācārāngasūtram and Sūtrakṛtāngasūtram, with the Niryukti of Ācārya Bhadrabāhu Svāmi and the Commentary of Silānkācarya. 1978. Ed. Ācārya Sāgarānandasūriji Mahārāja; re-edited with appendices etc. by Muni Jambūvijayajī. Delhi: Motilal Banarsidass.

Adiceam, Marguerite. 1967. *Contribution à l'étude d'AiyaNār-Śāstā.* Pondicherry: Institut français d'Indologie.

Ali, Daud. 2004. *Courtly Culture and Political Life in Early India.* London: Cambridge University Press.

Alsdorf, Ludwig. 1960. "Contributions to the Study of Asoka's Inscriptions." *Bulletin of the Deccan College Research Institute* 20 (*Sushil Kumar De Felicitation Volume*): 249–75.

Anargharāghavam of Murāri. Ed. and tr. Törzsök 2006.

Anargharāghavam with the Commentary (ṭīkā) of Rucipati. 1908. Ed. Durgaprasad and Wasudev Laxman Shastri Pansikar. Kāvyamālā 5. Bombay: Nirnaya Sāgar Press.

Andersen, Paul Kent. 1990. *Studies in the Minor Rock Edicts of Aśoka I: Critical Edition.* Freiburg: Hedwig Falk.

Aṅguttara Nikāya. 1885–1900. Ed. Richard Morris and Edmund Hardy. 5 vols. London: Pali Text Society.

Āpastamba Dharmasūtra. Ed. and tr. Olivelle 2000.

Aśvaghoṣa. *Saundarananda.* Ed. and tr. Covill 2007.

Āśvalāyana Śrautasūtra. The Srauta Sūtra of Āśvalāyana: with the Commentary of Gārgya Nārāyaṇa. 1874. Ed. Rāmanārāyaṇa Vidyāratna. Calcutta: Asiatic Society of Bengal.

Atharva Veda (Śaunaka). Ed. with Sāyaṇa's com. By Vishva Bandhu. *Vishveshvaranand Indological Series, 13–17.* Hoshiarpur: 1960–64. Tr. W. D. Whitney. Harvard Oriental Series, 7–8. Cambridge: 1905.

Âyâraṃga Sutta of the Çvetâmbara Jains. 1882. Ed. Hermann Jacobi. London: Pali Text Society.

Bailey, G. Forthcoming. "On the Buddha's Eightfold Noble Path in the Mahābhārata." Festschrift in Honour of Arvind Sharma.

Bākre, Mahādev Gangādhar. Ed. 1917. *Grihya-Sūtra by Pāraskar with Five Commentaries of Karka Upādhyāya, Jayarām, Harihar, Gadādhar and Vishvanāth.* Bombay: Gujarati Printing Press. Reprint, Delhi: Munshiram Manoharlal, 1982.

Baudhāyana Dharmasūtra. Ed. and tr. Olivelle 2000.

Baudhāyana Gṛhyasūtra. Maharṣibodhāyanapraṇītaḥ smārtakalpasūtraḥ. 1905. Ed. Maṇakkāl Rāmaśarmā Muddudīkṣita. Cennanagara [Madras]: Jñānasāgara Press. [In Grantha script.]

Baudhāyana Gṛhyasūtra. Śrī-Gṛhyasūtram, Maharṣi-Śrī-Bodhāyanācāryapraṇītam, Rāmacandra-Śāstri-Sūri-viracitayā 'Sañjīvinī'-samākhyayā vyākhyayā samalaṅkṛtam. 1986–89. Ed. Ananta Bhaṭṭa. 4 vols. Honnavar, Karnataka: Śri Subrahmaṇyaprācyavidyāpīṭham.

Baums, Stefan. 2009. "A Gāndhārī Commentary on Early Buddhist Verses: British Library Kharoṣṭhi Fragments 7, 9, 13, and 18." PhD dissertation, Department of Asian Languages and Literatures, University of Washington.

Bellah, Robert N. 1970. "Civil Religion in America." In *Beyond Belief: Essays on Religion in a Post-Traditional World*, pp. 168–189. New York: Harper and Row. Originally published, *Daedalus* 96 (1967): 1–21.

Benveniste, Émile. 1964. "Édits d'Asoka en traduction grecque." *Journal Asiatique* 252: 137–57.

Berger, Hermann. 1955. *Zwei Probleme der mittelindischen Lautlehre.* Munich: Kitzinger.

Biardeau, Madeleine. 2002. *Le Mahābhārata. Un récit fondateur du brahmanisme et son interpretation.* 2 tomes. Paris: Éditions du Seuil.

Bloch, Jules. 1950. *Les inscriptions d'Asoka: Traduits et commentées.* Paris: Société d'Édition "Les Belles Lettres."

Böhtlingk, Otto. 1879–89. *Sanskrit-Wörterbuch in kürzerer Fassung.* St. Petersburg: Kaiserliche Akademie der Wissenschaften.

———, and Rudolph Roth. 1852–75. *Sanskrit-Wörterbuch.* 7 vols. St. Petersburg: Kaiserliche Akademie der Wissenschaften.

Bollée, Willem B. 1977. *Studien zum Sūyagaḍa.* Part 1. Wiesbaden: Steiner.

Bolling, George Melville, and Julius von Negelein. 1909–10. *The Pariśiṣṭas of the Atharvaveda.* Vol. 1: *Text and Critical Apparatus.* Leipzig: Harrassowitz.

Bowles, Adam. 2007. *Dharma, Disorder, and the Political in Ancient India: The Āpaddharmaparvan of the Mahābhārata.* Leiden: Brill.

———. 2016. "Reflections on the *Upākhyānas* in the *Āpaddharmaparvan* of the *Mahābhārata.*" In *Argument and Design: The Unity of the Mahābhārata*, ed. V. Adluri and J. Bagchee, pp. 320–58. Leiden: Brill.

Bṛhadāraṇyaka Upaniṣad. Ed. and tr. Olivelle 1998.

Brockington, J. 1984. *Righteous Rāma: The Evolution of an Epic.* Delhi: Oxford University Press.

———. 1998. *The Sanskrit Epics.* Leiden: Brill.

Bronkhorst, Johannes. 1993. *The Two Sources of Indian Asceticism.* Bern: Peter Lang.

———. 2007. *Greater Magadha: Studies in the Culture of Early India.* Leiden: Brill.

———. 2016. *How the Brahmins Won: From Alexander to the Guptas*. Leiden: Brill.

Bühler, Georg, tr. 1879–82. *Sacred Laws of the Āryas*. 2 vols. Sacred Books of the East 2, 14. Oxford: Oxford University Press.

Buitenen, J. A. B. van, tr. 1973–78. *The Mahābhārata* (Books 1–5). Chicago: University of Chicago Press.

Chakravarti, Uma. 1996. *The Social Dimensions of Early Buddhism*. Delhi: Munshiram Manoharlal.

Chāndogya Upaniṣad. Ed. and tr. Olivelle 1998.

Charpentier, Jarl. 1908. "Studien über die indische Erzählungsliteratur," *Zeitschrift der Deutschen Morgenländischen Gesellschaft* 62: 725–47.

Cilappatikāram of Iḷaṅkovaṭikaḷ, with the commentary of Aṭiyārkkunallār. 2001. Ed. U. Ve. Cāminātaiyar. Reprint. Chennai: Dr. U.Ve. Cāminātaiyar Nūlnilaiyam.

Clarke, Shayne. 2014. *Family Matters in Indian Buddhist Monasticisms*. New Delhi: Dev Publishers & Distributors.

Cone, Margaret. 2010. *A Dictionary of Pāli*, pt. 2. Bristol: Pali Text Society.

Collins, Steven. 1990. "On the Very Idea of the Pali Canon." *Journal of the Pali Text Society* 15: 89–126.

Covill, Linda, ed. and tr. 2007. *Handsome Nanda by Aśvaghoṣa*. Clay Sanskrit Library. New York: New York University Press – JJC Foundation.

Cox, Whitney. 2017. *Modes of Philology in Medieval South India*. Leiden: Brill.

Daston, Lorraine. 2014. "Objectivity and Impartiality: Epistemic Virtues in the Humanities." In *The Making of the Humanities*, Volume 3: *The Modern Humanities*, ed. Rens Bod et al., pp. 27–41. Amsterdam: University of Amsterdam Press.

Daston, Lorraine, and Peter Galison. 2010. *Objectivity*. New York: Zone Books.

Daston, Lorraine, and Glen Most. 2015. "History of Science and History of Philologies." *Isis* 106, 2: 378–390.

Deo, Shantaram Bhalchandra. 1956. *History of Jaina Monachism, from Inscriptions and Literature*. Poona: Deccan College Postgraduate and Research Institute.

Deshpande, Madhav M. 2009. "Interpreting the Aśokan Epithet *devānaṃpiya*." In Olivelle 2009: 19–43.

Deussen, Paul. 1909. "Āśrama." In *Encyclopedia of Religion and Ethics*, ed. J. Hastings, Vol. 2: pp. 128–31. Edinburgh: T & T Clark.

Dhammapada. 1995. Ed. Oskar von Hinüber and Kenneth R. Norman. Oxford: Pali Text Society.

Dīgha Nikāya. 1890–1911. Ed. Thomas W. Rhys Davids and J. Estlin Carpenter. 3 vols. London: Pali Text Society.

Doniger O'Flaherty, Wendy. 1971. "The Origin of Heresy in Hindu Mythology." *History of Religions* 10, 4: 271–333.

Doniger, Wendy. 1976. *The Origins of Evil in Hindu Mythology*. Berkeley: University of California Press.

Dumont, Louis. 1960. "World Renunciation in Indian Religions." *Contributions to Indian Sociology* 4: 33–62.

Dundas, Paul. 2002. *The Jains*. 2nd ed. London and New York: Routledge. First published, 1992.

Durgâprasâd, Pandit, and Kâśînâth Pâṇdurang Parab, eds. 1889. *The Gâthâsaptaśatî of Sâtavâhana, with the Commentary of Gangâdharabhatta*. Kâvyamâlâ 21. Bombay: Nirṇaya-Sâgara Press.

Edgerton, Franklin. 1953. *Buddhist Hybrid Sanskrit Grammar and Dictionary*. Vol. 2: *Dictionary*. New Haven: Yale University Press. Reprint, Delhi: Motilal Banarsidass, 1993.

Einoo, Shingo. 1996. "The Formation of the Pūjā Ceremony." *Studien zur Indologie und Iranistik* 20: 73–87.

Falk, Harry. 2006. *Aśokan Sites and Artefacts: A Source-Book with Bibliography*. Mainz am Rhein: Philipp von Zabern.

Fausbøll, Viggo and Dines Andersen, eds. 1877–97. *The Jātaka, Together with its Commentary, Being Tales of the Anterior Births of Gotama Buddha*. 3 vols. Pali Text Society. London: Kegan Paul, Trench, Trübner & Co.

Fitzgerald, James. 2002. "Nun Befuddles King, Shows *Karmayoga* Does Not Work: Sulabhā's Refutation of King Janaka at *MBh* 12.308." *Journal of Indian Philosophy* 30: 641–77.

———. tr. 2004. *The Mahābhārata*. Vol. 7: *Book 11: The Book of the Women and Book 12: The Book of Peace, Part One*. Chicago: University of Chicago Press.

Fowler, James A. 1998. "Christianity is NOT Religion." http://www.christinyou.net/pages/Xnotrel.html, accessed October 17, 2017.

Freeman, J. R. 2003. "The Teyyam Tradition of Kerala." In *A Companion to Hinduism*, ed. G. Flood, pp. 306–26. Oxford: Blackwell.

Freiberger, Oliver. 2013. "Religionen und Religion in der Konstruktion des frühen Buddhismus." In *Religion in Asien? Studien zur Anwendbarkeit des Religionsbegriffs*, ed. Peter Schalk, Max Deeg, Oliver Freiberger, Christoph Kleine, and Astrid van Nahl, pp. 15–41. Uppsala: Uppsala University Press.

———. 2018. "Zu Hause beim Saṅgha: Bezeichnungen für Nicht-Asketen in frühen Pālitexten." In *Saddharmāmṛtam: Festschrift für Jens-Uwe Hartmann zum 65. Geburtstag*, ed. Oliver von Criegern, Gudrun Melzer, and Johannes Schneider, pp. 127–137. Vienna: Arbeitskreis für Tibetische und Buddhistische Studien.

Gaṇḍavyūhasūtra. 1960. Ed. P. L. Vaidya. Darbhanga: The Mithila Institute.

Ganguli, Kisari Mohan. 1993. *The Mahābhārata of Krishna-Dwaipayana Vyasa*. 4 vols. Delhi: Manoharlal Publishers. Originally published, Calcutta: Bhārata Press, 1886.

Gautama Dharmasūtra. Ed. and tr. Olivelle 2000.

Geldner, Karl Friedrich. 1951. *Der Rig-Veda aus dem Sanskrit ins Deutsche übersetzt und mit einem laufenden Kommentar versehen*. 3 vols. Cambridge, MA: Harvard University Press.

Gobhilagṛhyasūtra. 1884–86. Ed. Friedrich Knauer. 2 vols. Dorpat: C. Mattiesen.

Goldman, Robert, tr. 1984. *The Rāmāyaṇa of Vālmīki: An Epic of Ancient India*. Vol. 1: *Bālakāṇḍa*. Princeton, NJ: Princeton University Press.

Goldman, Robert P., and Sally J. Sutherland Goldman, tr. 1996. *The Rāmāyaṇa of Vālmīki: An Epic of Ancient India*. Vol. 5: *Sundarakāṇḍa*. Princeton, NJ: Princeton University Press.

———. tr. 2017. *The Rāmāyaṇa of Vālmīki: An Epic of Ancient India*. Vol. 7: *Uttarakāṇḍa*. Princeton, NJ: Princeton University Press.

Gómez, Luis O. 1976. "Proto-Mādhyamika in the Pāli Canon." *Philosophy East and West* 26: 137–65.

Gonda, Jan. 1977a. *The Ritual Sūtras*. History of Indian Literature 1.2. Wiesbaden: Otto Harrassowitz.

———. 1977b. "The Baudhāyana-Gṛhya-Paribhāṣā-Sūtra." In *Beiträge zur Indienforschung: Ernst Waldschmidt zum 80. Geburstag gewidmet*, pp. 169–190. Berlin: Museum für Indische Kunst.

———. 1980. *Vedic Ritual: The Non-Solemn Rites*. Leiden: Brill.

Goodall, Dominic, and Harunaga Isaacson, eds. 2003. *The Raghupañcikā of Vallabhadeva, Being the Earliest Commentary on the Raghuvaṃśa of Kālidāsa*. Vol. 1. Groningen: Egbert Forsten.

Das Gopatha Brāhmaṇa. 1919. Ed. Dieuke Gaastra. Leiden: Brill.

Grafton, Anthony. 1994. "Humanism and Science in Rudolphine Prague." In *Defenders of the Text: The Traditions of Scholarship in an Age of Science, 1450–1800*, pp. 178–203. Cambridge, MA: Harvard University Press.

———. 1999. *Cardano's Cosmos: The Worlds and Works of a Renaissance Astrologer*. Cambridge, MA: Harvard University Press.

Granoff, Phyllis. 2006. "Fathers and Sons: Some Remarks on the Ordination of Children in the Medieval Śvetāmbara Monastic Community." *Asiatische Studien / Études Asiatiques* 60: 607–33.

Grünendahl, Reinhold, ed. 1984. *Viṣṇudharmāḥ: Precepts for the Worship of Viṣṇu, Part 2, Adhyāyas 44–81*. Wiesbaden: Otto Harrassowitz.

Hacking, Ian. 2002. *Historical Ontology*. Cambridge, MA: Harvard University Press.

Hahn, Michael, ed. 2007. *Haribhaṭṭa in Nepal. Ten Legends from His Jātakamālā and the Anonymous Śākyasiṃhajātaka. Editio Minor*. Studia Philologica Buddhica Monograph Series 22. Tokyo: The International Institute for Buddhist Studies of the International College for Postgraduate Buddhist Studies.

———. ed. 2011. *Poetic Vision of the Buddha's Former Lives: Seventeen Legends from Haribhaṭṭa's Jātakamālā*. New Delhi: Aditya Prakashan.

Haradatta. 1969. *Ujjvalā* (commentary on the *Āpastamba Dharmasūtra*). Ed. Umeśa Chandra Pāṇḍeya. 2nd edition. Varanasi: Chowkhambha Sanskrit Series Office.

Heesterman, J. C. 1964. "Brahmin, Ritual and Renouncer." *Wiener Zeitschrift für die Kunde Südasiens* 8: 1–31.

Hiltebeitel, Alf. 2006. "Aśvaghoṣa's Buddhacarita: The First Known Close and Critical Reading of the Brahmanical Sanskrit Epics." *Journal of Indian Philosophy* 34: 229–86.

———. 2018. "From Ṛṣidharma to Vānaprastha: The Southern Recension Makeover of the Mahābhārata's Umā-Maheśvara Saṃvāda." In *The Churning of the Epics and Purāṇas*, ed. Simon Brodbeck, Adam Bowles, and Alf Hiltebeitel, pp. 14–45. New Delhi: Dev Publishers and Distributors.

Hinüber, Oskar von. 1996. *A Handbook of Pāli Literature*. Berlin: Walter de Gruyter.

———. 2001. *Das Ältere Mittelindisch im Überblick. 2., Erweiterte Auflage*. Vienna: Verlag der Österrichischen Akademie der Wissenschaften. Original edition, Vienna: Österreichische Akad. d. Wiss., Phil-Hist. Kl. no. 467, 1986.

Hinz, Walther. 1975. *Altiranisches Sprachgut der Nebenüberlieferung*. Göttinger Orientforschungen, III. Iranica Band 3. Wiesbaden: Harrassowitz.

———, and Heidemarie Koch, ed. 1987. *Elamisches Wörterbuch*. Berlin: D. Reimer.

Houben, Jan E. M. 1999. "Why Did Rationality Thrive, but Hardly Survive in Kapila's 'System'?: On the Pramāṇas, Rationality and Irrationality in Sāṃkhya. Part I." *Asiatische Studien* 53, 3: 491–512.

Hultzsch, Eugen. 1991. *Inscriptions of Asoka*. Corpus Inscriptionum Indicarum I (new edition). Delhi and Varanasi: Indological Book House. First published, Oxford: Clarendon Press, 1925.

Itivuttaka. 1889. Ed. Ernst Windisch. London: Pali Text Society.

Jacobi, Hermann. 2002. *Jaina Sūtras*. Part I: *The Âcârâṅga Sūtra, The Kalpa Sūtra*. Sacred Books of the East 22. Delhi: Motilal Banarsidass. First published, 1884.

———. 2004. *Jaina Sūtras*. Part II: *The Uttarādhyayana Sūtra, The Sūtrakararitâṅga Sūtra*. Sacred Books of the East 45. Delhi: Motilal Banarsidass. First published, 1895.

Jacobi, Hermann, ed. 1962. *Ācārya Vimalasūri's Paumacariyaṃ with Hindi Translation*, Part I. 2nd rev. ed. by Punyavijayaji, Hindi tr. Shantilal M. Vora. Prakrit Text Society Series 6. Varanasi: Prakrit Text Society, 1962.

———. ed. 1968. *Ācārya Vimalasūri's Paumacariyaṃ with Hindi Translation*, Part II. Prakrit Text Society Series 12. Ahmedabad: Prakrit Text Society, 1968.

Jacobsen, Knut A. 2008. *Kapila: Founder of Sāṃkhya and Avatāra of Viṣṇu*. New Delhi: Munshiram Manoharlal.

Jaimini Gṛhyasūtra. 1905. *De Literatuur van den Sāmaveda en het Jaiminigṛhyasūtra*. Ed. Willem Caland. Amsterdam: Johannes Müller.

Jamison, Stephanie W. 1996. *Sacrificed Wife/Sacrifer's Wife: Women, Ritual, and Hospitality in Ancient India*. New York: Oxford University Press.

———. 2006. "Women 'Between the Empires' and 'Between the Lines.'" In Olivelle 2006a: 191–214.

———. 2009. "Sociolinguistic Remarks on the Indo-Iranian *-ka Suffix: A Marker of Colloquial Register." *Indo-Iranian Journal* 52: 311–29.

———. 2011. "The Secret Lives of Texts." *Journal of the American Oriental Society* 131: 1–7.

———. 2016. "The 'Brahman's Wife' and the Ritual Patnī." In *The Vedas in Indian Culture and History: Proceedings of the Fourth International Vedic Workshop*, ed. Joel P. Brereton, pp. 207–20. Florence: Società Editrice Fiorentina.

———. 2018a. "Marriage and the Householder: *vivāha, gṛhastha*." In Olivelle and Davis 2018: 125–36.

———. 2018b. "'Sacrificer's Wife' in the Rig Veda: Ritual Innovation?" In *Creating the Veda, Living the Veda: Selected Papers from the 13th World Sanskrit Conference*, ed. Joel P. Brereton and Theodore N. Proferes, pp. 19–30. Helsinki: Finnish Academy of Science and Letters.

———. Forthcoming. "The Double Life of *gahapati*." To appear in a forthcoming Festschrift.

Jamison, Stephanie W., and Joel P. Brereton, tr. 2014. *The Rigveda: The Earliest Religious Poetry of India*. 3 vols. New York: Oxford University Press.

Jātakamālā of Ārya Śūra. Ed. and tr. Meiland 2009; Khoroche 1989.

Jātakamālā of Haribhaṭṭa. Ed. Hahn 2007; Hahn 2001; tr. Khoroche 2017.

Jātakas. Pāli. Ed. Fausbøll and Anderson 1877–97.

Jhā, Subhadra. 1981. *A Grammar of the Prākrit Languages*. Delhi: Motilal Banarsidass.

Kālidāsa. *Abhijñānaśākuntala*. Ed. and tr. Vasudeva 2006.

Kālidāsa. *Kumārasaṃbhava*. Ed. with Vallabhadeva's commentary by M. S. Narayana Murti. Wiesbaden: Franz Steiner Verlag, 1980.

Kālidāsa. *Raghuvaṃśa*. Ed. Goodall and Isaacson 2003; Nandargikar 1982; Poduval and Nambiar 1964.

Kāmandaka. 1912. *Nītisāra, Edited with the Commentary, Jayamangala of Sankarārya*. Ed. T. Gaṇapati Sāstrī. Trivandrum: Trivandrum Government Press.

Kamandakiya Nitisara, or the Elements of Polity (in English). 1979. Tr. Manmatha Nath Dutt. 2nd ed. Varanasi: Chowkhamba Sanskrit Series Office.

Kāmandakīya Nītisāra. Forthcoming. Tr. Jesse Knutson.

Kane, P. V. 1962–75. *History of Dharmaśāstra*. 5 vols. Poona: Bhandarkar Oriental Research Institute.

Kangle, R. P. 1969. *The Kauṭilīya Arthaśāstra*. Part I: *A Critical Edition and Glossary*. 2nd ed. Bombay: University of Bombay. First edition, 1960.

Keith, Arthur Berriedale. 1914. *The Veda of the Black Yajus School entitled Taittiriya Sanhita*. 2 vols. Harvard Oriental Series, 18–19. Cambridge, MA. Reprint. Delhi: Motilal Banarsidass, 1967.

———. tr. 1972. *The Kauṭilīya Arthaśāstra*. 2nd ed. Bombay: University of Bombay.

Khoroche, Peter, tr. 1989. *Once the Buddha Was a Monkey. Ārya Śūra's Jātakamālā*. Chicago: University of Chicago Press.

———. tr. 2017. *Once a Peacock, Once an Actress. Twenty-Four Lives of the Bodhisattva from Haribhaṭṭa's Jātakamālā*. Chicago: University of Chicago Press.

———, and Herman Tieken. 2009. *Poems on Life and Love in Ancient India. Hāla's Sattasaī*. Albany: State University of New York Press.

Kobayashi, Masato. 2004. *Historical Phonology of Old Indo-Aryan Consonants*. Tokyo: Research Institute for Languages of Cultures of Asia and Africa.

Kosambi, D. D., and V. V. Gokhale, eds. 1957. *The Subhāṣitaratnakoṣa compiled by Vidyākara*. Cambridge, MA: Harvard University Press.

Lariviere, Richard, ed. and tr. 2003. *Nārada Smṛti*. Delhi: Motilal Banarsidass.

Lingat, Robert. 1973. *The Classical Law of India*. Tr. J. D. M. Derrett. Berkeley: University of California Press.

Lubin, Timothy. 2011. "The Elusive *Snātaka*." In *Religion and Identity in South Asia and Beyond: Essays in Honor of Patrick Olivelle*, ed. Steven E. Lindquist, pp. 23–40. New York, London, Delhi: Anthem Press.

———. 2013. "Aśoka's Disparagement of Domestic Ritual and Its Validation by the Brahmins." *Journal of Indian Philosophy* 41, 1: 29–41.

———. 2016. "Baudhāyanīya Contributions to Smārta Hinduism." In *Vedic Śākhās: Past, Present, Future. Proceedings of the Fifth International Vedic Workshop, Bucharest 2011*, ed. Jan E.M. Houben, Julieta Rotaru, and Michael Witzel, 591–606. Harvard Oriental Series, Opera Minora 9. Cambridge, MA: Department of South Asian Studies, Harvard University.

———. 2018a. "The Vedic Student: *brahmacārin*." In Olivelle and Davis 2018: 98–112.

———. 2018b. "The Vedic Graduate: *Snātaka*." In Olivelle and Davis 2018: 113–124.

Lucian. 1925. "Alexander the False Prophet." In *Lucian*, Vol. IV, ed. and tr. A.M. Harmon, 174–253. Loeb Classical Library 162. Cambridge, MA: Harvard University Press.

Maes, Claire. 2015. "Dialogues With(in) the Pāli Vinaya. A Research into the Dynamics and Dialectics of the Pāli Vinaya's Ascetic Other, with a Special Focus on the Jain Ascetic Other." PhD dissertation, Ghent.

Mahābhārata. 1927–59. Crit. ed. V. S. Sukthankar et al. 19 vols. Poona: Bhandarkar Oriental Research Institute.

Mahadevan, T. P. 2008. "The Southern Recension of the Mahabharata, Brahman Migrations, and Brahmi Paleography." *Electronic Journal of Vedic Studies* 15, 1: 1–146.

Maitrāyaṇī Saṃhitā. 1881–86. Ed. Leopold von Schroeder. 4 vols. Leipzig: F. A. Brockhaus.

Majjhima Nikāya. 1888–99. Ed. Vilhelm Trenckner and Robert Chalmers. 3 vols. London: Pali Text Society.

Mānava Dharmaśāstra (*Manusmṛti*). Ed. and tr. Olivelle 2005.

Mānava Dharmaśāstra (*Manusmṛti*). *Edited with the commentaries of Medhātithi, Sarvajñanārāyaṇa, Kullūka, Rāghavānanda, Nandana, and Rāmacandra*. 1886. Ed. V. N. Mandlik. 2 vols. Bombay: Ganpat Krishnaji's Press.

Mayrhofer, Manfred. 1951–76. *Kurzgefasstes etymologisches Wörterbuch des Altindischen*. 3 vols. Heidelberg: Carl Winter.

———. 1986–96. *Etymologisches Wörterbuch des Altindoarischen*. 3 vols. Heidelberg: Carl Winter.

McClish, Mark. 2009. "Political Brāhmaṇism and the State: A Compositional History of the *Arthaśāstra*." PhD dissertation, The University of Texas at Austin.

———. 2019. *The History of the Arthaśāstra: Sovereignty and Sacred Law in Ancient India*. Cambridge: Cambridge University Press.

Meiland, Justin, ed. and tr. 2009. *Garland of the Buddha's Past Lives by Āryaśūra*. 2 vols. Clay Sanskrit Library. New York: New York University Press – JJC Foundation.

Modak, B. R. 1993. *The Ancillary Literature of the Atharva-Veda: A Study with Special Reference to The Pariśiṣṭas*. Delhi: Rashtriya Veda Vidya Pratishthan.

Monier-Williams, Monier. 1899. *Sanskrit-English Dictionary*. Rev. ed. Oxford: Clarendon Press.

More, Andrew. 2014. "Early Statements Relating to the Lay Community in the Śvetāmbara Jain Canon." PhD dissertation, Yale University.

Morrison, Kathleen. 2016. "From Millets to Rice (and back again?): Cuisine, Cultivation and Health in Southern India." In *A Companion to South Asia in the Past*, ed. Gwen Robbins Schug and Subhash R. Walimbe, pp. 358–73. West Sussex: John Wiley.

Murāri. *Rāma Beyond Price* (*Anargharāghava*). Ed. and tr. Judit Törzsök. Clay Sanskrit Library. New York: New York University Press – JJC Foundation, 2006.

Nandargikar, G. R., ed. 1982. *The Raghuvaṃśa of Kālidāsa With the Commentary of Mallinātha Edited with A Literal English Translation, Copious Notes in English Intermixed with Full Extracts, elucidating the text, from the Commentaries of Bhaṭṭa Hemādri, Cāritravardhana, Vallabha, Dinakaramiśra, Sumativijaya, Vijayagaṇi, Vijayānandasūri's Varacaraṇasevaka and Dharmameru, with Various Readings, etc. etc.* 5th ed. Delhi: Motilal Banarsidass.

Nārada Smṛti. Ed. and tr. Lariviere 2003.

Nikam, N. A. and Richard McKeon, tr. 1959. *The Edicts of Asoka*. Chicago: University of Chicago Press.

Nītisāra. See Kāmandaka.

Norman, K. R. 1966. "Middle Indo-Aryan Studies VI". *Journal of the Oriental Institute, Baroda* 16: 113–19. Reprinted in *Collected Papers, Vol. I*: 77–84, London: Pali Text Society, 1990.

———. 1972. "Notes on the Greek Version of Aśoka's Twelfth and Thirteenth Rock Edicts." *Journal of the Royal Asiatic Society* 2: 111–18.

———. 1985. *The Rhinoceros Horn and Other Early Buddhist Poems* (*Sutta Nipāta*). London: The Pali Text Society.

———. 2012. "The Languages of the Composition and Transmission of the Aśokan Inscriptions." In Olivelle, Ray, and Leoshko 2012: 38–62.

Obeyesekere, Gananath. 1984. *The Cult of the Goddess Pattini*. Chicago: University of Chicago Press.

Oldenberg, Hermann. 1879. *The Dīpavaṃsa: An Ancient Buddhist Historical Record.* London and Edinburgh: Williams and Norgate.

Olivelle, Patrick. 1974. "The Notion of Āśrama in the Dharmasūtras." *Wiener Zeitschrift für die Kunde Südasiens* 18: 27–35.

———. 1993. *The Āśrama System: History and Hermeneutics of a Religious Institution.* New York: Oxford University Press.

———. 1995. "Ascetic Withdrawal or Social Engagement." In *Religions of India in Practice,* ed. Donald S. Lopez, pp. 533–46. Princeton, NJ: Princeton University Press.

———. ed. and tr. 1998. *The Early Upaniṣads: Annotated Text and Translation.* New York: Oxford University Press.

———. tr. 1999. *Dharmasūtras: The Law Codes of Ancient India.* Oxford: Oxford University Press.

———. ed. and tr. 2000. *The Dharmasūtras of Āpastamba, Gautama, Baudhāyana, and Vasiṣṭha.* In *Sources of Indian Law,* ed. Patrick Olivelle. Delhi: Motilal Banarsidass.

———. ed. and tr. 2005. *Manu's Code of Law: A Critical Edition and Translation of the Mānava-Dharmaśāstra.* New York: Oxford University Press.

———. ed. 2006a. *Between the Empires: Society in India 300 BCE to 400 CE.* New York: Oxford University Press.

———. 2006b. "Explorations in the Early History of Dharmaśāstra." In Olivelle 2006a: 169–190.

———. 2006c. "The Ascetic and the Domestic in Brahmanical Religiosity." In *Asceticism and Its Critics: Historical Accounts and Comparative Perspectives,* ed. Oliver Freiberger, pp. 25–42. New York: Oxford University Press.

———. ed. and tr. 2008. *Life of the Buddha by Aśvaghoṣa.* Clay Sanskrit Library. New York: New York University Press.

———. ed. and tr. 2009a. *Viṣṇu's Code of Law: A Critical Edition and Translation of the Vaiṣṇava-Dharmaśāstra.* Harvard Oriental Series 73. Cambridge, MA: Harvard University Press.

———. 2009b. "Hindu Law: The Post-Formative Period, 400 BCE–400 CE." In *Oxford International Encyclopedia of Legal History,* ed. Stanley N. Katz, Vol. 3, pp. 151–55. New York: Oxford University Press.

———. ed. 2009c. *Aśoka: In History and Historical Memory.* Delhi: Motilal Banarsidass.

———. 2010. "Dharmaśāstra: A Textual History." In *Hinduism and Law: An Introduction,* ed. T. Lubin, D. Davis Jr., and J. K. Krishnan, pp. 28–57. Cambridge: Cambridge University Press.

———. 2011. "War and Peace: Semantics of *saṃdhi* and *vigraha* in the *Arthaśāstra.*" In *Pūrvāparaprajñābhinandanam: Indological and Other Essays in Honour of Klaus Karttunen,* ed. Bertil Tikkanen and Albion M. Butters, pp. 131–39. Studia Orientalia 110. Helsinki: Societas Orientalis Fennica.

———. 2012a. "Aśoka's Inscriptions as Text and Ideology." In Olivelle, Ray, and Leoshko 2012: 157–83.

———. 2012b. "Patañjali and the Beginnings of Dharmaśāstra: An Alternate Social History of Early Dharmasūtra Production." In *Aux abords de la clairière: Colloque en l'honneur de Ch. Malamoud*, ed. Silvia D'Intino and Caterina Guenzi, pp. 117–33. Bibliothèque de l'Ecole des Hautes Etudes—Sciences religieuses. Paris: Brepolis.

———. 2013. *King, Governance, and Law in Ancient India: Kauṭilya's Arthaśāstra*. New York: Oxford University Press.

———. 2017. *A Dharma Reader: Classical Indian Law*. Historical Sourcebooks in Classical Indian Thought, ed. Sheldon I. Pollock. New York: Columbia University Press.

———. 2018. "Orders of Life: *āśrama*." In Olivelle and Davis 2018: 78–85.

———. 2019. *Yājñavalkya: A Treatise on Dharma*. Murty Classical Library of India. Cambridge, MA: Harvard University Press.

Olivelle, Patrick, and Donald R. Davis, Jr., eds. 2018. *Hindu Law: A New History of Dharmaśāstra*. The Oxford History of Hinduism. Oxford: Oxford University Press.

Olivelle, Patrick, Himanshu Prabha Ray, and Janice Leoshko, eds. 2012. *Reimagining Aśoka: Memory and History*. Delhi: Oxford University Press.

Ollett, Andrew. 2017. *The Language of the Snakes. Prakrit, Sanskrit, and the Language Order of Premodern India*. Oakland: University of California Press.

Pañcaviṃśa Brāhmaṇa [=Tāṇḍya Brāhmaṇa]. 1870–74. *Tāṇḍya Brāhmaṇa with the commentary of Sāyaṇa Ācārya*. Ed. Anandachandra Vedantavagisa. Calcutta: Asiatic Society of Bengal.

Parthasarathy, R., tr. 1993. *The Cilappatikāram of Iḷaṅko Aṭikaḷ: An Epic of South India*. New York: Columbia University Press.

Patañjali. *Vyākaraṇa-Mahābhāṣya* (commentary on Pāṇini's *Aṣṭādhyāyī*). 1962–72. Ed. F. Kielhorn. 3 vols. 3rd rev. ed. by K. V. Abhyankar. Poona: Bhandarkar Oriental Research Institute.

Patwardhan, M. V. 1980. *Hāla's Gāhākosa (Gāthāsaptaśatī) with the Sanskrit Commentary of Bhuvanapāla. Part I*. Prakrit Text Series 21. Ahmedabad: Prakrit Text Society.

———. 1988. *Hāla's Gāhākosa (Gāthāsaptaśatī) with the Sanskrit Commentary of Bhuvanapāla. Part II*. Edited with an Introduction, Translation, Index of Stanzas, Glossary and Notes. B. L. Series 5. Delhi: Bhogilal Leherchand Institute of Indology.

Paümacariya. Ed. and Hindi tr. in Jacobi 1962; Jacobi 1968.

Pinault, Georges. 2000. "Védique *dámūnas-*, Latin dominus et l'origine du suffixe de Hoffmann." *Bulletin de la Société de linguistique de Paris* 95: 61–118.

Pischel, Richard. 1900. *Grammatik der Prakrit-Sprachen*. Tr. Subhadra Jhā, *A Grammar of the Prākrit Languages*. Delhi: Motilal Banarsidass, 1981.

Poduval, K. A., and C. K. Raman Nambiar, eds. 1964. *Raghuvamsa by Mahakavi Kalidasa with Prakasika Commentary of Arunagirinatha & Padarthadeepika Commentary of Narayana Panditha, Cantos 1 to 6*. Tripunithura: Sanskrit College Committee.

Pryzluski, J. 1929. "Hippokoura et Satakarni." *Journal of the Royal Asiatic Society* 2: 273–79.

Rāmāyaṇa. 1960–75. *The Vālmīki-Rāmāyaṇa*. Crit. ed. Govindlal Hargovind Bhatt, Umakant Premanand Shah, et al. 7 vols. Baroda: Oriental Institute.

Ratnachandraji. 1988. *An Illustrated Ardha-Magadhi Dictionary*. Reprint of 1923. 5 vols. Delhi: Motilal Banarsidass.

Rhys Davids, T. W., and William Stede, eds. 1921–25. *The Pali Text Society's Pali-English Dictionary*. Reprint, London: Pali Text Society, 1979.

Rigveda Saṃhitā. Ed. with Sāyaṇa's commentary by F. Max Müller. 6 vols. London: Wm. H. Allen & Co. 1849–74. Tr. Jamison and Brereton 2014.

Rocher, Ludo. 1985. "The Kāmasūtra: Vātsyāyana's Attitude toward Dharma and Dharmaśāstra." *Journal of the American Oriental Society* 105, 3: 521–29.

Roth, Gustav. 2007. "Vergleichende Beobachtungen zu Asokas Felsenedikt XIII." In *Expanding and Merging Horizons: Contributions to South Asian and Cross-Cultural Studies in Commemoration of Wilhelm Halbfass*, ed. Karin Preisendanz, pp. 143–166. Vienna: Verlag der Österreichischen Akademie der Wissenschaften.

Salomon, Richard. 2009. "Aśoka and the 'Epigraphic Habit' in India." In Olivelle 2009c: 45–51.

Sāmavidhāna Brāhmaṇa. 1873. Ed. A. C. Burnell. London: Trübner & Co.

Saṃyutta Nikāya. 1884–1898. Ed. Léon Feer. 5 vols. London: Pali Text Society.

Sanderson, Alexis. 1985. "Purity and Power among the Brāhmans of Kashmir." In *The Category of the Person: Anthropology, Philosophy, History*, ed. M. Carrithers, S. Collins, and S. Lukes, pp. 190–216. Cambridge: Cambridge University Press.

Śāṅkhāyana Gṛhyasūtra. Ed. Hermann Oldenberg. Das Çâñkhâyanagrihyam. *Indische Studien XV*, pp.1–166. Leipzig: F.A. Brockhaus, 1878.

The Śāṅkhāyana Śrauta Sūtra. 1888–1891. Ed. Alfred Hillebrandt. Calcutta: Bibliotheca Indica.

Śatapatha Brāhmaṇa (in the *Mādhyandina* recension). 1855. Ed. Albrecht Weber. Berlin: F. Dümmler.

Sattasaī. Ed. Albrecht Weber 1881; ed. and tr. Patwardhan 1980, 1988; Tieken 1983; Khoroche and Tieken 2009; ed. with Hindi tr. Durgāprasād and Parab 1889.

Sayers, Matthew R. 2012. *Feeding the Dead: Ancestor Worship in Ancient India*. New York: Oxford University Press.

Scharfe, Hartmut. 1993. *Investigations into Kauṭalya's Manual of Political Science*. Wiesbaden: Harrassowitz.

Schlumberger, Daniel. 1969. "Eine neue griechische Aśoka-Inschrift." In *Der Hellenismus in Mittelasien*. (*Wege der Forschung*, Vol. 91.), ed. Franz Altheim and Joachim Rehork, pp. 406–17. Darmstadt: Wissenschaftliche Buchgesellschaft.

Schlumberger, Daniel, and Émile Benveniste. 1967. "A New Inscription of Aśoka at Kandahar." *Epigraphia Indica* 37: 193–200.

Schneider, Ulrich. 1978. *Die Großen Felsen-Edikte Aśokas. Kritische Ausgabe, Übersetzung und Analyse der Texte*. Wiesbaden: Harrassowitz.

Schubring, Walther. 2000 (1962). *The Doctrine of the Jainas Described after the Old Sources.* Tr. from 1935 rev. German ed. by Wolfgang Beurlen. Delhi: Motilal Banarsidass.

———. 2004a. *Mahāvīra's Words. Translated from the German with much Added Material* by W. Bollée and J. Soni. Ahmedabad: L.D. Institute of Indology.

———. 2004b. (German edition, 1926). "Pure Life (*Bambhacerāiṃ*)" [Translation of the first book of the *Ācārāṅga Sūtra*]. In Schubring 2004a.

Shama Sastri, R. 1920. *Bodhâyana Gṛihyasutra.* Oriental Library Publications Sanskrit Series 32/55. Mysore: Government Branch Press.

Shatavadhani Jain Muni and Shri Ratnachandraji Maharaj, eds. 1923. *An Illustrated Ardha-Magadhi Dictionary.* Reprint, Delhi: Motilal Banarsidass, 2016.

Shaw, Julia. 2013. *Buddhist Landscapes in Central India: Sanchi Hill and Archaeologies of Religious and Social Change, c. Third Century BC to Fifth Century AD.* London: The British Academy.

Shaw, Julia, John Sutcliffe, Lindsay Lloyd-Smith, Jean-Luc Schwenninger, and M. S. Chauhan. 2007. "Ancient Irrigation and Buddhist History in Central India: Optically Stimulated Luminescence Dates and Pollen Sequences from the Sanchi Dams" *Asian Perspective* 46, 1: 166–201.

Sheth, Pandit Hargovind Das T., ed. 1963. *Pāia-Sadda-Mahaṇṇavo. A Comprehensive Prakrit-Hindi Dictionary, with Sanskrit Equivalents, Quotations and Complete References.* 2nd ed. Delhi: Motilal Banarsidass. First published, 1928.

Shulman, David. 2016. *Tamil: A Biography.* Cambridge, MA: Harvard University Press.

Sircar, D. C. 1975. *Inscriptions of Aśoka.* 3rd ed. New Delhi: Government of India.

———. 1986. *Select Inscriptions Bearing on Indian History and Civilization.* Vol. I: *From the Sixth Century B.C. to the Sixth Century A.D.* 3rd ed. Delhi: Asian Humanities Press.

Smith. Monica. 2006. "The Archaeology of Food Preference." *American Anthropologist* 108, 3: 480–93.

Subhāṣitaratnakoṣa. Ed. Kosambi and Gokhale 1957.

Sūryakānta. 1956. *Kauthuma-Gṛhya, Edited with Introduction, Notes and Indices.* Bibliotheca Indica 279. Calcutta: Asiatic Society.

Sutta-Nipāta. 1913. Ed. Dines Andersen and Helmer Smith. Oxford: Pali Text Society. Tr. Norman 1985.

Sūyagaḍa, for the First Time Critically Edited with the Text of Niryukti. 1928. Ed. P. L. Vaidya. Poona: Motīlāla.

Taittirīya Saṃhitā. Ed. with Sāyaṇa's commentary by Kāśīnātha Śāstrī Āgāśe. 9 vols. Ānandāśrama Sanskrit Series 42. Poona, 1900–08. Tr. Keith 1914.

Thapar, Romila. 1997. *Aśoka and the Decline of the Mauryas.* 2nd ed. Delhi: Oxford University Press.

Tieken, Herman. 1983. *Hāla's Sattasaī. Stemma and edition (Gāthās 1–50), with translation and notes.* PhD dissertation, Utrecht.

———. 2000. *Kāvya in South India: Old Tamil Caṅkam Poetry*. Groningen: Egbert Forsten.

Törzsök, Judit, ed. and tr. 2006. *Rama Beyond Price*. Clay Sanskrit Library. New York: New York University Press—JJC Foundation.

Turner, R. L. 1963. *A Comparative Dictionary of the Indo-Aryan Languages*. 3 vols. London: Oxford University Press.

Uttarādhyayanasūtra, being the First Mūlasūtra of the Śvetāmbara Jains. 1922. Ed. Jarl Charpentier. Archives d'Études Orientales vol. 18. Uppsala: Appelbergs Boktryckeri Aktiebolag.

Udāna. 1885. Ed. Paul Steinthal. London: Pali Text Society.

Vaiṣṇava Dharmaśāstra (*Viṣṇusmṛti*). Ed. and tr. Olivelle 2009a.

Van Den Bossche, Frank. 1999. *A Reference Manual of Middle Prākrit Grammar: The Prākrits of the Dramas and the Jain Texts*. Gent: Universa.

Vasiṣṭha Dharmasūtra. Ed. and tr. Olivelle 2000.

Vasudeva, Somadeva, ed. and tr. 2006. *The Recognition of Shakúntala by Kalidasa*. Clay Sanskrit Library. New York: New York University Press—JJC Foundation.

Vasudevahiṇḍi-prathamakhaṇḍa. 1930. *Pūjyaśrīsaṃghadāsagaṇi-vācakavinirmitaṃ Vasudevahiṇḍiprathamakhaṇḍam, tasyāyaṃ prathamo 'ṃśaḥ (dhammillahiṇḍigarb hitaḥ)*. Ed. Caturvijaya and Puṇyavijaya. Bhāvanagara: Śrījaina-ātmānandasabhā.

Vātsyāyana. *Kamasutra*. 2002. Tr. Wendy Doniger and Sudhir Kakar. New York: Oxford University Press.

———. 1900. *Kāmasūtra*. Ed. with Yaśodhara's *Jayamaṅgala* commentary by Durgaprasād. Jaipur: Nirnaya Sagar Press.

———. 1929. *The Kāmasūtra by Srī Vātsyāyana Muni, with the Commentary Jayamangala of Yashodhar*. Ed. Dāmodar Shastri. Benaṛes: Jai Krishnadas-Haridas Gupta.

Vetter, Tilmann. 1988. *The Ideas and Meditative Practices of Early Buddhism*. Leiden: Brill.

Vinayapiṭaka. 1879–83. Ed. Hermann Oldenberg. 5 vols. London: Pali Text Society.

Wackernagel, Jacob. 1896. *Altindische Grammatik*, vol. I: *Lautlehre*. Reprint, Göttingen: Vandenhoeck & Ruprecht, 1957.

Walzer, Richard. 1949. *Galen on Jews and Christians*. London: Oxford University Press.

Weber, Albrecht, ed. 1881. *Das Saptaçatakam des Hâla*. Leipzig: F. A. Brochhaus.

Wezler, Albrecht. 1977–78. "The True *Vighasāśins*: Remarks on Mahābhārata XII 214 and XII 11." *Annals of the Bhandarkar Oriental Research Institute* 58–59: 397–406.

Willis, Michael. 2008. "The Formation of Temple Ritual in the Gupta Period: *Pūjā* and *pañcamahāyajña*." *Prajñādhara: Essays on Asian Art History, Epigraphy and Culture in Honour of Gouriswar Bhattacharya*, ed. G. Mevissen and A. Banerji, pp. 1–22. New Delhi: Kaveri Books.

Winternitz, Maurice. 1999. *History of Indian Literature*. Volume II: *Buddhist and Jaina Literature*. Rev. ed. of 1983. Delhi: Motilal Banarsidass. Originally published in German, 1920.

Wynne, Alexander, tr. 2009. *The Mahābhārata. Book XII: Peace, Volume III, "The Book of Liberation."* Clay Sanskrit Library. New York: New York University Press—JJC Foundation.

Yājñavalkya Dharmaśāstra. Ed. and tr. Olivelle 2019.

Yājñavalkya Dharmaśāstra (Yājñavalkyasmṛti) with the Commentary Mitākṣarā of Vijñāneśvara. 1985. Ed. Nārāyaṇa Rāma Ācārya. Reprint, Delhi: Nag Publishers.

Yamazaki, Gen'ichi. 2005. *The Structure of Ancient Indian Society: Theory and Reality of the Varṇa System*. Tokyo: The Toyo Bunko.

Index

Note: Tables are indicated by *t* following the page number